Music and Black Ethnicity:
The Caribbean and South America

Edited by

Gerard H. Béhague

North·South Center Press
UNIVERSITY OF MIAMI

The publisher of this book is the North-South Center Press at the University of Miami.

The mission of the North-South Center is to promote better relations and serve as a catalyst for change among the United States, Canada, and the nations of Latin America and the Caribbean by advancing knowledge and understanding of the major political, social, economic, and cultural issues affecting the nations and peoples of the Western Hemisphere.

Library of Congress Cataloging-in-Publication Data

Music and Black Ethnicity : the Caribbean and South America / edited
   by Gerard H. Béhague
         p. cm.
      At head of title: North-South Center, University of Miami.
      Proceedings of a conference held in Miami, Jan. 16-19, 1992.
      Includes bibliographical references.
      ISBN 1-56000-708-7 (paper)
      1. Blacks—Caribbean Area—Music—Congresses. 2. Blacks—South
America—Music—Congresses. 3. Blacks—Caribbean Area—Race
Identity—Congresses. 4. Blacks—South America—Race Identity—
Congresses.   I. Béhague, Gerard.   II. University of Miami. North-
South Center.
ML3549.M87   1994
780'.899608—dc20   94-503
                                                                        CIP
                                                                        MN

ISBN- 1-56000-708-7 (Paper)
Printed in the United States of America
00 99 98 97   7 6 5 4 3

Contents

Foreword

In early discussions that my colleague, Robert Parker, and I had with Dean Ambler H. Moss about prospects for a music conference under the aegis of the North-South Center, the topic that gradually emerged was the influence of black ethnicity on the musics of Latin America. It was perceived that an examination of the presence and shape of this influence in various regions of Latin America could help to underscore and clarify some of its prominence, commonality, and diversity. It was envisioned that the conference would also afford a means of disseminating this information to the public and the academic community.

Directions taken in these discussions led to the selection of distinguished musicologist and Latin American specialist Gerard H. Béhague to develop a conference of the scope and magnitude required for this multi-faceted theme. Dr. Béhague's subsequent conference proposal drew upon his vast knowledge of this field and his working relationship with music investigators uniquely qualified to carry out regional components of the task.

The project enjoyed generous support from the North-South Center that resulted in a vibrant four-day colloquium in Miami in January of 1992, led by Dr. Béhague and involving sixteen lecturers from North and South America, the Caribbean, and Africa. Lively music by the Afro-Cuban *Ilu*, the Haitian *Kazak* troupe, Puerto Rico's *Atabal* conjunto, the Othello Molineaux Quartet, and University of Miami Percussion Ensembles complemented the lectures and discussions. Some two hundred auditors from the American and European continents joined presenters in the quest to illuminate the issue of black ethnicity in Latin American and Caribbean music and to unravel some of its complexities. The conference went a long way toward the accomplishment of these goals, exposed areas in need of further research and speculation, and at the same time entertained and strengthened the network of interest within this vital and far-reaching area of investigation.

Dr. Robert Parker, the University of Miami School of Music's Associate Dean for Graduate Studies, served with distinction as the local coordinator of the conference. His dedication, organizational skills, and attention to every detail resulted in a conference that was well planned and coordinated.

Presented here, thanks to the vivid insight of the individual contributors, monumental editing by Dr. Béhague, and editorial and publication support from the North-South Center, is the rich distillate of that conference.

William Hipp
Dean

Patricia L. Frost
Professor of Music
University of Miami

Acknowledgments

As the original proponent of the main theme of the conference and as both conference coordinator and editor of this volume, I wish to thank my colleagues who participated in the conference and in the preparation of this volume for the high quality of their work and their commitment to the study of music and ethnicity. I also extend warmest thanks to the musicians and organizers of the groups *Ilu* from Miami, *Atabal* from Puerto Rico, *Kazak* from Haiti, the Othello Molineaux Quartet, and the University of Miami Percussion Ensembles, whose members provided memorable performances during the conference; Dean William Hipp, dean of the University of Miami School of Music; Dr. Robert Parker, associate dean of the University of Miami School of Music; and Dean Ambler H. Moss, Jr., director of the North-South Center, for their subsequent unfailing support.

Gerard H. Béhague

Introduction

Gerard H. Béhague

"Mestizaje *is a powerful force of exclusion of both black and indigenous communities in the Americas today. As a consequence, black and indigenous awareness of exclusion and continuous struggle for ethnic power will remain prominent"* (Whitten, Jr., and Torres 1992, 21).

The role fulfilled by music in the construct of cultural identity (whether regional or national) and especially of ethnicity (along ethnic or social stratification boundaries) has received significant attention in recent anthropological and ethnomusicological literature, less so in musicological literature. As one of the most highly structured human cultural expressions, music encapsulates social groups' most essential values affecting individual members' worldviews or "cosmovisions." Such values are embedded in the enactment of music performance styles and occasions, as I have articulated elsewhere (Béhague 1984). In addition, there can be no doubt that the central issue in any type of ethnic grouping is *ethnicity*, as it relates to identity. The concept of ethnicity, however, requires specific explanation. In contemporary daily language, it is rather ambiguous. First, it appears crucial to differentiate between the concept of what Richard Adams refers to as an "internally defined ethnicity" from that of an "externally defined ethnicity" (Adams 1989). The first one represents a native group's definition of self-identity, the second an identity ascribed by outsiders. In effect, an "internally defined ethnicity" is "a population whose members self-define their collective survival by replicating a shared identity through cultural and biological self-reproduction," while an "externally defined ethnicity" is "a population whose collective reproduction is externally ascribed in terms of their replicating a shared characteristic through cultural and biological reproduction" (Adams 1989, 478). Such a difference is especially meaningful when applied to Caribbean and South American ethnic groups and to the specific expressions of their identity. Ethnic identities are adaptive and indeed do change. In addition, they certainly embody political agendas, in the sense of being reflective of power relations.

Numerous factors of black ethnicity remain highly problematic, particularly the wide diversity throughout the Caribbean and Latin America of criteria used to self-identify one's ethnicity in racial terms. This diversity explains the wide gaps between minimum and maximum percentages on the black population in the various countries. It is common knowledge that the meaning of terms used by people to identify themselves racially varies a great deal. The term *mestizo,* for example, is most frequently used to denote the mixture of white and native American, even when people identifying themselves as mestizos show a clear African ancestry. In addition, light-skin mulattoes frequently refer to themselves as whites, and darker-skin individuals as mulattoes or mestizos. This may result from the indoctrinary influence of the ideology of *blanqueamiento* (*branqueamento* in Portuguese), a racist, socio-political concept implying the "purification" of "whitening," accepting "the implicit hegemonic rhetoric of the United States with regard to 'white supremacy,'" and frequently blaming "those classed as black and indigenous for the worsening state of the nation" (Whitten, Jr., and Torres 1992, 18). While in many Caribbean countries, such as Haiti, Jamaica, Barbados, and the Bahamas, black ethnicities dominate; in Central and South American countries they are minorities, despite the varying regional distribution of the black population. In most cases, however, they are marginalized. Thus, black ethnicities often adopt the ideology of *négritude* as the essence of their cultural, sometimes class, identity. In so doing, they naturally develop counterhegemonic strategies toward the ultimate elimination of their political and economic subordination and exploitation. In this struggle, aspects of expressive culture such as music function as highly effective symbolic means of vindication.

Thus, it seems particularly relevant and timely to reflect in a more sophisticated manner on the relationship of music expressions and black ethnicity in the Caribbean and South America. The traditional approach of most studies on African-American-Latino music has focused on the scale of Africanisms retained in contemporary practices of such music and on various levels of syncretism resulting from the specific ethnohistorical considerations of a particular region, country, or social group, as seen in the works of Melville J. Herskovits and Isabel Aretz, among others. However, the search for Africanisms and the very concepts of syncretism and acculturation are to a great extent symptomatic of colonialist thought. Indeed, these concepts privilege the notions of socio-cultural assimilation and accommodation to the dominant segments of society. Thus, the study of the subtle continuum of the actual nature of African-American-Latino-créole music needs to consider seriously all of the rich dialectics of a particular tradition. Contrary to the general opinion, such music appears rather heterogeneous in the Caribbean and South American areas, as its various manifestations correspond to and result from highly complex processes of *mestizaje,* creolization, or explicitly black nationalism, at various periods of its history. It is still common to characterize "black" music in the New World in terms of performing media and stylistic factors related to an African heritage. But although certain associations of musical instruments and their playing techniques and certain features of style may carry significant markers of identification as historical referents, they are not the only means that define the essence of the relationship of music to black ethnicity. Some aspects of cultural expression in contemporary Afro-American communities in the Caribbean and South American may not be of historic African derivation at all, but fulfill an equally vital purpose of identity and sense of heritage. In addition, various forms in Afro-American cultures "may also exist in the living memory of people who no longer engage in them. Absence of on-going practice is not necessarily evidence of 'culture loss' or 'acculturation,' because talk of past customs may become a vehicle for cultural continuity. And such contemporary discourses may reveal far more about black or indigenous history and identity than reified inscriptions in learned volumes about 'genuine' (but 'disappearing') Africans and Indians in the New World" (Whitten, Jr., and Torres 1922, 22).

With these premises, an International Conference was held in Miami on January 16-19, 1992, under the sponsorship of the North-South Center and the School of Music of the University of Miami. The event brought together some fifteen European, American, Caribbean, and South American scholars from the disciplines of anthropology, musicology, ethnomusicology, sociology, and allied fields in the humanities, as well as a number of active musicians from Puerto Rico,

Cuba, and Haiti. The Conference explored some specific aspects of the relationships of music and black ethnicity, such as:

1. Changing nature of ethnicity: diachronic and synchronic perspectives:

    a) The configuration of stratification, in socio-cultural, economic, and political terms in areas such as Cuba, Puerto Rico, Dominican Republic, Haiti, Panama, Venezuela, Colombia, Ecuador, Peru, and Brazil;

    b) The "ethnic identity" viewed internally and externally, with case studies in the same selected areas, exploring the possible continuum Black-Latino-National current meanings in these areas;

2. Cultural expressions of identity/ethnicity through music: case studies in historical or contemporary perspectives;

3. Musical styles and aesthetics as reflective of and as identity/ethnicity:

    a) the blurring and/or invention of traditions in Caribbean and South American contexts,

    b) specific case studies of folk/traditional music,

    c) specific case studies of art-music trends,

    d) specific case studies of popular music trends and activities;

4. Common denominators and differences of expression of identity/ethnicity from the case studies examined;

5. Current state and future needs of this field of research in the areas studied.

Given the complexity of the subject matter and the specificity of the case studies, one could not expect a fully comprehensive coverage or treatment of the numerous imaginable factors. However, the conference addressed several facets of the current understanding of the complex mosaic of African-American-Latino musical traditions and their relationship to the mechanisms of cultural dynamics.

This volume contains the revised and amplified versions of the presentations. The first two chapters, by Anthony Seeger and Gerhard Kubik, deal with some of the theoretical premises and problems of music and identity/ethnicity. Seeger examines how members of any community may have a number of different potential identities. He argues that musical style is less a natural outgrowth of a given history than a chosen statement about the future through an interpretation of the past in the present, and that, in fact, members of a group may transform their "identities" and their musical styles quite suddenly. Although he draws his examples from his field research experience among South American Indians, he shows convincingly that the phenomenon is also relevant to considerations of African-American communities and their musical traditions.

The chapter by Kubik addresses a number of theoretical questions, including the concepts of identity, ethnicity, and ethnic identity, viewed from the vantage point of socio-psychological function and meaning in present day African-American societies. It also examines how the search for origins and linkages to Africa can in itself be an expression of ideologies centered around concepts of identity, black identity, and ethnicity, among others, as negotiated by cultural action groups in the Americas.

The Cuban scholars Victoria Eli Rodríguez and Olavo Alén Rodríguez provide specific examples of Cuban music and ethnicity, the first in broad historical terms applied to Afro-Cuban traditional religious musics and to *afrocubanismo* as an aesthetic trend, the second in connection with the French/Haitian presence in Eastern Cuba and its legacy in the *sociedades de tumba francesa*. Both papers exemplify the current state of ethnomusicological research in Cuba on the relationship of music and ethnicity. Additional case studies from the Caribbean are by Martha Ellen Davis and Gage Averill. Davis's paper emphasizes the contemporary musical culture of the Dominican Republic, providing historical background data regarding the development of both cultural composition and cultural/ethnic identity (that is, the attitude toward cultural composition) in the country. Variants in culture and cultural identity according to social class are stressed and related to folk, pop, and art music expressions, with specific examples to illustrate the main points. Averill's study examines the dramatic changes in spatial and territorial components of Haitian identity in the post-1986 Duvalier period, during which the gulf between insular Haitians and diaspora Haitians shrank. The paper considers evolving spatial (transnational) dimensions of Haitian identity, arguing that music has helped to define these new spaces, that it has articulated and popularized Afrocentrism with *vodou* and *rara* roots music, and that it has helped to structure popular rebellion with a pleasurable impulse.

Brazilian topics are presented by José Jorge de Carvalho and Kazadi wa Mukana. Carvalho sees black identity as a self-conscious movement as a recent issue in Brazil, mainly expressed through specific genres of popular music with little influence from traditional Afro-Brazilian religious music, but rather with direct connection to models of black ethnicity coming from modern Africa and the Caribbean. On the other hand, he considers Umbanda cults as a source of great influence in traditional Afro-Brazilian music styles and as having become a vehicle of expression of all the various ethnic identities in the country: whites, blacks, mulattoes, Indians, gypsies, Arabs, Turks, and Japanese, among others. Wa Mukana considers the relationship between style and ethnicity in the northern regional versions of the folk dramatic dance, *Bumba-meu-boi.* In spite of changes and the creation of new styles of this folk drama, the author sees the survival of the African style of the drama, *Boi de zabumba,* as a result of its ability to adapt and to assimilate regional elements without sacrificing the governing concept of organization of features of its ethnic identity. The chapter also delves into the African slave authorship of the *Bumba-meu-boi* in colonial Brazil, considering several factors of social function, musical instruments, rhythmic patterns, and the format of the dance presentation.

Specific case studies of syncretism and ethnicity in the music of the Atlantic and Pacific coasts of Colombia are taken up by Egberto Bermúdez. His consideration of the ritual music of Palenque and the tradition of *gaiteros* and *cañamilleros* and the *currulao* marimba dance music, among others, provides ample data for assessing the dynamic processes of identity and ethnicity in contemporary Colombia. Ronald Smith deals with the tradition of the *Sociedad de los Congos* as a significant example of Panamanian ethnicity and identity. Among people of Afro-Hispanic descent, *Congo* emphasizes mimetic dance-theater, outrageous costumes, songs rich in oral history, and contemporary observation of various kinds. *Congo* groups organize prior to the beginning of Carnival festivities. However, some groups maintain a communal sense of society throughout the year and exhibit a cohesiveness that often permits greater artistic development of both group and individuals within the tradition. The latter thus permits maintaining a strong sense of ethnic identity and reserves a place for commentary on the past.

Max Brandt focuses on specific drum ensembles of the central Venezuelan coast of Barlovento as symbolic of Afro-Venezuelan identity. Unlike some African-American communities, most Barloventeños had lost contact with their African past until the middle of the twentieth century, when scholarly investigations, especially concerning music, sparked interest among them in their African ancestry. The author shows how the drums of Barlovento and neighboring Afro-Venezuelan communities have become a focal point of Venezuelan pride in the rich African heritage of the country.

Despite the predominant native Indian ancestry of the Andean countries, the chapters by John Schechter and Raúl Romero give strong evidence of dynamic Afro-Ecuadorian and Afro-Peruvian musical traditions. Schechter's paper focuses on a group of Ecuadorian musicians of African descent widely acknowledged to be the finest representatives of the music of the Chota River valley in northern Ecuador. Based on fieldwork in 1980 and again in 1990, this study documents the development of the musicians' vocation and the changes that have taken place in the ten-year period with special regard to their approach to their repertoire. Romero presents an overview of past Afro-Peruvian musical traditions and explains how these expressions disappeared as a living tradition around the turn of the twentieth century. Since the 1950s, however, several urban musical groups have appeared, re-creating many of these almost extinct musical genres and disseminating them through the mass media. Today, black musical genres are performed and consumed by a wide range of audiences and social sectors. The author poses a number of key questions, such as, Why did Afro-Peruvian music disappear as a living tradition? Why were these traditions re-invented? And is this reconstruction linked to a black group, their relation the "creole" dominant culture, and issues concerning the existence, or absence, of a reinvigorated black identity in Peru.

As a whole, therefore, these chapters fulfill the main purpose of the conference, namely, to determine the current state of knowledge and research on the various topics presented and to explore and identify new directions in the study of African-American-Latino musics in the Caribbean and South America.

References

Adams, Richard N. 1989. "Internal and External Ethnicities: With Special Reference to Central America." In *Estado, Democratización y Desarrollo en Centroamérica y Panamá* (Asociación Centroamericana de Sociología). Guatemala: Impreso Serviprensa Centroamericana.

Béhague, Gerard, ed. 1984. Performance Practice: *Ethnomusicological Perspectives*. Westport, Conn.: Greenwood Press.

Whitten, Jr., Norman E., and Arlene Torres. 1992. "Blackness in the Americas." *Report on the Americas* 25, no. 4 (February): 16-22.

Whoever We Are Today, We Can Sing You a Song about It

Anthony Seeger

Pete Seeger composed a wonderful song about the mixing and mingling of our cultural traditions in the Americas. Here are some verses of it, which he sings to a calypso-derived melody, usually accompanying himself on the twelve-string guitar:[1]

> *You know this language that we speak*
> *Is part Latin, part German, and part Greek*
> *With a little Celtic and Arabic all in the heap*
> *Well amended by the man in the street.*
> *The Choctaw gave us the word OK*
> *Vamoose is a word from Mexico way.*
> *And all of this is a hint, I suspect,*
> *Of what comes next*
>
> Chorus:
> *I think that this whole world*
> *Soon ma-ma-my whole wide world*
> *Soon ma-ma-my whole world*
> *Soon gonna be get mixed up.*
> *I like Polish sausage, I like Spanish rice*
> *And pizza pie is also nice.*
> *Corn and beans from the Indians here*
> *All washed down with some German beer.*
> *Marco Polo travelled by camel and pony*
> *To bring to Italy the first macaroni.*

This paper was originally presented at the Symposium on Music and Black Ethnicity in the Caribbean and South America. I am grateful to the organizers of the symposium for the opportunity to reflect on these issues and to the participants for their comments on the original oral presentation.

And you and I, as well as we're able,
Put it all on the table.

Chorus
There were no red-headed Irishmen
Before the Vikings invaded Ireland.
How many Romans had dark, curly, hair
Before they brought slaves from Africa?
No race of man is completely pure,
Nor is anyone's mind and that's for sure.
The winds mix the dust of every land
And so will woman and man.

Chorus
Now this doesn't mean we must all be the same.
We'll have different faces and different names.
Long live many different kinds of races.
And difference of opinion, that makes horse races
But remember the rule about rules brother,
What's right with one is wrong with another.
Let's take a tip from la belle France,
"Vive la différence."

This song takes a whimsical approach to an important subject, demonstrating how the marks of our interdependence are revealed in our language, our cuisine, and our bodies. By extension (through its rhythm, melody, and instrumentation), it makes the same argument for our music.

Although the cumulative effects of the diverse influences on our bodies and our cultures are "all mixed up," the social processes that gave them to us are not mixed up at all. Violence, enslavement, exploitation, resistance, endurance, and creativity can all be documented in the history of the Americas. The food that any one of us actually eats, the music any one of us actually performs, and the ways any one of us actually speaks and any one of us classifies other people by physical type are parts of specific historical and cultural processes of which we are a part. While the results appear to be "all mixed up," the social sciences have amply demonstrated that people use their language, food, music, and physical appearance as markers of their community identity (or identities). There are patterns to be discerned in the mobilization of music, cuisine, hair styles, and body adornment by specific groups.

In a sense we are confronting two separate issues — issues that in some situations overlap. One issue is "ethnicity," with a focus on black ethnicity in the Caribbean and Latin America. The other issue is music. Sometimes they overlap, and sometimes they are quite distinct. At times, music may not be actively used by members of a group to create or represent a group identity. Music may simply be something you make at church, listen to at the bar, sing around the house, or complain about when the younger generation listens. Then, at some moment, you may begin to employ a musical style as a resource to say who you are and use it to interpret who other people are and to indicate what a community aspires to. Under which circumstances this happens and what happens to the music when it becomes a resource for group identification are significant issues.

The formation and maintenance of social groups is a topic to which social scientists have devoted considerable attention during the past century and a half. Ethnicity is just one resource for group formation, and the literature on it is more recent but almost as vast.[2] Group formation often involves what Davis calls "an image or myth with which a group can identify itself." He continues:

> The image can be provided by legend or history, religion, poetry, folklore, or what are more vaguely called "traditions." It need not be expressed in precise or absolute terms; on the contrary it is usually flexible and capable of being gradually transformed, but if a people is to be conscious of its identity it must have such an image (Davis, cited in Williams 1989).

Note that in the enumeration of traditions, the author does not even mention music. Social scientists rarely consider music in discussions of group formation. Even Royce (1982), a dance ethnographer, does not list either music or dance in her index. So what is the role of this unmentioned, oft-forgotten art form in group formation and interaction?

Discussions of music and ethnicity by ethnomusicologists have had a tendency toward simplicity and the isolation of music from other domains of social action. Too often it is said that the "X-people" perform a certain kind of music which is an expression of their identity. Three simplifications appear regularly about music and identity:

1. The identity of a particular group with a particular musical form is enduring over time, and each group has its own typical style. As demonstrated below, this is not always the case. And even when a musical style remains the same, its significance may change — as when church hymns are taken out of churches and onto the streets, and the "freedom land" and the obstacles that "we shall overcome" cease to be in the afterlife and become an ambition to realize in this life, in this country.

2. The simplistic notion that the relationship of music and ethnic identity can be analyzed outside the specific socio-political and historical contexts in which they belong — especially the relationships of domination among groups. The mobilization of ethnic identity almost always arises as part of a conflict.

3. Little or no thought is given to the role of researchers and research institutions in issues of music and ethnicity, when in fact they have been quite important, and continue to be so. The very fact that there is conflict among researchers and within research institutions signals our involvement in the processes of ethnicity.

The roots of some of these simplified assumptions can be traced to nineteenth-century social philosophy and the power of evolutionary and classification-oriented approaches to human societies. Anthropology presented us with a world of apparently distinct but internally homogeneous societies characterized by certain culture traits — including music with characteristic scales, rhythms, forms, and performance styles. We are still accustomed to the phrase "The music of the so-and-so is this-a-way." Yet pre-Colombian American Indian communities probably already performed several types of music, some of them learned from other groups. There were often distinct male and female musical genres. Shortly after their contact with Europeans, many American Indian groups adopted a new type of music — one that has rarely been collected, but has a form shared from Tierra del Fuego to the Arctic. Some Canadian communities even sent for hymn books before the arrival of missionaries (Diamond-Cavanagh 1992). With the addition of other musical traditions — from Africa, Asia, Europe, and elsewhere in the Americas — the possibilities for adapting new styles became even richer.

Researchers often ignored this complexity for a combination of reasons. First, they were often looking for a single (pure, original) tradition and recorded what they were looking for. As a result, we have very few recorded examples of hymns among American Indians, urban popular music genres performed in rural communities, European concert music from the Caribbean, and other examples of "impure" or "recently developed" musical forms. Second, since we have few if any recordings or written records from these communities, the recordings of a single visit by a researcher capture part of the musical life at a single instant in time. The result is a bit like seeing a single frame of a film, in which all movement is frozen for an instant. Third, researchers may have been lulled by repeated assurances of the people they recorded that "we have always done it this way" and assumed that people in fact always had performed music the way they did during the field research period. Fourth, relying heavily on recording technology permitted researchers to isolate single performances from the continuum of performances of which they were a part and to remove them from the cultural contexts in which they were inserted. Finally, researchers were sometimes directly involved in the creation of ethnic groups for administrative or other reasons, which influenced what they saw, heard, and were permitted to record.

To advance our discussions of music and ethnicity, it is necessary to look at the subject matter very carefully and examine our own role in the processes. I will give two examples from South America; the clarity of these cases will yield insight into similar cases elsewhere. They concern the Suyá Indians of Mato Grosso, Brazil, for whom I have sufficient knowledge to be sure of the relationship of music to the social processes of ethnicity, and the Kiriri Indians of the interior of Bahia, whom I visited briefly in 1982.[3]

An Amazonian Example of Shifting Identities

The Suyá story began in the eighteenth century, when a group of Gê-speaking Indians related to the Timbira groups began to move westward, away from the dangers of the advancing Brazilian frontier in Maranhão. They embarked on an exodus in which they migrated over a thousand miles and yet always recalled an earlier homeland in the East (see Figure 1). During their slow movement westward, then south, then somewhat to the north and east, the group encountered other Indian communities. With some of these groups they traded and learned songs along with new forms of material culture; with others they fought, and from their captives they learned new songs. In the nineteenth century, they appear to have been on the Tapajos River, fighting with powerful enemies, and they split into two parts. One part continued south to the Arinos River (where they became known as the Beios de Pau or Tapayuna) and the other moved east to the headwaters of the Xingu river, where they became known as the Suyá.

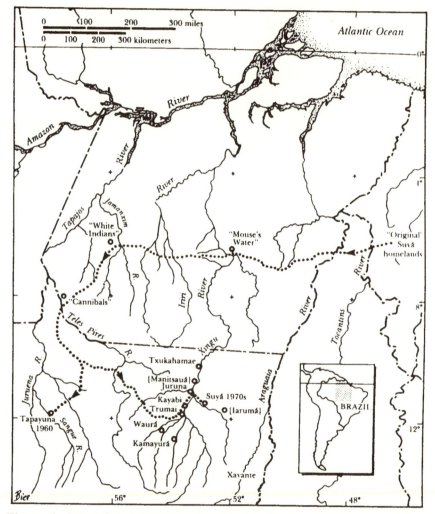

Figure 1 — *Map showing Suyá migration and approximate location of groups from whom they learned songs. Extinct groups in square brackets.*

The headwaters of the Xingu River were occupied by a distinctive group of Indian communities that spoke different languages, had different histories, but generally shared a single culture — technology, cuisine, belief systems, rituals, and music. For the next one hundred years the Suyá lived on the edge of that system and have interacted with it in different ways. At times the relations were peaceful; at others, hostile.

The first recorded European sighting of the Suyá was by Karl von den Steinen in 1884. At that time they were living on the banks of the Xingu River near the mouth of what is now known as the Suyá-missu River (sometimes written Sui-miu). Von den Steinen described them as having a less elaborate material culture than the Upper Xingu groups, and as having in their midst captives from the Manitsau Indian villages. He was impressed by the detailed geographical knowledge of the Suyá leader who even drew him a map in the sand and listed the other communities he knew about. Later, to his chagrin, von den Steinen discovered the Suyá had taken advantage of his visit to relieve him of a large quantity of material objects — knives, mirrors, and even the thermometer he used to measure the temperature of the water. The Suyá were once again taking advantage of a cultural contact to adapt themselves to a new situation by stealing something from powerful strangers. There is no indication, however, that they learned any songs from the Europeans.

Shortly after the 1884 visit of the German explorer, the Suyá were attacked by tribes to the north and moved up the Suyá-missu River to successively more isolated villages in an effort to escape their firearm-bearing enemies. They did emerge to trade or to attack other communities and take captives but were not seen by non-Indians again until 1959, when they entered into peaceful contact with Brazilians as well as with their former enemies in what was by then the Xingu National Park Indian Reserve.

In 1959, the Suyá moved to their earlier village sites near the mouth of the Suyá-missu River, into a greatly changed intertribal Indian reservation. They soon intermarried with an Upper Xingu group, the Trumai. During the ensuing ten years, they performed a great deal of Upper Xingu music — some of which they had learned from captives and some of which they learned from their new marriage partners. A Brazilian anthropologist who visited them in the 1960s characterized the Suyá as a pale reflection of Upper Xingu societies (Lanna 1966). In the late 1960s the Trumai group moved 120 miles upstream to escape local violence, and the Suyá were left to realign themselves with other groups in the region — the Kayabi, Juruna, and Northern Kayapo.

In 1970 a small group of Indians who spoke a language nearly identical with that of the Suyá were flown to the Xingu reservation. These few survivors of a tragic encounter with Brazilian society and government agents were probably descendants of the Gê-speakers, known as Tapayuna or Beios de Pau, who did not migrate east to the Xingu in the nineteenth century. For a variety of reasons they were taken to join the Suyá in their village. Each Suyá household took in some of the newcomers, fed them, taught them the ways of their new ecological and political environment, and spent hours listening to the newcomers recount the details of their culture. The Suyá said the newcomers were like their ancestors had been before they had encountered the Upper Xingu communities. The newcomers sparked a major renaissance of Gê culture, which was documented by another anthropologist, me. The two groups began to perform ceremonies together that pre-dated the Suyá contact with the Upper Xingu — dutifully recorded and discussed by myself as the resident anthropologist ("our Whiteman," as they sometimes referred to me).

In the early 1970s, the Suyá were carefully distinguishing their "traditional" Gê music from their more recent Upper Xingu repertory. I characterized the Suyá as basically a Gê-speaking society, not a pale reflection of the Upper Xingu, although there had been a clear Upper Xingu influence in women's culture, in material culture as a whole, and in some other areas.

The contrast between Lanna's description and my own is dramatic. We scarcely seem to be describing the same group. At the time I thought it was because we used different techniques. Since I had spent six or seven times more months among the Suyá than Lanna, I assumed that I was right and he was wrong, biased by his earlier encounter with the Upper Xingu communities. In fact, I think we were both quite accurate; the Suyá we were observing had changed. During Lanna's visit in the 1960s, the Suyá were identifying with the Upper Xingu culture area, marrying with members of those groups, and seeing them as the strongest allies in a complex new social and political situation. Shortly before I arrived that changed, and they began to identify themselves with an earlier past and with their Gê traditions. Lanna and I each presented what we saw as "the Suyá."

Suyá identity was not static, however. By 1980 the Suyá were making a less radical distinction between their Gê and their Upper Xingu ceremonies. The same person who had told me in 1972 that

Upper Xingu songs were not true Suyá songs said to me, "We have known those songs so long, they are really ours now." Shortly afterward the Tapayuna group moved out of the village and set up their own village some distance upstream. Around 1984 the remaining "old" Suyá village split — half of its residents moving far upstream from the rest. The reason cited for the split was that one faction wanted to perform "Old Gê songs" while the other "just wanted to sing Upper Xingu women's songs all the time." In other words, music itself became an object of contention and a point around which factional identities were formed.

The changes that occurred in this relatively short time span in a small Amazonian group have interesting implications for other communities as well. First, a community changed its cultural orientation and its music dramatically several times in three decades. Second, two researchers characterized the same group of people very differently, but neither was necessarily wrong — the group changed, each time emphasizing the traditional nature of what it was performing. Third, the community itself eventually broke up over the very difference that the two anthropologists noted. Whereas the Upper Xingu and Gê had apparently been sequential identities, at a later time the musical performances became the object of factional dispute and contributed to the dissolution of the community.

The Kiriri of Bahia: Toward an "Indian" Identity

Hundreds of miles to the east of the Suyá, in the dry interior of the state of Bahia, live the Kiriri Indians. Their history is entirely different from that of the Suyá. They have been in intensive contact with Brazilians for hundreds of years. During this period they ceased to use their language, practice their pre-Colombian religion, and perform their pre-Colombian music — among many other things. They also lost virtually all the land that had been set aside for them by decree in the eighteenth century. Living in close proximity and frequent contact with the Brazilian rural peasant population, they shared many social events with them. Some Kiriri were particularly admired for their performances of traditional Bahian music of the interior.

In the 1970s, probably in reaction to increased attention to Brazilian Indian rights around the country, and perhaps to internal developments as well, some Kiriri began to learn and to perform the Tor, a ceremony found among a number of Northeastern Indian communities. Although it may not have been originally "Kiriri," the Tor was demonstrably "Indian."[4]

In 1982, on election day, the Kiriri invaded the surrounding ranches and expelled the Brazilian residents. Announcing their determination to regain their former territories, they mobilized themselves to defend their regained lands. They cleared a large collective garden on a hill-top, built a structure at the highest point, and danced by the light of large fires, visible from some distance away.

I visited the Kiriri during this period, and there was no mention of their Brazilian musical expertise. All I heard about was the Tor, which I was invited to attend. The Kiriri were obviously in the midst of a re-activation of a Brazilian "Indian" identity. I, for my part, visited them to examine the success or failure of a program funded by a German non-governmental organization (NGO). The program had as its objective to increase the social and economic autonomy of the Kiriri. This kind of aid was rarely given to peasant groups. It is quite likely that the Kiriri particularly wanted to stress their difference from the surrounding communities for me and my colleagues. My own identity as a representative of the funding organization may well have given me a particularly focused view of the Kiriri.[5] My report dutifully stressed their distinctiveness from the regional population.

What might be the motivation for such a change of identity in this group of peasant farmers who to outsiders looked so much like any other rural Brazilian community? Why, after hundreds of years, did the Kiriri begin a revival of an "Indian" ethnic identity? There were probably several contributing factors. One was the definitely positive advantage of being considered "Indians" by the government and the general public. As "Indians" the Kiriri have a constitutional right to land; as Brazilian peasants they do not. By emphasizing their Indian past they could justify their forcible occupation of other people's land in a way that regional peasants could not.[6] As "Indians" the Kiriri could take advantage of international support and assistance; as peasants they were not likely to be noticed.

The mobilization of a given identity is often related to a wider political and legal framework, and that of the Kiriri was no exception. This does not mean that the Kiriri were insincere in their aspirations to be considered Indians. On the contrary, they may have been suppressing this identity for centuries. But there were also changes in the national image of Indians that encouraged them to take action in the 1970s and 1980s. The lessons to be drawn from the two Brazilian Indian cases are as follows:

1. The identity of a community can change quite rapidly, in ways often related to other changes in the social, political, and economic system of which they are a part. Members of a given community may have several alternative identities they can activate at different times, thus changing group affiliation.

2. Social scientists and other outside observers, because they lack an historical perspective and because they are actors themselves, may be quite misled by what they see.

3. The enactment of a given identity is related to specific contexts in which groups actively insert themselves as actors and in which they interpret the actions of others.

4. Musicologists and social scientists have also been actors in the creation of ethnic group or nationalistic processes. The roles we assume both as fieldworkers and as scholars may lead us to form certain opinions about ethnic identity that we then spread to wider audiences.

The first three points above were illustrated in the Suyá and Kiriri examples. The fourth has been particularly noted for folklorists, who were very active in nineteenth-century nation building throughout Europe. Michael Herzfeld provides a particularly thoughtful discussion of the role of folklorists and ethnologists in the formation of the Greek state:

> Most of what they did was a response to the ideological needs of their emergent polity. Indeed, they made distinctive and important contributions to the making of modern Greece, no less than the military and political leaders in their respective areas (Herzfeld 1982,9).

Anya Royce recognizes that one of the difficulties of the concept of ethnic identity is that it is a powerful phenomenon for observed and observers alike:

> It is powerful both at the affective level, where it touches us in ways mysterious and frequently unconscious, and at the level of strategy, where we consciously manipulate it. Its power is also perceived and interpreted differently by individuals and groups, whether they are users of ethnicity,

observers of ethnicity, or analysts of ethnicity. Presenting a coherent view of a field that revolves around such a phenomenon is a difficult, often frustrating, always exciting task. One would like to be fair. That is difficult because even scholars, who are, after all, human, are not neutral about ethnic identity (Royce 1982, 1).

To the extent that ethnomusicology overlaps with the study of folksong, we have had our nation builders and the champions of distinctive music for distinctive ethnicities, the most influential being John and Alan Lomax, whose collections emphasized the unique musical features of African-American style. Cantometrics is based on the establishment of enduring regional styles and deals less clearly with subsequent hybrids and "fusion" music that follow. Scholars describing music and relationships among social groups in this volume, as well as those who later read it, are inheritors of a long and mixed tradition of involvement with the concepts of nation, community, and ethnicity. In the books we write, the grants we recommend, the performers we invite to festivals and universities, and in our meetings, we participate in the same social processes we are studying. This is not necessarily bad — but we need to remember it and to reflect on our own activities as well as on those of the musicians and their other audiences.

Summary and Conclusion

To conclude, my title — "Whoever We Are Today, We Can Sing You a Song About It" — masks a serious topic that has implications not only for the objects of our study, but also for all the activities of ethnomusicologists.

On the one hand, everything is refreshingly mixed up. We can try to put it all on the table, turntable, or CD player. The Americas have seen a creative fusion of styles whose vigor and beauty have made their music known throughout the world. This process continues daily as musicians continue to create and perform. As old traditions are revived or new ones are created, music repeatedly serves as a resource for social group formation. On the other hand, musical performances of a particular genre or style often are the hallmark of a given group. Musical performances are used by composers, performers, audiences, critics, governments, oppressors, and liberators (in sum, by all social actors) in ways they find meaningful, which are not (for them) mixed up at all. And while each group may be characterized by one kind of music, a given individual may claim membership in various groups and perform a variety of musical styles appropriate to them. Musical performance is thus part of larger social processes — among them oppression, resistance, and the creation and affirmation of social identities.

In all research on the subject, we must distinguish carefully between the mixture of sounds and the singleness of purpose that characterize the traditions we discuss and the scholarship we produce. We want to explain not only the music people are performing today, but also what they are not performing today that they performed yesterday, and why they may be performing something different tomorrow. By examining music and ethnicity in their wider socio-political context as well as over time, we can present the complexity and the vitality of both music and human aspirations.

Notes

1. From the song "All Mixed Up" (Pete Seeger/Stormking Music, Inc., BMI). Used with permission.

2. See, for example, Royce (1982) for a general overview, and review articles by Williams (1989) and Foster (1991) that broaden the discourse.

3. My research among the Suyá Indians was mostly carried out between 1970 and 1982. I am grateful to the NIH, the Wenner-Gren Foundation, the Ford Foundation of Brazil, the Federal University of Rio de Janeiro, and FINEP for support for this research (see Seeger 1987, xix-xx for a more complete set of acknowledgments). My visit to the Kiriri was funded by the German organization Bröt für die Welt (Bread for the World), and made possible through the activities of the Centro de Trabalho Indigenista (CTI) of São Paulo, Brazil.

4. By putting the word "Indian" in quotation marks, I mean that it is a translation of a Portuguese word, in this case *indio. Indio,* like Indian, is a generic word and refers to a general "indian" identity rather than the more specific identity as "Kiriri," "Suyá," etc. Certain rights are guaranteed to all "Indians," and "Indians" have a certain symbolic power within the Brazilian political scene.

5. The situation with the Suyá was entirely different. The roles my wife and I played were far less focused, and even if the Suyá had been focusing our attention on certain matters, it would have been difficult to be consistent during the twenty-four months we lived with them over a period of eleven years. The depth I can provide for the Suyá changes of identity is entirely absent from my experience with the Kiriri as a representative of a funding agency who arrived during a crisis period in their relations with their neighbors.

6. As a Brazilian Air Force colonel once observed, if you wound a single Indian, the whole world hears about it; if you kill half a dozen peasants, nobody notices.

References

Davis, P. 1979. *The Normans and Their Myths*. London: Thames and Hudson.

Diamond-Cavanagh, Beverly. 1992. "Christian Hymns in Eastern Woodlands Communities." In *Musical Repercussions of 1492: Encounters in Text and Performance*, ed. Carol E. Robertson. Washington, D.C.: Smithsonian Institution Press.

Foster, Robert J. 1991. "Making National Cultures in the Global Ecumene." In *Annual Review of Anthropology* 20:235-260. Palo Alto: Annual Reviews Inc.

Herzfeld, Michael. 1982. *Ours Once More: Folklore, Ideology, and the Making of Modern Greece*. Austin: University of Texas Press.

Lanna, Amadeu D. 1966. "La division sexuelle du travail chez les Suyá du Brésil central." *L'Homme* 8:67-72.

Royce, Anya Peterson. 1982. *Ethnic Identity: Strategies of Diversity*. Bloomington: Indiana University Press.

Seeger, Anthony. 1987. *Why Suyá Sing: A Musical Anthropology of an Amazonian People*. Cambridge: Cambridge University Press.

Steinen, Karl v. den. 1940. "Entre os aborígines do Brasil central." São Paulo: *Journal of the Municipal Archives of São Paulo*, nos. 34-58.

Steinen, Karl v. den. 1942. *O Brasil Central*. São Paulo: Brasiliana.

Williams, Brackette. 1989. "A Class Act: Anthropology and the Race to Nation across Ethnic Terrain." In *Annual Review of Anthropology* 18:401-444. Palo Alto: Annual Reviews Inc.

Ethnicity, Cultural Identity, and the Psychology of Culture Contact

Gerhard Kubik

Introduction

This chapter examines some of the psychological forces that have generated "ethnicity" movements in the Americas and elsewhere, including "black ethnicity." Also discussed are popular notions about culture, race and "cultural identity," and their roles in cultural conflict. Some emphasis is given to accumulating evidence that individuals constantly change their cultural profiles during their lifetimes in processes of inner cultural reconfiguration; that is, individuals are not necessarily life prisoners of *one* culture learned during early enculturation. However, societal pressure may prompt individuals to demonstrate forms of behavior and "cultural identities" ultimately prescribed from the outside. The search for origins and linkages between the present-day cultural panorama displayed in the Americas and African cultures can in itself be an expression of ideologies centered around concepts of identity, ethnicity, black ethnicity, and so on. In this sense, cultural action precepts in the Americas, deliberately or unconsciously, may find themselves manipulating (present-day) African materials to create a semblance of historical continuity. Researchers provide, sometimes involuntarily, the materials for such aims.

Ethnicity Groups and Ethnicity

"Black ethnicity" is a composite term. As it is a centerpiece of this book, it seems justifiable to reflect upon the ideas expressed by this term. Is "black ethnicity" descriptive of a phenomenon, or does it express a mood or a particular psychological constellation to be encountered in our times? Why, for example, is there no parallel concept such as "white ethnicity"? Have we ever given some thought to that?

Let us first examine the term "ethnicity" in isolation, and later, in combination with the term "black." To my knowledge, the term "ethnicity" was first heard in America during the 1950s, but it became more current in the 1970s, not only in the academic world of anthropology, but also as a popular term. This coincided with the appearance of several articles and books directly or indirectly relating to the subject, such as E.H. Spencer's "Persistent cultural systems" (1971); *Urban Ethnicity*, edited by A. Cohen (1974); *Ethnicity: Theory and Experience* by Glazer and Moynihan (1975); and several other works listed in the references.

"Ethnicity" is not a term, however, that was coined for the description of any particularly new phenomenon detectable by anthropologists; rather, it came up to express a new consciousness about ethnic attachment. Historically, its rise paralleled another concept that gained increasing currency in the 1970s but had been used in America for some time, namely, that expressed by *Roots* (Haley 1977).

As so often in the ever-changing face of cultures around the world, the popularity and acuteness of terms and the concepts expressed by them can move diametrically in different geographical areas at the same time period. A concept — and this applies particularly to those with an emotional charge, either positive or negative — can become of central importance to some communities in one part of the world, while it is rejected in others. This has happened, for example, to the term "Bantu" in Africa, a word meaning "people" in many languages of east, central, and southern Africa. Its use is despised by many in South Africa, a country with a controversial history of "apartheid" and "pass laws," while it has become a symbol of a desired new cultural identity in some areas of Central Africa, particularly in formerly French-administrated territories. More recently, such consciousness culminated in the foundation of a *Centre International des Civilisations Bantu* (CICIBA) in Libreville, Gabon.

In Germany, during the era of the Third Reich (1933-1945) the term "Volk" became an emotionally and highly charged concept within the propaganda machine of Nazi Germany, with specific connotations and associations, such as "Volk ohne Raum" ("people without space, without living space"), which was used to justify colonialism and German expansionism at that time. In the course of these processes, the combination "das deutsche Volk" became a concept with strongly racist overtones, singling out an artificially created entity, namely the so-called "Aryans," as a genetically determinable populace, or "race."

If anything like the situation in Germany from the 1920s to the 1940s were recreated today, what kind of terminology would a present-day propaganda machine use to express such concepts? Would it speak of "German ethnicity"? Or "Aryan ethnicity"? Situations are never exactly duplicated in history and in different parts of the world, although a certain measure of comparability does indeed exist. It is significant that the term "ethnicity" has been used particularly in connection with the study of urbanized, highly industrialized, and pluralistic or multi-cultural societies, that is, societies composed of groups speaking different languages or dialectal variants and minorities who for one or another reason feel compelled to assert a separate cultural identity within the larger transcultural mold. This includes marginal areas of the society, groups aiming at alternative lifestyles, subcultures, and so on. Thus, the set of ideas expressed by the term "ethnicity" is connected with a certain social situation analogous today in many parts of the world. These ideas can also be understood as a response to such situations, as an attempt to come to grips with the challenges involved.

As expressed in titles of articles and books, the concept "ethnicity" is intimately connected with the related concepts of "cultural" or "ethnic" identity (see, for example, the title of A. P. Royce's book *Ethnic Identity: Strategies of Diversity*). "Ethnicity" is descriptive of a state of consciousness about ethnic bonds aiming at reconfirmation and reinforcement of dormant ethnic or cultural identities. Thus, it is not only a descriptive, but, in a sense, also an ideologically prescriptive concept. "Ethnicity" is not a higher-level abstraction of what in ethnology or cultural anthropology is called "ethnic groups." Actually, in areas of the world where the concept of "ethnic groups" still appears in the anthropological literature, as, for example, in sub-Saharan Africa, one rarely hears the word "ethnicity" in discussions. For Africa, the idea of "ethnicity" is strange and even suspicious, because it seems to promote identities which African governments are trying to discourage. To many African intellectuals "ethnicity" sounds as if it were just a new euphemistic surrogate term for "tribalism."

"Ethnicity" as a concept has, therefore, gained acceptance in cultural areas such as the Americas where the concept of "ethnic groups" has lost its original meaning because of a prolonged history of cross-cultural contacts leading to intensive amalgamation and transculturation and, as a consequence, to the emergence of new social groupings. Here, the term "ethnicity" is employed for the segmentation of large, essentially non-ethnic population clusters into smaller entities which are perceived as culturally related or even homogeneous. The stem of the word "ethnicity" derives from the Greek word "ethnos" which means "people" and by implication "groups having a common culture." "Ethnic" as an adjective means "what is connected or relates to *ethnos.*" With the additional suffix *-ity* in English, the word is transposed back into a noun. *-Ity* transmits the idea of "a quality of being," therefore, "ethnicity" describes something like the quality of being "ethnic," or a state of consciousness about being "ethnic."

Factual and Fictitious Ethnic Identities

On the cognitive level we can detect, however, a decisive differ- ence between the factual "ethnic identities" demonstrated by coherent ethnic groups, and the kind of fictitious ethnic identity postulated within the framework of a concept such as "ethnicity." The identity of an ethnic group is experienced by its members in a way that needs no further confirmation. A group of people at a particular time period shares a language, a set of common values, patterns of behavior and institutions, and that is taken for granted. It is not an issue to be discussed in the village's assembly pavilion. Sometimes it is even thought of as a heritage. In eastern Angola and northwestern Zambia, for example, the English or Portuguese words "culture," "cultura" — if the need arises to translate them — have been translated into the Ngangela languages of ZONE K (in the classification of Bantu languages by Malcolm Guthrie 1967-1971) as *chisemwa cha vantu* (see Kayombo ka Chinyeka 1973, 3). *Chisemwa*, etymologically analyzed, can be rendered as "what one is born with," and *chisemwa cha vantu*, therefore as "what people are born with." This proposes something like the existence of a genetically transmitted "ethnic character." It is a concept about culture that contradicts the results of modern anthropol- ogy, because we think that culture is precisely what one is *not* born with, but what one learns during one's lifetime in the environment in which one grows up and lives. But in the areas of Africa mentioned, and indeed also elsewhere, popular thought embraces a sort of "genetic" concept of culture. One is born Cokwe and committed to be a Cokwe all of one's life. Should there be any doubt about that, one gets one's tribal marks in time, such as having one's teeth chiseled to a point, thereby making it impossible to hide one's "ethnic identity." In a sense, the concept of culture as *chisemwa* is comparable to a concept which was also promoted in a culturally quite different part of the world and expressed in the adjective "arteigen" (compare "arteigene Kunst") during the Nazi regime in Germany.

The process of learning a culture by slow absorption, informal and formal training, while growing up, is called enculturation. But while it was often assumed in the past that individuals who share a culture — reinforced by a common language or common mode of verbal expression — continue to do so all their lives, more recent research undertaken on the psychology of enculturation, and culture contact (Kubik 1991a, 1991b) confirms that the cultural profile of an individual can change considerably during the individual's life span. Enculturation does not stop at any particular age, and in addition there is and has always been contact with other cultures, no culture having ever existed in total isolation. Depending on an individual's intellectual capacity and on the kind of contacts he or she has had, individuals — some of them more, some less — change their cultural profile during a lifetime in processes of inner cultural reconfiguration. In other words, we are not bound to one and the same culture during all of life. Sometimes there are clearly marked transitions. Sometimes there is an incision, a sudden leap. Sometimes the process of inner change is more gradual. In retrospect, I recall how my own cultural profile changed abruptly between 1945 and 1947 at the age of ten to twelve in Vienna, my city of birth, through intensive exposure to African-American cultural expressions of the time, while I lived with my mother in the American occupation zone.

Not too long ago, culture was considered something static, rigidly delineated. For Africa it was assumed that people there had been carrying on the same cultural traditions for centuries without any notable change. Africa was considered a "continent without history." These days are now over. We know that the regional expressions of sixteenth- and seventeenth-century African cultures were quite different from those of twentieth-century African cultures, and it is one of the axioms in current comparative research, for example, in Africa and in the Americas, to pay attention to the time span under investigation. For example, we may compare late eighteenth-century musical instruments of southwestern Angola with late eighteenth-century musical instruments in those regions of Brazil among contemporaneous communities where they were documented at the time. We can then proceed along the lines of a sequence of sources, to learn how these musical instruments (in their organology playing techniques, and so on) changed in the nineteenth and twentieth centuries during their independent histories in the two regions separated by the Atlantic. Although it is always done, again and again, a direct comparison of twentieth-century African traditions in Africa with African-American traditions in the twentieth century requires methodological prudence. Any possible stability of culture traits in the separate culture worlds has to be ascertained from case to case. Superficially recognizable similarities have to be submitted to more rigorous structural and historical scrutiny.

The set of ideas expressed in the concept of "ethnicity" does not include the notion of dynamic culture change in history. Rather it seems to promote arresting of cultural mobility by postulating a rigid liaison between culture and population groups. If looked at with the eye of a historian, the concept of "ethnicity" — much more than that of "ethnic groups" — is essentially non-historical. It assumes a somewhat eternal, unchanging "ethnic identity" for the groups singled out on the basis of language, physical outlook, or any other "identity markers."

If one looks comparatively across the popular cognitive landscape on earth today, one will find, of course, that ideas about static, unchanging "ethnic" behavior that would make a Frenchman remain French all his life, a German irreversibly German, and an African-American forever unchangeably African-American, are cultivated in the most diverse quarters. Such philosophies are the result of ancient human survival strategies, and — although they seem perhaps a little outdated on the verge of the twenty-first century — they still determine the worldview of many and the relationships between individuals.

However, while the idea of *chisemwa cha vantu* discussed above may be suited to the margin of experience accessible to a village population in Eastern Angola, problems emerge with acuteness for a believer in cultural genetics, if he or she is transplanted into a different cultural environment; in other words, if a scenario is created in which different cultures become tangible through contact. This is precisely what became operational in the Americas from 1600 onward, and it is now also increasingly being experienced in Europe.

Culture Contact

Much has been written about the mechanisms of culture contact, from the writing of the eminent anthropologist Melville J. Herskovits to more recent psychologically oriented studies such as those I have carried out (Kubik 1991b). Culture contact is always a deeply penetrating and transforming challenge to an individual's idea about self. Culture contact teaches relativity. A monolingual person suddenly transplanted into another language and cultural world learns painfully that his or her categorizations in the mother tongue, modes of behavior, and values are nothing absolute or universally valid, but rather are relative and often culture-specific. Such a person might feel as if relegated to a position at the edge of the galaxy instead of at its center. For many individuals — whatever culture and language group they come from — this can become difficult to accept. Two opposing forces then come into play: Curiosity and other motivations lead the individual into a process of learning about the other culture. Failure in quick learning, disappointment, and the inner resistance against giving himself up totally by devaluing and even erasing all previous experience in order to start anew in the other culture accumulate to constitute the counter-force. There is also fear of the unknown and additionally the unpredictable reaction by members of the contact culture. If they accept the newcomer, the process of transculturation can be facilitated. If the members of the contact culture reject the newcomer, the forces of inner resistance to transcend the cultural boundary will gain momentum. Individual experience of this kind becomes a socio-psychological pattern from the moment such an experience is multiplied.

Why, in culture contact groups, people reject each other is, of course, a very complex matter. It can only be discussed on an area and case basis. Unconscious processes of projection, however, play a great role in cross-cultural contact, namely that — expressed in psychoanalytical terminology — some of the contents of an individual's unconscious, particularly ideas and tendencies repressed in his own culture of origin, are regularly projected upon the contact culture (see Kubik 1991b for examples). If the idea of "black," for example, is charged with a negative content in one culture, as was historically the case in many Mediterranean and European cultures — hence surviving terms such as Black Death for the bubonic plague, black market, black cat, black magic, black sheep, to blackmail, blacklist, blackout, black widow, black spot, and so on — this can form the basis of reinterpretations in culture contact resulting in neurotically distorted images of reality. In contact with cultures upon which the negatively charged concept "black" can be projected for one or another reason, the outcome of the arising conflict is predictable.

In many circumstances, culture contact develops into relationships of ambivalence. The initial "cultural identity" brought by each of the interacting groups ends up being constantly questioned. Reinterpretation, described by Melville J. Herskovits as one of the cognitive reactions that begin to operate in culture contact, is in fact a group reaction ignoring the cognitional reality of the other culture. It is a kind of short-cut towards understanding (or rather misunderstanding) the other culture within familiar categories in one's own culture world. The abortive undertaking of understanding the other culture in its own emics* leads to ambiguous feelings of disappointment and deprivation. Successful attempts, on the other hand, can lead to joy in the new identity. Ideally, the different cultural contact groups eventually grow together to form a new culture.

Such processes of what Fernando Ortiz (1940) has described as "transculturation" have taken place in the culture history of several areas of South America and the Caribbean, at several historical stages. But in some areas, a high visibility of physical differences between the groups involved and emotional reactions attached to it have delayed or even held back indefinitely the transculturation process. Thus, it is not true that pronounced cultural differences (including language) inhibit transculturation; that can all be learned within a generation or two (consider, for example, the successful assimilation of pre-World War I Czech and Slovak immigrants into the mainstream culture of a place like Vienna). It is physical properties beyond an individual's control which can delay the process *if* they are targeted in segmentary societies to function as "ethnic" or "cultural" identifiers. From the concept of the "Jewish nose" in the mid-twentieth-century Germany of concentration camps, to mystical ideas about "blood," up to the familiar usage of skin color and type of hair as "identifiers" in racist societies, we get a broad panel of atavistic popular ideas about "human

---

* Emics mean analyzing linguistic or behavioral phenomena in terms of a system's own internal structural or functional elements.

classification." The daily individual experience of societal interaction proceeding from such popular ideas eventually accelerates segmentation processes within the larger society, leading to the formation of something like pseudo-ethnic groups. From the moment such existential traumas begin to be experienced in large numbers — as, for example, in the collective experience of groups of Germans in the 1930s who suddenly found themselves segmented and isolated as "Jews" — centripetal forces come into play, accelerating this process. The resulting polarization of society allows no alternatives. You become classified as "white," "black," "Aryan," "Jewish," and the like; supposedly you cannot be all at the same time. In a recent issue of *Time* magazine devoted to ethnic strife, one discovers that curious taxonomies have emerged in North America, evident from the categories exposed in an opinion poll whose text is printed in that issue, distinguishing among "Whites," "Blacks," and "Hispanics."

A pseudo-ethnic identity is thereby established for targeted population groups in a manner that leaves few choices for the individual, as few perhaps as the variety of merchandise displayed on the shelves of a Moscow supermarket in 1991. Pseudo-ethnic classification easily degenerates into an obsession with committing individuals to membership in some cultural, racial, professional, ideological, social or whatever group, while in reality the cultural environment of any area of the world is complex and characterized by smooth shades and transitions, quite apart from the significant factor of changing individual cultural profiles. Age-old processes of transculturation, softening or even breaking up cultural contrasts that may have formed at one time or another, are an important factor. It is fair to say that any culture in the world is a product of previous transculturation, and this has always been so in history. There have never been any "pure" cultures on our planet. For this reason we speak of cultural configuration and reconfiguration, rather than of "culture" as a rigid and singular term.

The delicate emotional connotations of the processes of identifying oneself can be brought to light in psychological tests of various kinds. For example, consider how you would feel or how others would feel if asked any of the following questions:

- Are you American or Hispanic? (Question to someone whose first language is Spanish)
- Are you White or Hispanic? (Same as above)

- Are you an African or are you a Black American? (Question to someone whose physical appearance suggests an African ancestry)

- Are you *Muntu* or West African? (Question that was posed to someone off-stage at an international conference organized by CICIBA in Libreville in 1985)

There are also notable counter-trends to the forces which eventually steer a society towards mass ethnic obsession and the resulting pressures upon individuals to follow suit. Paradoxically, nationalism at the level of nation-states can be such a counter-force. Communist and socialist ideologies proceeding from the notion of centralized control of the means of production and social life can also temporarily attenuate any tendencies towards ethnic segmentation, or discourage the political implications of existing ethnic identities, while excessively promoting their folkloristic aspects. In some countries of Latin America, Venezuela for example, strong state interference in cultural life, visible in the reorganization of almost any cultural activity around "grupos folklóricos" can also work in the direction of an attenuation of any ethnicity consciousness that might emerge. A classic example of such policies, however, was the former Soviet Union, where "ethnic identities" became officially reinterpreted as "nationalities." To a certain extent this model was copied in Angola during the late 1970s and early 1980s, when the languages of six Angolan ethnic groups became called "national languages," and Portuguese a "vehicular language" (*língua veicular*). But since centralized control of human activities frequently ends up in repression — examples could be cited from a number of one-party states in Africa where ethnic groups have been deprived even of their languages — ethnic strife is the likely outcome once the lid is taken off the pot. In present-day Yugoslavia — or rather what remains of it — one can witness the destructive outcome of a clash between opposing ideas about where an individual should belong. The question put to someone born in Zagreb of whether he or she is "Croatian" or "Yugoslavian" is about whether this individual identifies with his or her community sharing a small culture and language, or with the more abstract entity of a nation-state that came into being for certain historical reasons and circumstances, totally beyond the control of the individual.

Identity as an Issue

From what has been said so far, it seems that an intellectual atmosphere in which "ethnic identity" becomes an issue emerges precisely in situations where culture contact and the route toward transculturation have reached a dead end. A content analysis of the concept of "ethnicity" alone does not answer the question about how such concepts begin to develop in the first place. One has to consider the implications and then learn comparatively about their history, not only in the Americas, but elsewhere. From the viewpoint of a dynamic vision of culture, the concept of "ethnicity," therefore, can be submitted to psychological scrutiny. For psychological anthropology in particular, the basic question is not whether "ethnicity" is anything phenomenologically detectable, but rather an inquiry into the cognitional basis of such concepts. In simple words, why do people in certain places and at certain times in history conceptualize the way they do; why do they divide the human world in the manner they do, and then pressure individuals into the categories they have created?

What is the social and ideological function of the "ethnicity" concept? What is the energy underneath it that keeps it going? What are the psychological forces giving rise to discussions about "ethnicity" and "cultural identity"? We have said that in some rural areas of Africa the fact of belonging to an ethnic group that is identifiable by a common language and common life experience, values, and institutions, is something self-understood, without further questioning. There is no need to discuss "cultural identity" in an environment where the cultural identity of its inhabitants is obvious.

As I pointed out in a paper on the "identity" question (Kubik 1989), identities are not discussed in societies in which a living identity is in operation. Identities begin to be discussed precisely when for some reason — in at least a segment of the society — there is uncertainty about identities. In other words, identity begins to be discussed from the moment it has become somebody's problem. This includes "ethnic" or "cultural" identity. And like the rigorous controls at border posts in the former German Democratic Republic (GDR) — where in 1984 one of the GDR passport officials I met expressed doubts about the identity of the nose (!) of an African colleague with whom I was traveling — identity can become even more of a problem for the authority trying to identify than for the individuals to be identified.

In the Americas, ethnic identities of eighteenth- and nineteenth-century Africa have not survived as genealogically traceable units. In some parts of the Americas, however, African groupings have survived even under their original names, not as ethnic groups, but as associations perpetuating certain cultural traditions, as for example in Brazil in the Nagô, Jeje, and other relatively closed religious traditions of the Candomblé groups (Pinto 1991). While apparently nowhere in the Americas is there a direct continuation of any eighteenth- or nineteenth-century African ethnic group without considerable admixture from ethnically different families, African or non-African, cultural traditions can sometimes still be traced historically to quite specific regions of Africa, as I have been able to demonstrate repeatedly (Kubik 1979, 1990). The important point here is that those cultural traditions are carried on in the Americas by groups of people who are not necessarily traceable as a coherent group in their genealogy to the same regions. For example, in some Brazilian Candomblé religious groups one finds a set of predominantly Yoruba-(Nagô-) related cultural traits, in others, a configuration of traits that points to the Kongo/northwestern Angolan culture area; but that does not mean that those who perpetuate and perform these traditions in Brazil today are uniformly physical descendants of either culture area. In principle, the present-day carriers of apparently "ethnic" traditions can have any sort of genealogical profile and come from any stratum of the populace. On the other hand, it turns out that these traditions are transmitted by relatively tight groups. These are, however, new social groupings with their own criteria for in-group adherence. Although they are perpetuating ethnically identifiable cultural traditions, the carriers today are not an ethnic group.

In addition, a closer look at even small African-American communities will reveal to the observant eye that what sometimes appears to be culturally homogeneous is not so in reality. In Brazil I was repeatedly reminded of these realities in several rural communities researched in 1979 and 1980 in the states of Minas Gerais and São Paulo. For example, a small rural community of some seventy inhabitants, Bairro de Cafundó near Salto de Pirapora in the state of São Paulo, which I researched together with Guilherme dos Santos Barbosa, (Barbosa 1978, Kubik 1990) eventually turned out to be a cultural conglomerate. This community had attracted my attention because some of its members remembering a vocabulary of about three hundred to five hundred words from Angolan languages such as Umbundu, Kimbundu, Kikoongo, and "Ngangela." They used this vocabulary in deceptive conversations whenever foreign visitors penetrated their village. After staying in the village for some weeks I discovered how different the individual cultural profiles of the various group members were. One sub-group within the community showed behavioral and cognitional traits pointing to cultural patterns I was familiar with from my extensive research in Angola. But another group showed predominantly Iberian cultural traits, while yet another which had apparently formed from a stock of recent immigrants — in spite of some degree of transculturation — showed cultural links with the Brazilian northeast. In addition, all of this was embedded into a generalized culture of southern Brazilian make, familiar to us from people who speak the so-called "dialeto caipira" (*caipira* [São Paulo state hinterland] dialect; see Amaral 1976).

The cultural differences between the inhabitants of Bairro de Cafundó were independent of their physical appearance. A researcher proceeding consciously or unconsciously from the notion that physical appearance could be a diagnostic indicator of culture would run into a pitfall here. In other words, the most African-looking face in Cafundó would not necessarily belong to the mind in which most of the African remembrances were accumulating, although it must be said that two of our key informants, Otavio Caetano and Benedita Pires Pedroso, were also genealogically traceable as descendants of ancestors who had come from one distinctive Central African area (see Barbosa 1978, Kubik 1991).

Living Identity and Cultural Marginalization

Regarding cultural identity, it is significant to point out that the neo-African cultural groups in some rural areas of the Americas, like their counterparts in Africa, apparently have no identity problem. They have achieved a new living cultural identity which remains unquestioned. Psychologically, therefore, the origins of the ethnicity concept cannot be expected to be found in the general population. Ultimately, of course, any ideas are created by individuals, come from the individual experience, and can only become collective if they are propagated and if the experience is multiplied. But the social stratum that was fertile in creating ethnicity is quite specific. The fact that "ethnicity" and "cultural identity" are emotionally charged concepts points to an origin in individuals within a social stratum where "cultural identity" had become a problem. These individuals must have passed through the painful experience of hetero-cultural deprival and rejection giving rise to basic existential questions such as "Who am I? Where do I belong?" These are not questions a successful "capoeira" master is likely to pose. He knows who he is. These also do not come up in the general non-reflective population. But they come up regularly in individuals who are culturally marginal and who for this reason have gone through an existential trauma.

In psychological terms, the "ethnicity" movement can also be understood, therefore, as an essentially compensatory process, as a compensatory reaction to the absence of factual ethnic identities in certain sectors of a stratified society, and to the frustrations resulting from an abortive transculturation attempt.

Our research question, then, amounts to assessing the kind of societies in the Americas that make such traumas possible, on the one hand creating a fertile ground for cultural marginalization of some, on the other hand providing a psychological basis for certain traditions to remain rigidly associated with distinctive population segments or social strata. Why have some cultural traditions of African origin in the Americas not become a common heritage of all?

"Ethnicity" as a social response comes to the support of the second tendency. However, "ethnicity" as a cultural consciousness movement is by definition non-ethnic. It is an attempt at large-scale grouping beyond the relatively narrow variation margin of what in ethnology is defined as an "ethnic group" (see Hirschberg 1988). That a large population speaks the same language, and shares some common cultural characteristics, is not sufficient to lump its members together as an "ethnic group." That another population group displays similarity in some physical traits while it is culturally diverse does not make it a candidate either. "Ethnicity," therefore, is much closer to a prescriptive ideological program than it is a term descriptive of ethnic facts.

"Ethnicity" as a Collective Oppositional Response

During our recent fieldwork in Namibia,[1] in the southwestern part of Africa (14 October to 14 December 1991), we were able to make a few interesting comparative observations regarding ethnic identities. These observations can be used as an interpretive framework pertinent to the American scene and allow us to understand it better. Namibia had a prolonged struggle for political independence. Before World War I, it was a German colonial territory; then it came under the administrative power of the South African regime which later created apartheid, until Namibia gained independence under United Nations supervision in 1990. One can observe now a difficult readjustment process among Namibian individuals, a search for redefining identity. There would be no such need, of course, if it had not been made a problem through colonization and apartheid. At closer look, the whole South African system of apartheid was a device aimed at promoting ethnicity, although this word was never used; that is, the promotion of an ethnic consciousness on the basis of the original meaning of this word's root, namely "ethnos." The policy implied that ethnic groups in the country should become increasingly conscious of and interested in retaining their identity, hoping that the African population would thereby remain split according to languages and cultures, avoiding the only thing that the apartheid regime found dangerous for its own Boer ethnic survival, namely that — in spite of different languages and cultures such as Xhosa, Sotho, Zulu, Tswana, and so on — the people concerned might develop a feeling for identity and a common consciousness based on a totally different principle that is non-ethnic, namely the more atavistic concept of *race* (compare the "black consciousness" movement in South Africa during the 1970s). The great fear of the apartheid regime was that the different peoples of South Africa might in fact transcend their language-based ethnicity, to reach a common *black* consciousness based on racial identity. In such case, of course, they would reach immediately majority status in South Africa, while on the basis of maintaining ethnic divisions, the ethnic panorama of South Africa would remain much more segmented and thereby favor the Boer- or Afrikaans-speaking community.

In Namibia, the apartheid system is over. But the impact of the decade-long ideological indoctrination is still visible everywhere. Most of the land of Namibia was divided up into farms which attracted farmworkers who became permanently attached to the mostly German- or Afrikaans-speaking farm owners. In a sense, this late twentieth-century picture reminded our research team of circumstances described in the literature on nineteenth-century Brazil, with the large "fazendas" (plantations) economically dominant, and dependent slave-worker communities attached to each *fazenda*. We were surprised to discover that the institution of "Casa Grande" and "Senzala" (plantation home and slave quarters), described by Gilberto Freyre (1943), is still alive as a social situation in that remote part of southwestern Africa. Some of the farmworking families recruited from Nama and other authochtonous peoples of Namibia have been attached to those farms for three to four generations, and the children were born there. They know nothing else but farm life in dependency, the work they are expected to do and the family of the farm owners responsible for their lives and well-being.

But some communities in Namibia retained a certain independence throughout the colonial period by war and through fierce struggles — such as the Herero, who have remained psychologically traumatized until today from the times of the 1904 war of annihilation with German occupying forces. The Herero holocaust is a living experience in many Herero individuals and has greatly contributed to an ethnic consciousness that could be called "Herero ethnicity" — in opposition to the historical holocaust inflicted upon the Herero by German military personnel. It is not called by that term in Namibia, but could be described as such. From this example we can notice an important structural element in the state of consciousness described by the word "ethnicity." Ethnicity movements are always a form of collective response in opposition to some other community perceived as oppressive, and as an ethnic threat.

Gradually, we are also beginning to understand more extensively what fuels ethnicity. The whole concept begins with the experience of outside aggression, deprivation, discrimination, and holocaust. The traumatic collective experience of a group fuels the kind of consciousness called "ethnicity." And this seems to be valid not merely for the Herero in Namibia, but for many areas of the American scene in North, Central, and South America. Thus, a causal determinant for the rise of ethnicity as a simplistic, though ideologically powerful, concept is the previous experience by a community of an equally ideologically based, direct aggression by an oppositional community with which it came into culture contact, and the experience that such contact did *not* lead to transculturation (in Fernando Ortiz's term), but to rejection.

In the case of the Herero, the independence of Namibia has brought a new dimension to the conflict. By analogy, one may imagine a fictional scenario in which the United States of America would suddenly be ruled by a predominantly African-American government. In such a case, what would happen to the concept of "ethnicity"? Would it continue? Probably not. There would come something else. The new dimension among the Herero is that (what I have tentatively called) "Herero ethnicity" is no longer sufficient as an ideology, and also, some people seem to realize that the whole concept can be manipulated, identities can be "managed" (see Greverus 1981), and their maintenance can play ultimately into the interest of the former oppressor. The oppressor's interest in any stratified society is, of course, to subject people to predestined categories and roles, from birth to death, in order to exert control. But one can only control what has been defined clearly. What cannot be nailed down cannot be controlled. For example, if you are asked, on the telephone, to identify yourself, as black or white, or Jewish, or Hispanic, or Herero, or whatever, and your answer is "I am XY. Full stop.", then any potentially oppressive authority will have a problem. If you say: "Myself I am neither black nor white. I am not European. I am not American. I am nothing of that sort. I have no ethnicity at all. I am XY"; then your potential oppressor gets into a state of frustration. He will not know what to do, as he can't fit you into any of the slots he has prepared for you. He will say: "This is not possible. You must be *something*. You must be one of those things which I know." The oppressor will, of course, try immediately to eliminate you, to make you a non-person, because coming across somebody who is not black, not white, not yellow, not even green, nothing like that, approximates an encounter with a terrifying extraterrestrial. But for you to be nothing cements your freedom.

Ingestion of the Oppressor

Culture contact can lead to "syncretism" and cultural merger, but it regularly assumes oppressive or aggressive structures if one community with a strong cultural coherence thinks of itself as culturally superior to another, or if, in addition, it attempts hegemony. In such a case one encounters a relationship of tensions which makes a real merger, real transculturation, that is, acculturation from both sides, impossible for generations, although it might eventually occur. In East Africa there was such a situation in some areas of Uganda, Rwanda, and Burundi, when pastoral people invaded the areas from the fourteenth century on, coming from the East African horn, believing that their ways of life and value systems were superior to those of the settled agriculturalists, and consequently looking at them with contempt. That such feelings of superiority of one ethnic or racial group towards another involve varying degrees of ethnocentrism, lacking objectivity, is evident. For example, one could say that technologically, the settled agriculturalists of the interlacustrine area in East Africa in the fourteenth and fifteenth centuries, with a highly developed iron technology, were probably far superior to the invaders. But the invader is often blind, as ethnocentrism is characterized by the inability to acknowledge any values and achievements by groups other than those defined by the observer's own ethnic group itself.

Like recourse to physical "identity markers," ethnocentrism is, of course, part of a syndrome of antique survival strategies, ultimately necessary for weak groups whose culture is in danger of disintegration and who are afraid of that. The intracultural value system is thought of as universal. When such a group comes into contact with another group of different technological and cultural profile, it reacts with a defense mechanism (see Anna Freud 1936 for explanation of the term), developing ethnocentrism, seeing itself at the center of the human universe, and adhering to a policy which streamlines individuals in this group to conform with the ideology. The contact group, of course, sees the behavior of the invading group for what it is, an aggression. It cannot detect the motivations of that aggression in the invading group's own psychological structure.

A unique situation, however, was created through the Arab and Atlantic slave trade, when the conqueror came technologically into a position to use the conquered for his own aims as manual labor and to transfer whole populations to a New World, sealing their dependence upon him by depriving them of their old community support. In other words, when cattle-keeping invaders had swept through the interlacustrine areas of East Africa, the native inhabitants were able to react to the invasion by reinforcing their cultural coherence — which, for example, gave rise to the foundation of states such as Bunyoro-Kitara and later Buganda which can be seen as compensatory reaction to the invasion by the force of the autochthonous inhabitants. These states were not creations by the cattle-herding pastoralists, as was thought in ethnology in the late nineteenth and early twentieth centuries, but they might also not have come about without the cultural and political pressures exerted by the invader upon the native people, who reacted by finding or rather redefining their ethnic identity in reaction to the aggressor, eventually absorbing him. On the other hand, when large groups of people from various parts of Africa were geographically dislocated, transferred to the Near East or the New World, their possibilities for reinforcing their cultural coherence were somewhat smaller and less ethnically determined.

The reactions to a cultural invader or conqueror include various processes of identification with the latter, emphasizing one or the other realm. Identification by the oppressed with the oppressor is a common psychological reaction of oppressed groups to overcome and eventually overrun the oppressor. One could say even bluntly that the oppressed community reacts by psychological "ingestion" (internalization) and thereby elimination of the oppressor (see Kubik 1991a).

A common symptom of the identification is that the oppressed group adopts the oppressor's language: In Africa the most striking examples have been the rise of certain African languages to the status of trade languages and later even national languages; for example, Kiswahili, the language spoken originally by the highly Arab-influenced population of a small strip of the East African Coast, or Hausa, in certain parts of West Africa reflecting the results of Hausa hegemony, and later, in some parts of West and Central Africa, French, in the movements of "francophonie" and even "négritude." That all the liberation movements in the former Portuguese-dominated territories of Africa adopted Portuguese in their own bush schools right from the beginning of these movements, in Moçambique, Angola, and Guine-Bissau, and that in the post-liberation era Portuguese is even spoken more generally in these territories than it used to be during the colonial rule, is a similar symptom and a sign of an unconscious identification process of the oppressed with the former oppressor. Informants who are untrained in depth psychology will, of course, rationalize; they will say, Portuguese had to be adopted as a vehicular language in education because of a lack of availability of books in any African languages of the area, or, a frequent argument, the adoption of the language of the former colonial master is necessary to avoid promoting "tribalism" — one could also simply say to avoid promoting separate identities of any of the numerous ethnic-linguistic groups in the country. These are the usual arguments articulated in favor, but underneath there is another stratum, namely, that the secret desire of the oppressed is always to rise to the status and power of the oppressor. The tragedy is that the victims of aggression and torture later tend to identify with the victimizer's values, often the only way for a complete psychological "reconquista."

In other places, it is not the language of the oppressor which is perceived as the key to overcome and eliminate or "ingest" him, but his technology. The rise of Nama culture, which has a hunter-gatherer basis but a superimposed pastoral economy (in Namibia) is an example of such a reaction. The rise of Japan as a technological world power today can be explained, to a certain extent, as an extremely successful implementation of the same mechanism. The trauma of Hiroshima and Nagasaki only reinforced a tendency that had existed in Japanese culture from the nineteenth century on. Technological superiority of Japan at the end of the twentieth century is an expression and ultimate result of an unconscious identification with the original aggressor: the West.

What happens, then, if a cultural community identifies with the oppressor to the extent of doing almost everything to imitate him in order to obtain his recognition, and yet the oppressor shows no sign of recognizing the attempt? There is a great deal of evidence to assume that during the era of slavery many African descendants did not react at first with counter-aggression, but accepted tacitly the oppressor's claim that they were inferior human beings, and tried to "improve." In Brazil, for example, we can detect in the literature of the nineteenth century that those slaves hailed by the slavers as most useful, especially Angolans, were developing that attitude. For a number of reasons that cannot be analyzed in detail here, certain West African descendants — Yoruba, Hausa, Mandingo — responded with resistance to a greater extent.

Why then do the oppressed identify unconsciously with the oppressor? Because in the beginning the oppressor invariably succeeds in convincing the oppressed that he is superior: Where he does not succeed, he cannot function as an oppressor. The whole arrangement breaks down; he would only stand as a fool claiming unjustified superiority. The key for understanding the psychological state of the oppressed is therefore found in this reciprocity. Accepting the role of the oppressor in the initial stages of the encounter, the oppressed then tries a successful defense strategy first by identifying with him, his methods and ways of life. If that fails, as it often did in the Americas, then we get a set of more complex reaction patterns, among which the "ethnicity" movement is one.

Redesignations

In the study of culture contact, it is advisable to consider denominations and content of various concepts separately because very often ideas are simply renamed under varying circumstances, as is demonstrated, for example, by the modifications in meaning which the Fõ term *vodu* has undergone in various parts of the New World. *Vaudou* (in French spelling) in Haiti has a wider semantic field than the ancestral West African form *vodu*, while the content of the latter term — analogous to the Yoruba *orisa* — was transposed into the Haitian concept of *loa*. In other words, a researcher from Dahomey or Togo visiting Haiti will find that what he calls *vodu* is often called *loa* in Haiti. In Brazil, the concepts of Yoruba *orisa,* on the other hand, developed into a bilingual expressive form, in the sense that the Brazilian term *santo* and the Yoruba term *orixá* (in Brazilian spelling) became alternative and widely analogous denominations for the same set of ideas.

There are various historical forces and socio-psychological pressures that can generate such changes in denominations, not always accompanied by a change in the ideas themselves. In Africa, for example, the terms "tribe," "native," and "tribal" were very common in the colonial literature until they acquired a negative emotional charge and were changed to "ethnic," "indigenous," and the like. The term "ethnic group," however, is a mere euphemism of what was called "tribe" before, while the associated concepts have not changed at all. More recently, one can hear the term "cultural group," which is another substitute or surrogate term that is even more misleading.

Sensitive areas in human relations regularly undergo a revision in terminology, perpetuating the illusion that matters themselves have changed. Against this background we can now consider the composite term "black ethnicity."

In the United States, there has been a chain of terminological changes referring to populations of African descent, from "Negro" and "Colored," to "Afro-American," "black American," "black" and "African-American." The problem here is that terminology has changed, but not the referent (that is, who or what is referred to), although etymologically the new terms show a remarkable trend towards "decolorization." The term "African-American" — at least in its wording — makes no longer any reference to atavistic notions about physical properties such as skin color or the like, but it is a term referring to geographical ancestry.

The psychological forces behind the creation of surrogate terminology can best be described with Sigmund Freud's term "Verschiebung"
(approximately: "displacement") and interpreted from the viewpoint
of psychoanalytic theory. We can say that the psychological forces that
have replaced the term "Afro-American" with "black" and then
"African-American" are forces of the id (in psychoanalytical terminology), reacting to censorship that declares that a term is no longer
appropriate. Analyzed this way, however, the question is what does the
id want, and what does the censorship try to stop. To put it in rough
language: the id wants the "Nigger" to remain "Nigger," to maintain the
identity it has prescribed for him. The superego protests against the use
of such a terribly racist and searing epithet and creates a substitution
scenario in which apparently the "Negro" is seen transforming into
something else, while the paradoxical implication is that he still
maintains his "identity" (that is, he remains what the oppressor has
assigned him to be). He just gets another name.

The crucial question here is, Whose id and whose superego are
we talking about? Are they the victimizer's or the victim's? Or perhaps
both?

"Black ethnicity"

The term "black ethnicity" places ethnicity into a framework which
is by definition non-ethnic. "Black" as an adjective or noun (or its
counterpart "negro" in Spanish and Portuguese) when applied to
people, is *not*, in its etymology, a compelling reference to anything
ethnic, to any specific ethnic or cultural entity. It is a notion derived
from and based upon the concept of race. But since there is no causal
correlation between race and culture that could be traced scientifically
in any part of the world — although popular mythological thinking
would postulate precisely that — there is a logical problem with the
juxtaposition of the two terms. The combination "black" with "ethnicity"
is a contradiction in terms, because "black" is not an ethnic qualifier, and
"ethnic" is not a racial qualifier. However, this word combination exists;
it is still widely used and has therefore an impact on public intellectual
life. Moreover, although a person's physical appearance and cultural
background are, in principle, unrelated, they can be made to appear
being related when the surrounding society postulates a relationship.
If someone has red hair and freckles since birth, it has no connection
with his intellectual capabilities, or socio-cultural behavior unless the

society projects upon that individual a set of expectations, using those physical characteristics as "identity markers." Much the same can be said about the fate of albinos in various African societies, for example. Only different in physical outlook from the general populace, an albino can become a projection screen for the most varied social expectations. In most cases the victims will then begin to act as expected.

"Black ethnicity" is a concept based on two popular ideas unsustained by scientific data gathering: 1) that there should be a predictable causal or at least reciprocal relationship between a person's physical appearance and culture; and 2) that a group of human beings identified superficially by some common physical characteristics should be culturally homogeneous or at least similar.

Concept 2 is, of course, in relationship to concept 1 in the sense that if concept 1 did not exist, concept 2 could not exist either. The term "black ethnicity" thus implies that groups of people singled out by some common physical characteristics are expected to behave like an ethnic macro-entity spread out across the Americas from the United States to Brazil, having a common culture, a "black culture."

In 1981, when my friend and colleague David Evans and I visited the Ajanaku family in Memphis, Tennessee — a family that has tried to adopt a West African lifestyle in the United States — they blamed me for having used the word "black" in the title of my book *Angolan Traits in Black Music, Games and Dances of Brazil*, although in the book I had explained the somewhat unconventional manner in which I used it, not referring to people at all. I now agree with the Ajanaku family that it was a bad choice that should not have been made under any circumstances. About ten years later, the word "black" is apparently still with us. In South Africa it even seems to gain increasing currency with the creation of misnomers such as "black languages" instead of African languages.

Although the "black ethnicity" concept is something that has sprung up from North American soil, there were movements in Africa that are comparable to some extent. "Black ethnicity" is hardly heard in Africa, but several chiliastic and nativistic movements in twentieth-century Africa based on the undeclared but implied concept of "identity by race" are comparable. In Africa, the idea of racial identity was sometimes stretched as far as to embrace the physically most diverse populations, from the Kalahari steppe to the vanished populace of Ancient Egypt.

Even *négritude* was, in a sense, a movement comparable in concept to "black ethnicity," although we cannot overlook the differences in historical setting and content. Since the adjective "negro" (in Spanish and Portuguese) is widely congruent in its semantic field with "black" in English — although in Latin languages one sometimes gets two words translatable as "black," for example, "negro" and "preto" in Portuguese — the French term *négritude* could also be expressed in English with a construct containing the word "black," as in "blackness."

With regard to the considerable criticism to which the use of the word "black" has been subjected for some time in the United States, we can now try to identify the social and psychological setting which promotes its continuing use and projection into the cultural realm.

The overall analysis I have tried to give in this paper suggests that "ethnicity," and "black ethnicity" in particular, as a collective notion is a multifaceted response to a social situation involving disparate interests. Role interaction always demands the participation of at least two interactors. Therefore, it would probably be inaccurate to characterize "black ethnicity" as an exclusively African-American idea and movement. Several antagonistic components of the larger society have been drawn into the game, discovering a convergence of interests. The promotion of "black ethnicity" as mass consciousness may, therefore, serve the interests of quite opposing forces. If "black identity" means assigning roles of cultural behavior to individuals, who then assigns those roles? Pushing individuals into prepared conceptual slots throws up the question to what extent potentially oppressing forces play their part in the game. Strangely, but quite obviously, the game seems to be played in concert by parties with the most varied interests.

A neurotic societal arrangement always has some kind of advantage for the individuals and groups affected. A simple but basic advantage for the deprived individual is the facility to evade responsibilities. A person suffering from agoraphobia does not have to cross open, unprotected places. If my self-appointed stepfather tells me that I am an ape, and if he continues to tell me every day that is my identity, if he rejects me as a human being, what options do I have? At least I will not have to sweep the house, because apes don't sweep. I will not have to contribute as much as I could to the economic pie. If I cannot run away from him, one possible working arrangement will be that I behave exactly like the ape he created in his mind, perhaps like Tarzan's "Cheetah." I will mirror the image about me which he created and cultivates. If he says that apes have a special rhythmic talent and are born with it, then I will play the drum, I will try to satisfy his expectation, and perhaps he will pay me money for confirming his ideas about me. If he says that apes have African ancestry, I will try to get hold of everything I can obtain from Africa to make me look more African, and thereby even get away from him a little, although in my deep soul I know, of course, that I am *not* African; in fact, I hate the sight of any Africans if I meet them in the streets, for example, students from Africa who hold American scholarships, whom I may think of as "those slaves" ...(!)[2] If he expects apes to know much about *voodoo,* I will import all the *voodoo* quickly from the Caribbean to my home to play the role more convincingly....

This fictional narrative will make us aware, through symbols, of some of the deeper psychological strata that are activated in culture contact. It is not meant to simplify the complexity of the subject we are dealing with here and the variability of the results of culture clash. But as in the well-known movie series *Planet of the Apes,* symbolism sometimes transmits the essence of social structures much more directly than scholarly language can do. In this story I am dealing essentially with a neurotic constellation. Its structure does not apply to — and can therefore not diminish — the legitimacy of any genuine (that is, non-neurotically motivated) interest by many Americans of African descent in the African continent and its peoples, culture and history. Such interests are motivated differently; the motivations can be deeply personal and non-ideological. For example, my friend Donald Hopkins' intensive interest in and knowledge about African history, as demonstrated in his book on the world history of smallpox, *Princes and Peasants,* to whose eradication he contributed significantly, belongs to another realm. Such interest is genuinely scientific, non-emotional and motivated in a way hardly different from anyone else working on culture history in Africa, Europe, Asia, or elsewhere.

Summary

The social environment in which ethnicity movements arise can be characterized as culturally pluralistic, urban or semi-urban, and stratified. Emphasis on ethnicity in the population at large is a response to cultural conflict and aborted transculturation. I.M. Greverus at the I.U.A.E.S. (International Union of Anthropological and Ethnological Sciences) Congress in New Delhi in 1978 characterized what he called the "new ethnicity" (see also Bennet 1975) as essentially a dissident movement which can take the form of a strategy of disengagement and end up as "identity management." When the disengagement process becomes effective, centripetal societal forces of the kind that are also characteristic of other mass movements, nationalistic or the like, come into play and streamline individual behavior. Societal pressure may then push individuals into increasingly demonstrating forms of behavior and a cultural makeup ultimately prescribed from the outside.

Ethnicity, therefore, can develop into an ideological program, besides describing a state, or mood, or consciousness about collective cultural bonds. This proceeds at the expense of individuality. Individuals become manipulated by group pressure to demonstrate a "cultural identity" that is often merely stereotype-confirming. Even the stereotypes are not necessarily in their entirety those which the group has formed about itself, but very often they are hetero-stereotypes projected from outside (for example, a typical representative of Group X will not merely play the role Group X has assigned for him, but also the role created for him by oppositional contact Group Y).

In ethnicity movements proceeding from the notion of race, such as "black ethnicity," individuals identified by the larger society as "black" come under social pressure to behave precisely the way stereotypical expectations from outside suggest. Anyone identified by the opposing category, namely "white," comes under pressure to behave in a way that leaves no doubt about his or her assigned "cultural role" as "white" (that is, society will probably not expect him to spend his leisure time in trying to identify the wizard who killed his wife by communicating with her through a spirit medium). The methods exerted by group pressure include ridicule and other forms of discouragement of non-conformist behavior, deletion of all factual evidence for their existence from the mass media, and so on. (This also bears particular reference to musical groups that are non-conformist, for example, in the composition of their personnel.)

Segmentation of the society into cultural compartments by decree is not only the result of rigid black-and-white categorizing, with no room for shades and transitions, but also creates social pressures by which non-streamlined individuals are pushed into following suit, into identifying with one or the other group, rarely through their own decision. In this way, individuals can become captives not of what really is their culture, but of what the surrounding society expects their culture to be.

The ignorance of individual cultural profiles as a modifying force — reflecting the neglect of the individual in a collectivizing society — also contributes to the possible polarization of groups. Both sides of such an artificially polarized society then play the game with equal fervor. The victimized and also the victimizing play the game with unanimity.

Theoretically, therefore, it seems fair to summarize that the notion "ethnicity" can embrace a reactive, strongly ideologically oriented program which is prescriptive to individual behavior on the basis of fictitious "ethnic" groupings in whose formation both the communities affected as well as their opponents have a share. That such a psychological situation greatly influences the arts and artistic production — especially when they are drawn into the limelight — is doubtless. The study of cultures in South America and the Caribbean, as well as in North America, therefore must take the "ethnicity" concept into account as an important behavior-modifying factor. A volume such as the present one should bring clarification about the various routes by which the "ethnicity" concept affects the artistic production of individual artists and artistic groups in the hemisphere.

Notes

1. Research project P-8643 SPR carried out by G. Kubik and M. A. Malamusi, financed by the Foundation for the Advancement of Scientific Research, Vienna; in cooperation with the Ministry of Education and Culture, Windhoek, Namibia.

2. These are actual quotes from residents of some locations in New Brunswick, N.J., who often threatened African students when they detected them in their streets (personal communication by Richard Graham, New Brunswick, July 1991).

References

Amaral, Amadeu. 1976. *O Dialeto Caipira*. 3rd edition. São Paulo: Hucitec.

Barbosa, Guilherme dos Santos. 1978. "Cafundó, uma comunidade que corre o risco de dissolução." *Bulletin of the International Committee on Urgent Anthropological and Ethnological Research*, 20: 92-104.

Béhague, Gerard. 1980. "Brazil." In *The New Grove Dictionary of Music and Musicians*, ed. Stanley Sadie. Vol. 3. London: MacMillan.

Bennet, J. W., ed. 1975. "The New Ethnicity: Perspectives from Ethnology." *1973 Proceeding of the American Ethnological Society*. St. Paul: West Publication Co.

Chinyeka, Kayombo ka. 1973. *Vihandyeka vya mana — Sayings of Wisdom*. Vienna: Föhrena E. Stiglmayr.

Cohen, A., ed. 1974. *Urban Ethnicity*. London, New York: Tavistock Publications.

Depres, L.A., ed. 1975. *Ethnicity and Resource Competition in Plural Societies*. The Hague and Paris: Mouton.

Freud, Anna. 1936. *Das Ich und die Abwehrmechanismen*. Vienna.

Freud, Sigmund. 1900. *Die Traumdeutung*. Leipzig and Vienna: Franz Deuticke.

Freyre, Gilberto. 1943. *Casa Grande e Senzala*. Rio de Janeiro: José Olympio.

Glazer, N., and D.P. Moynihan, eds. 1975. *Ethnicity: Theory and Experience*. Cambridge: Harvard University Press.

Greenberg, Joseph. 1966 (2nd edition, 1973). *The Languages of Africa*. Bloomington: Indiana University Press.

Greverus, I. M. 1981. (Manuscript) Ethnizität und Identitäsmanagement. 10th International Congress of Anthropological and Ethnological Sciences (I.U.A.E.S.). New Delhi: 1978.

Guthrie, Malcolm. 1967-1971. *Comparative Bantu*. 4 Vols. Farnborough.

Haley, Alex. 1977. *Roots*. London: Hutchinson & Co.

Henry, F., ed. 1976. *Ethnicity in the Americas*. The Hague: Mouton.

Herskovits, Melville J. 1938. *Acculturation. The Study of Culture Contact.* New York: J. J. Augustin.

Herskovits, Melville J. 1941. *The Myth of the Negro Past.* Boston: Harper and Brothers.

Hirschberg, Walter, ed. 1988. *Neues Wörterbuch der Völkerkunde.* Berlin: Dietrich Reimer.

Hopkins, Donald R. 1983. *Princes and Peasants. Smallpox in History.* Chicago: The University of Chicago Press.

Kubik, Gerhard. 1979. *Angolan Traits in Black Music, Games and Dances of Brazil.* Lisbon: Estudios de Antropologia Cultural.

Kubik, Gerhard. 1988. Review of "Cuyagua, a film by Paul Henley, Granada Center for Visual Anthropology. University of Manchester, U.K. 1977," *Yearbook for Traditional Music,* 20: 255-257.

Kubik, Gerhard. 1989. "Afrikanische Musik, ideologischer Kolonialismus und die Identitätskrise der Zöglingsgeneration 1945-1970." In *Perspectives on African Music,* ed. Wolfgang Bender. Bayreuth African Studies Series, 9: 7-23.

Kubik, Gerhard. 1990. "Drum Patterns in the 'Batuque' of Benedito Caxias." *Latin American Music Review,* 11 (2): 115-180.

Kubik, Gerhard. 1991a. *Extensionen afrikanischer Kulturen in Brasilien.* Aachen: Alano Verlag, Edition Herodot.

Kubik, Gerhard. 1991b. "Documentation in the field. Scientific strategies and the psychology of culture contact." *Dialogue*(Montreal).

Ortiz, Fernando. 1940. *Contrapunteo Cubano del Tabaco y el Azúcar.* La Habana: J. Montero.

Pinto, Tiago de Oliveira. 1991. *Capoeira, Samba, Candomblé, Afro-Brassilianische Musik im Recôncavo, Bahia.* Berlin: Museum für Völkerkunde.

Royce, Anya. P. 1982. *Ethnic Identity. Strategies of Diversity.* Bloomington: Indiana University Press.

Spencer, E.H. 1971. "Persistent Cultural Systems." *Science* 171: x.

Stack, J.F., ed. 1981. *Ethnic Identities in a Transnational World.* Westport, Conn.: Greenwood Press.

The Camouflaged Drum: Melodization of Rhythms and Maroonage Ethnicity in Caribbean Peasant Music

Angel G. Quintero-Rivera
(In collaboration with Luis Manuel Alvarez)

Counter-Plantation Maroonage *and the Ethnic Amalgam*

The first book to be considered a "classic" in Puerto Rican "customs picture" literature, *El Gíbaro* by Manuel Alonso, published in 1849, described the dance music of the island at that moment as divided into two basic types: upper-class dances (*bailes de sociedad*), which are, he said, "a repeated echo of those from Europe" and *garabato* dances, which are those typical of the country (*propios del país*).[1] He also mentioned a third dance category:

> those of blacks from Africa or Creoles from Curazao (i.e.,
> the Black Caribbean) which do not deserve to be included
> in this description because, although they can be seen in
> Puerto Rico, they have never been generalized.[2]

In other words, the black dances, though present, were deliberately excluded from the "customs picture," from what could be considered to be the country.

This paper was presented originally at a conference, Born Out of Resistance — International and Interdisciplinary Congress on Caribbean Cultural Creativity as a Response to European Expansion, Utrecht University, The Netherlands, March 25-28, 1992. A longer version in Spanish was presented at the conference on Music and Black Ethnicity, in Miami, January 16-19, 1992.

This paper was prepared with the special collaboration of Luis Manuel Alvarez.

One of the most vivid cultural expressions of plantation society was its music, characterized by the importance given to rhythm, to the simultaneous combination of rhythms (or polyrhythm), and to some particular types of rhythms which the European musical tradition denominates *syncopated*. This character was reinforced with the protagonistic role of percussion instruments, mainly drums. Plantation music became so identified with drums that in many different places of the Americas — as distant as Paraguay, Ecuador, Santo Domingo, and Puerto Rico — it was called "bomba" (or words with similar sounds) after an African word for drum.[3]

The very meticulous studies of Alvarez Nazario on the history of language in Puerto Rico stress the nineteenth-century distinction in popular music between *bomba* dances, those accompanied by drums, and *garabato* dances, those popular dances (that is, non-high society dances) in which drums were not used. The interesting fact he adds is that the word "garabato" in this context comes from an African word referring to a stick instrument,[4] and, in fact, the institution of *el bastonero* (a person with a stick instrument who was in charge of indicating changes in figures in the dance) existed originally in this type of music. So peasant music, which was distinguished from African music by the absence of drums, acquired its name (*garabato*) also from an African instrument. Popular dances, even in the origin of their nomenclature, thus manifest the dialectical tension that characterized our first centuries of existence: plantation and counter-plantation, forced domestication and the camouflage of *maroonage. Garabato* denominates the (supposedly) non-African, though the word itself is African as well.

It is important, therefore, to examine further this dialectical tension, which is of fundamental importance for the analysis of Caribbean culture. Given the role of the Caribbean in European expansion, this tension was present throughout the region, although some societies contained both terms of the polarity, while others were basically either plantation or counter-plantation islands.

In previous writings I have tried to show that faced with the controlled areas that the slave plantation represented, rural Puerto Rico in those early centuries was basically populated anarchically by fugitives. These included runaway slaves from neighboring English- and French-dominated island plantations; Indians displaced by the destruction of their communities, their economies, and their way of life; and Spaniards seeking refuge from the repercussions of their peninsula's

then-turbulent atmosphere (internecine ethnic conflicts against descendants of Jews and Moors, the repressive Inquisition, and agonizing
trials of purity of blood).[5] This runaway or *cimarrón* ethnic amalgam
(of blacks, Indians, Moors, Sephardic Jews, and other Spaniards of
"suspicious antecedents"), that "tawny-moor" (*pardo*) world, as the
chroniclers called it, whose former cultures were menaced or in a
process of destruction, began shaping a rural society around the axis
of their fugitive nature — a society seeking to shake off oppression by
escaping, a society based on what we could call, in contemporary
terms, "the right to live in peace." Their runaway character fostered an
economy characterized by isolated dwellings and a family-based mode
of subsistence production, an agrarian structure radically different from
that which predominated in Spain (organized around small towns or
villages) and which state policy had attempted to reproduce in the
Americas.[6]

Much has been discussed in the Hispanic Caribbean around the
relative importance of the cultural backgrounds of the different ethnic
groups that formed Caribbean societies, and the analysis of music has
been strongly permeated by this discussion. Even more important than
these backgrounds was the fact itself of the ethnic amalgam and the
way it took form. Cultural elements of all these ethnic groups, of
course, remained, but our cultures and music cannot be seen simply
as a mixture of these remnants. The crucial matrix of Puerto Rican class
cultural formation was the counter-plantation nature of the society.

For analysis of the counter-plantation culture in the Caribbean it
is, thus, important to use the term "maroonage" in its broad original
meaning. Maroons have come to be identified basically with runaway
slaves of African descent, but this limits the concept to a particular type
of *maroonage*. Both the English word "maroon" and the French
"marron" come from the Spanish "cimarrón" which had originally this
broader meaning of "those escaping," escaping because of not having
accepted domestication.[7] It is very important, also, that the word used
in Puerto Rico since the late eighteenth century to name the rural folk
in this type of rural situation was "jíbaro," when in Cuba this word was
a synonym of *cimarrón*.[8] Several studies stress the relationship
between those words, as with the word "guajiro" used in Cuba to name
the country folk.[9]

The most rigorous and documented study of the history of the
word "jíbaro" was again done by Alvarez Nazario.[10] He stressed the

relationship of the origins of *jíbaro* and *guajiro* with *cimarrón*, quoting references from the sixteenth century to "Indians that ran away to the hinterland in order to elude forced serfdom."[11] In Ecuador the word "jíbaro" was used to name an Indian tribe characterized by being untamed or wild. The word later acquired a descriptive flavor of ethnic amalgam, probably due to the ethnic amalgam nature of this world of escape. In a 1753 Spanish book, the word is used for "Creoles and *mestizos* from Hispaniola, Puerto Rico, and other Islands;" in Brazil it came to mean a *mestizo* of *cafuso* and black ancestry (*cafuso* being a mixture of black and Indian); in eighteenth-century Mexico a *jíbaro* was the offspring of *lobo* and *china* (*lobo* being a mixture of black and Indian, and *china*, of Indian and white).

This very revealing etymology of the word, which is used to this day in Puerto Rico to denote the country folk, is important for study of the origins of peasant music. Since the Indian presence was from early times of post-Spanish history very weak in the Caribbean, and since "Hispanic" Caribbean peasant music uses almost no drums (use of which is identified with African presence in the Americas), but mainly guitar-type instruments, this peasant music has generally been characterized as basically Spanish. Most general histories of music in all three "Hispanic" islands stress this identification.[12] But the Caribbean peasantry was very different from that of European; it was a counter-plantation peasantry of a wide ethnic amalgam in *maroonage* (that is, also including people escaped from Spain).

The two basic genres of peasant music in Puerto Rico (*música jíbara*) are the *aguinaldo* and *seis*. In a doctoral thesis in ethnomusicology on *bomba* and *aguinaldo*, author James McCoy presents rhythmic similarities between these two types of music, concluding that

> while the African influence is not so strongly felt in the *aguinaldo* as in the *bomba*... it is nevertheless significant. The driving unrelenting strong rhythmic impulse found in the extant *aguinaldo* does not originate in Spain nor Arabia, but instead in the music brought by the slaves from Africa.
>
> Even though complexity in rhythmic structure exists in the music of Arabia and Spain... the force of powerful pulsation found in the Puerto Rican *aguinaldo* is not evident in the Spanish *villancico*....[13]

There are numerous variants of *seis*, but at the rhythmic level the research done by ethnomusicologist Luis Manuel Alvarez has shown four basic types: one whose rhythm seems to follow Amerindian forms, and three (the most popular, in fact) whose syncopation suggests African influences.[14]

Although many would like to hide it, *jíbaro* music (as the *jíbaro* itself) is an expression of ethnic amalgam. In order to go beyond this basic fact, to understand the particular forms and character that the mixture took, it is necessary to examine more closely the counter-plantation world from which it emerged.

Downgraded Identity and Camouflage: Our Contradictory Culture

...all Caribbeans know, more or less intuitively, that in the final analysis, the only sure possession the undertow of history has left them is their paradoxical culture.[15]

Counter-plantation cultures in the Caribbean (as all counter-cultures) vary also in terms of the nature of the presence of their opposites. In countries and/or periods of strong slave plantation economies, the counter-plantation was considered a menace because of the attraction it implied for working slaves. For that reason, runaways were fiercely chased, and runaway societies attacked. The runaways formed villages (*palenques*) for mutual defense and for the organization of an alternative, though endangered, way of living.[16] Also, plantation slavery differed from older forms of slavery in that the reproduction of its labor force was not generated internally, but externally, through commerce in the slave trade. (The intensity of exploitation was such that the life span of the slaves was very short, and they were replaced mainly by new slaves brought into the society by the slave trade.) This made the presence of Africa nearer in memory, and the counter-plantation in this situation could adopt forms closer to those of the African societies from which the slaves had been brought, though obviously modified by their different situation.[17]

In societies of weak plantation economies, but with a strong garrison city, as in Puerto Rico, *maroonage* was an opposite in retreat, not in active opposition. The military city dwellers did not see the rural world as a menace, but as a world of primitive indolence. The runaways thus did not feel a need to organize (which could have turned them into a menace) and their anti-urban nature hampered the formation of *palenques*. This type of counter-plantation society was characterized by isolated family dwellings involved within a family-based petty mode of production in subsistence agriculture. This continued mainly through shifting cultivation, which marked this form of life as seminomadic. This agrarian structure was, as already mentioned, radically different from that predominant in Spain.[18] It was basically a natural economy, the opposite of plantation commercialism. It developed, nonetheless, in an epoch and region of growing international trade. The presence of this commerce was channeled outside state jurisdiction through smuggling, whose importance is emphasized over and over in reports and descriptions of the period for all three Hispanic islands.

In spite of the primitive rebellious character of *maroonage,* the runaway world of our first peasantry was extremely vulnerable and contradictory. Its challenge was of escape, not attack, which was manifested in the individual type of escape and in the small-holders farming. Eighteenth-century descriptions of Puerto Rico[19] all emphasize the peasants' love of freedom, but this was the freedom of retreat, filled with inferiority complexes. For a Christian of some Moorish ancestry in Cádiz in 1492, there was nothing worse than his Moorish ancestry. The Spaniards were the conquerors and the Indians the defeated ones; black was identified with slave plantation, the opposite of *maroonage* liberty. Therefore, the world from which retreat was made, not because it was bad, but because it was the one that was victorious, took on clear racial tones, the most evident form of identification. The ethnic amalgam *jíbaro* world reflected a rural society tinted by self-downgrading feelings.

The aspiration to liberty through escape, and the self-downgrading feelings it nurtured, on the one hand, and the city-based military type of colonialism, on the other, fostered a first (tacit) social accord in the country. Urban colonialism needed to spread "subjects of the crown" throughout the island to defend it from attacks by foreign powers. And the fugitive country dwellers, faced with the possibility of a controlled countryside and the plantation-style colonialism that their foreign neighbors represented, began to take on valiantly the defense of the "Spanish crown," as evidenced by the many instances in which attacks by the Dutch, the English, and pirates were repelled.

This tacit social contract required special cultural patterns. Spanish scholars describe the contrast in the sixteenth century between "the ample freedom of the humble folk to speak and criticize, on the one hand, and on the other, the great intransigence against foreigners and in matters of faith."[20] Both kinds of intransigence were intrinsically related, since earlier internecine ethnic conflicts had produced an identification of religion with nationality. The desire of fugitives in Puerto Rico to preserve their freedom (of withdrawal, not confrontation), led, in this context, to contradictory efforts at using unofficial hispanization as a shield. In order to avoid the conflicts which such intransigence could generate, and to make possible the tacit social accord previously alluded to, it was extremely important not to appear to be a heretic or a foreigner. One of the most important efforts of unofficial hispanization was, therefore, through popular religion — a Christianity that was of basic importance to display, tinted, however, with the libertarian spontaneity of the new society shaped by the ethnic amalgam of fugitive country dwellers.

This non-institutional popular religiousness — through which country dwellers could manifest both their non-foreignness and, simultaneously and covertly, their spontaneous existence outside state domination — permeated and shaped their social life. They lived in daily isolation, and their social encounters took place chiefly around festive activities designed to show that they were not foreigners; that is to say, related to some Christian (or Christianized) celebration. The most important of "black feast days" honored the most Spanish of all saints, James the Moor-slayer, in Loíza. The most openly pagan of feast days — celebration of the summer solstice — honored the saint for whom Spain had named the island: St. John the Baptist. The most important celebrations of country dwellers were the patron saint feasts honoring the patron saints of their town parishes. Of the fixed holidays near the winter solstice, the Epiphany was more important than Christmas itself. It must not be forgotten that one of the Three Wise Men was an African black, and the other two were from imprecisely defined places generally referred to as "the East." In a world of ethnic amalgam, it was important to establish that a black could be a Christian and a king, and that kings and Christians could also be people of indistinct origin. For that *jíbaro* of the countryside whose origin, because of his own fugitive condition or that of his ancestors, it was best to keep indistinct, the Wise Men from "far-off lands" were a fundamental unifying symbol.[21] The Three Wise Men accurately represented the ethnic amalgam.[22] They were united in their adoration of the Christ Child, that is to say, in the hope for the future.

The Three Wise Men were also wanderers; this strengthened their symbolism in a society built around a seminomadic agriculture. In fact, the Three Kings celebrations stressed the importance of movement. *Parrandas* were organized — groups of friends visiting, with music and moving from hut to hut. Their Christmas present or *aguinaldo* was music, and the host's offering or *aguinaldo* was food and drink. Both these meanings were mingled with this name given to one of the two basic genres of peasant music.

An eighteenth-century chronicle very vividly describes the importance that Puerto Rican peasants attached to these social gatherings, and how, because of their isolated settlement pattern, they walked miles to participate:

> The most beloved diversion or amusement of these Islanders is the dancing parties... for which hundreds show up from everywhere, even if they have not been invited.... These dancing feasts usually last a whole week.... [T]hey travel two or three leagues (nearly eight to twelve miles) with no other purpose than to attend the *fandango* (feast) whose music, singing, and noisy kicks leave the most resistant head bewildered for a long time.[23]

In all these peasant celebrations, music and dance played a fundamental role, to the point that even today it is impossible to conceive a social gathering in Puerto Rico without dance and music.

The words used to name the principal music at these social encounters — "aguinaldo" and "seis" — are revealing as well. *Aguinaldo* is the Christmas offering, related, as previously stated, to the Three Wise Men; and *seis*, in the sixteenth and seventeenth centuries in Spain, was the music danced to at the most important religious celebrations.[24] It was danced in the church, in front of the altar, as an offering to the Eucharistic sacrament.[25] The dance movements of blacks and mulattos, or people influenced by them, were considered lascivious by the ecclesiastic authorities in the colonial city, and the *seis* was prohibited in the Cathedral of San Juan.[26] It is significant that the *seis*, or at least the nomenclature, took refuge in popular dance. *Seis* is the *jíbaro* dance music, which always must be danced inside the hut, as in a temple, never outside.[27]

The fundamental characteristic of social action in *maroonage* was camouflage, through which the libertarian values of spontaneity and freedom were maintained while confrontation avoided. That is why the phenomenon of masks (which are, together with *Santos,* our most important popular plastic arts expression) and carnival-type of feast performances[28] were, and are, so important in the rituals of social gatherings.

The Maroonage Drum

Camouflage is also present in *jíbaro* music. Both the *aguinaldo* and the *seis* encompass, at the vital level of rhythm, the clear but camouflaged presence of our racial amalgam. The rhythms, basically African and Afro-Arabic, are separated from the drums, which identified plantation music. The polyrhythmic combination was established in the interplay of other instruments: the guitar, the native lute (*cuatro*), the scraper (*guiro*), and human voice. The guitar, very much identified with Spanish culture (coming really from the Arab-Andalusian tradition) states the basic rhythm, while establishing, simultaneously, the harmonic pattern. In this way, syncopated rhythms are camouflaged through a harmony that "sounds" Spanish.

The only percussion instrument retained in the original *jíbaro* music was the *guiro*, which is identified in Puerto Rico with the Indian heritage. The instrument plays two functions in the rhythmic structure of this music. In the first place, following a basic pattern (which at times evokes, in fact, Indian rhythms), it establishes a rhythmic counterpoint to the guitar, which is of fundamental importance in the conformation of a polyrhythmic texture. Secondly, good *guiro* players depart at times from the basic pattern, making what in this tradition is called "repiquetear," or "repiqueteos," which are rhythmic improvisations very similar to what one of the two drums of traditional *bomba* does.[29] In its contribution to polyrhythm and through the *repiqueteo*, one of the *bomba* drums is camouflaged in *jíbaro* music through the "humble" *guiro* (as it was epitomized in the nineteenth century).

The chant is not call-and-response as in the African tradition of *bomba*, but done by a solo singer, which evokes the European troubadour tradition and manifests, from my point of view, the individualism of small-holding farming and Puerto Rico's type of *maroonage*. The chant is improvised in *décimas espinelas*, an old Spanish poetic form,[30] but the way it is sung also camouflages the Moorish heritage of *Zejel*[31] and marks the *décima* with its own syncopation, which contributes in its turn to the comprehensive polyrhythmic texture.

The most important instrument in *jíbaro* music, which has even become a national symbol, is the *cuatro*, whose sound resembles that of the Spanish lute or mandolin. All *seis* and *aguinaldos* start with an instrumental prelude in which the *cuatro* plays a melody that identifies the particular variant in which the troubadour will have to improvise his *décimas*. When the versification begins, the *cuatro* accompanies the singer with a sort of improvised *obbligato*[32] through subsidiary melodic phrases which are harmonic variations (or cadenzas) on the defining theme of the introduction. Through this improvised *cuatro obbligato*, the players of *jíbaro* music can show an enormous virtuosity in a "discreet" form, as an accompaniment which should not compete nor interfere with the singer's melody. It is especially significant that both the melodic prelude and this accompaniment *obbligato* transfer to the melodic sphere of music Afro-Caribbean rhythms.

The basic melodic phrase of one of the most traditional *aguinaldos* is structured, in fact, on one of the *bomba* variants.

Aguinaldo jibaro (Si me dan pasteles)

Another *bomba* rhythm is present in the melodic prelude of another of the most popular (to this day) *aguinaldos*:

Aguinaldo Cagüeño

The Afro-Caribbean rhythm identified today with *merengue* is melodically treated in the basic *cadenzas* of two of the most popular *seis*:

Mapeyé

Ritmo de merengue

And the *seis* most used for improvisation duels includes in its melody both *bomba* and *merengue* rhythms.[33]

Seis Fajardeño   Ritmo de bomba ...y ritmo de merengue

Ritmo de bomba "Bambulaé sea ya"

Bam-bu-lé se-a   ya se- a se- a   se- a

Bam-bu-lése-a ya-se-a pa-ramd no mas bam-bu-la-é se-a...

With a sound so radically different from the drums, a brilliant metallic sound which evoked the string instruments of Spanish music, the *cuatro* camouflaged in our contradictory counter-plantation world the African presence of its real, but denied, constitution. No one could imagine (except those living these rhythms) that *jíbaro* music was full of camouflaged drums.

Notes

1. Published in San Juan by Cultural, 1968. See pages 33-34.

2. Author's parenthesis and translation, 40.

3. See, for example, Edgardo Díaz, "La gomba paraguaya: un documento para el estudio de la bomba puertorriqueña," *Revista La Canción Popular* 1 (1) (January-June 1986): 8-14; Emilio Rodríguez Demorizi, *Música y baile en Santo Domingo*, Santo Domingo: Lib. Hispaniola, 1971, 55; and Pedro Henríquez Ureña, "Música popular de América," *Boletín de Antropología Americana* 9 (June 1984): 142.

4. For example, "Historia de las denominaciones de los bailes de bomba," *Revista del ICP* 4 (1) (March 1960): 61. Cuban ethnomusicologist Argeliers León, *Del canto y el tiempo* (Havana: Letras Cubanas, 1984), 73, points to this same origin of *garabato* in Cuba.

5. Angel Quintero-Rivera, "La cimarronería como herencia y utopía," *David y Goliath*, CLASCO 48 (November 1985): 37-51.

6. Carmelo Viñas Mey, 1969, "Las estructuras agrosociales de la colonización española en América," reprint of the *Anales de la Real Academia* 46, (n.p.): 173-230.

7. It is significant that the word was used first regarding animals that were supposed to be domestic, but were living wild, like wild cattle or wild dogs. The word referred later to persons whom others had tried unsuccessfully to domesticate, most evidently through slavery. The *Velázquez Spanish-English Dictionary* (Chicago: Follet Publishing Company, 1964), 162, very correctly defines *cimarrón* as "wild and unruly," also as "maroon" and "runaway slave." See also Richard Price, ed., *Sociedades cimarronas* (Mexico: Siglo XXI, 1981), 11, note 1. In this excellent book, although Price describes this original meaning of the word and though he is aware of the ethnic fusions in the "wild" (but mainly between Afro-Americans and Indians, p. 25), he uses the term basically with its English meaning of black runaway slave.

8. Esteban Pichardo, *Diccionario provincial casi razonado de Vozes y frases cubanas* [ed. 1836] (Havana: Academia Cubana de la Lengua, 1953), 408, defines "cimarrón" as "El perro o perra que se hace montaraz y su descendencia." Pichardo adds that in the eastern part of the island (i.e., the part closer geographically, ecologically, and socially to Puerto Rico), "jíbaro" refers to "alguna veces al hombre de modales o costumbres agrestes" and is used as synonymous to "montaraz, rústico e indomable." The twentieth century revision of this dictionary by Esteban Rodríguez adds that the word is used for "personas y animales cuando huyen del trato humano."

9. See note 8 and Francisco J. Santamaría, *Diccionario general de americanismos* (México: Ed. Robredo, 1942), Vol. 2, 145-6.

10. El *influjo indígena en el español en Puerto Rico* (San Juan: Ed. UPR, 1977), 67-69.

11. See also in this respect Jalil Sued Badillo, *Puerto Rico negro* (San Juan: Ed. Cultural, 1986), 171.

12. See, for example, María Luisa Muñoz, *La música en Puerto Rico: panorama histórico-cultural* (Sharon, Conn.: Troutman Press, 1966); Héctor Campos Parsi, *La música en Puerto Rico*, Vol. 7 of *La gran enciclopedia de Puerto Rico* (San Juan: Ed. R, 1976); Flórida de Nolasco, *Santo Domingo en el Folklore Universal*, Santo Domingo: Imp. dominicana, 1956); María Teresa Linares, *La música y el pueblo* (Havana: Inst. Cubano del libro, 1974); and Argeliers León, *Del canto y el tiempo*.

13. "The *Bomba* and the *Aguinaldo* of Puerto Rico as They Have Evolved from Indigenous African and European Cultures," Ph.D. dissertation, Florida State University, 1968, 82.

14. *La presencia negra en la música puertorriqueña* (in press).

15. Antonio Benítez Rojo, *La isla que se repite* (Honover: Ed. del Norte, 1989), 172.

16. This is the type of *maroonage* that Price's book, quoted herein, is mostly devoted to, as the subtitle of its original English edition states: "Rebel Slave Communities in the Americas."

17. Jean Casimir, *La cultura oprimida* (Mexico: Nueva Imagen, 1981), especially Chap. 4; and *Estudio de caso respuesta a los problemas de la esclavitud y de la colonización en Haití* in Moreno Fraginals, *Africa...*, Chap. 17, (Mexico, 1977) has convincingly argued that post-independence Haitian village society (*aldeana*) was a modified African presence in America through the counter-plantation ideology. It was the only case, to my knowledge, where counter-plantation social formation was not only predominant, but dominant, and the analysis of its relations with the new national state could provide important insights about its dynamics and contradictions. Jamaican post-emancipation society produced processes of a similar *aldeana* character. See, for example, Philip D. Curtin, *Two Jamaicas 1830-65* (Cambridge, Mass.: Harvard University Press, 1955).

18. Carmelo Viñas Mey, *El problema de la tierra en la España de los siglos XVI y XVII* (Madrid: Inst. Jerónimo Zurila, 1941).

19. Fray Iñigo Abbad y Lasterra, *Historia geográfica, civil y natural de la isla de San Juan Bautista de Puerto Rico* [1782] (San Juan: Ed. UPR, 1959); Fernando Miyares, *Noticias particulares de la isla y Plaza de San Juan de Puerto Rico* [1775] (San Juan: UPR, 1957); and Andree Pierre Ledrú, *Viaje a la*

Isla de Puerto Rico [1797] (San Juan: Imp. militar de J. González, 1963). See also Angel López Cantos, "Notas para una aproximación al carácter de los puertorriqueños (siglo XVIII)," *Cruz Ansata* 10 (1987).

20. Julio Caro Baroja, *Inquisición, brujería y criptojudaísmo* (Barcelona: Ariel, 1970), 17 (author's translation).

21. Ramón López, "Supplement on the Tradition of the Three Wise Men," *En Rojo, Claridad* (January 1990).

22. It is very revealing that all those regions in the Americas which attached more importance to Epiphany than to Christmas day were areas with important black elements in their ethnic configuration.

23. Abbad, 188-190.

24. Ludwig Pfandl, *Cultura y costumbres del pueblo español de los siglos XVI y XVII* (Barcelona: Araluce, 1942), 256.

25. Pfandl, 161.

26. Salvador Brau, *Historia de Puerto Rico* (New York: D. Appleton & Co., 1904), 158.

27. I am grateful to my colleague, ethnomusicologist Luis Manuel Alvarez, for calling the ritual of this tradition to my attention.

28. In the broad sense of Bakhtin, not necessarily during the carnival period. See, for example, *Rabelais and His Word,* 1968 (Cambridge, Mass.: MIT Press).

29. The *bomba* is usually played with two drums; one states the basic rhythmic pattern and the other improvises over that pattern. This second drum is sometimes called "repicador."

30. It is interesting that *décimas* is the form adopted by other black communities in Latin America. See, for example, Jean Rahier, *La décima: poesía oral negra del Ecuador,* ([Quito?]: Ed. Abya yala, n.d.).

31. Luis Manuel Alvarez, "African Heritage of Puerto Rican Folk-music: Poetic Structure," Manuscript, University of Indiana, 1979.

32. *The New Grove Dictionary of Music and Musicians,* edited by Stanley Sadie (London; Macmillan, 1980), Vol. 13, 460, defines the *obbligato* as "an independent part in concerted music ranking in importance just below the principal melody and not to be omitted."

33. More details in Luis Manuel Alvarez, *Antología de la música folklórica puertorriqueña* (San Juan: ICP, in press).

References

Abbad y Lasterra, Fray Iñigo. [1782] 1959. *Historia geográfica, civil y natural de la isla de San Juan Bautista de Puerto Rico.* San Juan: Ed. UPR.

Alonso, Manuel. [1849] 1968. *El Gíbaro.* San Juan: Cultural.

Alvarez, Luis Manuel. 1979. "African Heritage of Puerto Rican Folk-music: Poetic Structure." Manuscript. Indiana University.

Alvarez, Luis Manuel. In press. *Antología de la música folklórica puertorriqueña.* San Juan: ICP.

Alvarez, Luis Manuel. In press. *La presencia negra en la música puertorriqueña.*

Bakhtin, Mikhail. 1968. *Rabelais and His Word.* Cambridge, Mass.: MIT Press.

Benítez Rojo, Antonio. 1989. *La isla que se repite.* Hanover: Ed. del Norte.

Brau, Salvador. 1904. *Historia de Puerto Rico.* New York: D. Appleton & Co.

Campos Parsi, Héctor. 1976. *La música en Puerto Rico. La gran enciclopedia de Puerto Rico.* Vol. 7. San Juan: Ed. R.

Caro Baroja, Julio. 1970. *Inquisición, brujería y criptojudaísmo.* Barcelona: Ariel.

Casimir, Jean. 1977. "Estudio de caso respuesta a los problemas de la esclavitud y de la colonización en Haití," in *Africa en América Latina,* ed. Manuel Moreno Fraginals. Mexico: Siglo XXI, 398-420.

Casimir, Jean. 1981. *La cultura oprimida.* México: Nueva Imagen.

Curtin, Philip D. 1955. *Two Jamaicas 1830-65.* Cambridge, Mass.: Harvard University Press.

Díaz Díaz, Edgardo. 1986. "La gomba paraguaya: un documento para el estudio de la bomba puertorriqueña." *Revista La Canción Popular* 1 (1, January-June).

Henríquez Ureña, Pedro. 1984. Música popular de América." *Boletín de Antropología Americana* 9 (June).

León, Argeliers. 1984. *Del canto y el tiempo*. Havana: Letras Cubanas.

Linares, María Teresa. 1974. *La música y el pueblo*. Havana: Inst. Cubano del libro.

López, Ramón. 1990. Supplement on the Tradition of the Three Wise Men. *En Rojo, Claridad* (January).

López Cantos, Angel. 1987. "Notas para una aproximación al carácter de los puertorriqueños (siglo XVIII)." *Cruz Ansata* 10.

McCoy, James. 1968. "The *Bomba* and the *Aguinaldo* of Puerto Rico as They Have Evolved from Indigenous, African, and European Cultures." Ph.D. dissertation, School of Music, Florida State University.

Miyares, Fernando. [1775] 1957. *Noticias particulares de la isla y Plaza de San Juan de Puerto Rico*. San Juan: UPR.

Muñoz, María Luisa. 1966. *La música en Puerto Rico: panorama histórico-cultural*. Sharon, Conn.: Troutman Press.

Nazario, Alvarez. 1960. "Historia de las denominaciones de los bailes de bomba." *Revista del ICP* 4 (1, March).

Nazario, Alvarez. 1977. *El influjo indígena en el español en Puerto Rico*. San Juan: Ed. UPR.

de Nolasco, Flórida. 1956. *Santo Domingo en el Folklore Universal*. Santo Domingo: Imp. dominicana.

Pfandl, Ludwig. 1942. *Cultura y costumbres del pueblo español de los siglos XVI y XVII*. Barcelona: Araluce.

Pichardo, Esteban. [1836] 1953. *Diccionario provincial casi razonado de Vozes y frases cubanas*. Havana: Academia Cubana de la Lengua.

Pierre Ledrú, Andree. [1797] 1963. *Viaje a la Isla de Puerto Rico*. San Juan: Imp. militar de J. González.

Price, Richard, ed. 1981. *Sociedades cimarronas*. México: Siglo XXI.

Quintero-Rivera, Angel. 1985. "La cimarronería como herencia y utopía." *David y Goliath. CLACSO* 48 (November).

Rahier, Jean. N.d. *La décima: poesía oral negra del Ecuador*. Quito?: Ed. Abya yala.

Rodríguez Demorizi, Emilio. 1971. *Música y baile en Santo Domingo*. Santo Domingo: Lib. Hispaniola.

Sadie, Stanley, ed. 1980. *The New Grove Dictionary of Music and Musicians.* London: Macmillan.

Santamaría, Francisco J. 1942. *Diccionario general de americanismos.* Vol 2. México: Ed. Robredo.

Sued Badillo, Jalil. 1986. *Puerto Rico negro.* San Juan: Ed. Cultural.

Velázquez Spanish-English Dictionary. 1964. Chicago: Follet Publishing Company.

Viñas Mey, Carmelo. 1941. *El problema de la tierra en la España de los siglos XVI y XVII.* Madrid: Inst. Jerónimo Zurila.

Viñas Mey, Carmelo. 1969. "Las estructuras agrosociales de la colonización española en América." *Anales de la Real Academia* 46:173-230. Reprint.

Ethnicity, Identity, and Music: An Anthropological Analysis of the Dominican Merengue

Jorge Duany

Nowadays, the Dominican Republic is commonly known as "the land of merengue." But this was not always so. Merengue's massive popularity in the Dominican Republic dates from the beginning of the twentieth century. The Dominican elite did not accept merengue as a ballroom dance until the 1920s (Mercado 1983; del Castillo and García Arévalo 1988). Outside the Dominican Republic, merengues gained a solid audience in the 1960s. The current international vogue of the genre is largely due to the success of Juan Luis Guerra and his Group 4.40, both in the Dominican Republic and other Hispanic markets such as Puerto Rico, the United States, Mexico, Venezuela, and Spain.

Why did a rural folk dance become a symbol of national identity? How did merengue overcome the racial and class prejudice of the Dominican elite? To what extent does merengue embody the basic values of Dominican culture? How has the commercialization of the genre affected its musical and ideological structures? These are some of the fundamental questions posed by an anthropological approach to popular music (Davis 1982; Béhague 1985). Such an approach is based on the belief that popular music articulates the dominant themes and concerns of a national culture.

I appreciate the comments on an earlier draft of this paper by Frances Aparicio, Cristóbal Díaz Ayala, Nancy Morris, and Angel Quintero-Rivera.

The purpose of this chapter is to examine the historical background and contemporary significance of merengue in the Dominican Republic. To begin, the chapter will outline the development of ethnic relations in the Dominican Republic since the nineteenth century. Second, the chapter will describe the emergence of Dominican identity as expressed in both elite and popular culture. Third, the paper will explain the rise of merengue as the most popular music in the Dominican Republic. Finally, the lyrics of two songs by Juan Luis Guerra will be analyzed. My main argument is that merengue synthesizes many features of Dominican identity, especially in opposition to neighboring Haiti, based on racial and class conflicts.

Ethnicity in the Dominican Republic

The Dominican Republic is an interesting case of the changing nature of ethnicity and its musical expression. Unlike most Caribbean countries, the Dominican Republic has a long history as an independent state since 1844.[1] This history largely explains the early maturation of a national ideology shared by ample sectors of the population (Lewis 1983, 277-286). At the same time, Dominican ethnicity was complicated by the immigration of various groups since the nineteenth century, especially American blacks, Curaçaoan Jews, Cubans, Puerto Ricans, Syrians, Lebanese, Haitians, and West Indians (Hoetink 1985; González 1975). Thus, the Dominican Republic presents the apparent paradox of a growing sense of national identity along with increasing ethnic diversity.

The historical point of departure for an understanding of contemporary ethnicity in the Dominican Republic is the period of Haitian domination (1822-1844). As Harry Hoetink (1971, 99, 117) notes, Dominican historians traditionally consider this period a "death-like dream," "a traumatic collective experience," and "a black page in the history of a people that would have liked to be white." Prior to this period, Dominicans showed few signs of a national consciousness apart from Spain, the mother country. Historians agree that most Dominicans perceived themselves as Spaniards until the end of the eighteenth century (Moya Pons 1986). Dominicans defined their culture largely as a Creole version of Hispanic culture, based on the Spanish language and Catholic religion. However, the Haitian invasions of Santo Domingo in 1801, 1805, and 1822 helped to consolidate the Dominican nation and to reinforce anti-Haitian feelings (Silié 1988).

From its inception, Dominican identity was marked by racial and ethnic competition with Haiti.

Many scholars have noted the enduring impact of the anti-Haitian ideology on Dominican national consciousness (see, for example, Báez Evertsz 1986, 134-140). To begin, Dominicans defined Haitians as blacks, while they viewed themselves as whites or at least of European and Indian origin. (To this day, the popular term indio, not mulato, refers to a mixture of black and white in the Dominican Republic (Torres-Saillant 1991). Furthermore, Dominicans represented an advanced European civilization, whereas they considered Haitians as savage Africans. Dominicans often boasted of being "the cradle of the Americas," in reference to early Spanish colonialism, when Santo Domingo was the main European settlement in the New World. Moreover, Dominicans stressed their Catholic religion in opposition to the African cults practiced by Haitians, especially voodoo. Finally, Dominicans hailed the Spanish language as a symbol of their identity, in contrast to French and Haitian Creole, which Dominicans considered a patois rather than a language in its own right. According to Emilio Rodríguez Demorizi (1975, 290), "The struggle against Haitian domination contained three predominant elements: color, language, and race. The strongest and most decisive of these three elements was language."[2]

The entrance of new ethnic groups into the Dominican Republic after 1844 blurred the duality between Dominicans and Haitians.[3] First, Sephardic Jews immigrated from Curaçao and St. Thomas, initially specializing in urban commerce and assimilating rapidly into Dominican society. A continuous stream of Spanish settlers, mostly from the Canary Islands, became peasants, artisans, and merchants. In the 1870s, a wave of exiles from the Ten Years' War in Cuba gave a boost to the Dominican sugar industry. Toward the end of the nineteenth century, thousands of workers came from Caribbean islands such as St. Kitts, Nevis, and Anguilla — the so-called cocolos. A smaller number of Arab immigrants from Syria and Lebanon — the so-called turcos — joined the movement to the Dominican Republic (Hoetink 1971, 1985; del Castillo 1978, 1985).

Thus, the Dominican population expanded at both ends of the racial continuum: white and black. Most Sephardic Jews, Cubans, Spaniards, and Arabs assimilated into the white elite. In contrast, most West Indians and Haitians became part of the black working classes. A strong racial prejudice dominated Dominican ethnicity, favoring

Europeans and their descendants over Africans and their descendants. As several scholars have noted, Dominicans imported European evolutionary doctrines and applied them to their own society (see Bryan 1985). For example, Dominican immigration policy sought to increase the white element of the local population (Hoetink 1971, 117). As a result, the local government downgraded blacks as primitive and upheld whites as cultured.

By the end of the nineteenth century, Dominican society was sharply divided in racial and ethnic terms (González 1975; Hoetink 1971). On one hand, the "national" bourgeoisie was mainly composed of foreign immigrants from Cuba, Curaçao, and Spain — most of whom Dominicans perceived as white. White immigration also increased the middle classes of small merchants, artisans, and professionals. On the other hand, the bulk of the proletariat consisted of the descendants of black slaves and a growing number of Caribbean immigrants (Hoetink 1985). The vast majority of the Dominican people was mulatto by the middle of the nineteenth century. Hence, the immigration of both whites and blacks helped to polarize the racial composition of the Dominican Republic.

A cultural expression of Dominican ethnicity during this period (1880-1910) was the growing hostility toward the cocolos. Conflicts between Dominican workers and West Indian immigrants were based on economic competition as well as racial prejudice. Thus, the Dominican elite transferred its anti-Haitian ideology to other groups whom the elite deemed inferior because of their skin color, language, and culture. As Patrick Bryan (1985, 245) notes, "The cocolo and the Haitian, as a rule, proved excellent scapegoats" for class conflicts. Despite the important contributions of these two groups to Dominican culture, Dominicans generally rejected them as foreign and uncultured (del Castillo 1979; del Castillo and Murphy 1987).

The massive migration of Haitians to the Dominican Republic dates from the beginning of the twentieth century, especially the period of U.S. military occupation (1915-1934). Most of the immigrants came from the impoverished south-central regions of Haiti and went to the eastern sugar-growing regions of the Dominican Republic (Báez Evertsz 1986). Despite ethnic and racial prejudice, Haitians represented a viable solution to the scarcity of agricultural workers. The immigrants provided a cheap, abundant, and regular labor force for the expanding sugar plantations of the Dominican Republic. Popular stereotypes contributed to a system of ethnic segregation where Haitians performed the worst paid and least desirable jobs, such as cane cutting and construction work. According to Franc Báez Evertsz (1986, 165), Haitian immigrants today "constitute a true subproletariat, markedly differentiated and isolated from the national proletariat" of the Dominican Republic.[4]

To summarize, antagonism between native Dominicans (criollos) and black foreigners has characterized Dominican ethnicity since the nineteenth century. As Frank Moya Pons (1986, 239) points out, "One of the great paradoxes in the formation of the Dominican nationality is that as the Hispanic population blackens, the Dominican mentality whitens." In particular, anti-Haitian prejudice and Dominican identity developed side by side (Alcántara Almánzar 1987, 163). As Nancie González (1970, 331) puts it, many Dominicans "claim that Haitians are bloodthirsty, cannibalistic, demon-ridden, and inherently evil and jealous." The symbolic opposition between Haitian and Dominican culture justified the creation of an independent nation-state in the Dominican Republic. The myth of the Dominican Republic as a Hispanic, Catholic, and white country stood against the image of Haiti as a French-speaking, African, and black country. Such stereotypes formed the basis for a growing sense of national identity in the Dominican Republic.[5]

National Identity in the Dominican Republic

Literary critics have noted that Dominican writers initially sought the roots of Dominican culture in an idealized Indian past (Alcántara Almánzar 1987, 163). This romantic indigenismo minimized the African contribution to Dominican culture, from religion and dance to language and cuisine. Even today, Dominicans erroneously attribute many aspects of their culture to the Taíno Indians rather than to African slaves (see Davis 1987).[6] In the twentieth century, Rafael Trujillo's dictatorship (1930-1961) identified Dominican culture with a feeling of hispanidad.[7] Several generations of Dominican intellectuals were raised in this pro-Hispanic and anti-Haitian ideology, most prominently current president Joaquín Balaguer (1907-). In 1983, Balaguer published a book demeaning Haiti beginning with its title, *La isla al revés* (The Island Upside Down). This anti-Haitian environment culminated in the 1937 slaughtering of over twenty thousand Haitians near the Dominican border by Trujillo's military forces.

However, Dominican culture displays a strong African and Haitian influence as a result of the continuous immigration of black slaves and contract workers. The clearest example of this influence is popular religion. A recent study by Martha Davis (1987) documents the persistence of popular beliefs and customs that may not amount to a "Dominican voodoo" but bear the imprint of African and Haitian practices. In the nineteenth century, a representative Dominican writer had defined voodoo as "an African cult imported to our island by slaves brought from Guinea, and unfortunately perpetuated in Haiti until today with its obscene ceremonies and abominable rites" (reproduced in Rodríguez Demorizi 1975, 71). Contrary to official discourse, African cults such as voodoo and gagá are widespread in the Dominican Republic, often syncretized with Catholic and spiritualist practices (see also Deive 1981). The Dominican elite rejects such popular manifestations as evidence of the Haitian "invasion," much as in the past century it rejected merengue as black music. Historically, the elite associated popular music and dance with African religion (*Enciclopedia dominicana* 1978).[8]

Dominican culture, then, had at least two different expressions since the nineteenth century: the white orientation of the upper class and the predominantly mulatto identity of the lower class (Alcántara Almánzar 1990).[9] Whereas the upper class cultivated the Hispanic and Catholic heritage, the lower class combined Spanish, African, Haitian, and other customs. For example, the cocolos contributed significantly to folk dance and cuisine in the Dominican Republic, especially in San Pedro de Macorís and other sugar-producing areas. Arab immigrants also influenced local food habits and cooking techniques. Finally, Haitians lent Dominicans many words and phrases, and shaped the development of carnival in Santo Domingo (see del Castillo 1979; Hoetink 1985; Rodríguez Demorizi 1975; del Castillo and García Arévalo 1987).

An early example of the Hispanic bias of Dominican culture is provided in Rodríguez Demorizi's "Poesía popular dominicana" (1979). After noting that the Haitian domination of Santo Domingo was a period of "enormous moral and cultural backwardness" (p. 47), Rodríguez Demorizi reproduces a series of décimas by the popular poet Juan Antonio Alix (1833-1918). The title of one of Alix's longest poems is "Diálogo cantado entre un Guajiro dominicano y un Papá bocó haitiano en un fandango en Dajabón" (roughly translated, "A

Sung Dialogue between a Dominican Peasant and a Haitian Voodoo Priest in a Dance in Dajabón").[10] The entire dialogue revolves around the Haitian's insistence on dancing the vudú and the Dominican's equally strong resistance to the judú. Alix's verses portray Haiti as a savage land of African witchcraft, superstition, music, and patois, where black people "eat people" (come gente) for ritual purposes. In the end, the Dominican peasant kills the Haitian priest and triumphantly proclaims: "Como soy dominicano/Yo si no bailo judú" ("Because I am Dominican/I don't dance the voodoo").

A recent example of the Dominican image of Haiti is the massive deportation of Haitian immigrants and their descendants in the Dominican Republic (see Torres-Saillant 1991). Between June and September 1991, the Balaguer government sent back more than 50,000 Haitians to their country of origin. However, many deportees were Dominican nationals or were born in the Dominican Republic. This fact reveals the predominant view of Haitians as unassimilable elements into Dominican culture. From this perspective, Haitian origin becomes a tarnish on one's past that cannot be erased in one or two generations. As José del Castillo (1984,175) writes, "The prolonged period of Haitian domination, the wars and invasions by the 'Westerners,' the constant immigration of workers throughout the present century, have shaped the collective image of Haitians and their attributes as agents of evil [and] experienced practitioners of paid rites." The rise of merengue in the twentieth century must be understood in this historical context. As shown below, the legacy of racial prejudice, anti-Haitian sentiment, and pro-Hispanic ideas facilitated the elite's acceptance of merengue as the national music of the Dominican Republic.

Merengue as a National Symbol

Until several decades ago, the Dominican elite condemned merengue as undignified music because of its association with poor uneducated peasants. However, by the 1950s merengue officially became the typical music of the Dominican Republic. The government even created a Festival del Merengue to promote foreign tourism in the country. In the 1980s, merengue displaced salsa as the most popular dance in the Dominican Republic. In September 1991, Juan Luis Guerra recorded a merengue for a Pepsi-Cola TV commercial. This section will explain how merengue emerged as the undisputed musical symbol of the Dominican nation.

The historical origins of merengue date back to the middle of the nineteenth century, although experts disagree on the exact dates. Jacob Coopersmith (1949) notes that Dominicans danced merengues at the Battle of Talanquera against Haitians in 1844. The author of the entry on "Merengue" for the *Enciclopedia dominicana* (1978) asserts that the music was not well known prior to 1844, during the period of Haitian domination. Rodríguez Demorizi (1979) believes that merengue became popular around 1855, when the elite launched a poetic campaign against the genre in Santo Domingo's journals. In an often-cited poem, Manuel de Jesús Galván called merengue "awkward" and "despicable." An aging rural musician remembered that his father disliked merengues when they first became popular in the 1850s (Mercado 1983). In 1875, Ulises Francisco Espaillat launched another campaign against merengue, which by then had displaced other popular genres such as tumba and mangulina. In any case, merengue's growing popularity coincided with the consolidation of Dominican identity, prior to the massive immigration of cocolos and Haitians.

The geographic origins of merengue are a subject of controversy in the Dominican Republic. Some sources recognize the northeastern Cibao region as "the cradle of merengue" (*Enciclopedia dominicana* 1978, 240). Others argue that merengue was born near the city of Puerto Plata in the southeast coast (Mercado 1983, 86). Moreover, Davis (1980a, 260) suggests that merengues can be traced back to southwest Nigeria. Most sources agree that merengues originally came from the Dominican countryside and first became popular among the peasantry of mixed racial ancestry. However, scholars debate the precise origins of the accordion as one of merengue's main instruments, displacing local string instruments such as the tres and tiple.[11] According to one musician, the accordion was first used in Puerto Plata in the 1880s and from there spread to the Cibao (Mercado 1983, 86). Some versions attribute the importation of the accordion to Italian or German immigrants in 1881. Another version asserts that Spanish merchants introduced the instrument to Santiago de los Caballeros in the 1870s. Be that as it may, the accordion had become the principal melodic instrument of merengue orchestras by the 1890s (see Hoetink 1985, 64, 279; del Castillo and García Arévalo 1988, 24; Coopersmith 1949, 39). The addition of this instrument, as well as the saxophone in the first part of the twentieth century, increased merengue's popularity in the Dominican Republic. Thus began the era of merengue de orquesta, played by large urban ensembles, in contrast to merengue típico, played by small rural conjuntos (Pacini Hernández 1991).

In the 1920s, the upper circles of Dominican society slowly accepted merengues de orquesta. Arguably, the U.S. military occupation had exacerbated the nationalistic feelings of the Creole elite (Jorge 1982). "The first merengue that was danced in the salons of chic people was in 1924 or 1926," according to one informant (Mercado 1983, 107). However, merengues were performed in Santiago's Club de Comercio in 1920 and in La Vega's Casino Central in 1922 (del Castillo and García Arévalo 1988, 26). By then, merengues had moved to the cities, thereby improving their social standing. Nonetheless, the urban elite continued to scorn merengue as "the typical music of our countryside, with a very danceable and lustful rhythm" (Santiago 1922, in Rodríguez Demorizi 1975, 137). For many years, the upper class had objected to the sexual connotations of couples dancing close to each other's bodies.

In the 1930s, Trujillo incorporated merengue groups into his electoral campaigns (*Enciclopedia dominicana* 1978, 242). In this way, merengue lost its subversive character to openly support the established regime, especially in the compositions of Luis Alberti (see García 1947, 34; Jorge 1982). Under Trujillo, merengues achieved commercial diffusion through radio and television broadcasting.[12] During this period, Alberti's "Compadre Pedro Juan" and Alberto Beltrán's "El negrito del batey" became well-known emblems for the entire genre. In retrospect, Trujillo used merengue as a symbol of the Dominican nation (Pacini 1989, 72), as part of his campaign against Haitian influences (Moya Pons 1986, 245). The dictator and his allies hailed merengue as a Creole version of Hispanic folklore, with its preference for traditional Spanish poetry such as the copla and décima (see Valverde 1954, in Rodríguez Demorizi 1975, 83). Thus, merengue began to be considered the most typical manifestation of Dominican folk music. It was certainly the most popular dance in the Dominican Republic (Lizardo 1974).

The history of the Dominican carnival closely parallels that of merengue (see del Castillo and García Arévalo 1987). Since colonial days, black slaves celebrated the Catholic feast of Lent by masquerading and dancing in the streets of Santo Domingo. Carnival became increasingly popular during the Republican period when the feast was associated with two patriotic dates: independence from Haiti in 1844 and from Spain in 1865. Toward the end of the nineteenth century, the

Dominican elite began to celebrate carnival in private social clubs. However, this salon festival differed greatly from carnival in the barrios. While the elite imitated European fashions, the popular sectors mixed African and European traditions (see also González 1970). Nowadays, the Dominican government officially sponsors the celebration of carnival as an expression of national culture.

Merengue as well as carnival had to overcome its humble origins before being accepted by the Dominican elite. Popular musicians penetrated the urban elite by modernizing merengue's orchestration and imitating the American big-band style of the 1940s and 1950s (see del Castillo and García Arévalo 1988). Trujillo's patronage of merengue also gave a boost to local musicians. During Trujillo's regime, merengues reached a wider national and international audience. The large-scale commercialization of the genre began in the 1920s with the recordings of several musical groups from the Dominican Republic in New York City. By the time of Trujillo's assassination in 1961, merengue was firmly established as the national dance of the Dominican Republic, as well as a popular rhythm abroad. With the creation of a numerous Dominican colony in New York City in the 1960s, merengue expanded its international distribution circuit (McLane 1991).

Musically, merengue exhibits both African and European elements. The prevalence of the two-measure rhythmic pattern, played by percussion instruments such as the tambora, güira, and maracas, is an Afro-American trait. Melodic as well as rhythmic improvisation is also based on African tradition. The call-and-response structure of merengue is another African element, as is the combination of several meters in the same song, particularly the rhythmic formula known as cinquillo. Finally, most singers perform merengues in a clear, direct, and high tone. On the other hand, the Spanish influence on merengue is easily recognizable. Verbal improvisation by Dominican singers follows the traditional models of southern Spain and the Canary Islands. The predominant scale in Dominican music is the diatonic scale imported from Europe. The poetic forms are usually Spanish, especially the copla and cuarteta. Lastly, many merengues revolve around traditional Spanish tunes (see Davis 1980a; Coopersmith 1949). In this way, merengue reflects the Afro-European sources of Dominican culture. This syncretic character is a key to merengue's continuing popularity in the Dominican Republic.

In sum, several factors account for the rise of merengue as a symbol of Dominican culture. Historically, the genre developed at the same time that Dominicans consolidated their nation-state in opposition to Haiti. Geographically, merengues were associated with one of the country's most populous and wealthiest regions, the Cibao.[13] Socially, merengue represented a large class of Creole peasants who preserved many Hispanic customs. Culturally, the music combined African and European traditions. Politically, Trujillo used merengues as a propaganda tool to secure popular support. Economically, merengue became a lucrative merchandise for the music industry in the Dominican Republic and the United States.[14]

Since the 1960s, merengues have evolved in several ways (see del Castillo and García Arévalo 1988). To begin, most of the big bands of the 1950s were disbanded and smaller combos became the rule. Merengue's lyrics became more focused on the daily life of the Dominican people and often more critical of the established order. Most Dominicans did not associate merengue with the Trujillo dictatorship, because the genre continued to enjoy its status as the country's national music (Pacini 1989, 74).[15] Many orchestras added new technologies to their repertoire, such as the electric piano and bass. The tempo of the music itself accelerated. New groups proliferated not only in the Dominican Republic, but also in New York, Puerto Rico, and Venezuela, where large numbers of Dominicans have settled in the last three decades. As Deborah Pacini Hernández notes (1991, 9), "By the mid-1980s orquesta merengue began to replace salsa as the dance music of preference not only in the Dominican Republic, but in Puerto Rico and New York as well." By the end of the 1980s, the most popular of all merengue orchestras was Juan Luis Guerra and his Group 4.40. The final section of this paper explains the group's success in the Dominican Republic.

Juan Luis Guerra: The Poet of Merengue

At first glance, the music of Juan Luis Guerra follows the conventional formulas of the Dominican merengue. Guerra's compositions are usually divided into three sections: the introductory paseo, the main cuerpo or merengue proper, and the jaleo. The basic rhythm of merengue is a 2/4 meter. The preferred literary forms are Spanish coplas, décimas, and seguidillas. The instruments include Creole string instruments such as the tres or cuatro; wind instruments such as the accordion; and percussion instruments such as the tambora and güira. As in most merengues, the tempo of Guerra's music is generally Allegro or Andante (see Coopersmith 1949; Lizardo 1974; *Enciclopedia dominicana* 1978; Mercado 1983). In large measure, Guerra's music perpetuates Dominican folklore.

However, Guerra reshapes local tradition in several ways. As Rodríguez Demorizi (1975, 330) notes, "The lyrics of merengues were frequently quite pedestrian or nonsensical." In contrast, Guerra's lyrics contain carefully crafted verses, often with a social or political commentary. Above all, Guerra has a penchant for romantic love songs.[16] For this reason, he has been dubbed "the poet of merengue." Guerra has told journalists that one of his main sources of inspiration is the poetry of Pablo Neruda and Federico García Lorca, as well as oral traditions from the Dominican Republic. For example, one of Guerra's songs describes the customs of cocolo immigrants in San Pedro de Macorís, who drink guavaberry on Christmas eve and dance the guloyas during carnival (del Castillo and García Arévalo 1988, 61; 1987, 58). Another theme is the folk belief in an obscure substance called bilirrubina, which Guerra humorously depicts in a 1990 song with the same title. Hence, Guerra's music represents a return to the sources of merengue as a chronicle of daily life in the Dominican Republic. Still, this metaphoric return to oral, popular traditions is mediated by a complex series of poetic transformations (see Haidar 1991-1992 for an excellent discussion of this aspect of Guerra's songwriting).

For illustrative purposes, I will analyze two merengues with several of Guerra's leitmotifs. "Visa for a Dream" (Visa para un sueño) and "Let's Hope It Rains Coffee" (Ojalá que llueva café) combine Guerra's social awareness, lyricism, and melodious vocal arrangements (see the Appendix for transcriptions and translations of the lyrics). The two songs were released as part of the 1989 long-playing album, Ojalá que llueva café, which quickly became a hit in Santo Domingo, San Juan, New York, and other Latin American cities. "Visa for a Dream" deals with Dominican migration to the United States whereas "Let's Hope It Rains Coffee" concentrates on rural poverty in the Dominican Republic. The two songs reflect important popular concerns and aspirations.

"Visa for a Dream" consists of four coplas and a series of seguidillas. The first stanzas describe the long daily line of Dominicans hoping to secure an immigrant visa from the U.S. consulate in Santo

Domingo. Guerra observes that people of all social classes ("a seminarian, a worker") gather early in the morning to apply for a visa. He also notes their insincerity in filling out the forms to increase their chances of getting a travel permit. Guerra compares these people to docile animals ("one by one they went to the slaughterhouse") who sell themselves to achieve their dream: moving to the United States. The song's events take place on a particular day (January 8) in a specific place (the city of Santo Domingo). Many details of the scene — such as the need for a 2" x 4" photograph — form part of the Dominican folklore related to migration.

Thus, "Visa for a Dream" recreates a typical episode in the everyday life of urban Dominicans. Guerra portrays his characters with humor, sympathy, and irony. Toward the middle of the song, he assumes the point of view of a participant rather than an observer ("Who is going to find me?"). In his exchanges with the chorus, the singer voices the intimate concerns of the people standing in line: "I'm so furious," "What else can I do?" In the end, Guerra seems to justify the need to migrate to the United States, "never to return" to the Dominican Republic.

The song ends on a tragic note. Many Dominicans are unable to obtain a visa to the United States and are forced to migrate illegally to Puerto Rico (see Duany 1990). The dream often becomes a nightmare as many fragile boats (yolas) capsize in the Mona Channel and their passengers become "bait for the sea." The sound of a helicopter in the song's background reminds the audience that U.S. immigration authorities in Puerto Rico constantly capture and deport undocumented immigrants from the Dominican Republic. Without a visa, the dream of upward mobility for many Dominicans remains elusive.

Musically, "Visa for a Dream" combines traditional and nontraditional elements. Above all, the song follows the antiphonal structure characteristic of Afro-Caribbean music, such as salsa and reggae (see Duany 1984; Bilby 1985). After introducing the main theme, the soloist alternates with the chorus, which repeats the refrain, "Searching a visa for a dream." Moreover, Guerra sings in four-line coplas, one of the favorite forms of folk poetry in the Dominican Republic. The song's duple meter is also representative of traditional merengues. At the same time, "Visa for a Dream" has several modern elements. For one thing, the song's musical instruments include synthesizers and trumpets. For another, the topic of the song is very contemporary, for

Dominican emigration is a relatively recent phenomenon. Since 1965, thousands of Dominicans have moved to the United States, Puerto Rico, Venezuela, Spain, and other countries. Wherever they have settled, Dominicans have taken merengues with them, along with their food habits, speech patterns, and other customs.

"Let's Hope It Rains Coffee" has a more sentimental tone than "Visa for a Dream." "Let's Hope It Rains Coffee" contains several powerful metaphors of fertility: water, soil, honey, cereals, and fruits. The song's central image — a rain of coffee — condenses the writer's plea for a harvest of hope in the Dominican Republic. Contrary to "Visa for a Dream," here the atmosphere is rural, not urban; and the main protagonist is not people but nature itself. Guerra recreates the country's landscape by referring to local plants (yuca, mapuey, batata) and places such as Villa Vásquez, Los Montones, and La Romana. These three places are located in the northwest and southeast, representing a broad cross-section of the national territory. The song also contains local words and phrases, such as jarina (a light rain) and piti salé (a Haitianism). In sum, "Let's Hope It Rains Coffee" belongs to a long tradition of costumbrista poetry praising the Dominican land, people, and culture.

Like "Visa for a Dream," "Let's Hope It Rains Coffee" has a call-and-response structure. "Let's Hope It Rains Coffee" also consists of coplas and seguidillas. Similarly, this song has a polyrhythmic structure and an elaborate instrumentation. However, the melodic line is more sophisticated here than elsewhere. Overall, the text becomes the song's central focus, along with the music. As Guerra asserts, his aim is to write "merengue with a message."

The constant repetition of the refrain "Let's hope it rains coffee" gives the song a litany-like character, much like a responsorial chant. However, the song has a predominantly popular character rather than a religious one. The use of colloquial words such as pa' instead of para and phrases such as ay ombe creates an informal and conversational tone. Such literary strategies maintain the audience's attention on the author's message. The poetic image of raining coffee becomes a metaphor for a social utopia in the Dominican Republic, where peasants reap the fruits of their labor and children sing happily. As Julieta Haidar (1991-1992) has aptly noted, this song has a strong messianic undercurrent.

"Let's Hope It Rains Coffee" can also be read figuratively as a reflection on the social problems that lead to "Visa for a Dream." The metaphoric drought and infertility of the Dominican soil largely explain the drive to emigrate. Guerra suggests that the only solution to the mass exodus from the Dominican Republic is to improve his people's living conditions. Thus, Guerra's lyrics become a powerful vehicle for social protest and political consciousness in the Dominican Republic. Unlike Jamaican reggae and Trinidadian calypso, Guerra's merengues do not directly criticize the government. But the potential for ideological dissidence and popular resistance is clearly present in Guerra's lyrics. Guerra himself has called his songs "denuncias tiernas" (mild denunciations).

Together, the two songs give an overview of Guerra's musical tastes and interests. Most innovations take place in the song's texts and musical instrumentation. The songs emphasize melody without sacrificing rhythm. In most respects, Guerra stays close to Dominican folklore. Above all, his music represents an updated version of merengue de orquesta, influenced by electronic technology and contemporary Hispanic poetry. His music's wide appeal to young and old audiences is probably based on this mixture of traditional and modern elements.

In closing this section, it is worth noting what Juan Luis Guerra does not represent. First, his compositions do not downgrade women as sexual objects. In this sense, Guerra breaks away from a long list of merengue composers, from Johnny Ventura to Wilfrido Vargas. Second, Guerra avoids racial and ethnic stereotypes in his songs. Again, he differs from performers who commercially exploit this topic, particularly in its anti-Haitian form. Third, Guerra's lyrics show a deep sympathy for the poor and dispossessed. Although other songwriters have expressed social concerns, Guerra has placed such issues at the center of his writing. Finally, Guerra combines popular and elite culture without sounding elitist. Despite his cultivation of a poetic language, Guerra appeals to common men and women, especially his compatriots from the Dominican Republic.

Conclusion

Merengue was originally a folk dance associated with the peasants of the Cibao region in the Dominican Republic. However, the genre's growing popularity at the beginning of this century overcame the elite's racial and class prejudice. Since the 1920s, the mass media commercialized and exported merengues from the Dominican Republic. After thirty years of political manipulation by Trujillo's regime, the genre recovered its function as an expression of popular concerns and aspirations. Today, merengue is recognized as an essential part of Dominican identity, both in the Dominican Republic and abroad. Like carnival (González 1970), merengue has become a symbol of the Dominican sense of peoplehood.

The development of merengue reflects the history of the Dominican nation itself. From the beginning, merengue embodied Creole beliefs and customs, in contrast to Haitian influences. Later, merengue became an emblem of local tradition against foreign immigration from other Caribbean countries. Moreover, merengue synthesized the diverse elements of Dominican culture. Like other Caribbean popular musics, merengue represents the blending of African and European traditions (see Bilby 1985). Whereas African influences are most evident in the drumming style of merengue, European traditions have shaped its language, harmony, and melody. Even today, merengue reflects the rural folklore of the Dominican Republic.

In sum, merengue is clearly an Afro-Caribbean genre, which owes as much to Africa as to Europe. However, many Dominicans underplay African influences on their culture. Hence, merengue reflects a basic contradiction of the Dominican people. Although most Dominicans are mulattoes, they identify themselves as whites or indios, and others as blacks — Haitians and cocolos especially. Although many Dominicans practice Afro-Caribbean customs, they align themselves with Hispanic culture, the Spanish language, and Catholic religion. In essence, Dominican popular music expresses a hybrid identity that is neither black nor white but, as Cuban poet Nicolás Guillén likes to say, negriblanca.

Notes

1. The Dominican Republic lost its sovereignty to Spain in 1861 but recovered it after the War of Restoration in 1865 (see Moya Pons 1986). For an overview of ethnicity in Cuba and Puerto Rico during the nineteenth century, see Duany (1985).

2. All translations from the Spanish originals are mine.

3. During the first half of the nineteenth century, thousands of freed American slaves immigrated to the Dominican province of Samaná. Their cultural impact is still felt today in the city of Puerto Plata, especially through their English language and Methodist religion (see Hoetink 1985, 38; Davis 1980b).

4. Apart from Haitians, the Dominican Republic has several smaller ethnic minorities, such as Chinese, Japanese, German Jews, and Italians (González 1970; del Castillo and Murphy 1987). But the physical and social isolation of Haitians is much more extreme than that of other groups in the Dominican Republic.

5. In the 1980s, the popular merengue "El africano," performed by Wilfrido Vargas, recreated the stereotype of Haitians as sexually obsessed. The song persistently asked "Mami, ¿qué será lo que quiere el negro?" ("Mom, what does the black man want?"), in a clear reference to sex.

6. As Carlos Deive (1981, 116) writes, the traditional school of Dominican historiography underplayed the African influence on national identity, assuming that black slaves had completely assimilated into Spanish culture during the colonial period.

7. As Moya Pons (1986, 245) writes, "Between 1941 and 1961, Dominicans were taught to believe that they were mainly a white, Catholic, and Hispanic population, thanks to Trujillo's efforts to save them from a growing Africanization and from Haitian influence."

8. In 1849, the Spanish governor of Puerto Rico, Juan de la Pezuela, prohibited merengue dancing as "a cause of the depravation of customs" and "an object of scandal" (see Rodríguez Demorizi 1971, 129). In Puerto Rico as in the Dominican Republic, the Creole upper class preferred Europeanized dance forms such as danza to African-based rhythms such as plena and bomba.

9. This duality is not exclusively a Dominican phenomenon, but is typical of Caribbean cultures. In Puerto Rico, for example, the coexistence of danza and plena musically expresses two different versions of national identity: that of the white upper class and that of the mulatto lower class.

10. The fandango, a Spanish dance, was still performed in the Dominican Republic in the 1850s (Coopersmith 1949, 17). Dajabón is a Dominican town and province near the northwest border with Haiti.

11. Recently, Pacini (1989, 70) has pointed out that "When accordions were not available, however, Dominicans continued to play merengue with guitars."

12. In a personal communication (11 October 1991), Díaz Ayala noted that the Dominican radio station, La Voz del Yuna, began to broadcast merengues in the 1940s. Later renamed La Voz Dominicana, this station was a powerful tool in the international diffusion of merengue (see also del Castillo and García Arévalo 1988, 36).

13. The Cibao region has a large proportion of white settlers, a fact that helped merengues become popular. Many scholars have noted the relative purity of Spanish influence on the region's folklore (see Davis 1980a, 259; Coopersmith 1949, 37).

14. In an insightful paper, Pacini Hernández (1991, 5) argues that "*orquesta merengue* was clearly the best equipped to successfully compete in the market" in the post-Trujillo era, compared to *merengue típico* (rural *merengue*) and *bachata* (a romantic song type).

15. According to José del Castillo and Martin Murphy (1987), Dominican cultural policy since 1961 has maintained a Hispanic orientation, except during Juan Bosch's brief tenure as President in 1963.

16. According to Coopersmith (1949, 45), emotional problems are the main subject of Dominican folk songs, especially in the form of love, complaint, supplication, and dispute.

References

Alcántara Almánzar, José. 1987. "Black Images in Dominican Literature." *New West Indian Guide* 61(3-4): 161-173.

Alcántara Almánzar. 1990. *Los escritores dominicanos y la cultura.* Santo Domingo: Instituto Tecnológico de Santo Domingo.

Báez Evertsz, Franc. 1986. *Braceros haitianos en la República Dominicana.* 2nd. ed. Santo Domingo: Instituto Dominicano de Investigaciones Sociales.

Béhague, Gerard. 1985. "Popular Music." In *Handbook of Latin American Popular Culture*, ed. Harold E. Hinds, Jr., and Charles M. Tatum, 3-38. Westport, Conn.: Greenwood Press.

Bilby, Kenneth M. 1985. "The Caribbean as a Musical Region." In *Caribbean Contours*, ed. Sidney W. Mintz and Sally Price, 181-218. Baltimore: The Johns Hopkins University Press.

Bryan, Patrick E. 1985. "The Question of Labor in the Sugar Industry of the Dominican Republic in the Late Nineteenth and Early Twentieth Centuries." In *Between Slavery and Free Labor: The Spanish-Speaking Caribbean in the Nineteenth Century*, ed. Manuel Moreno Fraginals, Frank Moya Pons, and Stanley L. Engerman, 235-251. Baltimore: The Johns Hopkins University Press.

Coopersmith, Jacob Maurice. 1949. *Music and Musicians of the Dominican Republic/Música y músicos de la República Dominicana.* Washington, D.C.: Pan American Union.

Davis, Martha Ellen. 1980a. "Aspectos de la influencia africana en la música tradicional dominicana." *Boletín del Museo del Hombre Dominicano* 13: 255-292.

Davis, Martha Ellen. 1980b. "That Old-Time Religion: Tradición y cambio en el enclave "americano" de Samaná." *Boletín del Museo del Hombre Dominicano* 14: 165-196.

Davis, Martha Ellen. 1982. Folklore como antropología." *Eme Eme: Estudios dominicanos* 11(61): 61-78.

Davis, Martha Ellen. 1987. *La otra ciencia: El vodú dominicano como religión y medicina populares.* Santo Domingo: Editora Universitaria de la Universidad Autónoma de Santo Domingo.

Deive, Carlos Esteban. 1981. "La herencia africana en la cultura dominicana actual." In Bernardo Vega et al., *Ensayos sobre cultura dominicana*, 105-141. Santo Domingo: Ediciones del Museo del Hombre Dominicano.

del Castillo, José. 1978. *La inmigración de braceros azucareros en la República Dominicana, 1900-1930.* Santo Domingo: Universidad Autónoma de Santo Domingo.

del Castillo, José. 1979. "Las emigraciones y su aporte a la cultura dominicana (finales del siglo XIX y principios del XX)." *Eme Eme: Estudios dominicanos* 8(45):3-43.

del Castillo, José. 1984. *Ensayos de sociología dominicana.* Santo Domingo: Taller.

del Castillo, José. 1985. "The Formation of the Dominican Sugar Industry: From Competition to Monopoly, from National Semiproletariat to Foreign Proletariat." In *Between Slavery and Free Labor: The Spanish-Speaking Caribbean in the Nineteenth Century*, ed. Manuel Moreno Fraginals, Frank Moya Pons, and Stanley L. Engerman, 214-234. Baltimore: The Johns Hopkins University Press.

del Castillo, José, and Manuel García Aréval. 1987. *Carnaval en Santo Domingo/Carnival in Santo Domingo.* Santo Domingo: Radisson Puerto Plata/Banco Antillano.

del Castillo, José. 1988. *Antología del merengue/Anthology of Merengue.* Santo Domingo: Banco Antillano.

del Castillo, José, and Martin F. Murphy. 1987. "Migration, National Identity, and Cultural Policy in the Dominican Republic." *The Journal of Ethnic Studies* 15(3): 49-68.

Duany, Jorge. 1984. "Popular Music in Puerto Rico: Toward an Anthropology of Salsa." *Latin American Music Review* 5(2): 186-216.

Duany, Jorge. 1985. "Ethnicity in the Spanish Caribbean: Notes on the Consolidation of Creole Identity in Cuba and Puerto Rico, 1762-1868." In *Caribbean Ethnicity Revisited*, ed. Stephen Glazier, 15-39. New York: Gordon and Breach.

Duany, Jorge, ed. 1990. *Los dominicanos en Puerto Rico: Migración en la semi-periferia.* Río Piedras: Huracán.

Enciclopedia dominicana. 1978. "Merengue." *Enciclopedia dominicana.* Volume IV. (Second edition.) Santo Domingo: Enciclopédica Dominicana.

García, Juan Francisco. 1947. *Panorama de la música dominicana.* Ciudad Trujillo: Publicaciones de la Secretaría de Educación y Bellas Artes.

González, Nancie L. 1970. "Social Functions of Carnival in a Dominican City." *Southwestern Journal of Anthropology* 26(4): 328-342.

González, Nancie L. 1975. "Patterns of Dominican Ethnicity." In *The New Ethnicity: Perspectives from Ethnology,* ed. John W. Bennett, 110-123. St. Paul, Minn.: West Publishing.

Haidar, Julieta. 1991-92. "La música como cultura y como poesía: Juan Luis Guerra y el Grupo 4.40." *Claridad* (San Juan), Part I, 19-26 December; Part II, 3-9 January.

Hoetink, Harry. 1971. "The Dominican Republic in the Nineteenth Century: Some Notes on Stratification, Immigration, and Race." In *Race and Class in Latin America,* ed. Magnus Mörner, 96-121. New York: Columbia University Press.

Hoetink, Harry. 1985. *El pueblo dominicano: 1850-1900. Apuntes para su sociología histórica.* Santiago: Departamento de Publicaciones, Universidad Católica Madre y Maestra.

Jorge, Bernarda. 1982. "Bases ideológicas de la práctica musical durante la era de Trujillo." *Eme Eme: Estudios dominicanos* 10(59): 65-99.

Lewis, Gordon K. 1983. *Main Currents in Caribbean Thought: The Historical Evolution of Caribbean Society in Its Ideological Aspects, 1492-1900.* Baltimore: The Johns Hopkins University Press.

Lizardo, Fradique. 1974. *Danzas y bailes folklóricos dominicanos.* Santo Domingo: Fundación García Arévalo.

McLane, Daisann. 1991. "Uptown and Downhome: The Indestructible Beat of Santo Domingo." *Rock and Roll Quarterly* (Winter):13-15, 19.

Mercado, Dámaso. 1983. "Memorias de un músico rural." Parte II. *Eme Eme: Estudios dominicanos* 12(67): 83-111.

Moya Pons, Frank. 1986. *El pasado dominicano.* Santo Domingo: Fundación J.A. Caro Alvarez.

Pacini, Deborah. 1989. "Social Identity and Class in Bachata, an Emerging Popular Music in the Dominican Republic." *Latin American Music Review* 10(1): 69-91.

Pacini Hernández, Deborah. 1991. "La lucha sonora: Dominican Popular Music in the Post-Trujillo Era." *Latin American Music Review* 12 (2): 105-123.

Rodríguez Demorizi, Emilio. 1971. *Música y baile en Santo Domingo.* Santo Domingo: Librería Hispaniola.

Rodríguez Demorizi, Emilio. 1975. *Lengua y folklore de Santo Domingo.* Santiago: Universidad Católica Madre y Maestra.

Rodríguez Demorizi, Emilio. 1979. *Poesía popular dominicana.* Santo Domingo: Universidad Católica Madre y Maestra.

Silié, Rubén. 1988. "Aspectos culturales en la formación nacional dominicana." Paper presented at the Symposium on Culture and Society in Latin America, University of Puerto Rico, Bayamón, 26 October.

Torres-Saillant, Silvio. 1991. "Cuestión haitiana y supervivencia moral dominicana." Unpublished manuscript.

Appendix

Two Songs By Juan Luis Guerra
"Visa para un sueño/Visa for a Dream"

Eran las cinco 'e la mañana
Un seminarista, un obrero
Con mil papeles de solvencia
Que no le dan pa' ser sinceros

Eran las siete 'e la mañana
Y uno por uno al matadero
Pues cada cual tiene su precio
Buscando visa para un sueño

El sol quemándoles la entraña
Un formulario de consuelo
Con una foto dos por cuatro
Que se derrite en el silencio

Eran las nueve 'e la mañana
Santo Domingo, ocho de enero
Con la paciencia que se acaba
Pues ya no hay visa para un sueño

Coro: Buscando visa para un sueño
Buscando visa para un sueño

Buscando visa de cemento y cal
Y en el asfalto, ¿quién me va a encontrar?

Coro: Buscando visa para un sueño
Buscando visa para un sueño

Buscando visa, la razón de ser
Buscando visa, para no volver

Coro: Buscando visa para un sueño
Buscando visa para un sueño

Buscando visa
La necesidad
Buscando visa
¡Qué rabia me da!
Buscando visa
Golpe de poder
Buscando visa
¿Qué más puedo hacer?
Buscando visa
Para naufragar
Buscando visa

It was five o'clock in the morning
A seminarian, a worker
With a thousand documents trying to prove their solvency
That don't let them be sincere

It was seven o'clock in the morning
And one by one they went to the slaughterhouse
For everyone has his price
Searching a visa for a dream
The sun burning their entrails
An application form as their only consolation
With a 2 by 4 photograph
That melts away in silence

It was nine o'clock in the morning
Santo Domingo, January 8
With patience running out
Because there are no more visas for a dream

Chorus: Searching a visa for a dream
Searching a visa for a dream

Searching a visa of cement and limestone
And in the asphalt who will find me?

Chorus: Searching a visa for a dream
Searching a visa for a dream

Searching a visa, the raison d'être
Searching a visa, never to return

Chorus: Searching a visa for a dream
Searching a visa for a dream

Searching a visa
The need
Searching a visa
I'm so furious
Searching a visa
I wish I could have one
Searching a visa
What else can I do?
Searching a visa
To capsize
Searching a visa
Bait for the sea
Searching a visa
The raison d'être
Searching a visa
Never to return

Translated by Jorge Duany

"Ojalá que llueva café/Let's Hope It Rains Coffee"

Ojalá que llueva café en el campo
Que caiga un aguacero de yuca y té
Del cielo una jarina de queso blanco
Y al sur una montaña de berro y miel

Ojalá que llueva café

Ojalá que llueva café en el campo
Peinar un alto cerro 'e trigo y mapuey
Baja' por la colina de arroz graneado
Y continua' el arado con tu quere'

Ojalá el otoño en vez de hojas secas
Vista mi cosecha piti salé
Sembra' una llanura de batata y fresas
Ojalá que llueva café

Pa' que en el conuco no se sufra tanto
Ojalá que llueva café en el campo
Pa' que en Villa Vásquez oigan este canto
Ojalá que llueva café en el campo
Ojalá que llueva, ojalá que llueva, ay ombe
Ojalá que llueva café en el campo
Ojalá que llueva café

Ojalá que llueva café en el campo
Sembra' un alto cerro 'e trigo y mapuey
Baja' por la colina de arroz graneado
Y continua' el arado con tu quere'

Ojalá el otoño en vez de hojas secas
Vista mi cosecha piti salé
Sembra' una llanura de batata y fresas
Ojalá que llueva café

Pa' que en el conuco no se sufra tanto
Ojalá que llueva café en el campo
Pa' que en Los Montones oigan este canto
Ojalá que llueva café en el campo
Ojalá que llueva, ojalá que llueva, ay ombe
Ojalá que llueva café en el campo
Ojalá que llueva café

Pa' que to's los niños canten en el campo
Ojalá que llueva café en el campo
Pa' que en La Romana oigan este canto
Ojalá que llueva café en el campo

Let's hope it rains coffee in the countryside
A heavy shower of cassava and tea
A light rain of white cheese from the sky
And in the south a mountain of watercress and honey

Let's hope it rains coffee

Let's hope it rains coffee in the countryside
Combing a high mountain with wheat and agave trees
Falling down the hills of grained rice
And returning to plow with your love

Let's hope that fall dresses up my harvest real pretty
Rather than bring dry leaves
Planting the soil with sweet potatoes and strawberries
Let's hope it rains coffee

So the peasants don't suffer so much
Let's hope it rains coffee in the countryside
So the people of Villa Vásquez hear this song
Let's hope it rains coffee in the countryside
Let's hope it rains, let's hope it rains, man
Let's hope it rains coffee in the countryside
Let's hope it rains coffee

Let's hope it rains coffee in the countryside
Planting a high mountain with wheat and agave trees
Falling down the hills of grained rice
And returning to plow with your love

Let's hope that fall dresses up my harvest real pretty
Rather than bring dry leaves
Planting the soil with sweet potatoes and strawberries
Let's hope it rains coffee

So the peasants don't suffer so much
Let's hope it rains coffee in the countryside
So the people of Los Montones hear this song
Let's hope it rains coffee in the countryside
Let's hope it rains, let's hope it rains, man
Let's hope it rains coffee in the countryside
Let's hope it rains coffee

So all the children may sing in the countryside
Let's hope it rains coffee in the countryside
So the people of La Romana hear this song
Let's hope it rains coffee in the countryside
Oh, let's hope it rains, let's hope it rains, man
Let's hope it rains coffee

Translated by Jorge Duany

Cuban Music and Ethnicity: Historical Considerations

Victoria Eli Rodríguez

Introduction

In this paper, I will attempt to draw attention to two focal aspects: one which reflects, in general, the elements that make up Cuban ethnicity and determine the present character of the Cuban population as "mono-ethnic" and multi-racial; and another which underscores contemporary Latin American and Caribbean musicology's possibility and need to trace the paths of inter-influences between folk music and art music so as to arrive at a comprehensive vision of our musical cultures.

Of these aspects, this chapter will stress the so-called "stew" (*ajiaco*), as Fernando Ortiz (1881 - 1969) referred to Cuban culture. The chapter will then discuss the cultural continuity of those elements in their process of synthesis and show how, in the years between 1925 and 1940, they supplied the roots for the expression of Cuban national identity in the language of concert music. Both aspects will be drawn toward an indivisible convergence and conclusion that Cuban music is a form of cultural behavior of the Cuban people.

General Considerations

The integration of Cuban music took place through a long and complex process of inter-cultural relations. This process is intimately linked to the factors contributed by the different migratory waves of multi-ethnic Hispanic and African conglomerates that began to arrive on the island from the very beginning of colonization.

These two stand out as fundamental amid the heterogeneity of the cultural elements that converged in Cuba, where a number of different historical conditioning factors — moved by economic and political reasons — determined the incorporation of migrations from other geographical areas of Europe, Asia, the continental territories of the New World, and the neighboring islands of the Caribbean. All of these migrations, along with the Hispanic and the African, participated in the definition of the musical culture of Cuba.

The rather rapid genocide inflicted on aboriginal Cubans in the sixteenth century, in addition to the forced cultural and racial assimi-lation of those who survived, implied that their music should not be an element to be considered in the genesis of Cuban music.[1] And yet, during the third decade of the present century, the Cuban composer and musicologist Eduardo Sánchez de Fuentes (1874 - 1944) attempted to rescue the musical traditions of the Cuban Indians. His contention was that "the aboriginal roots had an influence, together with the melodic factor imported by the Spaniards and the rhythmic factor brought over by the Africans, on the shaping of our musicality," and he insisted that "the fact that our Indians left us no written testimony of their music, as opposed to what happened in the rest of the countries of Hispanic America, is not reason enough to deny their existence."[2] Following a rather heated debate — echoed in the Cuban press at the time — based on the fundamental research of Fernando Ortiz (1881 - 1969), Gaspar Agüero (1873 - 1951), and Alejo Carpentier (1904 - 1980),[3] the arguments used by Sánchez de Fuentes attempting to bestow authen-ticity on an alleged Anacaona *areito* to prove his point were finally destroyed. It was thus conclusively accepted that neither the sonorities nor the musical practices of the Cuban Indians were able to survive.

The Hispanic population came from many different regions and different social strata. The migratory flow from Spain was a permanent characteristic during the four centuries of colonial domination and even continued well into the twentieth century, after the establishment of the republic. During the first stage, essentially between the sixteenth and seventeenth centuries, the bulk of the migration came from Andalucía and the Canary Islands, but there were also Basques, Catalonians, Galicians, and others. In the nineteenth century and first half of the twentieth, the three most important regional groups were from the Canary Islands, Asturias, and Galicia.[4]

The influence of this heterogeneous population made itself felt in all orders of the spiritual and material culture. A varied range of song and dance expressions, as well as forms of musical behavior in salons, church, and the theater, blended to establish a tradition with its own life and profile on Cuban soil.

The Spanish presence was complemented by the Africans, who were brought over as slaves to replace the labor power of the rapidly disappearing Indians. Agriculture employed the great majority of these people because sugar, tobacco, forestry, coffee, and cattle raising were considerable sources of income. The growing importance of the sugar industry throughout the seventeenth, eighteenth, and nineteenth centuries not only reshaped the countryside and the economy, but also constituted the axis of social and cultural relations in the colony. The sugar plantations were the sites of the greatest concentrations of Africans in the rural areas of the western half of the island.

Other slaves were employed in domestic services and different urban jobs. In the sixteenth and seventeenth centuries, there were frequent cases of manumission resulting from inconsistencies in sugar exports. Thus a substantial number of African freemen and their descendants moved into the lower trades that were looked down upon by the population of Spanish origins. In the cities there appeared the *cabildos* and *cofradías*, organizations that grouped African freemen and slaves from the same ethnic community or "nation," as they were called then. These organizations were thought by the colonial authorities to be able to better control the black population and establish deculturation mechanisms to hamper inter-ethnic cohesion. They played an important role in the reconstruction and integration of the cultural values of the different ethnic groups on Cuban soil.

The Africans themselves had originated in a broad diversity of social and political structures. This, together with geographical and ethnic multiplicity, was the main characteristic of the black population. The largest numbers were taken from West Africa, although there were also groups from places as far removed as the coastal areas and hinterland of the Zambezi River. The fact is that Cuba received an amalgamation of human beings whose exact origins in Africa remain unknown even today. Ethnonyms and ethnic denominations were used helter-skelter by slavers and scribes and were rather thoroughly confused. Thus, to quote a single example, we are surprised to find associated under the term *Lucumí* no less than 137 different ethnic denominations that include men from the Yoruba people together with others that have nothing to do with them, such as Ashantis, Edos, Fulanis, Hausas, Ibos, and Malinkes, to mention just a few.[5]

Cuban ethnologists and musicologists have agreed, for the sake of avoiding this maze, to use meta-ethnic denominations based on sets of representatives of several ethnic groups who lived relatively close together and were the object of persecution, capture, and sale at a common or nearby shipping point.[6] Using these denominations as a criterion, we can single out the main groups — according to the areas of origin — that are bearers of cultural characteristics still discernible in the musical practices of Cuba:

Congo: People belonging to the Bantu ethnolinguistic group and coming from the region between the Congo River to the north and southern Angola to the south. Documentary sources (customs records, slave registers, and parish archives) indicate that this was the most numerous African population in Cuba. Several sub-denominations were grouped under the term "Congo," for example, Angola, Bacongo, Cabinda, Loango, Mayombe, Musundi, and others.

Lucumi: A human conglomerate with a significant Yoruba presence, coming from the areas on the west bank of the Niger River. This group is also numerically significant in the Cuban ethnogenesis. Some of the subdenominations that go under the name "Lucumi" are Iyesa, Oyo, Eguado, and many others.

Carabali: People originating in the region between the eastern bank of the Niger River, in southern Nigeria, and the mouth of the Rio de la Cruz, in old Calabar. This term was used to identify the Ewe, Fon, Magi, Cuevano, Sabalu, and others.

Aside from these three main groups, there was a long and varied list of origins, including Minas, Mandingas, Ganges, Macuas, and others, as well as Africans imported directly from Spain and Portugal and those brought over from continental and island territories in the Americas after a more or less prolonged stay there.[7] The successive waves that made up the direct African contribution to the culture of Cuba ceased with the abolition of slavery in 1886, although there was some clandestine trade for some years after that date. Close intra-ethnic and inter-ethnic fusions and syntheses and the normal reproduction of the African population in the country led to the appearance of new ethnic characteristics.

Factors such as the notion of territorial belonging, the generalized use of the Spanish language with its local characteristics and many place names and other words of Arawak origin, as well as a more limited group of African terms, and cultural and psychological features determined by a given economic and productive activity and closely linked to a permanent information transmission process at the interpersonal and family levels, all played a more significant role than the anthropological differences of the individuals in the formation of an ethnic type independent of historical progenitors.[8] This, plus the definition and concretion wrought by the independence wars of the nineteenth century, led to the definition of the "mono-ethnic" and "multi-racial" characteristics of the Cuban nation.

Continuity and Contributions of the African Cultures

For obvious reasons, the presence of Africa in the integration of the Cuban ethnos plays a very important role in this chapter. While it is true that the Cuban nation is today essentially mono-ethnic, one cannot ignore the evidence of studies aimed at revealing the particularities implicit in the participation of African cultures in the integration of the Cuban culture, and within it, its music.

There is no question but that the Africans contributed their own particular forms of communication to Cuba's expressive musical language in a singularly dynamic interaction with other ethnic components. In this case, following the notion of cultural African continuity in America proposed by the Cuban ethnologist and musicologist Argeliers León,[9] one can still find in Cuba a syncretization of the original social functions of Africa in diverse behaviors evident not only in music, dance, and religion, but also in the language and expressions of the visual arts.

Of all the expressions, it is in popular religions that the cultural elements of African antecedents have persisted most strongly. The *Regla de Ocha* or *santería*, the *Regla de Palo Monte*, the *Regla Arará* and the *Abakuá* or *Ñáñigo* societies are veritable complexes of ritual elements where music and dance play an essential role as a communication factor among the believers and the deities (this aside from the intensification of *voodoo, gaga,* or *rara* practices due to the Haitian emigration in the twentieth century). The Cuban ritual and ritual-festive music that takes part in the aforementioned religious expressions has differing degrees of similarity and affinity with the peoples of African origins.

One can still find, in different parts of the country, instrumental ensembles linked to the diverse expressions of the music of African origin. The organological study of these ensembles has been valuable, on more than one occasion, in helping us identify the presence of different cultural contributions.

The broadest typological heterogeneity is to be found among the instruments that accompany the songs and dances of Lucumi (Yoruba) descent. The *batá, iyesa, dundun,* and *bembé* drum ensembles, and the gourds (*agbe* or *chekere*) are an important Yoruba legacy to the organology of Cuba. The use of some of these instruments such as *batás* and gourds has gone beyond their ritual function linked to *santería*. They have been assimilated into the format of the dance band, chamber ensembles, and symphony orchestras, where they are used in the concert repertory.

Performance on the itólele, *drum of middle range in* batá **ensemble. Matanzas, Cuba.**

The instrumental ensembles and techniques of playing and singing associated with the Congo culture are not as diverse or highly developed as the Yoruba culture. However, the technique used to manufacture the congo instruments and to elaborate congo dance expressions have had a significant influence on the musical culture of Cuba. The most frequently used congo membranophones were made from hollowed-out tree trunks with nailed skins, but they were also made from staves in barrel or conical shapes. Tension by fire was soon replaced by metal hoops and screws, thus leading to the present *tumbadora,* also known as conga drum, an obvious reference to their ancestral origins. The ensembles made up of *yuka, makuta,* and *kinfuiti* drums are practically extinct, and at present the *tumbadora* is the instrument of choice to accompany the chants and beats of the *Regla de Palo Monte.*

The *Ñáñigo* or *Abakuá* associations, of Carabali descent, are characteristically very complex in organization and in their rituals. Two orders of instruments participate in their ceremonies. One of them has no musical function at all and is purely symbolic,

Performance on **tumbadoras***, widespread instruments in Cuba's folk and popular musical manifestations. Havana, Cuba.*

while the other order comprises the musical instruments, as such, of the *biankomeko* ensemble.

The practice of the *Regla de Arará* or *Arará* religion is rather rare today, but among the bearers of this tradition one may still find certain instrumental ensembles that denote the Ewe-Fon origins of their ancestors. Thus, the conservation of the instrumental typologies, music, and dances of their rituals has made it possible for us to identify the antecedent cultures today.

The drums used in the *Sociedades de Tumba Francesa* and in *voodoo* and *gaga* are morphologically very similar to the Arará drums, thus revealing the common ethnic

Bonkó-enchemiyá, *the lowest instrument of the abakuá drum group. Wedges are used for tuning the drumhead.* **Museo Nacional de Música, Cuba.**

origins of these practices, despite the fact that they arrived in Cuba at different times and by different routes.

Much More Than Drum and Rhythm

Within the general subject of the characteristics and contributions of African cultures, there have been more than a few simplistic judgments that tend to reduce them to the "drums" and the "rhythm," labeling the music, in general, in a marked derogatory sense as monotonous, redundant, primitive, and so on.

When approaching Cuban music of African antecedence, one must not attempt to find in it the organological and expressive models inherent in other cultures, particularly the European culture. For example, aspects as essential to music of the Old World as tonal and harmonic relations are not to be found in the same way in the structural conception of music of African origin, and it would be simply absurd to try to find in it the inevitable — for European music — tonic-dominant subordination of the sense of cadence.

Argeliers León has discovered a great many factors that allow us to understand how the deepest conceptions of Africans have projected themselves in their cultural continuity in the Americas and to extract from them generalization criteria applicable to the aforementioned diversity of African-antecedent music in Cuba.[10]

The instruments and voices, timbrically and rhythmically well contrasted, move in horizontally disposed sound strata. The instrumental planes are distributed essentially in three relative pitch levels: low, medium, and high. Each level is used to execute varied syntactical groups that reveal a sense of communication of particular connotations.

On the lower level, one finds the groups with the greatest rhythmic and improvisational diversity and a broader qualitative differentiation between the beats. The more fixed performing parts are executed in the middle and high pitch levels.

At present, although the differentiation among the different rhythmic-timbric levels is preserved, one finds in the execution of different beats a reversion of the functions with a transfer to the higher plane of the original improvisational function. This form of interpretation is adopted mainly by younger players who use in their playing the interpretational models characteristic of the *rumba*. In both forms there is a simultaneous implementation of the variability and stability criteria, as each stratum assumes different functions determined by metric, rhythmic, timbric, and expressive factors. Also present are the subordination and coordination factors among the strata occupied by the instruments and between the latter and the voices,[11] with elements that assume a referential function and are capable of governing the event in an overall manner.

Alternation between the soloist and the chorus is another of the expressive characteristics of the popular religions. At these events, the melodic line generally moves, rising and falling, around a fundamental sound relation or axis whose expressive tension is achieved by the delay in reaching the lower pitch level and whose conclusion or relaxation is attained with a shortening or synthesis of the motif occupying this level.[12]

The existence of the fundamental sound reference in the chants reveals another of the expressive particularities of the music of African origin in Cuba. As a logical consequence of the strong cultural interaction processes that have taken place, one can find tonal relations in the melodies, but they are not enough, in themselves, to consider the existence or use of major and minor scales in the chants. At present, there is a tendency toward the reproduction of scale organizations closer to the major tones, aside from the presence of pentatonic elements.[13] Regarding the much-bandied accusation of monotony, it is a fact that the repetition of short phrases appears as a characteristic of the music of African derivation, but this stylistic element plays a very precise role in the structure. While the preferred forms in European music are the so-called close forms, with contrasting parts, in the musical expressions indebted to African influences there is a predomination of open forms into which the communication timbric-rhythmic function of the event in question is fundamentally inserted.

Afrocubanismo: *An Option for a National Identity*

These are some of the stylistic elements of the music of the antecedent African cultures that have worked their way, through diverse uses, into the music of Cuba throughout the historical process of its integration. Genres and generic complexes developed in the area of folk and popular music that define the national musical language. But in concert or art music, the creative activity of professional composers carried the expression of the national identity to the works created amid the nationalist movements. Cuban musical nationalism has two important moments in the nineteenth and twentieth centuries. The first assumed urban folklore as its raw material, essentially the *danzas* and *contradanzas* that were the rage in the salons of the 1800s. The second, which developed approximately between 1925 and 1937, turned to blacks to find an intrinsically Cuban or national expression characterized by two key concepts, originality and independence, and capable of translating our own inside-outside accent and conveying *what* it had to say by means of a coherent *how* to say it in all the expressive means of the music.

This movement was part of a larger movement that affected the entire intellectual community of Cuba at the time. It was called "Afrocubanismo," and its focal point rested on rescuing the validity of the African cultural features present in Cuban culture. It was the artistic or aesthetic complement to the ethnographic studies carried out by Fernando Ortiz. As Alejo Carpentier has pointed out, the black man became suddenly the axis of our attention.[14]

Two composers, Amadeo Roldán (1900 - 1939) and Alejandro García Caturla (1906 - 1940), set the standard for the period, not only because they composed many essentially new works, but because of the conceptual implications of those works. Both were successful in synthesizing essential elements of Cuban music present in the *son, rumba, comparsas*, and ritual chants and beats in a noble balance with instrumental and vocal forms of a typically European nature.

Their music was nourished at once by the most authentic traditions and by the contemporary expressive and technical language of their time. Their starting points were the post-impressionistic current of the French school of composition and the folklorism of Stravinsky, but they created a music of cosmopolitan scope. The works of both composers allude to, quote, or re-create popular themes and motifs to achieve what was at the time an unquestionably Cuban character.

The main contribution of the period was that it put together a musical structure coherent in all its parameters, not only from the formal point of view but also from the consideration of the expressive resources to be used with the assimilation and re-creation of folk music.

The *Obertura sobre temas cubanos* (1925), by Amadeo Roldán, opened the door that allowed drums, claves, gourds, and rattles onto the concert stage together with violins and clarinets to conform a fusion and synthesis of core elements in the quest for a transculturized

Song to Changó. Transcription by Isabell Rosell. Havana, Cuba.

LA RUMBA
Voz y Piano
(1933)

Alejandro García Caturla's La rumba, *presenting stylistic elements from the Cuban folk rumba.*

La rumba, continued.

product that was essentially Cuban. In *Tres pequeños poemas* (1926), the same intention was woven in with the impressionistic stylistic model identified clearly with the creative world of Amadeo Roldán. *Oriental, Pregón,* and *Fiesta Negra* were an attempt to describe a given reality: Cuba. The functionality and balance between the timbric-rhythmic strata, as contributed by the African cultures, represent some of the stylistic characteristics best achieved by Roldán and Caturla on an unquestionably high level of abstraction and synthesis.

After working with orchestral color in his preceding works, in his *Tres toques* (1931), Roldán reduced the number of instruments — he did not use the entire symphony orchestra — contrasting harmony and counterpoint to achieve a solid structure based on the folk elements. To a certain degree, this was also Caturla's objective in *Bembé* (1929) and *La rumba* (1933). It was not a question of arranging the music of a festive ritual or a great *rumba* for a symphony orchestra, but of making the best possible use of rhythmic and timbric parameters to extract the essence of both and offer a totalizing vision. This is the same orientation followed in *Tres danzas cubanas* (1927). Caturla tried to extract a synthesis of the immense complex of the *danza* and made bold use of traditional elements — such as thirds and sixths — amid a range of complex harmonies. All means are justifiable if they solve the fundamental problem of creating the previously conceptualized sonority to underscore the autochthonous nature of our own music, clearly identifiable after a long and incomplete evolution process.

The fifth and sixth *Rítmicas* (1930) for percussion by Amadeo Roldán shook the concert world of the 1930s because until that time no one in Cuba had created a work using our own instruments as the main sound-producing means and based on the timbric and rhythmic functionality of percussion ensembles of African origin. The interdependence of the strata occupied by each instrument, the improvisational role assigned to the *timbales* and the *bongos*, the variations in the texture and the high degree of elaboration of the original models (in *son* and *rumba* polyrhythmic organization) are the determining factors among the procedures employed.

A glance at the catalogs of works of both composers reveals the importance of the elaboration of the musical material following the communicatory concepts of Afro-Cuban music, from which they extracted the very essence. Their incursion into the Afro-Cuban movement was not superficial, but a conscientious participation in an aesthetic current which in its times was synonymous with the reflection of the intrinsically Cuban elements of our national identity.

The works of these two composers laid the foundations for the subsequent development of contemporary Cuban concert music, because they provided the core element through which the nationalistic tendency could be combined with other stylistic languages. Thus, in the 1940s, after the death of Roldán and Caturla, composers had available new compositional techniques with which to shape a language in keeping with the evolution of the twentieth century.

Conclusion

The studies being carried out today by contemporary Cuban musicologists rely on an organic and coherent analytical approach of the ways of making music that practice and tradition have preserved to find the correlation that may exist with the elements and means of expression used by professional composers.

Interdisciplinary studies are being done on the specificities of Cuban organology and its instrumental ensembles to complete the *Atlas de los instrumentos de la música tradicional de Cuba* (Atlas of the Instruments of the Traditional Music of Cuba) and the *Estudio de las agrupaciones musicales tradicionales* (Study of Traditional Musical Groups), which comprise a large part of the expressions of Cuban music denoting a strong presence of original elements, both Hispanic and African.

A great deal of information compiled throughout the nation has already been assembled for the comprehensive analysis of the instruments and groups and their organization in the form of an atlas. The information reveals the way the instruments and groups exist at present, characterizes how they were used in the past, and establishes their zones of cultural influence.

Field research undertaken in the Republic of Angola gave us revealing insights into the presence and influence of the culture of the Bantu peoples in the music of Cuba. Together with the work done in Cuba in the areas with strong Congo settlements, this research has provided the platform from which to go on to an assessment, through musicological analysis, of the participation of this component in the popular music of Cuba. Work is also being done with the musical expressions of groups who have come to Cuba from other territories in the Caribbean, mainly the traditions preserved by the Haitians and their descendants in the eastern provinces of Cuba.

Comparative studies have also been carried out with the music of other islands and territories in the Caribbean basin. The basic aim of these investigations is directed toward discovering interrelations between Cuban and Caribbean music as demonstrated by the partial results obtained from work done in Grenada, Guyana, and Guadeloupe.

Cuban musicology has not limited itself to popular and folk research to the detriment of professional and academic music. In this regard, the musicologists and other specialists of the Centro de Investigación y Desarrollo de la Música Cubana (CIDMUC) (Center for Research and Development of Cuban Music) are following up on the research done heretofore with a new and ambitious project: a history of Cuban music that will reveal the complex system of social relations inherent to the formation and consolidation of the musical culture of the country and centering on the processes that led to the integration of the Cuban ethnos. Thus, in the immediate future, music and ethnicity in Cuba will continue to advance hand in hand.

Notes

1. Consider that the estimated Indian population in 1510 was close to 112,000, but was only 3,900 in 1555, which constituted a 96.5 percent drop in just half a century. (Juan Pérez de La Riva, "Desaparición de la población indígena cubana," in *Universidad de la Habana* No. 196-197: 61-84; Havana, 1972.)

2. Eduardo Sánchez de Fuentes, *La música aborigen en América* (Havana: Molina y Cia., 1938), 14.

3. Based on the following works: *Africanía de la música folklórica de Cuba* (Universidad de Las Villas, 1965); Gaspar Agüero, "El aporte africano a la música popular cubana," in *Revista de Estudios Afrocubanos* (Havana, 1946); Alejo Carpentier, *La música en Cuba* (Mexico: Fondo de Cultura Económica, 1946).

4. Jesús Guanche, "Tablas de composición regional de la inmigración hispánica Cuba." In the section "El poblamiento de Cuba," *Atlas de los instrumentos de la música popular tradicional de Cuba.*

5. Rafael López Valdés, "Notas para al estudio etnohistórico de los esclavos Lucumi de Cuba," in *Revista Anales del Caribe*, 6 (1986): 72-74.

6. Jesús Guanche, "Poblamiento africano," in the section "El poblamiento de Cuba," *Atlas de los instrumentos de la música popular tradicional de Cuba.*

7. Alejandro de la Fuente García, "Denominaciones étnicas de los esclavos introducidos en Cuba en los siglos XVI y XVII," in *Revista Anales del Caribe* 6 (1986): 93-94.

8. Jesús Guanche, "Etnicidad cubana y seres míticos," in *Revista Oralidad* 4 (in press).

9. Argeliers León, "Continuidad cultural africana en América," in *Revista Anales del Caribe* 6 (1986): 115-130.

10. León 1986, 115-130.

11. Mireya Martí, *El afrocubanismo: de la música folklórica a la profesional,* paper for diploma in musicology, Instituto Superior de Arte de Cuba, 1991 (unpublished).

12. Argeliers León, *Del canto y el tiempo* (Havana: Editorial Pueblo y Educación, La Habana, 1974), 50.

13. Mireya Marti, *El afrocubanismo* (see note 11).

14. Alejo Carpentier, *La música en Cuba* (Mexico: Fondo de Cultura Económica, 1946), 236.

References

Carpentier, Alejo. 1946. *La música en Cuba*. Mexico: Fondo de Cultura Económica.

Fuente García, Alejandro de la. 1986. "Denominaciones étnicas de los esclavos introducidas en Cuba en los siglos XVI y XVII." In *Revista Anales del Caribe* 6. Havana.

Guanche, Jesús. N.d. "El poblamiento de Cuba." In *Atlas de los instrumentos de la música popular tradicional de Cuba*. Unpublished.

Guanche, Jesús. Forthcoming. "Etnicidad cubana y seres míticos." In *Revista Oralidad*.

León, Argeliers, 1974. *Del canto y el tiempo*. Havana: Editorial Pueblo y Educación.

León, Argeliers. 1986. "Continuidad cultural africana en América." In *Revista Anales del Caribe* 6. Havana.

López Valdés, Rafael. 1986. "Notas para el estudio etnohistórico de los esclavos Lucumi de Cuba." In *Revista Anales del Caribe* 6. Havana.

Martí, Mireya. 1991. *El afrocubanismo: de la música folklórica a la profesional*. Havana: Instituto Superior de Arte. Unpublished paper.

Pérez de la Riva, Juan. 1972. "Desaparición de la población indígena cubana." In *Revista Universidad de La Habana* 196-197.

Sánchez de Fuentes, Eduardo. 1938. *La música aborigen de América*. Havana: Imprenta Molina y Cía.

The Afro-French Settlement and the Legacy of Its Music to the Cuban People

Olavo Alén Rodríguez

The emergence in Cuba of what has come to be known as Afro-Cuban music is the best possible indication of the changing nature of ethnicity. This fact is valid for the entire Caribbean region, where a music has developed which can increasingly, and with greater precision, be called Afro-Caribbean music. These two terms, "Afro-Cuban" and "Afro-Caribbean," indicate the existence of a Cuban culture and a Caribbean culture, both of which have in common the persistence of important elements in their respective identities whose origins are to be found in Africa.

On the basis of these elements, one may say that the Afro-Cuban and Afro-Caribbean cultures are part of the history of the Caribbean, but not necessarily that of Africa. Although they both may be considered specific projections of the African cultures in different social, economic, and cultural contexts, the transformations they have endured are so fundamental that they assume qualities which make them completely different from their African antecedents.

The culture of the Caribbean and the culture of Cuba, as well as their respective music, emerge from very recent historical phenomena. The first elements that indicate the appearance of the Caribbean individual whose economic, political, social, scientific, and artistic interests are rooted in the Caribbean itself. The consolidation of the identity of the Caribbean individual led to the development of a new culture that identified him, and his music formed part of that culture as its most relevant artistic expression. This happened not so very long ago.

In the case of Cuba, historians and scientists specializing in other branches of the social sciences have come to accept the second half of the eighteenth century as the period in which the Cuban nationality emerged as such. When compared with the history of other countries, the time elapsed since then is but a brief yesterday. Perhaps this may suggest that the longevity of a given aesthetic expression should not be taken to be an indicator of its authenticity.

It should be recalled that the original Indian population of the Caribbean was extinguished in a very short period of time, leaving us a few elements of its material culture, but hardly anything of its spiritual culture. Maracas, rattles made from sea shells, and xylophonic drums were some of the instruments used by our aboriginal populations, but what rhythms did they make with them? What melodies did they accompany? There are descriptions of the music of the aborigines in the diaries of travelers. But because they were not musicians, they only provided brief references; they had no way of preserving that music, and those descriptions generally underscore extra-musical features.

It may be useful to point out here that the most common and generalized way the Caribbean individual projects himself artistically is through music and the dances that go along with it. This is not denying the artistic capabilities of certain Caribbean individuals in the visual arts and in literature, nor the importance of the popular story or of poetry and the novel in our region. However, as a mass phenomenon, as the generic behavior of the aesthetic personality of Caribbeans, making music, listening to music, and moving to the beat of that music are incomparably more generalized characteristics than those projected in the other artistic expressions.

African slaves, no matter what their cultural origins, engendered a new social group in the New World at the very moment they achieved their freedom. It was precisely through the free Africans and their descendants that there was an intensification of deep change in the culture of African origin of which they were bearers. This led them to completely new forms in their aesthetic projection.

In the Spanish colonies of the Caribbean, African slaves were allowed to join in associations known as *cabildos*. These *cabildos* provided assistance, mutual aid, and protection of all sorts to their members. But they also helped preserve their rituals, religious practices, and the ancestral chants and dances linked to their myths and their magic. The great social significance of the *cabildo* as an institution was the preservation of many African customs and traditions that slowly worked their way into the aesthetic projections of the individual of the New World.

One particular case of a performance-recreational event related to African cultural elements within the framework of the *cabildos* is found in the *Sociedades de Tumba Francesa* (French Tumba Societies) in Cuba. Inasmuch as they are very representative of legitimate Afro-Cuban cultural expression, they deserve a closer examination.

The Haitians, black or mestizo, slaves or freemen, who came to Cuba in the late eighteenth and early nineteenth centuries as a result of the Haitian Revolution were known as *franceses* (French). The term was also applied to their descendants born in Cuba. The African slaves of all ethnic origins bought in Cuba by the French plantation owners who settled there were also called French.

The French language was assimilated as the language imposed by the masters, and the same occurred with a great many aesthetic customs, habits, attitudes, and behavior. The term *francés* was not only used for the people but for their entire cultural environment. Thus, their dances, musical instruments, societies and festivities were generally known as "French."

Being called French allowed these people to assume a higher social rank than the other slaves. In addition, any insistence in calling themselves Haitians might have put them in a bad light with the Spanish colonial authorities in Cuba because in the late eighteenth century Haiti was considered a center of subversion in the Americas by the European colonial powers.

The "French" immigrants who arrived in successive waves between 1790 and 1820 settled mainly in the mountainous regions of eastern Cuba, especially in the area bounded by Santiago de Cuba, La Gran Piedra, and the mountainous part of Yateras, Guantánamo. The main crop they cultivated in this region was coffee, and their contribution was decisive for the future of this crop in Cuba because the techniques they brought with them were superior to the ones employed in Cuba by the Spaniards. The other main reason that favored French settlements in this region was that land was cheaper there than in Cuba's western and central regions.

The initial integration of the groups that were later to become the *Tumba* Societies began in certain festivities celebrated by the slaves in the coffee-drying areas. At these festivities, dances, foods, costumes, and social behavior of different African ethnic groups intermixed — perhaps with a preeminence of the slaves from the Bantu linguistic areas — in addition to the customs, foods, dancing styles, and language of the French, who also participated.

Plantation festivities were the main element that attracted and brought these groups together until much later, when the first societies were founded in the small cities and towns in the vicinity of the French settlements.

The main objective of the societies was mutual aid and assistance among members, but they also provided recreation. Some even granted economic assistance for the education of the members' children. In this sense they were moved by the same objectives as the *cabildos*, also known as *cabildos de nación* ("nation *cabildos*"). They differed, however, in that while the nation *cabildos* admitted members exclusively of the same ethnic origin, the *Tumba Francesa* societies admitted slaves from very many African ethnic groups: their only common trait consisted in being, or having been, slaves of French masters. This essential difference between the *Tumbas* and the *cabildos* was decisive in the development, within the *Tumba Francesa* Societies, of a new ethnic typology in a relatively short time. They produced very well-defined musical and dance manifestations that differed distinctly from those that might be considered the African antecedents.

Feasts continued to be the center of the activities of the societies in which new habits and customs, new ways of dancing and playing the drums emerged and developed and later went on to enrich other expressions of Cuban music. Perhaps the clearest and most evident example of this development can be seen in the *congas* and *comparsas* (masquerades) of the carnivals in the eastern region of Cuba, especially in Santiago de Cuba, but elements of the music of the *Tumba Francesa* Societies may also be readily identified in certain groups of popular dance music in eastern Cuba.

Within the context of the festivities there are events, characters and forms of behavior that point very clearly to the cross influences of the original African ethnic groups and the musical cultures of the French. Also evident are the new elements that emerged from that mixture.

The *composé* is an essential character in the festivities. That is the name given to the lead singer, who creates or improvises the lyrics of his songs, directs the chorus that spontaneously emerges among the public, and eventually begins to alternate with it. The word *composé* may come from the French word *compositeur* since the function of the *composé* is to create through his improvisations songs that will later be repeated by other *composés*, or by himself, until they acquire more or less permanent forms that may reasonably be considered compositions.

Many believe that the *composé* is more of a poet than a singer because the beauty of his lyrics, his ability to improvise verses, and, often, his ability to answer other *composés* are essential elements in the evaluation of his talent. It often happened that competitions or duels between two or more *composés* would take place during the festivities, and in these cases criticism and satire played an important role in the improvised verses.

The lyrics of songs were generally in *patois*. In time, the Spanish language also began to be used. The main trend, however, was to use a mixture of both languages. *Patois* today has survived among these groups practically as a dead language whose use is restricted to the lyrics of the songs, but Spanish words are being used with increasing frequency. The contents of these songs have traditionally centered on daily events, and this is still the case today.

These songs are seldom written down, for the *composé* improvises them and keeps them in his memory. It often happens, however, that when he sings them again he introduces thematic material in the text that updates it and gives it a fresh meaning. Thus, the songs go through a process of change.

Some songs have come down to us just the way they were originally composed, as some of the *composés* have written them down in their notebooks to keep from forgetting them. However, this practice has not become generalized among the members of these societies.

The structure or form of the songs is the same for all the musical genres that have emerged among these groups, the *masón*, the *yubá* and the *fronté* or *frente* being the ones most frequently used today. In his song, the *composé* presents a text explaining the situations or problems he is going to sing about. This section has a closed form that is usually binary. Upon the conclusion of this section, the *composé* takes one of the phrases of the presentation and repeats it for the chorus to repeat as a sort of refrain. From then on the chorus uses the refrain to alternate with free improvisations on the subject announced by the *composé*, and this lasts as long as the public's interest endures. This practice produces a structure with an open form.

Thus, the structure of the song has two well-defined sections. The first has a closed form with an explicative text, and originates in the closed musical structures of Europe. The second section has an open form with an evident African derivation where the public plays a leading role because it participates in the song, by right, and especially because it decides when it is to end. Each verse is generally sung out on a single breath of air. This keeps the verses from being too long and influences the fact that the melodies tend to be descending and conclude on a low note. This element is also an obvious African derivation.

The relations between the *composé* and the chorus, as well as certain choreographic movements that are inserted into the general context of the dance, are also indicative of an African origin. The *composé* commands a circular displacement by the chorus around the room once the refrain begins. The costumes used by the participants are very attractive, as they allude to the form of dress of the French aristocracy of the eighteenth century. The women wear long dresses trimmed in lace and covered with embroidered ribbons. They use colored sashes, and all the dresses are perfectly ironed and starched. In their hair they wear bright colored kerchiefs tied in many different ways, and they generally use necklaces, fans, chains, fan cases, long earrings, bracelets, and some grand costume jewelry rings. The men wear white pants and shirts. Some use a jacket, dress shirt, and tie, but all wear low-cut comfortable shoes.

The instruments used in the accompaniment at these festivities are three large drums that are placed directly on the floor; these have individual names: *premier*, *bulá*, and *segón*. They also use a smaller drum know as the *tambora*, hung around the player's neck and struck with a stick. The last instrument is a xylophonic drum made from a hollowed out tree trunk, which is placed horizontally on a wooden stand and struck with two sticks.

The *premier* is the largest of the three drums, and its head has the widest diameter; thus, it plays the lowest notes. It is the last drum that joins in the polyrhythmic beat and its role — which makes it the musical center of attraction — is to play the virtuoso improvisations. The *bulá* is somewhat smaller than the *premier* and the diameter of its head is also smaller. It plays in the upper register, and its role is to execute a rhythmic pattern repetitively. The third drum or *segón* — also known as the *bulá-segón* — is approximately the same size as the *bulá* and generally plays the same beat, but occasionally introduces brief variants. These three drums are referred to by the generic name *tumba*, which is a word with a Bantu phonetic antecedent denoted by the phoneme *mba* included in the word. *Tumba* is a generic term for drum among different Bantu ethnic groups. In Cuba, this word was also used to denote the slave gatherings where they danced around their instruments. The term *bulá* has its antecedents in certain Bantu languages where it means to strike or to hit. The use of the xylophonic drum known as *catá*, as well as the cylindrical shape of all the drums in general, is also derived from the drums of the different Bantu ethnic groups in Africa.

The tension-tuning mechanisms used in these three drums follow the original model of the *arará* drums. A hook-shaped stake is driven into the body of the drum and used to stretch a cord that pulls on the ring bearing the skin.

Some elements of the instruments seem to indicate a local origin in Cuba. The traditional painting on the instruments with five-point stars, elliptical shapes, stripes, and triangles, the use of nuts and bolts in the tension system of the *tambora*, as well as the metal hoops used around the body of the drums to make them structurally stronger, all are strictly Cuban elements. In addition, the hanging of the *tambora* from the player's neck and striking it with a stick and not directly with the hand are elements whose origin can be found in Europe, possibly in France.

Generally speaking, the distribution of the rhythmic function of the different drums according to their registers in the *Tumba Francesa* ensemble has a clearly African character. In Cuban music — among the different drum combinations it comprises — the musical improvisation function is always assigned to the upper register. The medium- and low-register drums usually execute a set rhythmic accompaniment function. This particularity of the combinations of Cuban drums has its antecedent in the musical practice of Europeans and is not character- istic of the music of the *Tumba Francesa*. In the latter the lower-register drum, the *premier*, plays the improvisation role and the accompani- ment rhythms are played by the rest of the ensemble in a higher register. However, during field studies carried out in Santiago de Cuba in 1978 I attended a festivity given by the "La Caridad" *Sociedad de Tumba Francesa* and for the first time heard a *premier* tuned higher than the *bulá*. During the intermission, I inquired of the *premier* player — a young man of twenty-five who had been playing different drums in his society for some ten years — and his answer was decisive: "I tuned it that way so that it would be heard over the *bulá* and to make it sound more powerfully." He had been playing the *premier* for only a short time. The previous *premier* player had grown too old and was in ailing health, so this young man had to leave his *bulá* and take over the *premier*. Obviously, this young drummer could hear the improvisation of the *premier* better when it was played in a relatively higher register than the rest of the drums. This element is indicative of a change toward a new perception of the music, and it is logical for this change to occur among the younger musicians. I found the same situation once again in the mid-1980s during a festivity of the "Santa Catalina de Riccis" *Sociedad de Tumba Francesa* in Guantánamo. In that case the *premier* was also played by one of the younger musicians, and it was significant to notice that he, too, was filling in for the usual *premier* player, who was over seventy years of age.

This transition suggests that, sooner or later, the different drum combinations that exist in Cuban music adopt a distribution of registers following the European musical perception of the roles they are called upon to play.

In the case of the *Tumba Francesa*, this transformation may have come too late to save it from the stagnation it has been experiencing for the last thirty years. There are only two such Societies left in Cuba — one in Santiago de Cuba and another in Guantánamo — and both are experiencing the same difficulty: They are finding it increasingly difficult to bring in new members who will continue the traditions of their forebears. Many of these traditions are based on the aesthetic models of the French aristocracy of the eighteenth century and on the behavioral patterns and music of the African slaves, especially those of Bantu origins. These traditions are already too archaic for the young people who are growing up and living in the modern environment of salsa, rock, and the other popular music expressions of our times.

The situation of the *rumba* and the *comparsas* of the Cuban carnival is completely different. Fortunately for both of these genres, many elements of this music broke off, early in the twentieth century, from the original context in which they had emerged and developed a completely independent evolutionary line. The music of the *guaguancó* and the *comparsa* became an integral part of the mainstream of Cuban popular music and although *rumbas* are still played in slum yards and *congas* and *comparsas* are part of the traditional carnivals, the real enrichment and development of these genres has been taking place outside their original contexts. It should be noted here that salsa music has incorporated a great many elements taken from the *guaguancó* and the *comparsa* and combined them with other elements of contemporary popular Cuban music.

Other expressions of Caribbean folk music are rather close to the music of the *Tumba Francesa* societies. Among them are the *Big Drum* festivities I studied in the tiny island of Carriacou, a part of the Republic of Grenada. It is interesting to note that in this case the central drum, called the "cut-drum" — which played the same improvisation role as the *premier* — is tuned in a higher register than the later drums.

To summarize, the historical development of the music of the *Sociedades de Tumba Francesa* in Cuba reveals that this music was not brought over from Africa, but generated within the Cuban context. It is also evident that while this music does contain discernible events and elements whose direct antecedents are to be found among the different African ethnic groups that participated in the development of the *Tumba Francesa*, as well as easily discernible elements of the musical culture of the French aristocracy of the times, it also contains elements that belong to none of the antecedents as these appeared at a later stage.

One is, then, observing the appearance of a new cultural quality that might be indicative of a new ethnic group. This group is intrinsically linked to the most general concepts that point to the existence of an Afro-Cuban and Afro-Caribbean music that is very different from any expression of African music.

Music and Black Ethnicity in the Dominican Republic[1]

Martha Ellen Davis

The Caribbean Nation as Ethnic Group

In the United States, the concept of "ethnic group," that is, cultural group, implies a minority. Not so in the Caribbean. In the island states comprising the Caribbean, each nation is often viewed by its inhabitants as an ethnic group. This is actually a more accurate use of the term "ethnic," which is derived from the Greek word *ethnos*, meaning "nation," and implying synonymity between nation and cultural group. The nation as ethnic group is applied both to the Lesser and the Greater Antilles, the Dominican Republic being a case in point.

Certain Caribbean countries with an ethnic and political "minority" constituting up to half their populations actually may be politically segmented, with the division right down ethnic lines. Such is the case in Trinidad — as well as in Guyana, a de facto extension of the Caribbean Basin area — in both countries, East Indian is juxtaposed with black (plus white). In these countries, the question of which is the legitimate national culture lies at the crux of politics.

However, in most countries of the Caribbean and Caribbean Basin area, whose ethnic minorities are small in number and power, the nation is viewed, officially and popularly, as a quasi-ethnic group. Ethnic identity is national identity, and vice versa.[2] For the national/ ethnic groups of the region, there is little correspondence between color or race and culture. Thus, the U.S. term and model of "black ethnicity" implied in the title of this book and consequently this paper is not relevant to the Hispanic Caribbean because it implies a racial and ethnic *minority* and a covariance of race and culture.

The cultural content of national identity of the region is usually assumed to be a "Creole" identity, referring to a cultural conglomerate born of Old World parentage and tempered by New World circumstance and creativity. Elements of culture — language, the arts including music and dance, folk religion, food, and so forth — are pointed to as evidence of unique, Creole national cultures. Edna Manley, Jamaican sculptor and mother of Jamaica's Prime Minister Michael Manley, uses art to define Jamaican national identity (Springfield 1992). Here we address the use of another art as symbolic of national identity.

This general Caribbean view of nation as ethnic group often manipulates reality, reinforcing national mythology and enhancing or excluding certain components. One of the most complex ethnic configurations is represented, for example, by the Nicaraguan region of Bluefields, an impoverished area that is home to Native Americans of several ethnic groups and languages as well as Caribbean blacks whose lingua franca is an English Creole but whose elite speak English. This region is politically and culturally marginalized within a Spanish-speaking country of very complex and polemical political structure. However, even minorities in such Caribbean and Caribbean Basin countries tend to consider nationality as a primary, quasi-ethnic identifier.

Language, imposed by the various European colonial powers, is the determinant of trans-geographic cultural unity and divisiveness in the Caribbean Basin. Language demarcates the cultural areas within the region, and language competence is the main symbol of ethnic identity within the region and its constituent countries. Language competence is the key to assimilation of members of ethnic/racial enclaves and immigrant groups. It is said, for example, that during the Dominican elimination of thousands of illegal Haitians in 1937, Trujillo's troops distinguished Haitians who tried to pass as Dominicans by their pronunciation of the word *perejil* (parsley), which Haitians pronounced "pelegil."

Citizens of countries of the Hispanic Caribbean view their nations, politically determined ethnic units, as subsets of the linguistically determined macroculture area of the Hispanic Caribbean,[3] which is in turn a subset of Spanish America. Language thus allies this island region more with Latin America than with the rest of the Caribbean.[4] The implication of ethnic homogeneity is reinforced by the imposition of

"La Raza" by Spain (in other words, the new mestizo ethnic/cultural population in the colonies) and "Hispanic" by the United States, as the founding and current colonial powers in the region.

The Dominican Myth of the Spanish Past

This concept of "black ethnicity" as a frame of reference, although imposed perhaps from the United States, does have a special role as antithesis to the unrealistically defined official national identity. The country has long designated itself as white and Hispanic, the first colony in the New World, and in juxtaposition to neighboring Haiti, which is self-defined as a black republic. This official identity of Santo Domingo, established during the conquest and evangelization of the island five hundred years ago, was rekindled during the Haitian occupation of 1822-1844. In this century it has been a central feature of the ideology and cultural policy of Rafael Leónidas Trujillo, dictator from 1930-1961, and of his mastermind and heir, Joaquín Balaguer, president in 1966-78 and from 1982 to the present.

Balaguer recently reaffirmed *hispanidad* by building the colossal Columbus's Lighthouse (*el Faro a Colón*). The Faro is a pharaonic mausoleum for "the Admiral" which took up most of the national budget for several years. Symbolic of the European and Christian conquest, it was built in the form of a horizontal cross whose longer beam points between Spain and South America. It was inaugurated 6 October 1992, and validated by the Pope's visit and outdoor mass on 11 October. In his sermon, he preached of a "new evangelization" of the Americas, a sort of modern Holy Roman Empire.

Despite the continual affirmation by church and state of this official national identity, blacks have been present in Santo Domingo (the colonial name of the country) since about 1502. Yet the official view sees anything black, African, or Haitian[5] as a foreign intrusion, a contaminant tainting Dominican racial and cultural purity. Representing the views of the Hispanic elite, in *La isla al revés: Haití y el destino dominicano* (1983), Balaguer attributes Dominican problems in health, welfare, and morality to Haitian imperialism, which has turned the island "upside down and backward." He implicitly addresses the elite's latent fear of another Haitian armed invasion and refers to the more insidious continual infiltration of Haitian immigrants and culture. In the work he photographically portrays the white peasant of the north (Cibao) region as the prototype of the authentic Dominican.

Music has been used as symbolic evidence of Hispanic cultural authenticity and has been seen as a dangerous symptom of African infiltration. The late Emilio Rodríguez Demorizi, official historian for Trujillo, in his work, *Música y baile en Santo Domingo* (1971) and other writings, documents the elite view of cultural degradation through music and musical performance contexts, epitomized by the music and ritual of voodoo (*vodú*). He selectively cites historical proscriptive edicts as well as anti-Haitian folk verse such as *décimas* to justify the official position (see citations and commentary in Davis 1976 and 1987, partially replicated by Duany in this volume).

But for the past fifteen years or so, with some political liberalization following Trujillo's assassination, music has also been used by some researchers and aficionados as irrefutable evidence of the African presence, the antithesis to *hispanidad*. This antithetical position can be seen as a phase in the "reinvention" of Dominican identity which has not yet played itself out. Much less has a realistic synthesis yet been forged concerning the concept of a "Creole" culture which is not merely a revision of *hispanidad* but rather a hybrid, New World creation, still evolving. The justification of the Hispanic thesis, the substantiation of the African antithesis, and the ultimate expression of a Creole synthesis are all negotiated with music, both utilized and interpreted as symbolic of identity.

Dominican Cultural Composition

Beyond a national culture, albeit defined as Creole, as in every country, there is also quite a lot of complexity and diversity according to social class, region, and rural or urban location. With regard to class, the oligarchy (landed elite) are white and endogamous, the upper-middle class are white or light, and the lower-middle class and lower class vary according to the region. The peasantry of the southern region and the border area with Haiti are mostly black and African-influenced; those of the Cibao Valley (north), mostly Hispanic; and those of the eastern region, mixed. The cities and towns are traditionally white, ringed with black communities in the case of the capital and southern towns — a settlement pattern determined by economics and reinforced by racism. However, this pattern is changing with rural-to-urban migration, the tremendous influx of peasants into towns and secondary cities, and general influx into the capital and beyond to New York.

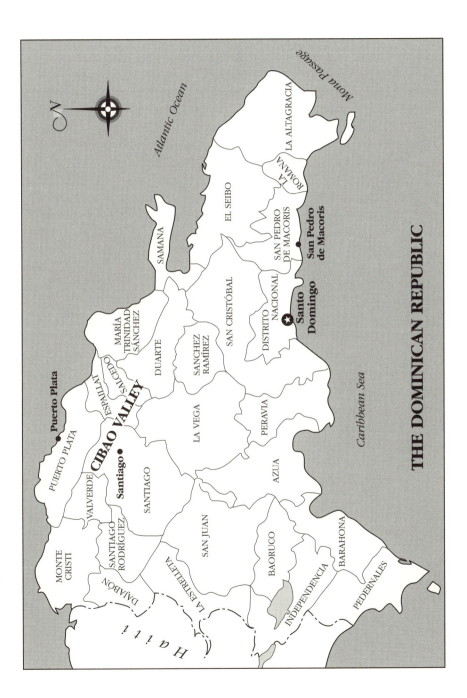

Within this racial and cultural constellation called the Dominican people, the country's black population and African-derived elements of culture represent the composite of superimposed strata laid down over a five-hundred-year history. The first blacks brought to Hispaniola were Christians from Spain.[6] The later introductions of blacks were directly from Africa from increasingly southerly points of origin: first from Senegambia, starting in the early seventeenth century from Guinea,[7] and starting in the mid-eighteenth century from the Bantu (Congo-Angolan) region (Larrazábal Blanco 1967; Curtin 1969).[8] Those aspects of musical culture considered "typically" Dominican may well be of an older, more extended and established origin, from the early Senegambia or Guinea influence; the folk *merengue* should be examined in this light. In contrast, the most obviously African customs, associated largely with black enclaves, are probably of the most recent origin — either from slaves from the Congo-Angolan area or, along the southern corridor, from Haiti during the 1822-1844 occupation.[9] Gerhard Kubik judged my Dominican audiovisual data on music, dance, and ritual, including data from the enclaves of Baní and Villa Mella (discussed below), to be of Congolese influence, and suggested specific areas of probable origin (personal communications, 1990 and 1991).

The black sector of the Dominican population is rendered additionally complex by immigrations from three foreign origins: Haiti (representing various historical periods of entry, up to the present), Afro-North America, and the Anglophone Caribbean.[10] Haitians in particular have contributed immensely during three centuries to the development and nature of Afro-Dominican music and Dominican "national culture" in general — ever since the division of the island with the French occupation of the western third in 1697. This is due to their length of influence, their numbers, and the fact that they are Catholic, which provides a channel of access into Dominican folk religion. At the same time, Haitian residents in the Dominican Republic, whatever their legal status or length of stay, have had to assimilate as an adaptive strategy, given their inferior position on the social pecking order due to color and national origin. The Haitian-Dominican acquisition of Dominican musical taste and behavior — a subject beyond the scope of this paper — constitutes a key symbol of their adaptation.

Given the current large Haitian presence (as many as 1 million of a Dominican population of 7.5 million) fed by illegal immigration of both economic and political refugees, and given the sectors of greatest national demographic growth, the Dominican population is darkening. Both this fact and the political liberalization of previously proscripted practices such as voodoo ritual are leading to an apparent racial and cultural Africanization of the Dominican Republic.

This is apparent to certain scholars who have occupied an intellectual niche in documenting Afro-Dominican history. And it is apparent to youths, who, in the context of neighborhood cultural clubs — a Caribbean phenomenon — and the public university (Universidad Autónoma de Santo Domingo), engage in a quest for the truth of their ethnic past and present. They antithetically redefine Dominican identity as Afro-Dominican. And they substantiate this with music, doing field observation and collection armed with audio cassette recorders, and playing drums as a form of communion with themselves. The details of this quest are described in a later section of this paper.

New York as a Crossroad for Afro-American Encounter

New York City, home to perhaps a half-million Dominicans,[11] is playing an increasingly important role in the redefinition of Dominican identity. For young Dominicans and immigrants from other Caribbean nations, New York provides the freedom from "down-home" regional divisions and class restraints, as well as the intellectual stimulus to explore, define, even to choose and create ethnic identity, which may be synonymous with national identity. Afro-Dominican youths, if schooled in New York, establish a bicultural identity with Afro-North Americans and have undoubtedly benefited from U.S. concepts of black pride and awareness (which in turn were influenced in their development by visionaries and spokespeople of Anglophone and Francophone Caribbean origin).

New York is acting as a crossroad of Afro-American, Caribbean, and Hispanic Caribbean encounter and reencounter, and a crucible of ideological evolution and articulation. New York is playing an important role in the reestablishment of the pan-Hispanic Caribbean cultural connection among the Dominican Republic, Cuba, and Puerto Rico — truncated at home by the political vicissitudes of the twentieth century — with the Dominican Republic a sovereign nation (though a de facto colony of the United States), Puerto Rico a de jure colony of the United states as "Commonwealth" or "Free Associated State," and Cuba, until recently a satellite of the former Soviet Union. The development in New York of salsa is a musical illustration of the progeny of this encounter:

born of Cuban rhythms, arranged for U.S. jazz band, and played largely by Puerto Rican musicians. "Latin jazz" is another genre of New York-bred multinational, transnational music (see Roberta Singer 1983 regarding tradition and innovation in Latin popular music in New York City).

New York is also providing a forum of cultural and musical encounter between the Dominican Republic and Haiti. For example, the New York Afro-Dominican folk and revival group AsaDifé has chosen a Haitian créole name. In the spring of 1994, the National Endowment for the Arts funded a performance, coordinated by the World Music Institute, by Afro-Dominican folk musicians representing three different genres, who played in ensemble with AsaDifé. They include the music associated with religious brotherhoods of two Afro-Dominican enclaves, the Sarandunga of Baní and the Congos of Villa Mella, as well as a group from La Romana of "*gagá*," the Dominican transliteration and version of Haitian *rará*, associated with sugar-cane plantation communities which characteristically use Haitian seasonal laborers (*braceros*).

Scholarship and Politics of Ethnic Identity

The hispanophilic bias of the Dominican intelligentsia of the late nineteenth and the twentieth centuries (see Davis 1976) is reflected in a total lack of interest and knowledge about Africa or Haiti, even though this is really necessary for a full comprehension of Dominican culture and sociocultural reality. Spanish culture, from a demographic point of view, is of course overrepresented in the constellation of today's national culture as the imposed culture of the conquest and evangelization. Yet the process of "creolization" through culture contact began virtually immediately upon the Spanish introduction of blacks into Hispaniola and their contact with Taíno Indians as well as Europeans.[12] The scholarly bias can be explained not only by the historical revisionism implied by the official national identity, but also by the traditional European orientation of academic disciplines such as folklore, and the class-determined Hispanic culture of local scholars as members of the urban elite. There is a tremendous cultural difference between the Dominican elite and the public in general. This is reflected in the unauthentic bases of nationalistic orchestral composition even of today, a barrier being overcome by the younger generation of composers in some other countries.

Given the local scholars' ignorance of the African presence, some non-European, exotic cultural traits such as certain musical instruments have been attributed to "the Indians," a view that has trickled down to the folk musicians themselves. In Latin American and Caribbean countries or regions where Native Americans are still present, they are situated by the elite at the bottom of the social pecking order. Where the indigenous population is no longer present, it may be romanticized, in contrast with the living black sector, ascribed in turn to the lowest social stratum. Such is the case in the Dominican Republic, where even a collective memory of an African past has been entirely lost or obliterated, very much in contrast with Haiti, where *Afrique Guinée* is frequently recalled in song texts as the mystical resting place of the souls of the ancestors. And, as elsewhere in Latin America, color is an encumbrance to social mobility, although ameliorated by money.

Scholarly studies of traditional music are crucial in molding and modifying the definition of national identities. In the Dominican Republic of the mid-twentieth century, the publications of Trujillo's official historian, Emilio Rodríguez Demorizi (1971), writing as the intellectual arm of a dictatorship, and musicologist Flérida de Nolasco (1939, 1948, 1956), writing as a scholar, have used music and dance to substantiate the myth of the Spanish past and justify the rejection of cultural "impurities." At the same time, ethnographic works documenting the African presence in the Americas have served as mighty political statements. In addition to the pioneering work of Melville Herskovits in various locales, Fernando Ortiz's extensive research on Afro-Cuban music and organology (the study of musical instruments) made a large impact on the Cuban redefinition of national cultural identity.[13] My own research on Dominican musical culture was initially conceived, in 1971, with the same purpose in mind. My field research, enhanced by Ortiz's etymological approach to organology, sustained the simple hypothesis that, given the racial statistics of Dominican demographic composition,[14] the country is probably a lot more African-influenced than the literature to date suggested, and this would be shown in the music.

Such works, entailing substantive documentation of the African presence in the Americas, as in some contributions in this volume, represent a first phase in scholarship on the cultural bases of ethnic identity. A second level of analysis, which interprets this data, is necessary to address the meaning of the data vis-à-vis ethnic identity

— for both the members of enclaves and, in a national frame of reference, for their compatriots — and the sociohistorical process involved in cultural extinctions, retentions, reinterpretations, and metamorphoses. This process entails the "dialectical tension" between a forced taming of *africanía*, on the one hand, and its camouflaged continuity on the other — which Angel Quintero Rivera (1992) calls *etnicidad cimarroneada*[15] — in which the African presence diffuses beyond enclaves and, unlabeled, becomes part of "national culture."

Following a summary of my documentation of Afro-Dominican and Creole musical culture, available in more extensive form in Davis 1976 and 1980, there is a preliminary analysis of these and other genres with regard to ethnic identity and symbols of identity. Discussed next is the recent trajectory of rectification of the official hispanophilic bias through recent field research and performance.

Traditional Afro-Dominican Musical Culture

Afro-Dominican religious music. The main features of African influence in Dominican musical culture and organology, in both enclaves and more regional or national musical culture, are outlined in Davis 1980; an overview of traditional musical culture as a whole may be found in Davis [1994]. To summarize, the most highly Afro-Dominican instruments and music are the long drums (*palos, atabales*), as well as certain group work songs and the songs in animal stories. These genres, the drums in particular, serve as conservators of an unwritten African past, useful in scholarship for historical reconstruction and, in the definition of an Afro-Dominican identity, as substantiating evidence of an African past.

The *palos* are largely associated with religious brotherhoods or confraternities — mutual aid and burial societies found throughout the country except in the central Cibao — as well as with individually sponsored saints' festivals. My research (1976) delineated musical areas of drumming, based on organological and musical features: the rapid *palo corrido* of the northeast, played on a set of two drums with pegged heads, accompanied by up to three *güiro* metal scrapers and a stick struck against the body of the master drum; the similarly named *palo corrido* of the southwest, played on a set of three wide drums with tacked heads and no idiophones; and the lugubrious *palo abajo* and *palo arriba* of the central-south, originally drums for the dead, played on a set of three narrow drums with tacked heads and no idiophones.

There are also two enclaves, the Brotherhood of the Holy Spirit of Villa Mella and the Brotherhood of St. John the Baptist of Baní, whose musical style and instruments are unique in the country: the *congos* of Villa Mella are a set of two drums, one large and one very small, with double-laced heads, accompanied by a wooden idiophone similar to the claves called *canoíta*, as well as single *maracas*; and the *tambores* of the *sarandunga* music of Baní are a set of three squat drums with double-laced heads, held between the knees or, for procession, under the arm, accompanied by one *güira*. The Haitian-Dominican *gagá* groups of cane settlements (*bateyes*) throughout the Dominican Republic during the Lenten season, are currently viewed by knowledgeable scholarship not as Haitian but as Haitian-Dominican (Rosenberg 1979).

A more Creole subgenre of religious music is the *Salve* of the central-south, where drumming is slow and somber; it is played at the altar in saints' festivals, accompanied by polyrhythmic ensembles of small drums and tambourines with *güira* metal scrapers and/or *maracas*. It represents an Africanized variant of the original type of *Salve,* called "*Salve de la Virgen*," the antiphonally sung, unaccompanied *Salve Regina* of archaic Spanish ecclesiastical tradition, passed into the oral tradition of Dominican folk Catholicism (see Davis 1981). Either the long drums or the *Salve* ensemble may be used for voodoo, a religious organization which, different from the brotherhood, serves as a medical cult and is characterized by spirit possession.

Creole recreational dance music. Recreational dance music, regionally specific in style and ensemble, which may also be played at folk-religious events, is marvelous evidence of the process of creolization. Its function as dance music renders it less resistant to change than religious music, which forms part of folk liturgy. Although some genres had died out by the mid-twentieth century, the surviving traditional dance ensembles include the eastern *baile de balsié* (the Dominican version of the ubiquitous Caribbean juba dance, onomatopoeically called *priprî*), which accompanies a variant of *merengue*, the *merengue redondo*, the southwestern *baile de balsié*, also called *priprí* but played with a different ensemble and entailing different genres (the triptych of *carabiné*, *mangulina*, and *danza* or *valse*); and the most well-known genre, the *merengue*, of the variant danced in the Cibao. While the other recreational dance genres are on the decline (the *zapateo* and its variants: the *guarapo*, the *sarambo*, the *yuca*, and the *callao*) (see Garrido 1961, Hérnandez 1969, and Coopersmith 1949)[16], the *merengue* of the Cibao (called *merengue típico,* or more correctly, *perico ripiao*) is flourishing in both its traditional ensemble and the modern, commercial version which is currently in vogue in Latin America and Spain.

Musical Symbols of Dominican Identity

U ses and functions of music, traditional and modern. Music performed in traditional contexts has meaning and symbolism tied to those contexts and their social uses and functions. For example, work songs are intended to coordinate and lighten group labor; lullabies are intended to put babies to sleep; ballads are intended as narratives; religious music is intended to fulfill a vow or allow the expression of devotion by mortals or self-expression by deities; music for the dead is intended to honor the deceased while disposing of mortal remains and dispatching the spirit; secular dance music is intended to provide courtship opportunities and fun, and make money for the musicians; and band marches are intended to coordinate military maneuvers, render homage to leaders, and express or engender patriotic enthusiasm.

It is in the context of the modern nation as ethnic group, as set forth above, that some or all of these genres acquire a new function: as symbolic of identity. "Identity" can refer to ethnic group (that is, cultural identity), geographical or political group (nation, region), social class, vocational or professional group, and so on. An individual's identity is comprised of various intersecting groups which may be viewed as sets and subsets of identity or, algebraically, as parentheses within parentheses.

Within the context of the modern nation, specific musical genres or styles, drawn from a compendium of traditional genres, may acquire the new function as symbolic of group identity. Most that come to represent national (or regional) identity, for projection outside the group, are social dances: the *samba* representing Brazil, the *tango* representing Argentina, the *cumbia* representing Colombia, the *joropo* representing Venezuela, the *sanjuanito* representing Ecuador, the *rumba, mambo, son,* and *chachacha* representing Cuba, the *tumba* representing Curaçao — and the *merengue* representing the Dominican Republic. Each such genre has its own history and trajectory with regard to selection, adaptation, and diffusion. As documented by

Stanley Brandes (1990) for the *sardana*, the musical symbol of ethnic and national identity of Catalonia (in juxtaposition to Spain, of which it unwillingly forms part), each of these Latin American and Caribbean genres really represents but one small part of the traditional musical culture of its respective country. And each is, to some extent, an "invented tradition" (*à la* Hobsbawn and Ranger 1983), in accord with the mythology of national history and cultural and racial composition. In addition, each, having been appropriated by the "music industry" as marketable commodity, has become fashionable, displacing a multitude of other traditional genres which originally fulfilled the same function of social dance, as well as other genres with other functions.

This trend parallels the loss within modern nations of dialects, victims of the linguistic standardization required by a "national language," as demanded in school and currently reinforced by the mass media of communication. For example, the Spanish language, *español*, is more correctly called Castillian, *castellano*, the language of the central region of Spain which became a national language with the unification of Spain and political domination by Castille. This trend in both language and music form part of a worldwide trend toward cultural simplification and standardization, which in turn parallels the biological loss of genetic diversity.

Within an internal, national frame of reference, however, there is more diversity of genre than that projected or known outside. Modernization, with its changes in values and technology, has of course led to the demise or obscurity of numerous genres of traditional music and dance. At the same time, others have developed or changed in function and symbolic meaning.

With regard to musical symbols of Dominican identity, I propose a preliminary taxonomy of musical categories within a national frame of reference, subject to amendment and revision.[17] The intermixed criteria for classification are region, rural-urban location, social class, educational level, profession, and age. A more detailed scheme should actually distinguish between participation in/attendance at live performance as opposed to consumption of recorded music. And it should show whether the symbolism of a given musical behavior is self-determined or ascribed by others.

Dominican Musical Genres as Symbols of Identity

Ethnic Identity

Hispanic or European

Literate tradition

- Art music (National Symphony founded in 1941)
- Some salon dances (archaic): for example, *vals, mazurka*

Non-literate tradition

- Spanish poetic forms that may be set to music: for example, copla, verso, décima

Afro-Dominican

- Long drum music (*palos*) and
- Music of the Haitian-Dominican *gagá*

Creole/national identity (the nation as ethnic group)

See also, in class categories below, middle class and lower class/rural:

- A genre of traditional secular dance music: the *merengue,* Cibao regional variant

    1. Rustic, peasant, quaint (marketed, performed internally)

        a. Subgenre: folk *merengue* (*merengue típico,* or more correctly, *perico ripiao*)

        b. Other regional social dances, less known and promoted

            1) "South" (=southwest): the *priprí* ensemble. Genres: *carabiné, mangulina, vals, danza*

            2) "East" (=northeast): the *priprí* or "*palo echao*" ensemble. Less well-known and not used as national symbol. Dance: a sort of "round" *merengue* (*merengue redondo*).

    2. Urban, commercial, trendy

        a. Subgenre: ballroom *merengue* (*merengue de combo* or *merengue orquestado*). Marketed, performed externally; used for international economic and cultural competition.

- Brass bands, military and civil (municipal, others, for example, firemen's band)

    1. Occasions of performance:

    a. Military marching, ceremonial functions, and in praise of flag or civil leaders

    b. Playing dances

        1) Exclusive Officers' clubs Town social clubs (*casino, club*)

        2) Popular Town *fiestas* for national holidays and local patron saints' festivals, including the *alborada* (pre-dawn procession prefacing patron saint's day)

        Sunday afternoon or evening concerts in town gazebo (*glorieta*) in central plaza

        Weekend all-day family social dances in local bar (*pasadías*)

2. Social function of musicians' participation in municipal bands and public "Academias de Música" (founded by Trujillo in the 1940s and 1950s)

    a. Social mobility through music literacy (parallel to social mobility provided by the military)

Class and Rural/Urban Identity

(For most musical categories below, note role of recording industry and radio broadcasting, in which "payola" has not been insignificant in conditioning tastes and developing markets.)

Urban upper class

- Art music (selected audience)
- Popular song (older adults — older genres, for example, *criolla* and older styles and repertoires of *bolero*)
- Rock 'n' roll (youths; selected audience)

Upper-middle class & intelligentsia

- Latin jazz (especially for expatriate community)
- *Nueva canción* (mainly youths; selected interest)
- *Bachata* (see lower class, below) becoming trendy due to recordings by Juan Luis Guerra, Sonia Silvestre (formerly of *nueva canción*), and others

Middle class (and aspirants)

(Also see genres under "Creole/national identity" above)

- Popular song, newer-style *boleros*, called *baladas* (recorded for large financial gain by international companies with Latin American and Spanish name-brand performers such as Julio Iglesias, JoséJosé, and others)
- *Merengue orquestado*
- *Salsa*
- The *ballet folklórico* (youths; selected interest)

Lower class (city and town) and rural
(Also see genres under "Creole/national identity" above)

- Oral tradition
    1. Rural: region-specific traditional genres in oral tradition, including religious, recreational, work songs (See above for Afro-Dominican genres; many, especially social dance genres, fallen into disuse)
    2. Region-specific (overview, main genres)
        a. Cibao (north): folk merengue, Salve
        b. East: *tonadas de toros* (of pilgrimage-brotherhoods); *son* (in San Pedro de Macorís), *pripří* (social dance); (northeast) long drums (*palos*); *Salve*
        c. South: long-drums (palos); unaccompanied *Salves*
        d. La Línea (northwest border): folk *merengue*
        e. Cane plantations: *gagá*, *bachata* (oral and radio)
- Radio transmission

(Note role of Radio Guarachita as local recording company and broadcaster for *bolero*, *bachata*, and folk *merengue*; operates under single cash payment for recording, no royalties)

    1. Folk *merengue* of Cibao region (*perico ripiao*), now of national rural popularity, but especially in the north and north border area (La Línea) where also played
    2. *Bachata*:[18] (1980s) local recording and distribution for local consumption by local companies, sometimes self-financed; (1990s) trendy, (now on CDs produced in New York), especially popular in the south (=southwest) and sugar-cane plantation areas
    3. *Ranchera mexicana*: especially popular in the north

4. *Son*: mainly in and near capital and San Pedro de Macorís, among both old and young, where also played

5. Ballroom *merengue* and *salsa*: urban

Latin American Pan-Regional Identity

(juxtaposed with U.S. and multinational political, military, and economic domination)

Socialistic, human-rights orientation

- *Nueva canción* — protest, social commentary intended to enlighten; (counterpart of *nueva trova* in Cuba; in a specific pan-Latin American style). New modality: wordiness and ideology of *nueva canción* within "Afro-pop" rhythmic idiom of *salsa, à la* Rubén Blades; for example, Juan Luis Guerra

Specifically Hispanic-Caribbean focus

- Latin jazz (for example, Michel Camilo's piano jazz)

The Merengue as Ethnic Marker

The question of the historical origin of the *merengue* is a metaphor for the cultural origin of the Dominicans (Pacini Hernández 1991,116). Some Dominicans are offended by implications that the Haitian *méringue* may be the original variant or a concurrent regional variant, or that the rhythm and instrumentation of the Dominican *merengue* may exhibit African influence. But the truth is that the style and very instrumentation of the *merengue típico* or *perico ripiao*, as well as other traditional recreational dance ensembles, symbolically represents the hybrid, Creole nature of Dominican culture. For example, with regard to the ensemble, the *perico ripiao* utilizes a European melodic instrument played by the vocal soloist — a Hohner button accordion (which replaced the guitar around 1890 due to trade with Germany); an African-derived *tambora*, a horizontally held, double-headed drum, beaten on one skin by the hand and the other skin by a stick; a *güira* — the Dominican metal version of the archaic *güiro,* the gourd scraper, which may represent syncretism between Taíno and African instruments; and a *marimba* (the same *marímbula* of Puerto Rico or Cuba), an African *mbira* on large scale which serves as a bass, imported in the 1930s with the Cuban *sexteto*.

The development of the commercial ballroom *merengue* as the typical Dominican salon dance is attributable to its promotion by dictator Trujillo over the European and Hispanic-Caribbean salon dances. In a masterful manipulation of musical symbolism, Trujillo justified this adoption of the *merengue* by viewing it as a "Creole version of Hispanic folklore" (Rodríguez Demorizi 1975, 83). Given the official definition of national character as Spanish, the concept of "Creole" could be viewed as an official-level manipulation or revision of "Spanish" so as not to be in dogmatic denial of obvious racial and cultural reality. This definition of the term implies the colonial racial definition: born in the New World of European parentage. On the other hand, youths may implicitly define "Creole" as it is taken now, to mean a hybrid developed in the New World of mixed parentage, the African component standing out as very significant. Their definition includes the Dominican concept of the hybrid as tougher than its components — as biological hybrids indeed are.

It is the revised, Creole national identity that is symbolized by the *merengue* as ethnic marker (although some scholars such as myself, and youths consider the drum-dance a more accurate symbol of identity). Both versions of the *merengue*, the folk and the commercial, are now taken as symbolic of national identity, the *perico ripiao* representing a rustic, peasant identity (inferring the white peasant of the Cibao, considered prototypic of Dominican peasantry and of the Dominican people as a whole), and the big-band *merengue orquestado* representative of urban, modern identity. Both together form the popular image of national identity — on the one hand rooted in charming (white) rusticity, but also progressive, modern, and even internationally trendy.[19]

Jorge documents composers' adjustments of form over several decades, seeking the best adaptation to a dance hall context as well as "translation" to the medium of art music (1980, 35).[20] Trujillo had his own dance band — the final one being the Santa Cecilia — and many *merengues* were composed and played in his honor (see Rivera n.d. and Tejada 1978). And he founded an official radio station, "La Voz Dominicana" (formerly "La Voz del Yuna," which followed the first official station, HIX, founded 1929), which served not only his ends but also encouraged artistic development in the country. About 1960 he also founded the television station, HIN (today Radio HIN Televisión, shortened as "Rahintel").

Trujillo also founded municipal bands (*bandas de música*) and public music schools (*academias de música*) in the 1940s and 1950s in towns and cities throughout the country. His intention was to develop education and the arts as well as industry. Feeling competition with Cuba, known as "the Athens of the Americas," he developed the *merengue* to be recognized as an artistic symbol of Dominican identity.[21] In addition, the *academias* taught young people music in order to play in his honor. For them, the acquisition of music literacy through the *academias* served as a symbolic means of social mobility — as does the military in Latin America, with which marching bands are associated.

The ballroom *merengue* actually bridges the oral and literate traditions. It taps oral sources for inspiration, fixed in composers' adaptations in scores. Recordings and dance halls serve as other sources of ideas and means of modern oral transmission from one band to another. Since their music, once played, is considered to be in the public domain, it is customary for other bands to pirate hit tunes and make their own arrangements, with no concept of music as "intellectual property." The American Society of Composers, Authors, and Publishers (ASCAP) in New York is trying to raise musicians' awareness of composers' and musicians' rights (Bruno Aguancha, personal communication, 1987).

As a symbol of identity, the masses have also invoked the *merengue* when threatened from outside. Jorge suggests that a preference for the *merengue* over foreign genres in dance halls during the first U.S. Occupation (1916-1922) had a nationalistic connotation (n.d., 37). During the 1970s the commercial *merengue* was modified (such as by an acceleration of tempo) to make it more attractive to the musical taste of urban youths in response to the inroads of rock 'n' roll as well as the commercial competition of *salsa* (see Pacini Hernández 1991, 109-110). During the last five years or so, the *merengue* has surpassed *salsa* as the Afro-Caribbean dance rhythm in vogue not only in New York but in Latin America and Spain. With New York as its commercial axis, the *merengue* has become a significant export product of the Dominican Republic in the form of recordings, shows, and dances. Its current fashion is also a motive for national pride as the musical symbol of a modern, trendy national identity. Although many of the main *merengue* bandleaders and lead singers of the 1960s and 1970s are black (such as Johnny Ventura, Cuco Valoy, Joseíto Mateo, and singer Rafael Colón) and some texts (especially those of Johnny Ventura) may make reference to that fact, the commercial *merengue* neither addresses nor symbolizes an Afro-Dominican identity. On the contrary, it is played simply for enjoyment and profit, and at the same time is invoked as a musical symbol of national identity.

Recent Afro-Dominican Studies and Performance

Much recent Dominican scholarship on Afro-Dominican history, culture, and musical culture, as well as performance of Afro-Dominican music outside its traditional contexts, takes into account the politics of ethnic identity. With an increasing liberalization of oppression regarding African heritage, especially during the two periods of rule of the Partido Revolucionario Dominicano (PRD) — the seven-month government of President Juan Bosch (1963), and from 1978 to 1986 — the country enjoyed a cultural renaissance. Two types of activities developed in regard to the Afro-Dominican heritage: On the one hand, certain Dominican scholars, of the class and color who would previously have rejected the subject, moved into Afro-Dominican studies as an unexploited, intellectual niche. On the other hand, a generation of students and young people, through neighborhood cultural clubs (a Caribbean phenomenon) and the public university, Universidad Autónoma de Santo Domingo (UASD), began to explore the roots and reality of their Afro-Dominican heritage through field research and performance. They were backed in spirit by government spending priorities which favored cultural endeavors.

The cultural policy of President Balaguer (1966-1978 and 1986-present) was and is a continuation of the *hispanidad* of Trujillo. This was reflected in his appointment of the architect José Antonio Caro Alvarez, an amateur archaeologist and collector, as director of the alabaster Museo del Hombre Dominicano (inaugurated 1973),[22] which Caro Alvarez had designed as part of the deluxe public-works project, the Plaza de la Cultura.[23] It is not coincidental that Balaguer's anti-Haitian book of 1983 was dedicated to Caro Alvarez and published by his foundation. The Museo del Hombre Dominicano was originally graced with two huge bronze statues representing the progenitors of the cultural composition of the country: the Taíno "Enriquillo" representing the Native American heritage, and Father Bartolomé de las Casas representing the Spanish heritage.

It was not until the economist, industrialist, and amateur archaeologist and collector Bernardo Vega took over the directorship of the museum that a third statue, of the African rebel "Lemba," was added,

Afro-Dominican heritage having become more politically correct among the intelligentsia, and to mark scholarly turf. Vega also ordered a permanent exhibit be prepared[24] on the history of slavery in the country and supported research and museum publications on Afro-Dominican history and custom. These included the armchair works of Carlos Esteban Deive:[25] on "voodoo and magic" (1979) (comparative rather than ethnographic) and an encyclopedic, two-volume work on African slavery in Santo Domingo (1980).[26] Previously, the only available published materials on the subject were the biased but well-documented historical compendia of Emilio Rodríguez Demorizi and *Los negros y la esclavitud en Santo Domingo* (1975) by Carlos Larrazábal Blanco.

Vega's policy was sustained and expanded by the subsequent director, sociologist José Del Castillo, a specialist on sugar-cane plantations, the epicenters of Haitian presence in the country. In addition to a major exhibit on the culture of the cane plantations and industry, he instituted a fortnightly folklore series of traditional musicians and dancers, "Sábados Folklóricos," which I coordinated, following suit after a couple of series under Vega. The series under Del Castillo, unlike the previous ones, were not outdoor entertainment with performers enshrined and inaccessible on stage. Rather, they were demonstrations and facsimile ritual and recreational interactive events, held indoors in the Hall of Folk Religion and utilizing the life-sized model home altar. Their purpose was intended to laud traditional artists and their culture and to bridge social classes through public education.

The series represented a renewal of the same public support of research and performance of authentic Dominican folk arts expressed in 1963 by the government of Juan Bosch, during the first period of rule of the Partido Revolucionario Dominicano[27]. During the course of his seven-month rule before Bosch was deposed by military interests with U.S. support, a major folk dance festival with traditional artists from throughout the country was organized in the Agua y Luz Theatre, located in the Feria de la Paz built under Trujillo in 1952.[28] A research trip was also sponsored for ethnomusicologists Isabel Aretz and Luis Felipe Ramón y Rivera of Caracas, whose perspective and data attested to the African presence in Dominican musical culture; unfortunately, their recordings are unavailable in the Republic and their data appeared in an obscure Venezuelan publication (1963).

With regard to other liaisons between scholarship and performance as educational extension, in 1945 Edna Garrido Boggs (b. 1913)
founded the Sociedad de Folklore Dominicano, following a folklore
course offered by American professor R.S. Boggs, as well as a short-
lived research-based folk dance ensemble she established at the
Universidad de Santo Domingo.[29] Garrido Boggs, an excellent and
thorough scholar, was and is interested in folklore of all sorts, but her
European-oriented training in folklore conditioned her selection of
research topics — Spanish-derived ballads (1946) and children's songs
(1955) — and limited her background for analysis of Afro-Dominican
lore. In her recording mission and study of Dominican folk dance, she
was aware of the presence of African influence, but she had to call on
others to discern the significance. Manuel J. Andrade (1930), sent by
Franz Boas to collect Dominican tales in the late 1920s, saw and
collected apparently without recognizing the African presence in
Dominican lore and without developing any taxonomy based on
cultural origins. He included an appendix on folk music with no
mention of the African origins or style of the songs which undoubtedly
accompanied collected animal tales. J. M. Coopersmith, well aware of
the cultural composition of the country, made good field recordings
and, given the brevity of his trip, wrote an amazingly good monograph
on Dominican folk and art music for the Pan-American Union (1949).
But the work had minimal circulation in the Dominican Republic until
a translation was published in 1974.

Also during the 1940s, a self-taught dancer and folklorist, René
Carrasco (d. 1978) was conducting research throughout the country,
financed by his meager earnings as a tailor in Las Cañitas, Miches
(northeast, on the Samaná Bay). Establishing himself in the old sector
of Santo Domingo on the Calle Arzobispo Meriño in a thick-walled
colonial house nicknamed "La Cueva Colonial" (the Colonial Cave), he
established a private dance academy and sort of folk museum. It was
decorated in folk motifs, such as polka-dots all over, and included a
special room with a functioning shrine to the spiritual healer and
messianic leader, Liborio.[30] During the 1960s and 1970s he gave nightly
classes at the "Cave" to neighborhood youths, and occasional public
performances, playing an important role in training and stimulating
research and performance by young people. During Bosch's brief
presidency, he received a pension in support of his work. Carrasco's
knowledge of Dominican folk music and dance was encyclopedic.

Through his readings in anthropology, he was ahead of his time in being fully aware of the African component of Dominican culture; one of his favorite topics upon which he frequently expounded was the tripartite composition of Dominican national culture.

But Carrasco was also an artist; his troupe's performances unconsciously fused ethnographic observation with artistic creativity. For example, every piece was accompanied by accordion — even the *congo* dance of Villa Mella, defined above. The sound of the north (Cibao) region is implicitly and erroneously popularly taken as the sound of Dominican "typical" (peasant) music, associated with the white peasant of the region, discussed above. Carrasco's sound and style set the precedent for the Dominican "*ballet folklórico*" as a new music/dance genre, replicated by such well-known groups as that of Josefina Miniño. His invented tradition is still seen and heard in clones of clones throughout the country, including small-town "cultural clubs" where this genre and style, legitimized by television, sometimes displaces those transmitted through the oral tradition.

In 1973, folklore aficionado Fradique Lizardo of San Cristóbal returned from self-imposed exile in Cuba and became active both in field research and performance. His forte is neither as artist nor rigorous scholar, but rather as promoter. He founded a performance group which he lobbied into appointment as the official Ballet Folklórico Nacional, although he later left it and returned to his own private-sector ensemble. Accrediting himself through the publication in 1975 of a volume on Dominican folk dance, based in part on a 1950s manuscript by Garrido Boggs, he made his name a household word by launching an attack in the newspapers on folklore enthusiasts René Carrasco and Casandra Damirón (d. late 1980s), an upper-class pop singer from Barahona who had her own troupe, charming but unauthentic.

Lizardo's trademark, on which he capitalized to the maximum, was the discernable African presence in Dominican folk music and dance, and he published a newspaper column and press releases with his continual "discoveries," some actually being resurrected or perhaps invented traditions. He enjoyed a flurry of fame and income following his troupe's performance for the 1977 Miss Universe pageant. His promotional skills have been very important in developing public awareness about the African heritage. He has attracted many youths of the capital to his folk dance troupes, and many have gone their own way to continue active in folk music performance at home and in New York. Cases in point include drummer Isidro Bobadilla, who directed a group in New York called "Los Amigos del Ritmo," and earlier "La Cofradía," and Bony Raposo, lead drummer for the currently active New York group AsaDifé, mentioned above. Meanwhile, Lizardo, tireless and devoted, continues active in publication and direction of his folk dance troupe.

The Universidad Autónoma de Santo Domingo, the state university of the country, has played an important role — as it did in the 1940s — in the scientific documentation and authentic representation of Dominican traditional culture. But its redefinition in 1965 as a popular rather than elitist institution,[31] and its internal structure which permits management of personnel and funds autonomous from governmental control,[32] has allowed inquiry into Afro-Dominican culture and heritage. In August-September 1973, a symbolically important conference was celebrated on the African Presence in Santo Domingo. Also in the 1970s, a university folk dance troupe was founded, Afro-Dominican in orientation, directed by José Castillo.[33] It is probably the most authentic in the country because it is founded in field observation by its director and some of its members.

In about 1978, the major in anthropology was created at the Department of History and Anthropology, attracting dynamic students interested in documenting their national ethnography and tantalized by their African past; however, if the course on Africa in their curriculum is actually taught, it is probably the only such course in the entire university and probably in any university in the country. June Rosenberg, versed in African studies and an expert on Haiti, was the first professor of anthropology, starting in the mid-1960s; she has influenced an entire generation of sociology and now anthropology students, and although retired she still advises students. Recently, she oriented and wrote the prologue for a collection of essays, *Gagá y Vudú en la República Dominicana: ensayos antropológicos* (1993) by the late Puerto Rican anthropologist, José Francisco Alegría-Pons (son of anthropologist Ricardo Alegría). And she also oriented Cuban writer, Mayra Montero (resident in Puerto Rico), in the field research used as the basis for her novel on *gagá*, *Del rojo de su sombra* (1992), which is dedicated to Rosenberg, Alegría, and his wife, Soraya Aracena.

Currently a professor of anthropology, Carlos Andújar is conducting an ongoing study of the *gagá* of the area of La Romana and has done minor video documentations of Afro-Dominican practices in the capital and Villa Mella as well. Many graduates and students of the program, such as Alejandro Peguero, have pursued similar interests. The social-science research unit of the University, el Centro de Estudios de la Realidad Social Dominicana (CERESD) under the directorship of Luis Gómez in the 1980s, supported research on Dominican culture, including my own five-semester study of Dominican voodoo (1987), as well as imparting relevant courses, such as a master's course in rural sociology sponsored by the Facultad Latinoamericana de Ciencias Sociales (FLACSO — Latin-American university consortium).

A sociology professor and university and government administrator, Dagoberto Tejeda has been influential since the 1970s in the documentation and projection of traditional Dominican music, starting with his founding of a research-performance group called "Convite" in 1976 (now defunct). The dual purpose of the group and its human-rights orientation made it unique and still much mentioned. Convite produced only one LP recording, *Convida*.[34] The political climate and the magnitude of their social mission is suggested by their arrest for a performance of the "Salve de Mamá Tingó,"[35] a song from the oral tradition which commemorates a black peasant from Yamasá who faced troops with a shotgun when she was going to be dislodged as a squatter. The main performance locale of Convite was the Casa de Teatro, founded about the same time in the colonial city, owned and directed by banker and oligarch Freddy Ginebra. The Casa de Teatro, which has a small gallery as well as a stage, has significantly served as a home for avant-garde and counterculture graphic artists and musicians. Thus, since the mid-1970s, Ginebra has played a crucial role in the support of both traditional and new music and arts.

Tejeda has continued with field observation of traditional musical performance contexts, especially in his hometown area of Baní. Involved in various projects in applied sociology, social work, and teaching thereof, he continues to take students and other enthusiasts to the field whenever possible. Although notably unproductive in publishing, Tejeda, like Rosenberg, has played a critical role in providing an initial opportunity for young people to launch into field observation of Dominican, especially Afro-Dominican, traditional musical culture. Both he and Lizardo currently teach folklore in hotel-management curricula in private universities. They are thus opening a new vocational niche for folklorists and graduates of the anthropology program at the UASD, as well as doing important "extension" work by providing knowledge about traditional culture to future figures in the tourist industry.[36]

The guitarist for Convite, Luis Díaz (sometimes spelled Días), was the only real musician for the group — which explains why every piece used guitar (the counterculture's counterpart of René Carrasco's ubiquitous accordion). He continues in the mode of Convite, now known as Luis "Terror" Díaz, garnering his artistic inspiration directly from observation of folk music performance in the field as well as other elements of the soundscape, now in New York, as components and ideas for his own creations. Díaz has a special interest in Afro-Dominican music, and in fact used the *congos* ensemble from Villa Mella in the videoclip of his best-known recording, "Ay, hombe" (ca. 1988)[37] — though the sound was overdubbed with a rhythm influenced by the *Salve*.

Despite his Afro-Dominican interests and identity, Luis Díaz's music epitomizes the eclectic, Creole nature of Dominican national culture. This is reflected in "Baile en la calle," another well-known but simple piece commissioned for the capital's carnival also in the late 1980s, later recorded by *merengue* singer Fernando Villalona, whose simple repetition is apropos to the carnival *comparsa*. Díaz has in fact internalized the Afro-Dominican musical idiom and creates new utterances in its modalities, often fusing various genres and rhythms. He takes creative risks, some of them not understood or appreciated by his audiences (such as his recent experimentations with rock 'n' roll, politically incorrect for the Latin-American counterculture and in Cuba). He terms the political risks he takes with his Afro-based musical fusions *la lucha sonora* — the sonic struggle.[38]

A new group in New York attempting to do the same is AsáDifé, mentioned above, directed by Tony Vicioso. He, like Díaz, bases his work on field research. He spends a great deal of time listening to, internalizing, and subjectively analyzing field recordings made at personal expense. He uses field recordings both for prescriptive purposes, to be replicated by the group, and, like Díaz, as the basis for composition. His source material is drawn mainly from the most atypical fringe of Afro-Dominican musical culture — the enclaves which play the *sarandunga* of Baní, the *congos* of Villa Mella, and the Dominican-Haitian *gagá*. The musical style of the group's musical creations, still in development, is characterized by Afro-Dominican rhythms, played at a faster tempo than in their traditional renditions, with conga (Afro-Cuban) and Dominican drums supplemented by band aerophones. Their text — in Spanish, English or "Spanglish" — is a wordy articulation of the ideology which inspired their musical mission, akin to the pan-Latin *nueva canción* of leftist social commentary. Their musical creations fall thus in the mode of the social commentary of Panamanian Rubén Blades, set to *salsa*, and some of the repertoire of Dominican Juan Luis Guerra, director of the internationally popular 4-40, which makes *merengue* and *bachata* (defined in the musical-genres scheme above) palatable to the aesthetics of the bourgeoisie. The creative style of AsaDifé is still evolving.

Again, what sets Convite, AsaDifé, Luis Díaz, and some other musicians apart from traditional, commercial, and avant-garde/*nueva canción* musicians is the fact that their art is rooted in field observation. And they use these materials and the understanding acquired through participant observation in the field to redefine Dominican national identity through music.

Current Trends in Afro-Dominican Music Not Associated with Ethnicity

In the meantime, other areas of current growth and activity in Afro-Dominican music which are *not* associated with ethnicity or any sort of consciousness about an Afro-Dominican identity, include the following:

1. Voodoo: A home-industry of recordings to accompany Dominican voodoo (*vodú, espiritismo*) ceremonies is slowly developing in the style of the old recordings (ca. 1950s) of the well-known Cuban duo, Celina y Reutilio, associated with spirit cults in the Dominican Republic and Puerto Rico. The Dominican recordings, like the Cuban, are string-accompanied, thus bearing a resemblance to *bachata* and serving a similar social sector. With regard to live drumming, the main traditional context of long-drum music and dance (*palos, atabales*), brotherhood or confraternity (*cofradía*), which has served as a mutual-aid and burial society for black Dominicans since colonial times, is on the decline. Meanwhile, voodoo, a healing cult, is on the rise, for reasons explained above. Within the major enclaves which play the *sarandunga* of Baní and the *congos* of Villa Mella, I have observed music for the *cofradía* now played for voodoo events characterized by spirit possession. So the two sorts of extra-official religious societies are merging.

2. *Gagá*: (the Dominican transliteration of the créole *rará*), a Lenten carnivalesque voodoo-related society associated with Haitians in cane-plantation settlements (*bateyes*), as mentioned above, is becoming increasingly Dominicanized and nationally well-known and popularly accepted as a dimension of Dominican music. *Gagá* has in fact been characterized since 1979 by expert June Rosenberg as "Haitian-Dominican." Now, with a generation of Dominican-born offspring of Haitian cane workers, *Gagá*, in Dominicanized, urban areas such as Haina (near the Capital) and La Romana, may sing in Spanish rather than créole. This genre is becoming trendy with young researchers and musicians, as evidenced in the support of it as Dominican by the performance group AsaDifé.

3. Commercial *merengue*: Haitian and Dominican musics exert mutual influence on each other in the commercial realm, as they do in the traditional, with the Haitian-to-Dominican influence being dominant over the reverse. In particular, the Dominican-based Haitian *merengue* group, Los Diplomáticos de Haití, whetted the Dominican appetite for the Haitian sound in *merengue*, which has continued until today.

Conclusion

This paper has suggested that in the case of many Caribbean countries, the nation is officially construed as synonymous with ethnic group, whether or not this reflects reality. Music is utilized and interpreted as symbolic of national cultural identity. Certain genres, usually for social dance, are selected, modified, and promoted for this purpose. Other genres may be ignored as useless for this purpose, or rejected as atypical, in a sort of official cultural revisionism to sustain national mythology. In the Dominican Republic of the twentieth century, as previously, the national myth is that of *hispanidad*, which defines Dominican racial and ethnic identity as white and Hispanic, in juxtaposition to neighboring Haiti, self-defined as a black republic. The justification of this Hispanic thesis and the development of an Afro-Dominican antithesis can and do use music as symbolic of identity.

The white peasant of the northern region of the Cibao is taken officially as the prototype of the Dominican. But it is not the Cibao peasant's most Hispanic music (which might be sung rosaries or certain work songs) which has been taken as musical symbol of identity, but rather his recreational music, the *merengue*, a hybrid with regard both to style and instrumentation. The selection of this genre represents a sort of reinterpretation of *hispanidad* as a creole identity — meaning in this case born in the New World of European parentage. Both types of *merengue*, the traditional and the orchestrated ballroom type, coexisted and continue to coexist as dual symbols of national and ethnic identity — a traditional identity tied to the earth on the one hand, and a modern, progressive, internationally admired identity on the other. At the same time, within an internal frame of reference, various genres of music transmitted in the oral tradition or through broadcasting carry various symbolic meanings with regard to ethnic, regional, class, rural/urban, and other domains of identity, several of which intersect in a single person.

Within the past two decades, certain scholars and many Dominican youths have expressed a view of the creole national identity as not a New World incarnation of European race and culture, but rather as a New World creation born of influences from Africa as well as Europe. Their position strikes a radical, antithetical pose to counterbalance *hispanidad.* The truth of their quest for identity is found in the detail of historical and ethnographic research and expressed through both publication and performance of Afro-Dominican music and dance.

New York City, where Afro-American pride has already been worked out, is playing an important role in this quest. It is here that leaders in Afro-Dominican musical creativity, such as Luis Díaz, have a forum and following. For New York is a place of Afro-American and Caribbean cultural encounter, transcending island barriers of politics, class, and race. It is thus a place of cultural evolution and a place which allows the creative risk necessary for the reinvention, through music, of Dominican national identity.

Notes

1.   Many thanks to Gerard Béhague of the University of Texas at Austin, Robert Parker and staff of the School of Music of the University of Miami, and the North-South Center for the sponsorship and organization of the 1992 conference of which a preliminary version of this paper formed a part. Thanks to René Fortunato, Dominican filmmaker, for information on the Dominican recording and broadcast industries and to Juan Miguel Matos for his information on Dominican commercial music, past and present, and his critique of my taxonomy of Dominican musical genres as symbols of identity. Thanks to Annie Davis of Technology Training Associates, Milton, Mass., for her technical revision of the manuscript.

2.   As illustrated by the papers in this volume of Victoria Eli Rodríguez on Cuba and Egberto Bermúdez on Colombia.

3.   The unity of the Hispanic Caribbean can be called *antillanismo.*

4.   Illustrated by the topics of unifying international conferences such as the IIº Encuentro del Seminario International/Identidad, Cultura y Sociedad en las Antillas Hispanoparlantes, sponsored by the Universidad Aútonoma de Santo Domingo and the Museo Nacional de Historia y Geografía, celebrated in Santo Domingo, 4-6 June 1992.

5.   The association is stated by a Dominican folklore aficionado in defining Haiti as "Africa camuflageada de francesa con el nombre indígena de Haití" (Africa camouflaged as French with the indigenous name of Haiti), translated by Pacini Hernández (1991, 115), citing Ysalguez 1976.

6.   Having resided there since the late 1300s.

7.   When the Senegambians became too rebellious and their cost, as acquired in Cape Verde Islands, became too high (Larrazábal Blanco 1975, 74, 77).

8.   Following the division of the island in 1697, the French development of Saint-Domingue (today Haiti) required a much greater African work force for the sugarcane industry. Their slaves were obtained through different commercial channels than those of the Spanish. Therefore, the predominant ethnic component of Haiti today is from the former French colony of Dahomey (today Benin), creating a different African-derived cultural composition than in the Dominican Republic, where Congo-Angolan (Bantu) influence apparently predominates.

9.   The icon and *sarandunga* drums of the brotherhood of St. John the Baptist of Baní are attributed to Port-au-Prince, through a detailed genealogy of the oral tradition (see Davis 1976). The brotherhood of Our Lady of Sorrows of Los Morenos, San Felipe, and Villa Mella, and the people of this community are also apparently of Haitian origin. Both probably date to the time of the

Haitian occupation, though slaves also escaped from St. Domingue to better conditions in Santo Domingo, and the border was probably more fluid for commerce than imagined (as it is now). I attribute the larger brotherhood of the Holy Spirit of Villa Mella, which plays the *congos*, to maroon origin, ultimately from the Sierra de Bahoruco.

10. The Haitian presence is composed mainly of slaves who escaped from the French colony of Saint-Domingue (1697-1804) border area, settlers with land grants for underinhabited areas (for example, Samaná) and others (southern corridor) during the Haitian occupation of the entire island (1822-1844), and sugar-cane laborers in the southeast, central south, southwest, and central north (twentieth century); today, more and more are moving into the capital as construction and domestic workers. Six thousand Afro-North American freedmen were repatriated to Hispaniola during the Haitian occupation of 1822-1844, as refugees from the system of slavery in the United States (see Davis 1980-83 regarding their history, culture, and musical culture). Immigrants from the English-speaking Lesser Antilles came in the early twentieth century to San Pedro de Macorís as stevedores and cane workers, and secondarily to Sánchez, Samaná, and Puerto Plata, some in professional service roles as teachers and preachers.

11. There must be almost one million Dominicans by now in the United States; census figures cannot be accurate because of the increasing number of illegals (since 80 percent of Dominican applications for all types of U.S. visas are denied). The traditional locus of disembarcation is New York City, but now there are satellite Dominican settlements in Providence and Massachusetts (Jamaica Plain, Lynn, Lawrence, and Lowell). These tend to be Dominicans of lower-class origin, while middle- and upper-class Dominicans prefer to settle in Miami. At present, Dominicans represent the fastest-growing immigrant sector in Manhattan, at twice the rate of the second group (Taiwanese).

12. For example, despite the rapid demise of the large *Taíno* (Arawak) native population (of at least a half million), the *Taíno*-African contact is apparent today because certain Afro-Dominican enclaves are the best conservators of Native American cultigens and food processing techniques (such as *casabe* or cassava torts made from manioc and *chola* rolls made from the starchy tuber, the *guáyiga*).

13. See Carlos del Toro González, "Identidad y cultura en Fernando Ortiz" (1992).

14. Recent (mid-1980s) figures (from the 1981 national census or national identity card data) indicate that the country is approximately 73 percent mulatto, 16 percent white, and 11 percent black (Haggerty 1991, xxviii).

15. *Cimarrón* (Anglicized as "maroon") means wild, untamed, a term used in this sense for plants and animals, and applied to runaway slaves. Since

the first fugitive slave settlement in the New World was in its first colony, Santo Domingo (Maniel Viejo in the Bahoruco mountain range, la Sierra de Bahoruco), Quintero Rivera (1992, 14) may be correct in suggesting a Taíno origin for the word, *símaran*, which refers to a shot arrow.

16. Garrido's and Coopersmith's field recordings are at the Archive of Folk Song at the Library of Congress, but without notes; one must consult their publications, which are not housed at the same place.

17. Many thanks to Juan Miguel Matos for his extensive observations regarding Dominican commercial music with special reference to black ethnicity, to René Fortunato for information about the history of the Dominican recording and broadcast industries, and to Tony Vicioso for comments about contemporary Afro-Dominican performance groups in Santo Domingo and New York.

18. Aptly termed by Pacini Hernández (1989) as "music of marginality."

19. In fact, the current vogue and financial success of the ballroom *merengue* is alleviating the ingrained national inferiority complex, which is continually compensated. For example, the red velvet program booklet for the inauguration of the National Theatre in 1973 favorably compared its dimensions with the Bolshoi of Moscow and La Scala of Milan, to indicate that the Dominican Republic is as important and as cultured as Russia and Italy.

20. For example, in 1927, Julio Alberto Hernández (1969) structured it as introduction (*paseo*), *jaleo*, two sections of *merengue*, coda; his pianistic variant, including *paseo, "copla" (=merengue), pasatiempo, jaleo*. Luis Alberti (1975, 79), the best-known and most successful diffuser of *merengue*, in 1954 reduced the ballroom form to *paseo, merengue, jaleo*; and he said that the *paseo* must be shortened for commercial recordings in order to reach the danceable part quickly. In the 1970s and 1980s, the *paseo* was eliminated, the tempo accelerated, and even the *merengue* reduced, emphasizing the *jaleo*.

21. Observation by Juan Miguel Matos (personal communication).

22. Where I have held an appointment as researcher, sometimes honorary, since 1976, and directed the Department of Sociocultural Anthropology from 1981 to 1984.

23. Includes the Museo del Hombre Dominicano as the national anthropology museum, said to house the largest collection of Pre-Columbian artifacts in the Caribbean, the National Library, the National Theatre, the National Gallery of Modern Art, and the museums of history and geography and natural history.

24. With designer Patricia Reid as museographer.

25. Dean of humanities at the private Universidad Nacional "Pedro Henríquez Ureña," a Spaniard who is a naturalized Dominican.

26. His later and shorter, but more specific and better, works have been based on his research in the Archive of Indies in Seville, during the period of rule of the Partido Revolucionario Dominicano when he served for four years as Dominican cultural attaché in Spain.

27. Founded by Bosch in exile in 1939, which he subsequently left as too populist in 1973 and founded the Partido de la Liberación Dominicana (PLD).

28. Coordinated by Fradique Lizardo.

29. The national public university, renamed the "Universidad Autónoma de Santo Domingo" in 1965, following the populist "Movimiento Renovador" which also provided autonomy from external political control over appointments and fiscal apportionments.

30. From Maguana Arriba, San Juan de la Maguana; killed as a political threat during the first American Occupation on 19 April 1922. But still a leader in spiritual form; practitioners of voodoo (a healing cult characterized by spirit possession) in the region call themselves "*liboristas.*" The messianic character of the cult was renewed in 1962 with the Movement of Palma Sola (see Martínez 1991), terminated again militarily with the army's assassination of one of the two leaders ("*Los Mellizos de Palma Sola*" — The Twins of Lone Palm).

31. Through an act of reform called the "Movimiento Renovador."

32. Hence the addition in 1965 of the term *autónoma* (autonomous) to the name, Universidad de Santo Domingo.

33. A staff member appointed to University Extension; not to be confused with José Del Castillo, mentioned above as former director of the Museo del Hombre Dominicano, who is a professor of sociology.

34. The term *convite* refers to an agricultural work party (a Dominican word adopted from the Haitian creole term for the same). *Convida* has an ambiguous meaning: *con vida*, meaning "lively," and *convida* from the verb *convidar*, "to invite."

35. "Son de Dios, son de Dios, son de Dios las Salves de Mamá Tingó" is an adaptation in the oral tradition of the old *Salve*, "Son de Dios, son de Dios, son de Dios las Salves que canto yo" (since the *Salve* as a genre invites modification and innovation).

36. Second revenue producer for the country after sugar.

37. "Hombe" is a Dominican interjection, obviously derived from the word *hombre*; "Ay, hombre" is more or less a melancholic "Gee whiz," with different meanings (such as sympathy) in different occasions.

38. See Pacini Hernández 1991 regarding the context of post-Trujillo popular music.

References

Alberti, Luis. 1975. *De música y orquestas bailables dominicanas, 1910-1959.* Santo Domingo: Museo del Hombre Dominicano.

Alegría-Pons, José Francisco. 1993. *Gagá y Vudú en la República Dominicana: ensayos antropológicos.* Puerto Rico, Santo Domingo: El Chango Prieto.

Andrade, Manuel J. 1930. *Folk-lore from the Dominican Republic.* Memoirs of the American Folklore Society. Vol. 23. New York: American Folklore Society. Reprint. Santo Domingo: Sociedad de Bibliófilos, 1976.

Aretz, Isabel, and Luis Felipe Ramón y Rivera. 1963. "Reseña de un viaje a la República Dominicana." *Boletín del Instituto de Folklore* 4 (4): 157-204. Caracas: Ministerio de Educación, Dirección de Cultura y Bellas Artes.

Austerlitz, Paul. 1992. Dominican Merengue in Regional, National, and International Perspectives. Ph.D. diss., Department of Music, Wesleyan University.

Balaguer, Joaquín. 1983. *La isla al revés: Haití y el destino dominicano.* Santo Domingo: Fundación José Antonio Caro.

Brandes, Stanley. 1990. "The Sardana: Catalan Dance and Catalan National Identity." *Journal of American Folklore* 103 (407): 24-41.

Coopersmith, Jacob Maurice. 1949. *Music and Musicians of the Dominican Republic: A Survey.* Washington, D.C.: Pan-American Union. Spanish translation: 1974. *Música y músicos de la República Dominicana.* Santo Domingo: Dirección General de Cultura, Secretaría de Educación, Bellas Artes y Cultos.

Curtin, Philip D. 1969. *The Atlantic Slave Trade.* Madison: University of Wisconsin Press.

Davis, Martha Ellen. 1976. Afro-Dominican Religious Brotherhoods: Structure, Ritual and Music. Ph.D. diss., Department of Anthropology, University of Illinois.

Davis, Martha Ellen. 1980. "Aspectos de la influencia africana en la música tradicional dominicana." *Bol. Museo del Hombre Dom.* 13: 255-292.

Davis, Martha Ellen. 1980-83. Series on the structure, culture, and religious musical culture of Afro-North American Protestants repatriated to Hispaniola in 1824-25. *Boletín del Museo del Hombre Dominicano* (Santo Domingo): 1) "'That Old-Time Religion': Tradición y cambio en el enclave 'americano' de Samaná." No. 14, 1980: 165-196. 2) "La cultura musical religiosa de los 'americanos' de Samaná." No. 15, 1980: 127-169. 3) "Himnos y anthems (coros) de los 'americanos' de Samaná: Contextos y estilos." No. 16, 1981: 127-169. 4) "Cantos de esclavos y libertos: Cancionero de anthems (coros) de Samaná." No. 18, 1983: 197-236.

Davis, Martha Ellen. 1981. *Voces del Purgatorio: estudio de la Salve dominicana.* Santo Domingo: Museo del Hombre Dominicano.

Davis, Martha Ellen. 1987. *La otra ciencia: el vodú dominicano como religión y medicina populares.* Santo Domingo: Universidad Autónoma de Santo Domingo.

Davis, Martha Ellen. Forthcoming. "Oral Musical Traditions of the Dominican Republic." *The Universe of Music: A History* vol. 9. Paris: UNESCO (43 pages, photos, recordings).

Del Castillo, José, and Manuel A. García Arévalo. 1992. *Antología del Merengue.* Santo Domingo: Corripio.

Deive, Carlos Esteban. 1979. *Vodú y magia en Santo Domingo.* Santo Domingo: Museo del Hombre Dominicano.

Deive, Carlos Esteban. 1980. *La esclavitud del negro en Santo Domingo (1492-1844).* 2 vols. Santo Domingo: Museo del Hombre Dominicano.

del Toro González, Carlos. 1992. "Identidad y cultura en Fernando Ortiz," paper presented at the Segundo Encuentro del Seminario Internacional on Identidad, Cultura y Sociedad en las Antillas Hispanoparlantes, Santo Domingo, 4-6 June 1992. 22 pages.

Garrido, Edna. 1946. *Versiones dominicanas de romances españoles.* Ciudad Trujillo: Pol Hermanos.

Garrido, Edna. [1955] 1980. *Folklore infantil de Santo Domingo.* Santo Domingo: Sociedad de Bibliófilos. Originally published in Madrid by Cultura Hispánica. Musical transcriptions by Ruth Crawford Seeger.

Garrido, Edna. 1961. "Panorama del Folklore Dominicano." *Folklore Americas* 21 (1-2): 1-23.

Haggerty, Richard A., ed. 1991. *Dominican Republic and Haiti: Country Studies.* Washington, D.C.: Library of Congress (U.S. Government Printing Office #550-36).

Hernández, Julio Alberto. 1969. *Música tradicional dominicana.* Santo Domingo: Julio D. Postigo.

Hobsbawm, Eric, and Terence Ranger, eds. 1983. *The Invention of Tradition.* Cambridge, London: Cambridge University Press.

Incháustegui, Arístides. 1988. *El disco en República Dominicana.* Santo Domingo: Amigo del Hogar.

Jorge, Bernarda. 1980. Bases ideológicas de la práctica musical durante la Era de Trujillo. Final paper, social sciences postgraduate course, Universidad Autónoma de Santo Domingo.

Jorge, Bernarda. 1982. *La música dominicana: siglos XIX-XX.* Santo Domingo: Universidad Autónoma de Santo Domingo.

Larrazábal Blanco, Carlos. 1975. *Los negros y la esclavitud en Santo Domingo.* Santo Domingo: Julio D. Postigo.

Lizardo, Fradique. 1975. *Danzas y bailes folklóricos dominicanos.* Santo Domingo: Museo del Hombre Dominicano and Fundación García Arévalo. (Introduction by Martha Ellen Davis, 17-31).

Lopes, Nei. 1993. "Afro-Brazilian Music and Identity." *Conexões* (Michigan State University, African Diaspora Research Project) 5, no. 1 (April): 6-8.

Martínez, Lusitania. 1991. *Palma Sola: opresión y esperanza (su geografía mítica y social).* Santo Domingo: Ediciones CEDEE.

Montero, Mayra. 1992. *Del rojo de su sombra.* Barcelona: TusQuets.

Nolasco, Flérida de. 1939. *La música en Santo Domingo y otros ensayos.* Ciudad Trujillo: Montalvo.

Nolasco, Flérida de. 1948. *Vibraciones en el tiempo.* Ciudad Trujillo: Montalvo.

Nolasco, Flérida de. 1956. *Santo Domingo en el folklore universal.* Ciudad Trujillo: Impresora Dominicana.

Pacini Hernández, Deborah. 1989. *Music of Marginality: Social Identity and Class in Dominican Bachata.* Ph.D. diss., Department of Anthropology, Cornell University.

Pacini Hernández, Deborah. 1990. "Cantando la cama vacía: Love, Sexuality and Gender Relationships in Dominican bachata."

Popular Music 9 (3): 351-367.

Pacini Hernández, Deborah. 1991. "La lucha sonora: Dominican Popular Music in the post-Trujillo Era." *Latin American Music Review* 12 (2) (Fall/Winter): 105-123.

Quintero Rivera, Angel G. 1992. "El tambor en el cuatro: la melodización de ritmos y la etnicidad cimarroneada." Paper presented at the Segundo Encuentro del Seminario International on Identidad, Cultura y Sociedad en las Antillas Hispanoparlantes, Santo Domingo, 4-6 June 1992.

Rivera, Luis. N.d. *Antología musical de la Era de Trujillo, 1930-1960.* 5 vols. Ciudad Trujillo: Secretaría de Estado de Educación y Bellas Artes.

Rodríguez Demorizi, Emilio. 1971. *Música y baile en Santo Domingo.* Santo Domingo: Librería Hispaniola.

Rodríguez Demorizi, Emilio. 1975. *Lengua y folklore de Santo Domingo.* Santiago: Universidad Católica Madre y Maestra.

Rosenberg, June C. 1979. *El gagá: religión y sociedad de un culto dominicano.* Santo Domingo: Universidad Autónoma de Santo Domingo.

Singer, Roberta L. 1983. "Tradition and Innovation in Contemporary Latin Popular Music in New York City." *Latin American Music Review* 4 (2): 183-202.

Springfield, Consuelo López. 1992. "Edna Manley's *The Diaries*: Cultural Politics and the Discourse of Self." *Explorations in Ethnic Studies* 15 (1) (January): 33-46.

Tejada, Adriano Miguel. 1978. "El folklore como mecanismo de control político en Heureaux y Trujillo." *Eme-eme: Estudios dominicanos* 6, no. 34 (January-February): 19-39.

Ysalguez, Hugo Antonio. 1976. "Merengue se deriva de contradanza española." *Ahora!* 637 (January 26): 48-50.

"Se Kreyòl Nou Ye"/"We're Creole": Musical Discourse on Haitian Identities

Gage Averill

The conference title that inspired the present volume of studies, "Music and Black Ethnicity in the Caribbean and South America," is problematic in the Haitian context. When Haitians discuss Haitian identity, they generally are concerned with something that might best be termed national identity. Only in the population centers of the Haitian overseas diaspora does ethnicity emerge as an indigenously or analytically significant concept. Moreover, the relationship of Haitian national identity to a racial marker ("black") is, as this chapter will demonstrate, complex and contradictory. Because Haitian identity can be regarded as either national or ethnic depending upon the context, I prefer to employ the more general concept of cultural identity.

Contemporary theories of national and cultural identity formation increasingly focus on the artifice by which they are produced and reproduced and on the necessity to ground collective identities in historical narratives. As Lowenthal states, "Nations and individuals habitually trace back their ancestry, institutions, culture, ideals to validate claims to power, prestige, and property" (1985, 52-3). The "subjective antiquity" of Anderson's "imagined [national] communities" (1991, 5), the implied "continuity with the past" of Hobsbawm and Ranger's "invented traditions" (1983, 1) and Giddens's "distant imagining" of nationalism (1985, 209-21) all emphasize the socially constructed nature of various types of peoplehood and their tenuous links to historical formations. In the views of these theorists, national and cultural identity hover in and around the realm of ideology. As social and historical constructions, identities are layered and multiple, capable of shifts and transformations, and conditioned by historical circumstances and social context. Despite the importance attached to differentia such as class, race, gender, age, ethnicity, and subcultural affiliation, all of these markers are considered, within this vein of scholarship, as socially activated components (and not static determinants) of identity.

Given this theoretical mutability of identities, it was intriguing to determine the extent to which Haitian identity has been in transition in the politically volatile epoch after the fall of the Duvalier dictatorship (1986-1992) and to explicate the part that expressive culture — popular music in particular — has played in this chaotic transition. This chapter approaches popular culture — specifically the popular music industry, its artists, its products, and its audiences — as a site of ideological contest over the content and representations of cultural identity. The underlying question remains: What is the relationship of music to cultural identity? To examine how popular music is implicated in recent changes in Haitian identity, this chapter charts the emergence of two musical formations in the post-Duvalier era, *mizik rasin* (roots music) and *nouvel jenerasyon* (new generation), both of which have vied with *konpa*[1] and imported musics for audiences and popularity.

Identities in Conflict

Haitian identities have formed within a historical drama of class, racial, and political antagonisms and struggles; they reflect the contours of these struggles. In Haiti, ideologies of African descent help both to construct the nation (i.e., "The Black Republic") *and* to deconstruct it. As many authors have pointed out (Buchanan 1980, Labelle 1978, Averill 1989b, Trouillot 1990), Haitians have a finely nuanced system of racial classification that attaches status differences to racial characteristics and associates race with class. However, since the Haitian revolution of the late eighteenth and early nineteenth centuries, Haitians have also developed a racially based discourse about nationhood, as in the use of the term *nwa* (black) — or more colloquially, *nèg* — for all Haitians, regardless of skin color, and the term *blan* (white) for all foreigners. There is also a patriotic strain in Haitian literature, and in music as well, that encourages all Haitians to unify and work together: to *met tèt ansanm* (literally to put heads together, to cooperate), to *kole zepòl* (glue shoulders together, march together), *met men kont men* (put hands together), and to *fè konbit* (cooperate like an agricultural work brigade). These corporeal images reflect the ideal of a united, integral nation[2] — an ideal frequently stated precisely because it contradicts such a deeply-rooted habitus of social division.

The ideology of the natural superiority of *klè* or light-skinned Haitians — a master narrative inherited from colonial discourse — has been under persistent attack in the twentieth century. The counter-ideologies, including *indigènisme, noirisme,* and *négritude,*[3] created the conditions for the rise of a black middle class as a cultural and political force (embodied in Duvalier rule) and for the more recent anti-elite movements of peasants and urban poor, such as the Lavalas movement of Father Jean-Bertrand Aristide. An earlier work of mine (Averill 1989b) addressed the large impact of the *indigène* movement (and its notion of Afro-Haitian authenticity) on popular music in Haiti. This concern is also evident in Lois Wilcken's study of Haitian folkloric dance troupes (Wilcken 1991), in Michael Largey's 1991 work on the autochthonous style in elite art music, and in Michael Dash's work on the literature of Haitian négritude (Dash 1981). These studies chart the emergence of an Afro-centric vision of Haitian identity among an influential segment of Haiti's middle class and intelligentsia.[4] It is precisely among these groups — which are urbanized, in contact with members of multiple racial and class groups, politically active, and educated — that the issue of cultural identity is most problematic. It is the same groups that constitute the producers and chief consumers of commercial popular music and popular culture in general, and thus it is these groups with which I am most concerned in this study.

Early Afro-Centric Musical Movements: *Voodoo-Jass and* Kilti Libète

African identity movements have typically arisen in the Americas during periods in which the exploitation and oppression of blacks is socially highlighted by political struggle. These movements foster oppressed group solidarity, link local exploitation to larger struggles of black peoples, and create a cultural space to articulate anti-hegemonic counter narratives (new histories, new genealogies, and new links with time and place) — tales told *about* the oppressed *by* the oppressed. Racially based, essentialist identities have competed prominently in the post-Duvalier cultural scene with more metropolitan visions of Haitian identity.

Anrasinman (back to the roots) movements in pop music signal (both sonically and textually) a relationship to traditional Afro-Haitian culture. In the twentieth century, there have been three distinct periods of cultural production that fall within this rubric: voodoo-jazz of the 1940s and 1950s, the *kilti libète* (freedom culture) organizations of the early 1970s, and the post-Duvalier *mizik rasin* movement.

Voodoo-jazz groups such as Jazz des Jeunes (Jazz of the Youth) and the Orchestre Issah el Saïeh fused traditional peasant rhythms from voodoo and *rara* processionals[5] to an ensemble style closely related to Cuban big bands. These groups tended to ally with the *noirist* movement that carried into power both Dumarsais Estimé (1947) and François Duvalier (1957). Jazz des Jeunes was the first group to incorporate *rara* — and the single-note *vaksin* bamboo trumpets peculiar to *rara* groups — into urban dance music with a well-known peasant *rara* song they orchestrated called "Kote Moun Yo?" ("Where are the people?"). The arrangement begins with the ostinato produced by the hocketed *vaksins*. This ostinato (the pitch structure of which is discordant with the tonal harmonic arrangement of the song material) is then buried under the sound of the full orchestra until it emerges during a break later in the piece. This use of incorporated traditional materials as framing devices in musical compositions is typical of experiments with roots musics.

The lyrics of "Kote Moun Yo?" criticize hypocrisy and incorporate a Haitian proverb as the song's final line. This use of proverbs (*pawol granmoun*, or the words of the elders) is also characteristic of neo-traditionalist compositions.

> *Kote moun yo, woy? Mwen pa we moun yo e*
> *Kote moun kap pale moun mal?*
> *Mwen pa we moun kap pale moun mal*
> *Woy woy woy woy woy woy*
> *Woy, devan byen, deye mal o!*
>
> *Where are the people? I don't see the people*
> *Where are the people speaking badly of others?*
> *I don't see the people speaking badly of others*
> *Nice in front (of you), but malicious behind!*
>
> (*Jazz des Jeunes, Ibo ILP 113*)

The voodoo-jazz movement could be considered the dominant proto-commercial music movement in the decade and a half before the Duvalier dictatorship commenced in 1957. It was eclipsed, however, in the early years of the dictatorship by the *konpa*, a newer style of dance music, based to a large degree on the Dominican *merengue*. Haitian dance pieces based on *rara* and *voodoo* rhythms continued to be performed by Jazz des Jeunes, but the group was relegated to folkloric troupe status.

The *indigène* movement and the debate over peasant and neo-African cultural expression were marked by a division between leftist and rightist tendencies. Right-wing noirists and Haitian communists shared common roots in the *indigène* movement of the 1920s and 1930s, but the two camps' split over the role race was to play in the class struggle. Despite the rift between the two camps, some personal ties persisted. For example, Duvalier's brother-in-law was a communist; and so was at least one member of Duvalier's early cabinet. Although his revolution was, in general, ardently anti-communist, Duvalier tolerated a small, disunited left which he used as a card in his dealings with the United States. He jettisoned this strategy in 1968 after the two major communist factions united to form PUCH (the United Haitian Communist Party) to wage armed struggle against him. Duvalier resolved to destroy the movement and to expose its sympathizers.

Among possible sources of left-wing discontent he targeted schools and universities, Haitians returning from abroad, workers' groups, the church, and the movement for Creole literacy and expressive culture.[6] In 1969, on the advice of his ally Edouard C. Paul, the anti-communist director of the state literacy bureau (ONAAC, National Organization for Literacy and Community Action), Duvalier ordered Paul to disband his own organization because of reputed communist influence within the group (Abbott 1988, 148). Along with ONAAC, Duvalier moved against private groups called "Karako Blè" (blue peasant dress), "Vaksin" (bamboo trumpet), and "Lanbi" (conch shell trumpet, believed to have been the instrument used to call slaves to rebellion), organizations working to develop a popular culture utilizing Creole and materials drawn from peasant culture. These groups were inspired by the Haitian *indigène* movement, the Latin American new song movement (*nueva canción*), the French student rebellion of 1968, and the U.S. Black Power Movement.

By 1969, Duvalier had broken up the creole literacy projects and cultural organizations and many survivors had joined the exile communities in New York and Montreal (Desgranges and Juste 1989). In general, these political refugees were intellectuals from middle-class and elite backgrounds. They constituted a new expatriate political movement distinct from the conservative opposition under the influence of former Haitian presidents Magloire and Fignolé.

Cultural groups in the mold of Karako Blè arose in the diaspora and took creole names (a change from the French names of the commercial *konpa* bands of the 1960s on). The best known of these were three New York groups: Atis Endepandan (Independent Artists), Solèy Leve (Rising Sun), and Tanbou Libète (Drum of Freedom). Other groups in the movement included Ayiti Kiltirèl (Cultural Haiti, Boston), Gwoup Kiltirèl Vaksin (Vaksin Cultural Group, Montréal), Kiskeya (an Indian name for the island of Hispañola), Grenn Banbou (Bamboo Seeds), Kouto Digo (Blue Knife), and Troupe Kouidor. These groups need to be distinguished from the less political folkloric troupes that performed in the diaspora at *galas* and *spèktaks* (multi-group cultural presentations with singers, bands, comedians, and folkloric troupes). They believed in the Maoist outlook on the revolutionary potential of the peasantry, and they advocated redistributing wealth and restructuring relationships of power. They offered the peasant *konbit* (collective work brigade) as model for collective struggle and national reconstruction.

The *kilti libète* groups' choice of acoustic music set them apart from commercial, middle-class *mini-djaz*. Their model drew from a tradition of *twoubadou* (troubadour) music, a guitar-based tradition that owes a debt to Cuban *sones* and *boleros* as well as to older Haitian rural song traditions. In many cases, the groups rewrote and radicalized peasant songs, transforming them into weapons to use against the dictatorship. In the liner notes to their 1975 album, the group Atis Endepandan wrote:

> We believe that a strong Haitian people's music exists, beginning with voodoo, rara, troubadours and other musical forms which had origins in slavery times... We try always to popularize the struggles of the masses, to make revolutionary propaganda and political education, but also to pay particular attention to the music itself (Atis Endepandan 1975).

The tune "Dodinen" (Rocking) on Atis Endepandan's record was a traditional lullaby whose lyrics were transformed to focus on the exploitation of Haiti's impoverished workers and peasants and their potential as a revolutionary force. The song features a *rara* rhythm and a whistle (an important ritual instrument in *rara* groups) in the introduction to alert the listener to the simulated *rara* environment. The acoustic guitar imitates the *vaksin* parts, playing an ostinato that uses four pitches. In the transition to the song, the guitar drops the *vaksin* imitation and uses the main pitch of the *vaksin* ostinato — E — as the root of the tonic E-minor chord. The *rara* is used only in the introduction, interlude, and coda, again framing the verses.

Group leader Max Antoine, a lawyer with a radio show on WKCR in New York, collaborated with guitarist Tit Pascal on the arrangements for guitars and traditional instruments. The second line paraphrases a Haitian proverb: *Fèzednat-la fè mat men se li ki domi atè* (The mat-maker makes the bed but it's he who sleeps on the ground):

> Se nou ki boulanje a, se nou k boule nan fè
> Se nou ki fèzednat la, se nou k domi atè
> Bagay sila pa kapab dire, travayè di yon mo
> Gran mesi pa nou se kout baton li ye
> Men zòt chita sou do n yap dodinen
> Dodinen mon konpè, wa dodinen
> Na rale chèz la, wava kase ren ou

> We're the bakers, but we bake in the fire
> We make the mats, but we sleep on the ground
> This can't go on, workers are complaining
> The big thanks we get is a blow from a stick
> But others are sitting on our backs rocking,
> Rocking, my friend, you're rocking
> We'll yank the chair and you'll break your butt

> (Ki-sa Pou-n Fe? Paredon P-1027, 1974)

Tit Pascal was, at the time, a music teacher and adviser to some of New York's commercial Haitian *konpa* bands including Tabou Combo, and he attempted, unsuccessfully, to convince Tabou Combo to record a *rara*-style piece. In 1984 — frustrated with the unwillingness of commercial bands to play *rara* — Pascal formed the first neo-traditional Haitian band in New York City, Ayizan (named after the voodoo deity of marketplaces and public gatherings).

Musik Rasin

The third period of neo-traditional music production is contemporaneous with the post-Duvalier era, although many of the important groups evolved in the years before Duvalier's exile. The best-known groups in this movement (within Haiti) were Boukman Eksperyans, Foula, Sanba-yo, and later Boukan Gine, Ran, and Koudyay. The first four of these groups had their origins collectively in 1978, when groups of young, urban musicians, influenced by roots music movements outside of Haiti, especially Jamaican Rastafarianism (to which they were exposed through the music of Bob Marley), began searching for a more "authentically Haitian" musical experience than that afforded by *konpa*.[7] In the following passage from their song "Nou Pap Sa Bliye" ("We Won't Forget This"), Boukman Eksperyans recalls their first experience with *mizik vodou*:

> *Nou sonje; nou pap sa bliye*
> *Jou ke nou di nou pral jwe*
> *Mizik peyi-an-nou*
> *Jwe mizik Vodou*
> *Nou tout te santi nou fè younn*
> *Ak tout lòt frè-n kap viv kilti-n*
> *Nou te santi nou Ayisyen*
> *Gen anpil moun ki wont pou nou*
> *Yo tap di se mizik lougawou*
> *Men nou konnen se manti*

> *We remember; we won't forget*
> *The day we said we were going to play*
> *Our country's music*
> *To play the music of voodoo*
> *We felt that we became one*
> *With all our other brothers who live the culture*
> *We truly felt we were Haitian*
> *There are many who were ashamed for us*
> *They were saying that it's werewolf music*
> *But we know that it's a lie*

(Vodou Adjaye, *Mango 16253 9899-2*)

Note that the spiritual closeness they speak of is juxtaposed to a (textually absent but logically necessary) state of separation or alienation from this culture by virtue of their the middle-class backgrounds. For the middle class and the elite, to participate in this form of cultural revival is to, as the song says, "become one" with a heritage and with millions of Haitians they had been taught to revile, shun, or pity.

This roots-oriented activity took place during the Duvalier period, when this type of music was all but entirely marginalized by the dominant middle-class ideology of the time. This ideology was rabidly anti-voodoo, stressing French-style education and marriage into more light-skinned sectors as paths for social advancement.[8] A member of Boukman summed up the negative attitudes toward the band during the dictatorship:

They used to say, 1) "You play music of Satan," 2) "It's not commercial music. You're not going anywhere with it," and 3) "The message is not for relaxing people," they said, "You say too much in the music" (Beaubrun 1989).

These attitudes were encountered in the diaspora as well. In New York, two groups formed in 1985, Sakad and Ayizan, both focusing on producing a commercially palatable blend of roots music with jazz, rock, and Haitian *konpa*. Both of these groups were headed by musicians who had performed with *kilti libète* cultural organizations mentioned above: Nikol Levy of Sakad (Solèy Leve) and Tit Pascal of Ayizan (Atis Indepandan). Nikol Levy explained the attitude of conservative Haitians in the diaspora toward the new sound:

I know some very good Haitian musicians who don't want to play this kind of music because they say "That's voodoo," because of their religious beliefs. They'll play Brazilian music, without realizing that it comes from Brazilian cult music! But they won't play their own music (Levy 1988).

Boukman Eksperyans excoriated these kinds of Francophile and anti-voodoo attitudes among middle-class and elite Haitians in their African identity manifesto "Se Kreyòl Nou Ye" ("We're Creole"), a song that was intended to influence debates over cultural identity:

Ayisyen yo, pito pale Fwanse
Olye yo pale Kreyòl! ...
Nèg Kongo nou ye, fò n pa wont sa
Nati Kongo nou ye, fò n pa pè sa
Nati Kongo, nèg Ginen, nèg Nago
Nèg jan Petwo, nèg Dahome, nèg Kongo yo
Se Kreyòl nou ye
Ala nou pap janm wont sa...
Kote w sòti? Lafrik!
Kote w pwale?
Kilès ki manman w? Lafrik!

Haitians prefer to speak French
It's better if they speak Creole!
We're people of the Kongo, don't be ashamed of it
Children of Kongo, don't fear it
Born in Kongo, Guinee, Nago
People of the Petro way, Dahomey, Kongo
We're Creole
We'll never be ashamed of it...
Where have you come from? Africa!

> *Where are you going?*
> *Who is your mother? Africa!*
>
> (Vodou Adjaye, *Mango 16253 9899-2*)

The semiotics of Boukman Eksperyans performances are complex, signifying traditional affiliations through musical structure, timbre, melodic contour, instrumental resources, choreography, and dress. The rhythm to the song above is a local variant of a well-known rhythm from the Rada rites of voodoo. The melody is hexatonic, typical of voodoo songs, and there is a short call-and-response in the *"Kote w sòti? Lafrik!"* section. Singer Eddie François uses a consciously rough, *abitan* (peasant) -style timbre, especially on the last solo passage. This contrasts sharply with the vocal style of almost all the *mini-djaz* singers as it does with the romantic and patriotic singers, most of whom use considerable vibrato for a warm, rich, romantic sound that could be classified in Haiti as *dous* (sweet). The band employs a traditional battery of three voodoo drums along with an iron *ogan* and a *tcha-tcha* (rattle). They dress in bohemian (by Haitian standards), neo-peasant, and African-identity garb. In Haitian *mini-djaz*, one finds the older style of sci-fi fantasy outfits (*a la* the Commodores), dress suits with ties, or the loose-fitting Parisian silk suits that Zairians call the "sapeur" look, but never the counter-cultural look of Boukman Eksperyans. Bands like Boukman and the others were instrumental in popularizing fashions that stressed downward social mobility. I quote a member of the band:

> There was a change in Haiti, even in the mentality of the people, because you can see now in Haiti how young people are dressing differently: they have *djakout* (traditional peasant bags), more traditional hats...All this is a part of the movement that Boukman helped to launch along with Foula and Sanba-yo. After 1986, the youth began to get tired of the traditional konpa — they wanted a new music to represent what they were feeling. They wanted artists who could express this for them. They were listening to what we were saying (Beaubrun 1989).

The possibilities for new codes in personal appearance didn't negate the disdain in which many of the "counter-culture" were held by more conservative Haitians who saw them as drug addicts or communists. Indeed, after the Army coup of September 1991, counter-cultural garb and Rasta-like hair exposed young Haitians to renewed repression.

Nikol Levy described the thorough-going cultural changes taking place in the period of *dechoukaj*, the "uprooting" of the Duvalier dictatorship:

> After Duvalier, they feel they can do something. At all levels you can see things happening... in music, too. The groups now, even the lyrics are different. Not only that, but the lyrics talk about reality, they're not talking about nonsense. We're going to have a popular music when the people — let's say the people from the countryside — can get access to the media, when the peasants can express themselves, when they can go on the stage, go on the radio and play their music (Levy 1988).

I have said that *mizik rasin* works to create a historical counternarrative; this narrative creates a history not of dates and Haitian presidents but of slavery and oppression and of a struggle for cultural survival. The songs of *mizik rasin* work to make slavery a contemporary concern, relating it to neo-colonial patterns, international relations, and current Haitian politics. The group Boukman Eksperyans is named after Boukman, a Jamaican-born leader of the Haitian slave rebellion at the end of the eighteenth century. A member of Boukman Eksperyans discussed the resonance that the concept of slavery has in contemporary Haiti:

> Mental slavery is much more serious than the physical. That's why we always say that Dessalines [a leader of the Haitian revolution] took away the physical slavery, but the slavery inside has not yet left us. We are slaves still (Beaubrun 1989).

Rara Machine, a New York Haitian roots band, entitled their first major label release *Break the Chains*. In doing so, they echoed a popular Boukman Eksperyans song (based on a *rara* rhythm) called "Pran Chenn, Wet Chenn" ("Get Angry, Remove the Chains") that had won a contest (the American Airlines Konkou Mizik) for best Haitian song of 1989:

> *Pran chenn, wet chenn*
> *Wa kase chenn-nan ki fè n paka ini nou*
> *Pou n ka sekle lakou-n*
> *Woy woy woy woy woy, o!*
> *Depi Lafrik nap soufri*

Nan bo isit se pi rèd
Sa fè rèd, o wayo

Get angry, remove the chains
Break the chains that keep us from uniting
So that we can weed out our homes
Woy woy woy woy woy oh!
Ever since Africa, we've been suffering
It's so much harder here
It's really difficult, oh wayo

(3èm Konkou Mizik MM 1001)

With the end of the dictatorship, *mizik rasin* bands began to play in nightclubs in the suburb of Petionville, in hotels, and in downtown theaters. The owner of one hotel frequented by foreigners started his own house voodoo-roots rock band (Ram). *Mizik rasin* advanced in popularity through a series of events that provided national exposure. Boukman Eksperyans won Carnival 1990 with a political rara called "Kèm pa sote" ("My heart doesn't leap"), a song that had a significant impact on the popular political discourse and struggle that year (the year in which United Nations- and Organization of American States-sanctioned elections were held). The major campaign songs of 1991 were almost uniformly based on *rara*, and the majority of popular carnival songs in 1991 were *rara* or contained *rara* sections. This activity points to the widespread acceptance and social impact of the genre, although local (Haitian) commercial production hasn't achieved the dimensions of that of the well-established *konpa* bands, in part because the pop *rara* is so closely linked in Haiti to carnival season.

Interest among foreigners in *mizik rasin* has impacted the demand and popularity of the genre, an effect that Mark Slobin has dubbed "validation through visibility" (Slobin 1992, 11). Foula has played at festivals in Louisiana and in Mexico; Sanba-yo has a single on the compilation *Konbit: Burning Rhythms of Haiti* (A&M CD 5281), and both made appearances in Jonathan Demme's film, *Haiti: Dreams of Democracy*. The first albums ever to be produced of individual Haitian groups by mainstream American labels featured Boukman Eksperyans (Mango Records) and Rara Machine (Shanachie Records) respectively. As of January 1993, four out of five of the Haitian albums that have been released by American labels are from this tendency in Haitian music.

Sensationalist and primitivist fantasies about Haiti have conditioned the reception of this music outside of the Haitian audience, giving it a selective advantage over less "authentic" expressions such as konpa and nouvel jenerasyon among cross-over audiences. For example, the record label press release for Rara Machine contains a virtual compendium of images of bodies out of control (overpower, ecstasy, feverish, energy, trance, irresistible, voodoo magic), claiming that band members

> ...almost overpower the audience with their onstage energy, their ecstasy elevating to a feverish pitch as they seem to go into a trance. Listeners may not be able to stop dancing to the irresistible music of Rara Machine, but it won't be because of voodoo magic! (*Break the Chain: Kase Chenn*, Shanachie Records 64038)

More restrained and supposedly enlightened support for the *mizik rasin* movement from abroad also appears to draw on neo-colonial attitudes concerning the allowable limits for expression in what used to be called the Third World, stressing the local and essential in Third World musics. *Konpa* and *nouvel jenerasyon* performers are regularly rejected by American festivals and record companies for not sounding "Haitian enough." My point here is that Haitian identities are shaped and negotiated among both internal and external actors. In commercial music, the inordinate economic power and draw of foreign markets (and the resulting intercession of foreign mediators) works to shape products to conform to foreign expectations.[9] Haitian identities are being formed partly in the representation of Haiti and things Haitian to an external world (primarily to a Euro-American audience), in the misrepresentations that arise between these cultures (e.g., exoticism, primitivism, demonization, and ethnic stereotyping), and in the projection of these representations and misrepresentations back onto Haiti. There is as yet little research on this subject, although Michael Dash's book, *Haiti and the United States: National Stereotypes and the Literary Imagination* (1988) has opened the way. Lois Wilcken's article on the tourist drum of Haiti (1988) and Alan Goldberg's dissertation on tourism and commercial folklore (1981) all contribute to an increasingly sophisticated sociology of insiders and outsiders in Haitian expressive culture.

It is not only *mizik rasin* groups that have experimented with *mizik vodou* and *rara*. As this movement has gained ground, *konpa* bands and *nouvel jenerasyo*n artists have incorporated traditional materials into selected compositions. The New York-based Haitian arranger Dernst Emile was responsible for a number of these experiments. Emile, convinced that *rara* rhythms could be used to produce a danceable disco-like Haitian music, arranged pieces for Mystik Band, System Band, Ti-Manno, and Skah Shah, among others. Producer Fred Paul (Mini Records) also wrote a neo-*rara* called "Raraman" for his studio band Mini All Stars, later included on the cross-over compilation *Konbit: Burning Rhythms of Haiti* (A&M 16235 9899-2). In this song, *rara* becomes a metaphor for African cultural survival despite the hardships imposed by the system of slavery:

> *Jouk nan kè Lafrik bato yo vin chaje*
> *Sou do Karayib la èsklav yo debake*
> *Yo pat gen anyen pou yo te pote*
> *Sèlman ti mizik yo pou yo te chante*
> *Woy, yo se raraman*

> *From the heart of Africa, the boats came full*
> *Slaves disembarked on the back of the Caribbean*
> *They couldn't carry anything with them*
> *Only songs for them to sing*
> *Oh, they're raramen*

> (*Raraman Mini Records MRS 1191*)

The most successful *mini-djaz* in the diaspora, Tabou Combo, recorded a *rara* in response to the popularity of Boukman Eksperyans and other groups, reprising the Jazz des Jeunes song "Kote Moun Yo?," this time with synthesizer patches, electric guitars, and an electric bass representing the sound of rara *vaksin*s. Emeline Michel, probably the best-known *nouvel jenerasyon* performer, also crossed over into *mizik rasin* with a *rara*-like song composed by Beethova Obas that was itself *about rara* bands. The song dealt with the role of *rara* festivities as respite from the misery and hunger of peasant existence.

> *De vaksin, de tanbou, Ayisyen anraje...*
> *Nanpwen tan pou chodyè monte*
> *Vant timoun yo ap kòde*
> *Denmen lè bann ap pase*
> *Na bliye vant kòde*

> *Two vaksin, two tanbou, Haitians turned on*
> *There's no time for the pot to heat up*
> *The children's stomachs are knotted*

> *Tomorrow when the rara band is passing*
> *We'll forget the knotted stomachs*
>
> *(Douvanjou Ka Leve SHAP 1002)*

The commercial video that accompanied this release attempted to occupy semiotic territory claimed by *mizik rasin*, and yet interesting contradictions emerged from the texture of the presentation. For instance, Michel's earrings, lipstick, and stylish hair contrast with the message conveyed by the torn, lumpen-proletariat garment. In the video, well-trained, choreographed, cosmopolitan, modern dancers are used to represent peasant *vodouwizan*.

The Musical Dynamics of Mizik Rasin

For musicians in all of these groups, developing a neo-traditional commercial sound entailed a difficult "apprenticeship" in traditional musics, exploring tradition-specific compositional principles. Tit Pascal spoke of his own early experiments in the genre:

> I practice the *rara* and try to get the bamboo sound. The problem has been harmonizing to *rara*, because *rara* is untempered. The peasants make their own instruments, so what you have is a pentatonic scale with the quarter tone influence. That's why when the Haitians try to harmonize the *rara*, they change its color [rather than] subduing themselves to the quarter tone. This is why I have been looking at *rara* the way we say *an kan* [on edge]; you look at it sideways and just let it go by. Every time you try to get involved, you get your fingers cut, and say, 'No, that's the wrong chord; it doesn't fit, doesn't blend.' The first song I wrote with the guitar in hand ended up being a kind of cliche of my own work that didn't reflect any *raborday* or *rara*. I realized I had to lay the instrument down because your fingers go in cliches. I had to close my eyes and think of the voodoo ceremonies and the *rara* bands that I'd seen and write the melody. I have never thought that I'm going to modernize *rara*. It is far more modern than anything modern we have. It is avant-garde. They used to think that the peasant doesn't know anything, but they carry with them thousands of years of African culture. So I said to myself, 'This is no ignorance, this is complex stuff. This is

heavy stuff going down. Like when I heard Coltrane' (Pascal 1988).

Each musician has a different approach to the incorporation of traditional symbolic elements in their music. Nikol Levy spoke of coming to grips with Haitian traditional music and his own distillation of important acoustic symbols of the tradition, especially the prominence of dialogue:

> There are specificities that you'll find only in voodoo music. The melodies we compose... we're trying to get them as close as possible to popular [traditional] music. Even in the form — the call-and-response — there's something very African, very voodoo ... a dialogue between the lead vocalist and the chorus. Even between the instruments, between the guitar, keyboards, and the bass. We're trying to do that, trying to dialogue all the time... polyrhythm, different lines at the same time (Levy 1988).

In neo-traditional musics, commercial performers have attempted to evoke through incorporation something of the music sound and ethos of the traditional models. Textual evocations are common in the songs I have been discussing so far, and they include the use of traditional proverbs ("Dodinen"), quotations from voodoo songs ("Ke M Pa Sote"), or entire *rara* texts ("Kote Moun Yo?"). Timbral evocations include use of traditional instruments such as the *rara vaksin*s ("Kote Moun Yo?") or voodoo drums (Boukman Eksperyans, Foula et al.) or the imitation of such sounds on guitar ("Dodinen"), synthesizers ("Plezi Mizè"), or other instruments. Evocation through traditional-styled melodic contours and rhythmic patterns is widespread and was the basis of the Jazz des Jeunes big band sound. Musical structure itself, especially in the use of responsorial structures, can also signify and evoke in this way.[10]

Finally, there is also a range of performative semiotic strategies for signifying a musical tradition. In a 1988 concert at New York's Ritz Theatre, Tabou Combo significantly changed their choreographic, kinesic, and interpersonal dynamics immediately upon beginning their *rara* piece. The *rara*, apparently, constituted permission to "act up" and to break out of a mold: The front group of band members ran back and forth on the front of the stage, moved their hips more (the *rara gwiyo*), and threw their arms in the air, dancing with other members of the band; in other words, incorporating aspects of traditional rara processional behavior and ambience into the staged presentation.

As I have mentioned, many early experiments with neo-traditional popular musics used framing as the primary tool for integration of traditional and contemporary materials. The discrepancies between styles were avoided by enclosing them within discrete sections (i.e., an introduction, break, and coda in a roots style). Later, as musicians mastered compositional principles of *mizik vodou* and *rara*, entire compositions in these styles emerged with more rigorous methods of integrating discrepant musical materials. One could label this approach "compositional-integration." An example of a compositionally integrated piece over which is dubbed a discordant jazz solo occurs with the recording of Sanba-Yo's "Vaksine" on *Konbit: Burning Rhythms of Haiti* (A&M 16253 9899-2).[11] When these kinds of neo-traditional compositions become springboards for improvisation *within* the style (i.e., with a culture-specific training or deep knowledge of local principles such that improvisation respects the enabling and conditioning parameters of the style), one can speak of an improvisationally integrated form. This is especially true of the more recent work of the group Foula, a group that has gone further than any other in exploring the potential affinities of African-American jazz and Haitian traditional music.

Nouvel Jenerasyon

Although many *mizik rasin* musicians come from the middle class, they see their music as supporting the aspirations of Haiti's lower class, the *pitit pèp-la* (literally, small people). Some of them have engaged in a low-key polemic with nouvel jenerasyon performers whose music leans more firmly in the direction of Euro-pop. Chico Boyer, bassist for the groups Foula and Rara Machine, distinguished their music from that of the *nouvel jenerasyon* artists, even when the latter, too, incorporate traditional materials:

> The *nouvel generasyon* represents a bourgeois tendency. The bourgeois class in Haiti was working with the political class in Haiti and they took a conscientious stand only after the 7th of February 1986 [the end of the dictatorship] when all the bourgeoisie wanted to become patriots too. Everybody was talking about democracy. It's an opportunistic music. Now, they're trying to play *rara* too (Boyer 1990).

The *nouvel jenerasyon* movement was profiled by Haitian writer Ralph Boncy (1987), who considered it together with the neo-traditional groups. Although there is still notable overlap in the two tendencies, they have consolidated as separate movements in the last few years. *Nouvel jenerasyon* performers can be distinguished best by a constellation of concerns that motivate their work: the poetic quality of their lyrics, technological sophistication, and cosmopolitan pop influences. The groups tend to be smaller (three to five members) and heavily dependent upon sequenced synthesizers and drum machines. In addition, the length of compositions is conditioned by expectations of radio play rather than by the dictates of the dance hall, carnival, ideological content, or extended improvisational sections.

Nouvel jenerasyon musicians cite early influences such as bandleader Michel Desgrottes and the early *mini-djaz* Ibo Combo, a group that appealed more to the upper class than other *mini-djaz* at the time. They also cite a later incarnation of Ibo Combo called Caribbean Sextet. In their name, the Sextet highlighted their affinity for jazz; their music, too, reflected a stronger jazz training with more complex chord progressions and exploratory solos. Their appearance in Haiti in 1977 was one of the first indications of movement away from the dominance of *mini-djaz konpa*, but their music lacked a commercial orientation:

> The audience that responds to the Caribbean Sextet style is perhaps better educated. It's certainly an audience that listens to imported music a bit more than local music. This audience sees in Caribbean Sextet a music that's better constructed, that's capable of being danced or listened to. We listen a lot to jazz and Brazilian music, but we don't play imported music. Moreover, we don't neglect our roots, because certain of our songs are influenced by our folklore, but with a more studied approach to harmony (Lavironn Dede, Delta DR 2014, translated from French).

Composer and music critic Gérard Merceron attempted to coin a new popular music for Haiti with his album *L'Energie mystérieuse*, the outgrowth of a sound track he wrote for the filmmaker Bob Lemoine (Boncy et al 1987, 169). He envisioned a *"nouvelle musique populaire haïtienne qui adapterait la langue créole aux exigences de la modernité"* ("a new popular Haitian music which would adapt the Creole language to the needs of modernity"). The intergenerational core group, called

Haiti 2000, was composed of Merceron, Herby Widmaier, and novelist/dramaturge Frank Etienne, along with vocalists Boulo Valcourt and Lionel Benjamin. They set out to produce a more refined and complex popular music. A follow-up album entitled *Têt san kò* (Head without a body, GM 003) was released in 1981 with four members of Caribbean Sextet. Merceron's chord progressions, frequent modulations, and use of instruments such as the cello and flute and even a chamber ensemble on one cut assured limited circulation for the albums. Their importance is better measured by their influence on the growing dialogue about musical directions, signaled by Merceron's use of the subtitle: "La nouvelle musique haïtienne" (The New Haitian Music).

The group Zeklè (Lightning) was formed in 1982 and recorded their first album the next year (*Joel + Zeklè: Cé ou minm'!* ZR 701). Zeklè and their jazz-combo alter-ego Lakansyèl (Rainbow) were projects of the Widmaier brothers[12] and a group of musicians that included keyboard player Raoul Denis, Jr., lyricist Ralph Boncy, bassist Joe Charles, and Caribbean Sextet guitarist Claude Marcelin. In performance, the band was often supplemented by percussion and wind players from Caribbean Sextet. Zeklè wanted to bridge the gap between dance and concert engagements:

> We opened a new world as far as concerts for bands were concerned — because before, the only people who did concerts were Ansy Derose [a romantic singer] and people like that. For a dance band to do that had never been possible. We had a light show and everything. A new era was starting (Widmaier 1988).

Zeklè blended *konpa* with funk and American jazz-rock (in the tradition of Weather Report, to whom they were often compared in the Haitian and French press). They used the bass as a more prominent instrument, freed from the two-beat metronomic role of the bass in *konpa*, and incorporating a percussive funk-like technique with pops and slaps. They also adopted a dual synthesizer sound, resembling that of the French West Indian group Kassav'. The reference to Kassav' is important here; The success of Kassav', whose dynamic new music (*zouk*) was heavily reliant on Haitian konpa, had disrupted the market for Haitian music in the French Antilles and had startled Haitian musicians. As I have argued elsewhere (Averill 1993), the *zouk* shock was a crystalizing force for changes in Haitian music.

Zeklè found an eager reception in France, but in Haiti, they were unable to go beyond a narrow audience bounded by class and geography. Their interest in a concert music was problematic due to the lack of halls in Haiti other than the Rex Théâtre and because of the limited audience for concert music. As Mushi Widnaier explained:

> We started doing the *bals* [dances] because we couldn't beat the system. After three or four concerts in Rex Théâtre, we had already taken five thousand people. That's the minority who can afford to buy LPs. You can't go anywhere in Haiti beyond the five thousand. If you sell six thousand records in Haiti, that's big. And the extra thousand is from people who like the band and buy the LP to give it as a gift. With the number of phonographs that exist still in the country, you can't go far (Widmaier 1988).

An article after a New York tour in 1984 criticized the restricted nature of their appeal, as follows:

> An appreciable dose of snobbery explains in part the craze for Zeklè among the petite bourgeoisie of Port-au-Prince, on account of the social composition of the members of the group and of the more sophisticated character of their music. Lots of city kids recognize themselves in this cosmopolitan, fast-changing music, which reflects the so-cial malaise and the uncertainty of the youth ("Zeklè: Annonce-t-il l'Orage?" *Haïti-Observateur*, 13-20 October 1984, translated from French).

By the words "social composition," the author raises the specter of the disproportionately light-skinned or upper-class composition of the group. After 1986, the efforts of the group were increasingly directed toward promoting new artists and personal projects of various sorts, including the production collective called SHAP (Haitian Society for Art and Production).

A 1988 release by a trio from Miami called Skandal had as its title track a piece called "Nouvelle Génération" (*Nouvelle Génération*, Melodie Makers SMLP001), which quickly became a new "handle" for the *"nouvelle musique haïtienne."*

> *Pou demen, gen lajwa, fò nou gen lespwa*
> *Koripsyon a mizè, nou bouke o*
> *Si demen nou vle rive, fò n deside*

Son nouvel jenerasyon kap pense o
Chorus: Si nou vle chante, ede m chante o
Si nou vle danse, leve danse o, konsa konsa
Si nou vle chanje, na chanje o
Si nou vle sonje, annou sonje o, konsa konsa

For tomorrow, there is joy, we have to hope
We'll stop the corruption and poverty
If we want tomorrow to come, we must decide
It's a new generation that is thinking!

[Chorus:]
If you want to sing, help me sing
If you want to dance, get up to dance, like this!
If you want to change, we'll change
If you want to remember, remember like this!

(Nouvelle Génération *SMLP001*)

The optimistic lyrics embrace social change, but the vision encoded in musical sound is cosmopolitan, light-hearted, and technocratic. The group had a string of hits on Haitian radio and their soft vocals and synthesizer sound were imitated by later groups (e.g., Papash, Zin, Sakaj).

Backed up by musicians associated with Zeklè and Caribbean Sextet, Emeline Michel has achieved some notable successes in France and Japan. As with many *nouvel jenerasyon* musicians, Michel refuses to restrict herself stylistically to Haitian indigenous formulas, and yet uses her nationality as a mark of *difference* in foreign markets. In "Flanm," she explored female sensuality with a kind of frankness that would have been thought overly forward for women in previous periods and that reflects a focus on deeply personal experience absent from most *mizik rasin* compositions:

Mwen jwenn yon zanmi
Dous tankou mango mi...
Lanwit nou pou n jemi
Nou pa sa dòmi
Nou mèt joure
Nou mèt kraze brize
Lè kòk ap chante
Na fè n ki kare ap danse
Lanmou se flanm ki klere devan m
Lanmou se kan m, se sa m vle defann
Lanmou se zanm ki fè m santi fanm
Lanmou se san m

I've found a friend
Sweet like a ripe mango
At night, we're like night owls
We don't sleep
We start swearing
We start breaking and smashing things
When the rooster crows
We'll square off dancing
Love is a flame that clears before me
Love is my edge, it's what I want to defend
Love is a weapon that makes me feel
like a woman, Love is my blood

(Flanm, *Cobalt JD 160239*)

Conclusion

During the revolutionary period that accompanied *dechoukaj*, pro-democracy advocates commonly associated *konpa* with the period of the dictatorship and many suggested that it should be *dechouke* (uprooted) as well. I have outlined the two musical movements that coalesced in the post-Duvalier period to take its place — *nouvel jenerasyon* and *mizik rasin* — and I conclude that the popularity and visibility of both movements can be directly linked to the demise of the dictatorship. In this period in Haiti's history, commercial musicians have served as cultural innovators with considerable influence over processes of change in ideology and identity. Through performances and recordings, these musicians have created the collective affective states that have helped to define and galvanize subcultures (in the stricter sense promoted by the "Birmingham School" of cultural studies, in which there exist homologies of style, ideology, and social organization; see Hebdige 1979) and, demographically more important, extensive audiences connected by affinity and outlook.

These developments in music are not isolated from changes in the rest of society. The effort to create a roots music culture in Haiti after the fall of the dictatorship is a musical corollary to populist political movements[13] and represents a musical discourse that has the potential to cross class and geographical lines in Haiti, that is, to bridge the vast chasm between *moun lavil* (city people) and *moun andeyo* (country people). The *nouvel jenerasyon* is more closely linked to liberal, technocratic political initiatives. Its exponents envision a Haiti less constrained by the past and by Haiti's history of suffering and victimization. In the turbulent post-Duvalier period, *mizik rasin*, with its appeal rooted in Afro-centric nationalism, has become the most talked-about musical phenomenon in Haitian music. This would seem to reinforce Tomlinson's observation that "in societies and at times in which there is uncertainty, dissent, or active struggle over national or regional identity, or where the nation is under external threat, the 'distant imaginings' of national or regional identity may become foregrounded in consciousness" (Tomlinson 1991, 88).

In fact, the two musical movements that I profiled have a considerable amount in common. The musical setting of *mizik rasin* is in most cases thoroughly dependent on modern technology and often owes a debt to international pop aesthetics. Similarly, *nouvel jenerasyon* music, while internationalist in its outlook, remains iden- tifiably Haitian, demonstrating significant rhythmic continuities with *konpa* and other forms. Both musical formations are based primarily in the urban middle and upper middle class, and both have exponents within insular Haiti and in the diaspora. Significantly, both movements accept the basic *imported* features (or ground rules) of commodified, commercial pop music as a given, such that they are restricted to manipulating flexible expressive codes within a rigid, globally homog- enized framework.

It is primarily in their affiliation with different socio-political outlooks and semiotic strategies that the musical movements diverge. Such choices are encoded in musical sound, style, texts, performance practice, dress, and behavior, and such strategies have wielded influence in recent years in the midst of Haiti's national political trauma.

Notes

Some of this material has appeared previously in my column in *The Beat* magazine, in a paper delivered at the 1990 International Association for the Study of Popular Music (U.S.) Annual Meeting in New Orleans, and, of course, in a paper for the 1992 conference "Music and Black Ethnicity in Latin America and the Caribbean," hosted by the University of Miami North-South Center. For Creole spelling, I use the IPN (Institut Pédagogique National) Creole orthography except when directly quoting from written texts that use other systems.

I would like to thank Dr. Gerard Béhague for his encouragement and for his persistence in organizing this volume and the conference that inspired it; Giovanna Averill, who proofread this article; Dr. Christopher A. Waterman, who helped to guide some of the early research that went into this study, and the many wonderful Haitian musicians and friends who have aided my work from the beginning and who continue to provide me with fresh challenges, feedback, support, and criticism.

The title of the paper is also the title of a song by the Haitian roots music group Boukman Eksperyans that addresses the conflict over Haitian identity.

1.   *Konpa*, originally *konpa-direk*, has been Haiti's most popular commercial dance music from the mid-1950s until the contemporary era. See Averill (1993) for a description of its origins and stylistic characteristics.

2.   The Haitian national motto is "L'Union Fait La Force" (In Unity There Is Strength). The 1990 presidential campaign of populist priest Jean-Bertrand Aristide employed a similar gesture in the slogan *"Yon sel nou feb, ansanm nou se lavalas"* (Alone we're weak, together we're strong, united we're a deluge).

3.   In practice, these three philosophies combined freely in Haiti of the 1940s and afterward. *Indigènisme* was a movement advocating ethnographic study of peasant life with the goal of reshaping expressive culture to reflect an African cultural inheritance. *Noirisme*, which was ascendent in post-World War II Haiti, was a political philosophy of black majority rule. *Négritude*, as articulated by Martiniquan author Aime Cesaire, was a complex pan-Africanist ideology of black identity and liberation. All three had racially essentialist underpinnings, seeking an "essence" of black identity.

4.   These studies deal with expressive culture in urban Haiti and in the diaspora. The question of identity, however, has seldom been examined in research on traditional, peasant, and liturgical musics (e.g., Courlander 1962, Dauphin 1986, and Fleurant 1987), which have been descriptive in nature or have engaged other sets of theoretical concerns. The attention paid by Herskovits (1937) and Bourguignon (1969) to questions of snycretism and

"socialized ambivalence," both intimately tied to identity, can perhaps be considered an exception to this pattern.

5. Voodoo refers to a widespread syncretic religion in Haiti that combines African pantheistic and animistic beliefs (including spirit possession) with Catholicism. The best known music of voodoo uses a three-drum battery with iron bell and rattle to accompany liturgical responsorial songs. This religion is practiced in formal and informal (household) settings, primarily by Haiti's peasants and urban proletariat. *Rara* is a peasant processional ritual most commonly encountered in the season during Lent and Holy Week before Easter. Although often steeped in voodoo beliefs and practices, *rara* processionals are considered more secular than *peristil*-based voodoo ceremonies, parading primarily through public roadways. The music is characterized by a hocketed accompaniment of single-note trumpets made from bamboo (*banbou* or *vaksin*), tin trumpets called "piston" or "kone," and various percussion instruments that accompany responsorial songs dealing with topical, political, derisive, or obscene subjects. Both *rara* and voodoo represent a peasant culture that is, historically and by nature, oppositional in relation to elite culture and foreign domination. They thus often serve as sources of potent political symbols (Averill 1991).

6. Haiti is a diglossic country. The elite and educated middle class speak French in more formal and official contexts and use creole widely for informal discourse. Haitian peasants and the urban proletariat are, in general, monolingual creole speakers.

7. The antecedent of Boukman Eksperyans, a group called "Moun Ife" (roughly "people of the abode of voodoo deities") had transformed itself from a loose-knit interest group into a performing ensemble in the mid-1980s, recruiting voodoo drummers from Port-au-Paix and expanding the group's electric instrumentation. Foula (their name comes from a Ki-Kongo word meaning "breath of life") and Sanba-yo ("rural song leaders") underwent similar trajectories, starting out together as a single ensemble in 1978, learning and practicing traditional music. They added guitar and bass in 1981 and in 1982 formed the group SA. Foula came about from a split in this group in 1985. Then after a disagreement over musical direction, Sanba-yo split off from Foula to create a more traditionalist counterpart to Foula's more avant-garde voodoo-jazz.

8. This ideology coexisted in very complex ways with Duvalier's state ideology of *noirisme*. While *noirisme* buttressed the social advancements made by blacks in civil service and professional careers, and while it helped to rally peasant and lower-class support for the Duvalier government (which was seen as an anti-elite force), the emergent black middle class adopted mulatto hegemonic ideals to a great extent and dissociated itself from the lower classes as severely as had the mulatto elite.

9. I should note my own involvement in these processes. I participated as associate producer on the *Konbit: Burning Rhythms of Haiti* (A&M CD

5281), an album mentioned above, and was responsible for much of the song translations and liner notes. I also translated lyrics and wrote liner notes for the Boukman Eksperyans album *Vodou Adjae* (Mango 16253 9899-2). I wrote liner notes and translations for the Smithsonian Folkways re-release of Verna Gillis's *Caribbean Revels: Rara in Haiti and Gaga in the Dominican Republic.* In my semi-monthly Haitian music column in the magazine *The Beat*, I gave prominent coverage to *mizik rasin.* Thus, my scholarship on Haitian music coexists — sometimes uncomfortably — with these rather "engaged" journalistic and promotional activities.

10. This particular constellation of evocational modes was suggested by Wesleyan graduate student Rob Lancefield, as was a nomenclature for modes of integration ("framing, contextually integrated, improvisationally integrated") that I use below, albeit in modified form.

11. This solo was performed by Cyrus Neville of the Neville Brothers in a studio with only a recording of the composition to play over. He was otherwise unfamiliar with *rara* tonality and structure.

12. The Widmaier brothers (there are three involved in music and another who runs the family radio station) come from a family of German Swiss origin with three generations of experience in Haitian radio, recording, and music production. Their grandfather, Ricardo, began two radio stations and produced the first audio recording made in Haiti. Their father, Herby, was an arranger, singer, producer, and recording engineer who was responsible for recording many of the bands in the 1950s and early 1960s. The family station, Radio Metropole, is considered to be among the most musically experimental, with a mix of local and international selections. Zeklè, and indeed many of those in the *nouvel jenerasyon*, were stigmatized by their competitors because of this ready access to the media and industry.

13. These movements are exemplified by the Ti-Legliz or small church; the radicalized peasant movement as represented by groups such as MPP, the Mouvman Peyizan Papaye; Zantray, a movement to promote voodoo; and the Lavalas movement of Reverend Jean-Bertrand Aristide.

References

Abbott, Elizabeth. 1988. *Haiti: the Duvaliers and Their Legacy.* New York: McGraw-Hill.

Anderson, Benedict. 1991. *Imagined Communities.* London: Verso.

Atis Endepandan. 1975. *Ki Sa Pou-N Fe?* Recording and liner notes. Paredon P-1027:4-5.

Averill, Gage. 1989a. "Haitian Dance Band Music: The Political Economy of Exuberance." Ph.D. dissertation, Department of Music, University of Washington.

Averill, Gage. 1989b."Haitian dance bands, 1915-1970: Class, Race, and Authenticity." *Latin American Music Review* 10(2), 203-235.

Averill, Gage. 1991. Notes to *Rara in Haiti, Gaga in the Dominican Republic.* Folkways/Smithsonian (SF 40402).

Averill, Gage. 1993. "Toujou Sou Konpa: Issues of Change and Interchange in Haitian Popular Music." In *Zouk: World Music In the West Indies,* by Jocelyne Guilbault and Gage Averill. Chicago: University of Chicago Press.

Beaubrun, Theodore "Lolo," Jr. 1990. Interview with author.

Boncy, Ralph, et al. 1987. "Nouvelle Musique Haïtienne: De Nemours... à Beethova." *Conjonction, Revue Franco-Haïtienne* 176: 160-176.

Boukman Eksperyans. *Voudou Adjaye.* Mango Records 16253 9899-2.

Bourguignon, Erika. 1969. "Haiti et l'Ambivalence Socialisée: Une Reconsideration." *Journal de la Societé des Americanistes* 58: 173-205.

Boyer, Yves "Chico." 1990. Interview with author.

Buchanan, Susan. 1980. "Scattered Seeds: The Meaning of the Migration for Haitian in New York City." Ph.D. dissertation., New York University.

Courlander, Harold. 1962. *The Drum and the Hoe: Life and Lore of the Haitian People.* Berkeley: University of California Press.

Dash, J. Michael. 1981. *Literature and Ideology in Haiti, 1915-1961.* Totowa, N.J.: Barnes and Noble.

Dash, J. Michael. 1988. *Haiti and the United States: National Stereotypes and the Literary Imagination*. New York: St. Martin's Press.

Dauphin, Claude. 1986. *Musique du Vaudou: Fonctions, Structures, et Styles*. Québec: Editions Naaman de Sherbrooke.

Desgranges, Farah Juste, and Jean-Claude Desgranges. 1989. Interview with author.

Fleurant, Gerdes. 1987. "The Ethnomusicology of Yanvalou: A Study of the *Rada* Rite of Haiti." Ph.D. dissertation, Department of Music, Tufts University.

Geertz, Clifford. 1973. *The Interpretation of Cultures*. New York: Basic Books.

Giddens, Anthony. 1985. *The Nation-state and Violence: Volume Two of a Contemporary Critique of Historical Materialism*. Berkeley and Los Angeles: University of California Press.

Goldberg, Alan Bruce. 1981. "Commercial Folklore and Voodoo in Haiti: International Tourism and the Sale of Culture." Ph.D. dissertation, Department of Folklore, Indiana University.

Haïti-Observateur. 1984. "Zeklè: Annonce-t-il l'Orage?" 13-20 October.

Hebdige, Dick. 1979. *Subculture: The Meaning of Style*. London and New York: Methuen.

Herskovits, Melville J. 1937. *Life in a Haitian Valley*. New York and London: Alfred A. Knopf.

Hobsbawm, Eric, and Terence Ranger. 1983. *The Invention of Tradition*. Cambridge: Cambridge University Press.

Jazz des Jeunes. Ibo Records ILP 113.

Konbit: Burning Rhythms of Haiti. A&M Records CD 5281.

Labelle, Micheline. 1978. *Idéologie de Couleur et Classes Sociales en Haïti*. Montréal: Université de Montréal.

Largey, Michael. 1991. "Musical Ethnography in Haiti: A Study of Elite Hegemony and Musical Composition." Ph.D. dissertation, Department of Folklore, Indiana University.

Levy, Nikol. 1988. Interview with author.

Lowenthal, David. 1985. *The Past Is A Foreign Country*. Cambridge: Cambridge University Press.

Merceron, Gérard, and Haiti 2000. *L'Energie Mystérieuse*.

Merceron, Gérard, and Haiti 2000. *Tèt san kò*. GM 003.

Michel, Emeline. *Douvanjou Ka Leve*. SHAP Records 1002.

Mini All Stars. *Raraman*. Mini Records MRS 1191.

Pascal, Alix "Tit." 1988. Interview with author.

Policard, Reginald. 1985. Liner notes to Caribbean Sextet's *Lavironn Dede* (Delta DR 2014).

Rara Machine. 1991. *Break the Chain: Kase Chenn*. Recording and liner notes. Shanachie Records 64038.

Skandal. *Nouvelle Génération*. Melodie Makers SMLP 0010.

Slobin, Mark. 1992. "Micromusics of the West: A Comparative Approach," *Ethnomusicology* 36(1): 1-87.

Tomlinson, John. 1991. *Cultural Imperialism*. Baltimore: Johns Hopkins University Press.

3èm Konkou Mizik. Melodie Makers MM 1001.

Trouillot, Michel-Rolph. 1990. *Haiti, State Against Nation: The Origins and Legacy of Duvalierism*. New York: Monthly Review Press.

Widmaier, Mushi. 1988. Interview with author.

Wilcken, Lois. 1988. "Hosts, Guests, and Sacred Souvenirs: The Tourist Drum As a Measure of Intergroup Understanding in Haiti." In *Come Mek Me Hol' Yu' Han': The Impact of Tourism on Traditional Music*, 45-56. Kingston: Jamaica Memory Bank.

Wilcken, Lois. 1991. "Music Folklore Among Haitians in New York: Staged Representations and the Negotiation of Identity." Ph.D. dissertation, Department of Music, Columbia University.

Zeklè. *Joel + Zeklè: Cé ou minm'!* Zeklè Records ZR 701.

Black Music of All Colors: The Construction of Black Ethnicity in Ritual and Popular Genres of Afro-Brazilian Music

José Jorge de Carvalho

The aim of this essay is to present an overview of Afro-Brazilian identities, emphasizing their correlations with the main Afro-derived musical styles practiced today in the country. Given the general scope of the work, this chapter will sum up this complex mass of data in a few historical models, running through four centuries of social and cultural experience. The aim is to establish a contrast between the traditional models of identity of the Brazilian black population and their music with recent attempts by various black movements, expressed by popular commercial musicians, to formulate protests against their historical condition of poverty and injustice and to forge a new image of Afro-Brazilians that is more explicit, in both political and ideological terms. To deal with such a vast ethnographic issue, the chapter analyzes how these competing models of identity are shaped by the different song genres and singing styles used by Afro-Brazilians. In this connection, this study also explores theoretically the more abstract problems of understanding the efficacy of songs; in other words, how in mythopoetics, meaning and content are revealed in aesthetic structures which are able so powerfully to mingle verbal with non-verbal modes of communication. Finally, the present discussion of Afro-Brazilian music is a case study to show the importance of these theoretical issues to a new assessment of the established views of the role of music in the construction of identity and ethnic differences.

Afro-Brazilian Cults

Undoubtedly, the main matrix of Afro-Brazilian identity is still the traditional cults of African origin, such as the *candomblé* of Bahia, the *shango* of Recife, the *tambor de mina* of São Luís, and the *batuque* of Porto Alegre. They concentrate some of the most popular symbols shared or at least known by most Brazilians: the *orishas* or *santos* — the African gods that take possession of cult members — and the drum ensembles, among which the better known are the *atabaques* of Bahia. From the point of view of ethnic identity, the *candomblé* does not establish social, racial, or color distinctions: everyone is a potential member, since all human beings have *orishas*; so, blacks or non-blacks, "preto" or "negro," Brazilian or non-Brazilian, are oppositions that do not make sense in the world of the *orishas*; they are just African, on the mythological level; and on the level of individual identification, they are simply universal. As discussed largely elsewhere (Carvalho 1988), the traditional cult's historical discourse keeps absolute silence about slavery in Brazil. It tells about the *orishas* in Africa (where they were all powerful) and then tells the heroic saga of the great leaders who established the Afro-Brazilian religious traditions since the last quarter of the nineteenth century up to the present day. From the point of view of the cults, therefore, the *orishas* are neither black nor white: Their images are preponderantly those taken from the Catholic iconography, and their music is uncompromisingly African.

Coherent with its universal religious view, *candomblé* and *shango* music (as well as *batuque* and *mina*), with its percussion ensembles of a high technical complexity, has never been used outside a ritual setting; it is only in appearance that Brazilian popular music has incorporated these cult rhythms. As a matter of fact, all the incursions we have seen so far show the adaptation of drum rhythms used in the more syncretic kinds of cult (such as *candomblé de caboclo, umbanda, macumba,* and so on), which are more compatible with the song structures used in popular music. Another factor which prevents the cults from "reflecting" more explicitly the black experience is the language factor: Their entire repertoire is still sung in African language (especially Yoruba and Ewe), so that biographical and human associations, so common in *macumba* songs (as we shall see later on), are totally impossible to formulate.

Shango music certainly concentrates Afro-Brazilian identity, but not to a point of helping to construct ethnic differentiation. This is so because, as we have seen, its religious outlook is universal. Its dominant way of processing identity is that of conditional inclusiveness: Anyone can join this powerful Afro-Brazilian identity, provided that he or she is linguistically, melodically, rhythmically, and choreographically competent. In other words, *shango* identity is defined fundamentally in aesthetic terms and, especially due to the complexity of its art, its demands on the individual are higher than those of any other form of Afro-Brazilian culture. Finally, if *shango* moves towards an African identity, it is certainly a religious identity and not an ethnic one, as it is sometimes (mistakenly in my view) argued.

Black-White Conciliation

The other traditional model of Afro-Brazilian musical culture is well represented by the *congadas,* or *congos*, or *ticumbis*, folk groups which express the conciliation between the social sponsors (the white men) and the devotees (usually, humble descendants of slaves and mulattoes). The "kingdom" of Congo is one of the main allegorial structures of the small amount of power (as temporary as a day in the year) guaranteed for the black man in Brazil. This mythico-historical kingdom is built by the blacks on the basis of a Catholic celebration. The congos are mostly the expression of the experience of the *pretos.* Although the main symbols of a clear evocation of Africa — the king and queen of Congo — and their practitioners are blacks, the *congadas* use the expression "meus irmãos" (my brothers) as well as "meus pretinhos" (my little black ones); it is always an implicit community, conditioned fundamentally by social position — poor, humble, illiterate, peripheral dwellers of the small towns.

The musical material of the *congadas* is not as deeply rooted African as that of *candomblé* — it changes from one state to another, and in many cases it combines quite openly Western musical structures and instruments with Afro-derived rhythmic patterns.

Here is a fascinating example from a congo group from Pombal, Paraiba:

> *Zabelinha vira pão*
> *Vira eu, vira você*

> *Quand'os branco*
> *Stão olhando*
> *com seus olhos*
> *de muçambé*
> *Dança dança meus pretinhos*
> *Depressa, sem mais tardá*
> *Quanto mais depressa andá*
> *Mais depressa acabará*
> *Pilunguinha pilunguinha*
> *Olê olê pro nossos reis*
> *Aqui'stá nossos pretinhos*
> *Dançando cum'é de ser*
> *Aqui'stá nossos pretinhos*
> *Tocando cum'é de ser.*

> *(Little Isabel turns into bread*
> *turns into me, turns into you*
> *When the white folks*
> *are watching*
> *with their eyes of* muçambé *flower*
> *Dance dance my little black ones*
> *Hurry, with no further delay*
> *The faster you walk*
> *The sooner you will finish*
> *Pilunguinha pilunguinha*
> *Hello hello for our kings*
> *Here are our little black ones*
> *Dancing as it should be*
> *Here are our little black ones*
> *Playing as it should be.)*

"Pretinhos" here can mean any one of the participants, regardless of color: After all, if a blond man is participating in a group of congos, he is bound to be as poor and socially inferior as any black person in the same group.

As to the text, it is a good example of what I call "the aesthetics of opacity": The vocal style is chosen to hide the words as much as possible; jumping, dancing, turning, drumming, and keeping the mouth half closed make it difficult for the outside observer to appreciate exactly which words are being sung. Apart from that, in most *congadas* the text itself is highly undefined linguistically, with broken Portuguese words combined with Bantu words, some of them perhaps also broken.

The congos, who are not necessarily blacks, are addressing themselves — and those who want to join them — as "pretinhos":

happy, fond of dancing, united in the act of participation. "Pilunguinha" means a little and lousy mule, and what exactly is this animal doing is not clarified by the ethnographer, so we can only guess. Perhaps it is evoking a character in the similar totemic folk-drama of the Bumba-meu-boi.

As to the white man, he is watching the dance, possibly marveling at the transformations taking place, with his light eyes, sweet as the *muçambê* flower! Such a lyric picture of the white man does not seem to imply resentment or confrontation, but rather a distance in role playing, expressed in a beautiful and tender image.

In the congos model, we have therefore blacks and whites occupying explicit positions: The blacks dance, the whites watch. One must bear in mind that this symbolic structure is not aimed at defining in racial terms who is dancing and who is watching: There are people of all colors on both sides of the divide.

In another curious form of Afro-Brazilian tradition — the *pemba* from Minas Gerais, a cult which is exactly midway between a *congada* and a modern *umbanda* possession cult — it is frequent to use the expression "meus irmãos" (my brothers) in many ritual songs.

> *Boa noite meus irmãos*
> *Ai meu Deus boa noite*
> *Viva todos meus irmãos*
> *Viva Deus viva meus irmãos*
> *Meus irmãos adeus adeus*
> *Visitei os meus irmãos*
> *Paz de Deus fica conosco*
> *Até quando eu voltar.*
>
> *(Good night my brothers*
> *Ah my God good night*
> *Hail all my brothers*
> *Hail God hail my brothers*
> *My brothers goodbye goodbye*
> *I visited my brothers*
> *Peace of God be with us*
> *Until I come back.)*

Due perhaps to the cult's isolation — both geographical and cultural — from the great centers of African influence in Brazil, *pemba's* songs are much poorer and simplified, in musical as well as in literary terms. This symbolic isolation can also explain why *pemba* members are not capable of stating overtly at least some of the divisions —

economic, social, racial — which deeply mark their lives as poor and oppressed people. They seem to have encompassed them (although it is difficult to prove that they have neutralized entirely these divisions) in this repetitive and apparently empty formula "my brothers," which works, therefore, as a kind of secret code: those who are like us recognize themselves as our brothers.

Syncretic Cults

The third powerful model of Afro-Brazilian musical culture which reveals all the subtleties and ambiguities of black identity in Brazil is the syncretic style of cult, called either *macumba* in Rio, *jurema* in Recife, *pajelança* in São Luís do Maranhão, *candomblé de caboclo* in Salvador, or, in more general terms, *umbanda*. *Umbanda* is possibly the extreme case of inclusiveness and incorporatedness, following the strategy of implicit community to the extreme; to caricature (and at the same time being accurate), in some *umbanda* temples, even a Japanese is a black! A bit like the Divine Comedy, the *juremas* and *macumbas* are an allegory firmly rooted in history: the characters (or dramatis personae) who are worshipped as supernatural entities are human types, equivalent to people who have actually lived, and it is with them that one can build a mythopoetic view of the whole Brazilian experience and, most especially, of the Afro-Brazilian experience.

All these syncretic cults (which are, obviously, institutions for cultural synthesis) make a strong effort to leave the problem of black ethnicity undefined, their symbolic and political strategy being the opposite of the new black movements, which want to define, to affirm, and, if possible, to solve it once and for all, according to explicit ideological lines.

Of all the dozens of types of supernatural deities which are worshipped in these cults, there is one kind of spirit which I take as the most relevant for the present discussion: the spirits known as "Preto Velhos" (the Old Blacks). *Macumbas, juremas, umbandas* are the home of *pretos* par excellence. I must explain from the start that there are two Portuguese words to call someone a black person — *preto* and *negro* — and, as far as I know, they differ ideologically in a way that I do not think the word "black" differs from the English word "Negro." Nor can I find an equivalent pair in the Spanish vocabulary. The difference between *preto* and *negro* has been already explored by Renato Ortiz (1977), but I believe there is still a lot more to be said about it.

"Preto" is the traditional Brazilian black person. It is the word we find more frequently in the *congadas, vissungos, moçambiques, catopês, candomblés* (in Minas Gerais), and other folk groups of similar description.

The "Preto Velho," however, is anyone, whereas the "negro," referred to contemporarily by the new cultural expressions inspired by the black movements (under the clear influence of Caribbean and North American black movements) is a definite person; the "Preto Velho" is a collective image, an archetype which is available for everybody: he does not reflect biological distinctions, but symbolic, psychological, philosophical ones.

The ambiguity (or avoidance of definition) behind the "Preto Velho" is one of the key factors for the centrality and diffusion of *umbanda* in Brazilian society. Being the religion of negotiations, it stresses a figure which literally comes from the bottom of the social ladder and offers it, allegorically, as a place where people can exercise their displacement within this same society (this displacement can be defined in many ways or dimensions — spiritually, aesthetically, sexually, politically, and so on). In other words, the suffering of the "Preto Velho" is the suffering of every human being. The image of the "Preto Velho" is definitely black, whereas its music is compromising, incorporating secular genres, especially those rhythms that remind us of the festive (even if stereotypical) trajectory of the Brazilian black people: *samba, samba de roda, coco, maculelê, capoeira, baião* and *jongo,* among others.

Instead of denouncing black experience, "Preto Velhos" express it, with all its miseries and glories. Symbolically polarized and even contradictory, the "Preto Velho" has served so far to postpone *sine die* the decisive confrontation of the Afro-Brazilian people with a white post-slavery society that has treated them so unjustly. To compensate this lack of opportunity for a real challenge to the Brazilian elite, this mythical figure becomes a locus of speech, from which various discourses can be built and radical plurality can be exercised, politically, semantically, and aesthetically. Consistent with this, these cults speak to each individual, leaving up to each one the decision to build whatever collective utopia he might want to pursue.

Apart from this, one needs to stress that the ideal of *macumba* is to build a fortress; its main symbolic expression of power is a castle, a city, a fortified building (perhaps even a state), with its defensive guard and an attacking army. It is what I call a warrior model. It differs from the model of war proposed by the new black movements in the fact that, for the former, it is always a war of one individual against the others, whereas for the latter the war to be fought is a collective war of liberation. The various entities worshipped in the *macumbas* might represent variables, conditions, exemplars, rules of conduct, and strategies for this war. However, they never define a specific collective arena from which to speak nor a collective field against which one is fighting. Consequently, there is no room for ideological exclusion or witch hunting.

This aesthetic and symbolic model has to be all-inclusive and its war-like character justifies the inclusion of secular musical genres such as *maculelê* and *capoeira*, both being a sort of war dance music associated with defense and attack.

The following example of a *jurema* song from Recife shows precisely this constant compromise with duality as well as the defense-attack aspect of this singular worldview:

> *Meu pilão tem duas bocas*
> *trabalha pelos dois lados*
> *na hora do aperreio*
> *Valei-me pilão deitado.*

> *(My mortar has two holes*
> *It works on both sides*
> *in the moments of trouble*
> *help me, laid down mortar.)*

Jurema's attitude towards negotiations and ambiguities does not always mean silencing oppression suffered by blacks. The following song even uses the significant "negro," certainly more appropriate for what is being said than the softer "preto:"

> *Negro não entra no céu*
> *nem que seja rezador*
> *tem o cabelo duro*
> *vai furar nosso Senhor.*

> *(A black man does not go to heaven*
> *even if he is a good prayer*
> *he has very thick hair*
> *is gonna hurt Our Lord.)*

The following "preto Velho" song from an *umbanda* temple of Minas Gerais reflects the traditional imagery associated with the roles of colonial society. Words like "sinhô," "sinhá," and "iaiá" cut across styles, epochs, and genres, being found in nineteenth-century literary classics and in Brazilian popular music since the beginning of the twentieth century.

> *Aiuê meu cativeiro*
> *meu cativeiro, meu cativerá*
> preto Velho *tá cansá*
> *ia pra senzala batia o tambor*
> *dava viva a Iaiá, dava viva a Iôiô*
> *dava viva ao Sinhô.*

> (*Aiuê my captivity*
> *my captivity*
> preto Velho *is tired*
> *went to the senzala and played the drum*
> *he gave greetings to the lady*
> *he gave greetings to the young lord*
> *he gave greetings to the master.*)

From this very same "terreiro" (cult center) the next "Preto Velho" rhythm shows a clear influence of the second historical model in Minas Gerais, that is, rhythmic patterns taken from *congadas* and *catopês*.

> *Lelé ulélé*
> *Rei de Congo lélé ó.*

> (*Lelé ulélé*
> *King of Congo lélé ó.*)

The following *umbanda* song is unmistakably from Rio de Janeiro, sounding very close to a carnival tune:

> *Eu fui na beira da praia*
> *pra ver o balanço do mar*
> *eu vi um retrato na areia*
> *me lembrei da sereia*
> *comecei a chamar*
> *Oh Janaína vem ver*
> *Oh Janaína vem cá*
> *receber suas flores*
> *que eu vim lhe ofertar.*

> (*I went near the beach*
> *to see the movement of the sea*
> *I saw a portrait in the sand*
> *It made me think of the mermaid*
> *I began to call:*
> *Oh Janaína come to see*

> *Oh Janaína come here*
> *to receive the flowers*
> *that I came to offer you).*

As I have argued elsewhere (Carvalho 1984), the production of *umbanda* songs in records, especially in Rio de Janeiro and São Paulo, has become a small sector of popular commercial music. Small wonder, then, that one finds an LP dedicated to spirits which utilizes practically all the rhythmic genres that form part of the carioca popular music (*batucada, jongo, samba, pagode,* and so on).

The next song, coming from the *tambor de mina* of Maranhão, is the paradigm of the kind of ambiguity and paradoxicality which characterizes the whole of Afro-Brazilian cultural tradition.

> *Eu sou banzeiro eu sou banzeiro*
> *Banzeiro grande é o tombo do mar*
> *ê mar ê mar ê mar*
> *Banzeiro grande é o tombo do mar.*
>
> *(I am banzeiro I am banzeiro*
> *big banzeiro is the clash of the sea*
> *Oh sea oh sea oh sea*
> *big banzeiro is the clash of the sea.)*

First of all, the melody allows for constant extemporization, since it is constructed upon a simple major chord which leaves the endings open to equivalences between thirds and sixths. Moreover, there is always a certain "imprecision" in the intonation of the ending thirds, which oscillate between minor and major. If we turn now to the text, we see even more oscillations and contradictions. In the first verse, the poetic subject states: "I am banzeiro." "Banzeiro" is a tricky word: it comes from "banzo," a Bantu word that means the lethal nostalgia which caught the African slaves as soon as they arrived in the Brazilian coast. They would sit immobile, in front of a house, sometimes staring at the sea, and would die there out of an absolute apathy. However, "banzeiro" means also the oscillating movement of a drunken man. And more precisely, in this ritual context, it means the movement of the sea waves. The problem is that the same word is used to express both the calm sea as well as the sound of the violent waves resulting from the clashing of the Amazon River waters against those of the Atlantic Ocean. Apparently the subject has chosen to identify himself with the violent waves, for in the second verse it is said "Big banzeiro is the clash of the sea." Then the sea is celebrated in the third verse; and finally the presence of the big "banzeiro" is once again stressed.

From the point of view of identity, therefore, we are dealing here with a gray area, as far as a process of subjectivation is concerned: The I, the immaterial subject of the song, comes and goes, as if he were, in this manner, playing second fiddle to other three material subjects: the *banzeiro* (the oscillating movement), the *tombo* (the clashing act), and the sea itself.

There is still another contradiction present in this song text: "Banzé" means trouble, confusion, so that a "banzeiro" can also mean a trouble-maker, an agitator. Thus, "banzeiro" is a conflicting adjective, pointing to radically opposite qualities experienced by the poetic subject. "To have banzé" is to reach a state of uncontrolled euphoria, quite the contrary of the depression which comes with "banzo."

But this song has captured even more semantic and mythological associations. Although present now in the city of Brasília, it comes from the *mina* tradition, where African deities are worshipped in the same festival as the local ones (*caboclos*, or *encantados*). As it combines a wobbling melody on top of a markedly *mata* rhythm (a rhythm for forest spirits) and at the same time emphasizes the semantic paradox of "banzeiro," it seems to unite the calmness, nostalgia, and sense of loss generally associated with Iemanjá (the national goddess of the sea, worshipped throughout the country) with the vivacity, strength, and overt aggressiveness that is sometimes shown by the spirits of *caboclos* and *encantados*.

Affirmation of Black Pride

As I have already indicated at the beginning, the real change in this model of aesthetic construction of black identity in Brazil has been presented in certain styles of popular (understood as commercial) music, coming especially from Bahia, which explicitly and self-consciously wants to identify itself with the "negro." I cannot trace here all of its history, but one of the pillars of this movement was the creation, about twenty years ago, of some *afoxés* (groups which appear in the Bahian carnival) that accept only blacks as their members. Moreover, their costumes and hairdos are taken from African styles, expressing a strong will to affirm and assert black pride in Brazil. For these associations (the most famous being the Filhos de Gandhi and the Ilê Aiyê), a man (or woman) of black color is a "negro," like an African, and not a *preto* (the oppressed and unliberated Afro-Brazilian who still calls a white man his master, as we have already seen in the *umbanda* song from Belo Horizonte).

The following song, which was quite successful in commercial terms, shows well this new attempt to foster "negro"-African pride. It is highly didactic, in the sense of celebrating the prowesses of African kingdoms, and it aims to instruct the Brazilian black about ethnic groups, history, and costumes of mother Africa.

Madagascar Olodum

Criaram-se vários reinados
O ponto de imerinas ficou consagrado
Rambosalama o vetor saudável
Ivato, cidade sagrada
A rainha ranaialona
Destaca-se na vida e na mocidade
Majestosa negra
Soberana na sociedade
Alienado pelos seus poderes
Rei Radama foi considerado
Um verdadeiro meiji
Que levava seu reino a bailar
Bantos, indonísios, árabes
Se integram à cultura malgaxe
Raça varonil, alastrando-se pelo Brasil
Sankara, Vatholay
Faz deslumbrar toda nação
Merinas povos tradição
E os mazimbas foram vencidos pela invenção
I ê ê ê é sakalavas onaé
Iá a a sakalavas onaá
Madagascar, ilha, ilha do amor.

(Various kingdoms were created
Imerinas point became famous
Rambosalana the healthy vector
Ivato, sacred city
The ranavalona queen
Exudes in life and youth
Majestuous black woman
Society's sovereign
Estranged by his powers
King Radama was regarded
A true meiji
Who led his kingdom to dance
Bantus, Indonesians, Arabs

All merge themselves into Malagasy culture
Brave race, spreading throughout Brazil
Sankara, Vatholay
Fascinates the whole nation
Merinas peoples tradition
And the mazimbas were conquered by invention
Ie ê ê ê sakalavas onaê
Ia a a sakalavas onaa
Madagascar, island, island of love.)

As I said, this song has reached some popular success; it is doubtful, however, whether it depended directly on this "Africa" message. Most likely it is the rhythm, the nice and easy *estribilho* (refrain), and so on. We shall return to it in a moment.

Another strong influence for this new generation of black musicians in Brazil is the Jamaican reggae. This connection, which only now is being more visible, was started by Gilberto Gil, one of the main exponents of our popular music, who introduced Jimmy Cliff to the Brazilian public more than ten years ago. Of the national reggae singers, Edson Gomes is considered one of the best. He calls his work "reggae resistência" (reggae of resistance) and is politically committed to the black cause. Here is one of his songs:

História do Brasil

Por isso é que a gente não tem vez
Por isso é que a gente sempre está do lado de fora
Por isso é que a gente sempre está lá na cozinha
Por isso é que a gente sempre está fazendo
Um papel menor um papel menor
Um papel menor um papel pior.

(That's why one hasn't got a chance
That's why one is always out
That's why one is always there in the kitchen
area
That's why one is always playing
A minor role, a minor role
A minor role, the worst role.)

We are dealing here with a typical protest song: serious, complaining, defining the enemies very clearly, lining up forces and calling out for a reversal of order. In the case of reggae in Brazil, perhaps the main effect it has had so far in advancing the black cause is in the absorption of the Jamaican giants of this music (Bob Marley, Jimmy Cliff, and so on), more than in the work of the Brazilian bands, which have not yet assimilated it to a point of acquiring a musical personality of their own.

Now, the main problem with this explicit movement in music is that faced by all genres and attempts at making "musique engagée" or protest songs. There is a fundamental contradiction between trying to control the polysemy of a song text (so that it is "right" politically, sexually, ethnically, racially, and so on) and the process of identification, which together form the basis of the relationship between the listener and the composer in the area of popular music. For all these reasons, the problem is solved not by politicians or ideologues, but by musicians themselves. Ultimately, the more effective black songs are those composed by the best composer, regardless of the degree of explicitness of the protest written in their lyrics. Take, for instance, the following song by Gilberto Gil.

Sarará

> Sara sara sara sarará
> Sara sara sara sarará
> Miolo
> Sara sara sara cura
> Dessa doença de branco
> De querer cabelo liso
> Já tendo cabelo louro
> Cabelo duro é preciso
> Que é prá ser você crioulo.
>
> (Heal heal heal will heal/sarará
> Heal heal heal will heal/sarará
> Brains
> Heal heal heal cures
> This white man's disease
> Of wanting to have thin hair
> When you already have blond hair
> Thick hair is necessary
> For you to be a black man.)

This is one of the most direct songs written by Gil towards the development of black pride. His solution is much better than those presented above because of its humor, of his tongue-in-cheek approach to color prejudices in Brazil. Sarará is a kind of blondish hair, found among some people of African descent in Brazil, which preserves the typical thickness of black hair. Gilberto Gil introduces here a play of words: sarará (thick blond hair) also means "will heal." By praising thick hair he is elegantly answering the *jurema* song from

Recife mentioned earlier which excludes the "negro" from heaven on the grounds that the thickness of his hair will damage Our Lord.

Of course, Gilberto Gil delves into this rather touchy area without being serious, without tragedy. He deconstructs reified habits by reminding us of the possibility of joining in one person the two extremes of social contrast: a blond man and a black man. This way, although himself committed to the black movement, he is using practically the same symbolic structure of inclusiveness and negotiation which characterizes the tradition of Afro-Brazilian culture. For instance, he even uses the word "crioulo," another stereotypical word for a white person to use to address a black man (again, white here understood as a subject of speech, a position which can be occupied also by a black). In the end, many of his songs demonstrate his capacity as a lyricist and a musician to invite us to join whatever theme of protest, accusation or affirmation he wants to express. What he offers is, first and foremost, excellent popular music; the "negro" or black cause, which he embraces as well, is located within his aesthetic explorations.

> *Babá Alapalá*
> *Aganju Xangô Alapalá*
> *Alapalá Alapalá Xangô Aganju*
> *O filho perguntou pro pai*
> *Onde é que tá o meu avô*
> *O meu avô onde é que tá*
> *O pai perguntou pro avô*
> *Onde é que tá meu bisavô*
> *Meu bisavô onde é que tá*
> *Avô perguntou bisavô*
> *Onde é que tá tataravô*
> *Tataravô onde é que tá*
> *Tataravô bisavô avô*
> *Pai Xangô Aganju*
> *Viva Egun Babá Alapalá*
>
> *(Aganju Xangô Alapalá*
> *Alapalá Xangô Aganju*
> *The son asked the father*
> *Where is my grandfather*
> *My grandfather where is he*
> *The father asked the grandfather*
> *Where is my great-grandfather*
> *My great-grandfather where is he*
> *Grandfather asked great-grandfather*
> *Great-great-grandfather where is he*

> *Great-great-grandfather great-grandfather grandfather*
> *Father Xangô Aganju*
> *Hail Egun Baba Alapalá.)*

Here, Giberto Gil managed to make up a song which is at once Bahian, Brazilian, African, and, finally, black or "negro." The text does not deal with human history — be it slave experience, black resistance, and so on — but with divine history instead. That is exactly why it was successful: A mood of ancestrality, of the awe present during an apparition of *eguns* (the frightful ancestor spirits still worshipped in some Bahian candomblés), expressed iconically by the cries and wails heard at the back during the entire song, is put together with a celebration of Aganju (the youngest of the various gods known as "Shango"), expresses in the accentuated and percussive rhythm of the bass. The rhythm of the song is also innovative in terms of traditional Afro-Brazilian drumming. Moreover, Gil sings this song (or "interprets" it, as we say in Portuguese) as if it is *shango* himself who is singing! His performance conveys all the character of this youngest version of the thunder god: fun-loving, spirited, cheerful (although not peaceful), juvenile, restless, full of energy to be externalized.

To recollect what has been shown so far, there are some elements demonstrating that the assumption of a correspondence between a certain musical genre and a social or ethnic identity has to take into account the way musical parameters and song texts are put together. Curiously enough, ethnomusicologists heretofore seem to have understood better the role of musical parameters (rhythmic structure, instruments, tonal organization, and so on) in the support or confrontation of ethnicity than the song texts themselves.

And the world of song texts takes us, willing or not, necessarily to the more general problem of mimesis, which Erich Auerbach (1987) defined as the different ways through which reality is represented in literature — in the case of song, in poetry. Let us take the song "Olodum Madagascar," for instance.

We know enough about the musicians who wrote it and played it to get their intentions: a clear "negro," African song, to foster black pride in Brazil. Now, one can fairly guess that 90 percent of the listeners of this song could not really follow this awkward description of a remote people with a remote history (it goes without saying that the Malgaches did not come much to Brazil; more of them went to the United States). What "caught" people was the refrain "Madagascar";

many listeners, however, would have equally applauded (and some might even have understood) an expression like "vamos dançar" ("let's dance") instead! In other words, they could do with Reflexu's what Rita Pavone did with the Peter Seeger protest song "If I Had a Hammer," as Umberto Eco has brilliantly shown some time ago (Eco 1987).

Watching Reflexu's performance of the song in a Chacrinha show (a grotesque TV entertainment program) gives another clue to the problem of its "real" meaning: the African message is diluted in sheer "aestheticized difference," which is the fundamental law followed by the commercial media. Reflexu's played just after a third-rate stereo-typed romantic singer and just before another Menudo-type group of teenagers, most of them absolutely unliberated mulattoes! So, the media accepts these products first and foremost for their entertainment value.

The field of popular music is bigger than the field of black music, and this explains the difficulty in trying to uncover value, meaning, and identity markers in songs which, because they are popular songs, potentially address everybody, regardless of their author's intentions or wishes. This is not to say they have no efficacy in identity building; on the contrary, either they are more efficacious than this, or they are not efficacious at all.

As Simon Frith (1987) has rightly argued, it is usually the assumption of a realist convention which lies behind most of the content analysis of popular music. He is also right when he says that in popular music one is listening to someone's accent. However, what is also important to say is that there are different literary (or poetic) conventions used by different singers. Gilberto Gil, for instance, seems closer to the Hebrew approach to mimesis as described by Erich Auerbach (1987) than Reflexu's, for instance, whose work is not lyrical, but clearly epic in intent. If Reflexu's is closer to Homer (just to follow Auerbach's analysis a bit further) in his detailed description of Ulysses meeting with Euriclea, Gil's clever "Sarará" takes as its subject the whole context of race relations, beauty values, and social status in Brazil: The text advances rapidly, as if Gil were, like Abraham, answering someone who has just put a big question to him.

Granted this, we must see how the musical material reinforces or shatters these poetic conventions. Reflexu's certainly diluted the epic side of their song by stressing its refrain, making it thus closer to common sense expectations of how a Bahian dance tune should sound.

Another point central to these symbolic processes of identification is who is trying to communicate to whom by means of the song. For instance, if popular music is based on the assumption that the singer is addressing every one of his listeners individually, that is not the case in the other models we have discussed. The singer of the congos is not singing for the public, but rather for a group of people selected from a larger community. In the *shango* case, the singing is certainly not primarily directed to the public or to any individual part of it, but to the deities being worshipped; since the language is hermetic, no social divisions are allowed to appear, but only ritual ones. The case of *umbanda* and similar forms is possibly the most complex, for since the practitioners are Portuguese speakers, they are not merely reproducing a musical structure which precedes them, but are mainly producing it. The linguistic competence gives room to the expression of differences that cannot appear in the other models.

In conclusion, these are some of the theoretical questions to which we should be addressing ourselves at present. The new technologies of identity construction (what Foucault used to call "technologies of the I") spread by the media might give us an illusion of ethnicity just where it is being dissolved into fashion and temporary identification. If the traditional approaches to ethnicity and identity were criticized on the ground that they reified social groups and cultural expressions, we should be aware that not all of the new musical identity markers are necessarily consistent with or different from the deeper structures which generate them. In other words, the main problems in the area of verbal and nonverbal communication run equally through the traditional and the contemporary models of Afro-Brazilian culture.

Discography and Recordings

1. *Shango* song of Oshun. Recorded July 1980 by José Jorge de Carvalho and Rita Laura Segato in Recife.

2. Congos of Paraíba. 1977. Compact record. Instituo Nacional do Folclore, Rio de Janeiro.

3. Pemba cult from Ipanema. Recorded January 1980 by José Jorge de Carvalho and Rita Laura Segato in Minas Gerais.

4. Jurema cult of Recife. Recorded March 1976 by José Jorge de Carvalho and Cristina Mata Machado.

5. Jurema song from Recife. Recorded March 1976 by José Jorge de Carvalho and Cristina Mata Machado.

6. "Aiuê meu cativeiro." N.d. Pai Guiné de Arruda. LP. Nelson Mateus de Nogueira com Côro da Cabana Espírita Umbandista Nossa Senhora da Glória, Belo Horizonte, MG. Fermata 22.512.1985.

7. "Rei do Congo." N.d. Pai Guiné de Arruda. LP. Nelson Mateus de Nogueira com Côro da Cabana Espírita Umbandista Nossa Senhora da Glória, Belo Horizonte, MG. Fermata 22.512.1985.

8. "Louvação a Janaína." N.d. Faramin Yemanja. LP. SOM SOLP 40464.

9. "Song for Water Spirit." Recorded 1 January 1992 in Brasilia by José Jorge de Carvalho and Rita Laura Segato.

10. Reflexu's. 1987. "Madagascar Olodum." Reflexu's da Mãe Africa. LP.

11. Gomes, Edson. 1988. "História do Brasil." Reggae Resistência. LP. EMI.

12. Gil, Gilberto. 1977. "Babá Alapalá." Refavela. LP. Philips, 6349329.

13. Gil, Gilberto. 1979. "Sarará Miolo." Realce. LP. WEA BR32.038.

References

Auerbach, Erich. 1987. A Cicatriz de Ulisses. Em: *Mimesis*. São Paulo: Perspectiva.

Benjamin, Roberto O. 1977. *Congos da Paraiba*. Rio de Janeiro: Instituto Nacional do Folclore.

Carvalho, José Jorge. 1984. "Music of African Origin in Brazil." In *Africa in Latin America*, ed. Manuel M. Fraginals, 227-248. New York: Holmes & Meir.

Carvalho, José Jorge, and Rita Laura Segato. 1986. "Musik der Xangô-Kulte von Recife." *In Brasilien. Einführung in die Musiktraditionen Brasiliens*, ed. Tiago de Oliveira Pinto, 176-192. Mainz: Schott.

Carvalho, José Jorge. 1987. *El Culto Shango en Recife, Brasil.* Caracas: Centro para las Culturas Populares y Tradicionales.

Carvalho, José Jorge. 1988. "La Fuerza de la Nostalgia. El Concepto de Tiempo Histórico en los Cultos Afrobrasileros Tradicionales." *Montalbán* (Caracas) 20:167-197.

Carvalho, José Jorge. 1991. "Sistemas abertos e territórios fechados. Para uma nova compreensão das interfaces entre música e identidades sociais." Paper delivered at the International Colloquium on Music, Knowledge and Power, sponsored by the ICTM, Florianópolis, at University of Santa Catarina.

Eco, Umberto. 1987. "A Canção de Consumo." In *Apocalípticos e Integrados*. São Paulo: Perspectiva.

Frith, Simon. 1987. "Why Do Songs Have Words?" In *Lost in Music. Culture, Style and the Musical Event*, ed. Levine White Avron, 77-106. London: Routledge & Kegan Paul.

Ortiz, Renato. 1977. "A morte branca do feiticeiro negro," *Religião e Sociedade* 1:43-50.

Sotaques: *Style and Ethnicity in a Brazilian Folk Drama*

Kazadi wa Mukuna

S ince its first presentation in the eighteenth century (ca. 1780) during the so-called "Civilização de Couro" period when cattle raising was at its peak in Brazil, Bumba-meu-Boi (a Brazilian dramatic dance of totemic character) has evolved, despite persecution by those in authority, by adapting to social changes. Bumba-meu-Boi was created by African slaves in colonial Brazil. This assertion is sustained by several facts, but primarily by the function for which the drama was created: to serve as a vehicle of social control to denounce and ridicule colonial slave owners. Other styles came into existence at later periods, created by other segments of the population in imitation of the African by maintaining the story line of the play and its dramatization without necessarily adhering to the original raison d'être; each of the new styles incorporated features which reflected its ethnic identity. The argument for African authorship of the Bumba-meu-Boi is also sustained by the chronology of appearance of the African style called Boi de Zabumba, the Indian style known as the Boi de Matraca introduced in Maranhão in 1868, and the most recent style called Boi de Orquestra (1958) with strong European influence — as well as by musical instruments, rhythmic organization, costumes, and the format of dance presentation. With changing times, modifications such as the religious overtone and a shift in the application of social control focused on the community as a whole became vital to the survival of the Bumba-meu-Boi, as its original functions became obsolete.

Definition and Origin

F or decades, the quest for the origin of cultural practices was a major obsession among students of Brazilian culture, who concentrated most of their effort on this issue to the point of ignoring other pertinent aspects of cultural analysis. Often, those caught in the web of this intellectual exercise were led into error, tending to confuse the principles of creation with those of innovation. The belief that all existing cultural practices in a society such as that of Brazil originated from other cultures with which contacts were made, or from which members came, not only is absurd but also fosters an archaic theory of diffusionist extremists that all cultural practices originated from one group in one area of the world, with dissemination due to contacts made possible by the rise of navigation.[1] To believe the contrary, diffusionists argue, is to perpetuate the isolation of societies.

In recent decades, the formulation of theories concerning the scrutiny of Africanism in the music of Latin America and the Caribbean has become an urgent priority for individual researchers and institutions. Their efforts have resulted in a variety of methodological guidelines which differ in expression but agree on the value of considering the conceptual level of the carriers of cultural material, as affected by the history of the new society, in order to reach a deeper understanding of the persistence and continuity of African cultural elements in the music of the New World.[2] Expanding this idea, the "Grupo de Trabajo" has asserted:

> The identification of African elements in the musical fabric of Latin America should also take into consideration the historical aspect which includes the impact of all phenomena, social and economic, on the carriers of the cultural material. This sustains the fact that a musical expression is indeed a product of the influence of these phenomena on the conceptual level of its makers. To the latter, music is not conceived as mere organization of sounds, but rather as integral parts of a total expression, which include languages, dances, movements, games, and special behaviors, pertaining to a dynamic society.[3]

Implicit in this methodological concept are the three focuses of interpretation, each of which requires a precise analysis of historical, cultural, and conceptual processes of evolution of Africanisms in the Americas. These are a) persistence/continuity, b) innovation/transformation, and c) creation/concept. In the first category, one searches for physical materials (musical instruments, rhythmic patterns, dance steps, cultural manifestation, religious practice, and so on) which have been maintained in the New World. In the second, African musical/ cultural elements have been modified morphologically or re-interpreted conceptually in the new society. In the last aspect physical African elements are absent, but the new musical/cultural expression is structured according to the African concept of organization. Discussing Africanisms in African-American music, Portia Maultsby concluded:

> A study of African-American music from the seventeenth through the twentieth centuries reveals that African retentions in African-American music can be defined as a core of conceptual approaches. Fundamental to these approaches is the axiom that music-making is conceived as a communal/participatory group activity. Black people create, interpret, and experience music out of an African frame of reference — one that shapes musical sound, interpretation, and behavior and makes black music traditions throughout the world a unified whole.[4]

It is within the framework of these methodological guidelines that the argument about the Africanism in the Bumba-meu-Boi in Maranhão is formulated, seeking evidence for the principles of organization of musical expression which continue to perpetuate Africanism in the diaspora, and identifying possible traces in musical instruments, dance steps, and other elements.

An examination of existing literature dealing with the origin of Bumba-meu-Boi reveals some conflicting theories. The first, advanced by Guilherme Theodoro Pereira de Melo (1908), attributed the origin of Bumba-meu-Boi to Portugal and affirmed that it is a variation of a sixteenth-century play, Monólogo do Vaqueiro (The Cowboy Monologue), presented by author Gil Vicente 8 June 1502, on the occasion of the birth of Prince Dom João, King Dom Manuel's first born (Melo 1947, 59). In Brazil this theory is given credence in Bahia and Pernambuco, where Bumba-meu-Boi is associated with Christmas. According to M. I. Perreira de Queiroz, Bumba-meu-Boi is part of the Reisados celebrated during the Epiphany (6 January), composed of short sketches whose story revolves around the ox. She wrote:

> The small drama which is now being presented probably originated in Portugal. During ancient religious processions in this country burlesque characters paraded intermingled with saints and angels.... In Brazil, the ox of processions and of ancient bull races in Portugal had transformed itself into

the principal character of a dramatic dance...(Queiroz 1973, 158).

The second theory, formulated by Arthur Ramos (1954), dismissed de Melo's suggestion and indicated that Bumba-meu-Boi has three likely origins: African, Amerindian, and European. Discussing the African origin, Ramos argued that Bumba-meu-Boi contained totemic survivals from Africa. He stated:

> It won't be necessary to insist too much on the meaning of popular feasts of totemic origin.... Recall that psychoanalytically the totemic animal is the symbol of the Father.... But, it is in the Bumba-meu-Boi that the totemic complexes reveal themselves with more evidence.... In this manifestation, the death of the ox is the leitmotif. The African black kept these ritual feasts in his subconscious and, through the principle of repetition, expanded them periodically in popular manifestations which he encountered in the new home (Ramos 1937, 115-116).

The third theory, suggested by Domingos Vieira Filho, asserted that Bumba-meu-Boi was born in Portugal's colony as a logical consequence of colonialism, influenced by the three races which forged the Brazilian nation (Vieira Filho 1968, 102). The choice of the ox for the drama, concludes Vieira Filho, was made by the African slave because "the Negro slave was the ox's brother in suffering and in work" (Vieira Filho 1968, 102-103).

The third theory is the most cogent, but not for the reasons advanced by its author. As conceived and celebrated in Brazil, Bumba-meu-Boi can be defined as a folk drama with music and dance which reflects an image of interaction among social classes in colonial Brazil. In more precise terms, Bumba-meu-Boi was a collective statement of retaliation voiced by the oppressed members of the society to denounce and ridicule their oppressors. It reflects character and structure different from its alleged prototypes. It is both a social/secular and psychological/religious, as well as a collective and personal manifestation sustained by the complex nature of its objectives. While Bumba-meu-Boi allows participants to exteriorize aggressions through hilarious displays of social sanctions, nowadays it also provides them with an opportunity to express profound devotion to Saint John, Saint Peter, and Saint Marçal.

As a collective and social manifestation, a presentation of the Bumba-meu-Boi is an occasion for communal merrymaking. As a personal and religious expression, it has become a personal affair during which individuals participate to keep private promises made to the saints and to renew their covenants with them. The ox, symbol of power and wealth during the Leather Civilization, is utilized in the drama as the catalyst for deep-seated satire against the ruling class. It is only with time that the ox became an object of devotion which is adorned, sanctified through baptism, and sacrificed to Saint John to serve as a link of covenant between the saints and the participants.

Subtle satire is incorporated into the roles of characters representing social authorities and into the manner in which these authorities are addressed in the play by those considered to be of the lowest order in the social hierarchy. Ridiculed characters vary from one region to another, but the most prominent in Maranhão are the priest, the Portuguese master (Amo), and the captain (Cavalo Marinho) who represent the ruling class and slave owners in colonial Brazil.

In order to gain a better understanding of the origin and the definition of the Bumba-meu-Boi, it is necessary to examine the legend that provides the story line for the drama. In this legend, three racial groups and two social classes are represented. The Portuguese Amo, owner of the ranch on which the story unfolds, the priest, and the capitão represent the ruling class; Pai Francisco, the daring African slave, the Indian medicine man, the cowboys, and the servants represent the lower class. The interaction of these social classes and racial groups is triggered by the chain of events and the intervention of each racial character in the resolution and the restoration of social harmony. The following version of the legend was recorded during 1980-1981 field trips in the district of Pindaré located 250 km south of São Luís, capital of the state of Maranhão:

> On a ranch owned by a Portuguese master (known in the play as Amo) and his wife, Dona Maria, dwelt the slave Francisco (also called Nego Chico), his pregnant wife (Mãe Catirina), and other slaves. Amo has a favorite ox, referred to in the legend as "Boi Estrela" (Star Ox) and "Fama Real" (Royal Fame). One day, Mãe Catirina has an urge to eat of an ox's tongue. Making her desire known to her husband, Mãe Catirina specifies that the tongue must be that of the master's favorite animal. Concerned for the life of his

unborn child, Pai Francisco leads the ox into the woods, where he kills it and takes the tongue to his wife, who cooks and eats it. The next day, Amo, realizing that his favorite ox is missing, summons all his cowboys and slaves together to ask if anyone has seen it. One of them informs him that he had seen Pai Francisco taking the Star Ox into the woods, from whence minutes later a gunshot was heard. Searching the woods, they encounter the remains of the ox. Infuriated by the sight of his dead animal, Amo orders the director of Indians to arrest Pai Francisco. Before undertaking such a dangerous mission, the director of Indians seeks blessing from the priest. Addressing Pai Francisco, Amo orders him to bring his ox back to life or die himself. A Portuguese doctor enters the scene and makes several attempts to resurrect the ox, but in vain. Finally a shaman (Indian medicine man) is summoned. He lays his hands on the animal, which arises, and they all dance joyfully through the night.[5]

Authorship

From the sociological point of view, Bumba-meu-Boi was a vehicle for direct social control, utilized primarily by the oppressed members of the society as a means of challenging the authority of the ruling class. Closer examination of the essence of the play reveals that, having no other recourse to vindicate their rights, the oppressed members of the society created a play in which despised authorities were caricatured and denounced. The objective of the drama, then, was denunciation of the ill-behaved members of the ruling class and the carrying out of deep-seated satire of them and all slave owners in a comical fashion.

Starting with Mãe Catirina's unreasonable request and Pai Francisco's daring compliance with it, every scene of the drama depicts ridicule of the authorities in one form or another. The killing of the master's favorite ox is indeed an act of provocation of his anger. But the solution adopted to pacify the situation reflects lower class mockery of the white man's medicine. In the play, the Portuguese doctor's attempts to resurrect the ox fail; the Indian shaman's magic succeeds in bringing the ox back to life. In light of this interpretation, which reveals the hidden satirical pun embedded in the themes of the drama's two most significant contrasting episodes (provocation and pacification, tension and resolution), it can be deduced that Bumba-meu-Boi was created as a challenge to social injustices as seen by its author.

Addressing the question of authorship of the Bumba-meu-Boi in a round table debate held in Maranhão (July 1986), Américo focused on the inner structure of the play:

> It is evident that Bumba-meu-Boi has a learned origin. This origin is implanted in the catechism cycle of the Jesuits who took advantage of the amusement which was also educational. It contains a moral lesson while at the same time it has all the characteristics of a theatrical piece.

Jomar Moraes is correct in asserting that external aspects of the tourinha and other European elements concerning the ox are not sufficient to determine that "our Bumba-meu-Boi comes from European origins. I believe," he concluded, "our Boi has a popular origin; it is of the people."[6]

The Brazilian origin of the Bumba-meu-Boi has been established and is no longer an issue for debate. However, there is conclusive evidence which indicates that this folk drama could not have originated among the ruling class, but rather is a creation of the lower class. In this lower class, it is certain that the African slave, who was considered inhuman and necessarily enslaved to protect the Indian whose soul was being saved by the Jesuits, would be more likely than the Indian to have come up with such an expression resulting from the conditions of his daily interaction with members of the ruling class. Describing Bumba-meu-Boi in 1840, Padre Lopes Gama provided the ethnic identity of the first performer and author of the drama. "Of so many popular diversions, frolics, and amusements that exist in our Pernambuco," wrote Padre Lopes Gama, "I do not know one so foolish, so stupid, and insipid, as the incidentally well-known Bumba-meu-Boi.... A Negro hidden inside a shaggy fabric made of wool is the ox..." (Padre Lopez Gama 1840). Further evidence of the slave authorship of the Bumba-meu-Boi is encountered in the statement of an author who called himself "A Friend of Civilization," requesting that the performance of the Bumba-meu-Boi be abolished:

> When a large portion of the population takes upon itself to end with those firecrackers for being deadly, an authorization is granted to the stupid and immoral merrymaking of slaves called Bumba-meu-Boi (O Imparcial 1861).

It is not the symbolic death and resurrection of the ox which constitute the essence of the Bumba-meu-Boi; it is the function for which it was conceived — the vehicle of retaliatory expression of the lower social class. As such, Bumba-meu-Boi could only have been created in Brazil by those for whom this purpose had to be served. In the course of time, the basic structure of the drama was expanded to meet new social needs, which included, but were not limited to criticism of the ruling class.

Within the drama itself, one can also find sufficient evidence which indicates that Bumba-meu-Boi was created by an African slave. First, there is the identification of the daring slave and his wife by name — in Francisco and Mãe Catirina. Second, the mode of delivery chosen is satire through singing. This form of dramatization of satire, when addressed to a superior, is a widespread practice in African cultures. "In song," Alan Merriam has said, "the individual or the group can express deep-seated feelings not permissibly verbalized in other contexts."[7] Such practice is commonplace among the Bashi in Zaire, the Luo in Kenya, and the Zulu in South Africa, to name just a few. The "Omangbetu Olya" of the Mangbetu people in northeast Zaire, for example, is a repertoire of court songs that are sung to the king by his subjects and members of the court to indicate a problem, make a request, criticize him, or simply ask for drinks. Discussing similar practices among the Chopi of Mozambique, Hugh Tracey wrote: "You can say publicly in songs what you cannot say privately to a man's face... and so this is one of the ways African society takes to maintain a spiritually healthy community."[8] It is only through this genre of songs that subtle satires can be addressed to the king without fear of losing one's head. In Bumba-meu-Boi, satires of members of the ruling class were delivered within this African concept.

Sotaques/*Styles and Ethnicity*

"Sotaque" is a generic term used to distinguish the variety of styles of Bumba-meu-Boi in Maranhão and Piauí. There are three major styles, reflecting characteristics peculiar to each of the racial groups which compose the Brazilian population: African, Indian, European. These peculiarities are apparent in the choice of musical instruments, costume design, rhythmic patterns, and choreography. The coexistence of the three Bumba-meu-Boi styles in Maranhão began in 1958. The testimony recorded in the field and from written documents attests that the first Boi de Zabumba was the first style to be identified in Maranhão. "The first 'bois' [dance groups] on the Island (São Luis)," writes Cyro Falcão, "were called De-Zabumba-Tambor. Their history developed alongside the drum implanted here by the African" (Falcão, 19). In time, this style became also identified with the district of Guimarães, once a major slave center, thus giving rise to the expression Boi de Guimarães.

In 1861 the celebration of the Bumba-meu-Boi was prohibited statewide, and in 1868 it reappeared. João Domingos Perreira do Sacramento wrote: "In this year's frolic they introduced the Matracas sound with the accompaniment of dull shouts and dissonance which shivered bodies to hear them, without a minimum recollection of such things having been used in Bumba-meu-Boi" (Sacramento 1868, 7).

Boi de Orquestra, the newest of the three styles and the only one for which all circumstances of its creation are documented, was founded in 1958 by Francisco Paiva, leader of a brass ensemble in the Axixa district. The orchestra style came into being when Paiva and his musicians were accompanying a local Bumba-meu-Boi group in the street after their rehearsal.

When and where Bumba-meu-Boi was first performed remains unknown. However, available written documents from the past point to the seventeenth- and eighteenth-century sugar mills and plantations of Bahia and Pernambuco as the period and sites of the first setting. José de Jesus Santos wrote: "The fact is that the seventeenth and eighteenth centuries witnessed the coming up of Bumba-meu-Boi, for this was the golden period of the cattle cycle in Northeast, North, and South, when the lives of the inhabitants of these regions were profoundly interrelated to the cattle raising" (Santos 1971, 14).

The dissemination of Bumba-meu-Boi in Brazil did not occur simultaneously with the expansion of cattle raising, although it did follow the same paths. From the valley of the São Francisco River, the site of the earliest mention of the merrymaking, Bumba-meu-Boi followed the cattle into the states of Ceará, Piauí, Maranhão, and Pará. Discussing the introduction of the Boi in Maranhão, Cyro Falcão dates the first rehearsal during the tangerine expansion period, which corresponded with the 1838-46 uprising in the interior of the state, known as the Balaiada War.[9] Domingos Vieira Filho also wrote: "Bumba-meu-Boi represents a remainder of the pastoral phase in the colony during which the ox was the important economic agent, driving herds of cattle in the vast pastures of the country's inland, implanting ranches and corrals which were often the initial nucleus of the important settlements."[10]

Vieira Filho (1974) concludes: "In Maranhão, Bumba-meu-Boi dates from the latter years of the eighteenth century as merrymaking for slaves on ranches and sugar mills." In 1858, the Maranhão newspaper *O Globo* published an article qualifying Bumba-meu-Boi as indecent, barbarous, grotesque, and worthy of being banned.

Instrumentation

The instrumentation of the Boi de Zabumba style is composed primarily of percussive musical instruments. The principal instrument, the zabumba *(Photo 1)*, is a cylindrical, double-headed drum with ox or goat skin on both heads. Originally the body of this drum was made from a carved tree trunk or from plywood. Today, metallic barrels are substituted for these materials. In the original form, the skin heads were attached to the body of the instrument by wooden rings; in the more modern version, these wooden rings are replaced by metallic ones.

The zabumba is played in a fixed location, with the weight of the instrument resting on a peg *(Photo 2)*. During the procession, the

Kazadi wa Mukuna, 1983

Kazadi wa Mukuna, 1982

Photo 1. Zabumba drum

Photo 2. Position of the Zabumba during performance

zabumba is hung on a stick and carried on the shoulders of two people while a third plays it freely.

The origin of this instrument and its association with Bumba-meu-Boi are still unknown. However, despite the lack of supporting evidence, there is speculation attributing the zabumba to Africa. Similar assertions about remnants of African cultural traits in Brazil have been judged very misleading, and should be dismissed for failing to specify the African cultural area of the alleged origin, and for failing to provide us with insights about changes which might have occurred during a given period of time, leading to the attained structures, functions, and forms of expression in the new milieu with which the element is associated. The ambiguity surrounding the origin of the zabumba stems from its name and its morphologic structure. On the one hand, the structure of its modern version resembles that of the bass drum in the European music tradition — but what must be kept in mind is that this new version derives from a process of substitution of construction materials. On the other hand, the original structure of zabumba is more closely related to the array of double-headed drums encountered in several West African cultures. In Nigeria, for example, there is the *atete* drum *(Illustration 1)* from Ogun State, which is used for worship of Orisha during Egungun festivals. This drum is also used during social gatherings (Echezona 1981, 125).

Lynne Menturwerck

Illustration 1. Atete *drum used in Nigeria for the worship of* Orisha *during Egungun festivals and for entertainment during social gatherings*

The zabumba varies in size, ranging between sixty to eighty centimeters in diameter and thirty to forty centimeters in depth. The body is painted in solid colors or adorned with geometric figures and other decorative motifs. Tuning is accomplished by tightening the rope holding the two rings around the drum heads. The number of zabumba drums in an ensemble is unlimited. They provide heavy straight beats, and their variations are similar to those of the Tambor de Crioulo of African derivation practiced in the region. The Africanism of the Boi de Zabumba style is also corroborated by the use of the friction drum and the organization of the rhythmic material. In contrast to samba and other carnival manifestations in which this drum is referred to as cuíca,[11] in the Bumba-meu-Boi it is known as Tambor Onça.

Costumes

The designs and materials used in costumes worn by dancers, musicians, and special characters who compose a Bumba-meu-Boi troupe constitute a significant stylistic distinction among ethnic groups in the region. There are several elements common to all the styles, but certain features reflect ethnic peculiarities of a troupe.

Kazadi wa Mukuna, 1982

Photo 3. The making of the Boi de Zabumba hat

There are several types of hats worn in the African style of Bumba-meu-Boi, but this style is best identified by the largest hat worn by the dancers. This hat is made of the inside of a young babacu of the palm tree family branch *(Photo 3)*, sewn together in a regular top-hat shape and reinforced with wire. The hat is covered with ribbons which hang from the top center all around the hat leaving a space of about ten centimeters in front, for the face. This interval is secured by a dome-like additional piece sewn to the hat and adorned with geometric patterns such as the star, as desired by the owner *(Photo 4)*.

Kazadi wa Mukuna, 1983

Photo 4. Completed* Boi de Zabumba *hat with its decorations

Hats worn by other dancers and by zabumba players are made from the common regional straw hats covered with black velour cloth and decorated again with designs according to individual preference, elaborated with colorful glass beads. Still another type of hat is found in the African style of Bumba-meu-Boi. This is a straw hat to which is sewn a dome-like front piece on which are depicted motifs in colorful glass beads. The back of the hat is covered with hanging ribbons from the top center of the hat to the individual's thighs.

There are some feathers in the African style of Bumba-meu-Boi, and these are worn by the Indian characters in the drama. Their hats are adorned with a small amount of feathers, but the bulk of hats for little Indians are made of cardboard covered with glossy, colorful paper and topped with synthetic rafias. According to Laurentino,[12] these synthetic materials have been infiltrating the Bumba-meu-Boi because the authentic materials are becoming scarce. In the case of the feathers, for example, the Ema Austriche bird has been declared an endangered species by the government and can no longer be killed for its feathers. As a result, feathers used today for Indians, especially among troupes in the capital city, come from different birds.

The peitoral blouse worn by members of the African style of Bumba-meu-Boi is like a cape. Its normal size stretches from the neck line to mid-forearm, extending two to three centimeters lower in front and back. The hem is finished with glass beads. The saiote skirt, however, is made of one single piece of cloth. Both the saiote and the peitoral are made of black velour cloth hemmed with glass beads and decorated with flowers and other motifs in glass beads. Underneath the skirt and the blouse are worn a white long-sleeved shirt, red pants, and black shoes covered with white spats *(Illustration 2).*

Choreography

The third category of stylistic distinction is the choreography, which includes dance steps and the presentation format. Beginning with the latter consideration, each Boi style has adopted specific dance formations during sections of the drama known as Cordão. In the Boi de Zabumba style, dancers in circle move in a counterclockwise motion while the accompanying ensemble remains station-

Lynne Menturwerck

Illustration 2. Complete costume for the Boi de Zabumba style.

ary outside the circle. The Zabumba dance reflects the dance movements of the Tambor de Crioulo with its gingas (moves/figures) characteristic of African dances that have survived in Brazil in conjunction with the religion.

Summary and Conclusions

The analysis of the components of the Bumba-meu-Boi provides a framework for the examination of stylistic creations from which stylistic distinctions emerge. Each style is derived from interaction of the legend, maintained as the unifying story line, with features derived from the cultural-racial backgrounds of the participants. Stylistic elements such as musical instruments, costume designs, and dance choreography are strongly influenced by, if they do not derive their basic structure from, the three basic racial groups which interacted at the creation of Brazilian society. The African influence can surely be detected in the Zabumba style in the morphological structure of the drum by the same name, and by the heavy-sounding strokes and rhythmic patterns produced on this drum. Further African presence still can be detected in the dance movements of the Boi de Zabumba style, which contains gingas similar to those of Tambor de Crioulo dance characterized by periodical spins. This is how Jeovah Silva Franca (1981, 47) expressed the Africanism of this style: "It is marked by the presence of the rumbling of the rustic percussion, profoundly felt by its followers like a distant echo of African drum beats heard at night in the houses-of-mina...." Strong indigenous (Indian) influences cannot be overlooked in the Boi de Matraca style, including its prominent musical instrument (the matraca, which provides its metronomic meter pulse) and the predominant feathers which form part of the costume design, decoration, and choreographic patterns of the dance steps. These steps bring to mind Indian dance steps often witnessed at pow-wow events. The European influence is apparent in the Boi de Orquestra through musical instruments and dance movements resembling contredances of Europe. In short, the ethnicity of the Bumba-meu-Boi style, as discussed above, does not reflect the racial background of a single group but rather shows the ongoing influence of several sources, beginning with the African slaves of colonial Brazil.

Notes

1. Leo Frobenius, "The Origin of African Civilization," in *Smithsonian Institution Annual Report*, 1898; see also G. Elliot Smith, *In the Beginning: the Origin of Civilization*, 20-31.

2. Grupo de Trabajo, "The Study of African Music Contribution to Latin America and the Caribbean: A Methodological Guideline," *The World of Music* 3 (1990):103.

3. Grupo de Trabajo, 103.

4. "Africanisms in African-American Music," in *Africanisms in American Culture*, ed. Joseph E. Holloway, 205. See also J. Kwabena Nketia, "African Roots of Music in the Americas: An African View," in *Report of the 12th Congress*, London, International Musicological Society (1981): 82-88.

5. At the last presentation of the year, the shaman's magic does not work, and the ox is dissected and its meat symbolically distributed among those present (participants and audience). This version of the legend was told by José Vale, the founder and leader of the "Rei da União" group, and his colleagues.

6. Jomar Moraes, 1986. Personal communication.

7. Alan Merriam, 1964: 190.

8. "The Social Role of African Music," *African Affairs* 53: 234-41.

9. A revolution was led by Manuel Francisco dos Anjos Ferreira (known as Balião) from 1831, which was ended in 1846 in the district of Caxias, Maranhão, by the national army under the command of Luis Alves de Lima e Silva. De Lima e Silva was then given the noble title of Duke of Caxias by President Vicente Pires de Camargo and was immortalized as the Patron of the Brazilian armed forces after his successful campaign in the Paraguayan War; see also Astolfo Serra, *A Balaiada*.

10. Domingos Vieira Filho, 1974: 60.

11. For a discussion of the origin of the cuíca and its uses in Africa and Brazil, see Kazadi wa Mukuna, 1979.

12. Interviewed in São Luís, Maranhão, December 1982.

References

Cascudo, Luís da Câmara. 1962. "Bumba-meu-Boi." In *Dicionário do Folclore Brasileiro*, 2d. ed. Rio de Janeiro: Instituto Nacional do Livro.

Castelo Branco, R. P. 1942. *A Civilização do Couro*. Teresina: Departamento Estadual de Imprensa e Propaganda.

Echezona, W. W. 1981. *Nigerian Musical Instruments: A Definitive Catalogue*. Lansing: The Apollo Publishers.

Falcão, Cyro. n.d. *Bumba-meu-Boi do Maranhão*. São Luís: Universidade Federal do Maranhão.

Ferretti, Sergio Figueiredo, ed. 1979. *Tambor de Crioulo: Ritual e Espetáculo*. São Luís: SIOGE.

Franca, Jeovah Silva. 1981. "O Meu Bumba-meu-Boi." *Cultura Popular* (July): 37-50.

Frobenius, Leo. 1898. "The Origin of African Civilization." In *Smithsonian Institution Annual Report*.

Gama, Padre Lopes. 1840. "A Estulotice do Bumba-meu-Boi." *O Carapuceiro* 2 (11 January).

Gottheim, Vivian I. 1988. "Bumba-meu-Boi: A Musical Play from Maranhão." *The World of Music* 30, no. 2.

Goulart, J. A. 1966. *Brasil do Boi e do Couro*. 2 vols. Rio de Janeiro: Edições GRD.

Grupo de Trabajo. 1990. "The Study of African Musical Contribution to Latin America and the Caribbean: A Methodological Guideline." *The World of Music* 3: 103-104.

Kazadi wa Mukuna. 1979. *Contribuição Bantu na Música Popular Brasileira*. São Paulo: Global Editora.

Kazadi wa Mukuna. 1986. "Bumba-meu-Boi in Maranhão." In *Brasilien. Einfuhrung in Musikkulturen Brasiliens*, ed. Tiago de Oliveira Pinto, 108-20. Mainz, Germany: Schott.

Kazadi wa Mukuna. Forthcoming. "The Ox and the Slave: Bumba-meu-Boi in Maranhão." *Progress Report in Ethnomusicology*.

Kubik, Gerhard. 1979. *Angolan Traits in Black Music, Games and Dances of Brazil: A Study of African Cultural Extensions Overseas*. Lisbon: Junta de Investigações Científicas do Ultramar.

Maultsby, Portia. 1990. "Africanisms in African-American Music." In *Africanisms in American Culture*, ed. Joseph E. Holloway, 185-210. Bloomington: Indiana University Press.

Melo, Guilherme de. 1947. *A Música no Brasil.* 2d ed. Rio de Janeiro: Imprensa Nacional.

Menezes, Bruno de. 1958. *Boi-Bumbá: Auto Popular.* Belém.

Merriam, Alan. 1964. *The Anthropology of Music.* Evanston, Illinois: Northwestern University Press.

Meyer, Marlyse. 1963. "Le Merveilleux dans une Forme de Théâtre Populaire Brésilien: le Bumba-meu-Boi." *Revue d'Histoire du Théâtre* (January-March): 94-101.

Nketia, Kwabena. 1981. "African Roots of Music in the Americas: An African View." In *Report of the 12th Congress*, 82-88. London: International Musicological Society.

O Imparcial (15 June 1861). São Luís, Maranhão.

Prado, Regina de Paula Santos. 1977. "Todo Ano Tem: as Festas na Estrutura Social Camponesa." Master's Thesis, Universidade Federal do Rio de Janeiro.

Queiroz, M. I. Pereira de. 1973. "O Bumba-meu-Boi, Manifestação de Teatro Popular no Brasil." *O Campesinato Brasileiro.* Petrópolis: Editora Vozes.

Ramos, Arthur. 1937. *As Culturas Negras no Novo Mundo.* Rio de Janeiro: Civilização Brasileira.

Ramos, Arthur. 1954. *O folclore negro do Brasil.* 2d ed. Rio de Janeiro: Casa do Estudante do Brasil.

Sacramento, João Domingos Perreira do. 1868. "Chronica Interna." *Semanário Maranhense* 1(45)(July): 7-8.

Santos, José de Jesús. 1971. *O Bumba-meu-Boi do Maranhão.* São Luís: Gráfica São Paulo.

Tracy, Hugh. 1954. "The Social Role of African Music." *African Affairs* 53: 234-41.

Vieira Filho, Domingos. 1968. "Bumba-meu-Boi do Maranhão." *Brasil Açucareiro* 36 (72, 2) (August): 102-3.

Vieira Filho, Domingos. 1974. "Folclore do Maranhão." *Revista Maranhense de Cultura.* Ano 1, 1 (January-June): 45-62.

Syncretism, Identity, and Creativity in Afro-Colombian Musical Traditions

Egberto Bermúdez

The main objective of this chapter is to present a synthetic view and some conclusions about syncretic musical traditions among Afro-American communities in Colombia, especially as these relate to the processes of identity search within these marginal communities. Moreover, it also proposes a reflection on the definition of the concept of syncretism regarding particular Colombian musical styles.

For this purpose, the syncretic cultural traditions involving Afro-American elements will be treated from three different perspectives: 1) the structural, examining the existing African retentions and the confluence of native American, African, and European elements in certain musical traditions, 2) the inter-ethnic relations between Afro-American communities and others (such as Indian and *mestizo*), and 3) the place of these particular musical traditions in the context of contemporary musical activity, especially regarding commercially recorded music.

Introduction

From the perspective of cultural history, music has played a very important role in processes of conformation, revival, and even

This work is the result of my participation and the discussions generated in the Conference "Music and Black Ethnicity in the Caribbean and South America," organized by Gerard Béhague with the support of the North-South Center and the School of Music of the University of Miami on January 16-19, 1992. Some of its material was also presented in one of the study groups of the VI Colombian Congress of Anthropology, "The construction of the Americas," Universidad de los Andes, July 22-25, 1992.

225

invention of identities. On the other hand, innovation and creativity in music acquired a special interest in the eighteenth and early nineteenth centuries, when people of new territorial entities (with their corresponding emergent nationalities) were trying to adapt their native musical traditions to the social, political, and cultural contexts brought about by the new order. They were also trying to shape particular cultures with clear and definite markers which could strengthen the coherence of those regional or national collective identity projects.[1]

The case of the Americas, especially since the last quarter of the nineteenth century, provides sufficient evidence for a discussion of the complex (and sometimes contradictory) relationship between creativity, musical innovation, and the above-mentioned processes of search of collective identities. From the musical point of view, the cases referring to the population of African descent (with its corresponding racial mixture with other ethnic groups) are the best paradigms because, at the international level, the musical products generated by them (jazz, rap, *salsa*, mambo, *cumbia*, samba, reggae, *merengue*, and so on) had become markers of "African-ness," "Afro-Americanism," and even "latinity," *par excellence.*

In the case of Colombia, George List was one of the first scholars to call attention to the study of syncretism in Afro-Colombian music. His work on the musical activity of Evitar, a village of around fifteen hundred inhabitants located on the Northern Colombian coast, had as its main hypothesis the importance of the contribution of Amerindian, African, and European elements to the conformation of *costeño* musical culture.[2] This was an interesting departure in an environment in which until the 1950s the African contribution to Colombian music was taken superficially in the best of cases. In the first half of the century an overtly racist perspective prevailed. For Daniel Zamudio,[3] Afro-Colombian music was apish and did not deserve the name of "music." However, List's idea of "tri-ethnicity" is difficult to sustain if we approach the complexities of the presence of the different elements of this particular musical culture. Linguistic, historical, and anthropological evidence has shown a more complex cultural picture in which the balance of the ethnic elements is not what appears to be and where inter-ethnic conflict, cultural manipulation, and external pressure are important factors to take into account.

In the 1960s, and particularly through the activity of the brothers Zapata Olivella, there was a reassessment of Afro-Colombian culture.

Regarding music, their approach was well-intentioned but still too ideological and uninformed about African musical traditions, and about the history and dynamics of slavery, maroon societies, and the history of the presence of Afro-American groups in Colombia.[4] Around the same time the work of Robert West, Norman Whitten, and Aquiles Escalante tackled the study of these phenomena from an anthropological perspective.[5] Whitten[6] recognized the social and cultural importance of music, musicians, dance, poetry, and songs in the marginal Afro-Colombian societies of the Pacific lowlands.

Continuing these scholarly approaches, Germán de Granda, Nina de Friedemann, William Megenney, and Carlos Patiño explored the cultural, inter-ethnic, historical, and linguistic aspects of the culture of these groups.[7] De Granda proposed and explored the dominance of Bantu lexical elements in the creole language of the Palenque de San Basilio, one of the most culturally consistent Afro-American communities in Colombia. Subsequently, the findings of Friedemann, Meggenney, and Schwegler[8] have confirmed this hypothesis. These authors attempted analysis of the texts of ritual songs with African (Bantu) vocabulary.

Historical Evidence

The first mentions regarding the musical activities of Africans in Colombian territory come from different sources. From the early sixteenth century there were slaves and free individuals of African origin or descent who inhabited in the lands discovered and conquered by the Spaniards. From the 1520s onwards archival records mention blacks (slaves and sometimes freemen) in Santafé, Cartagena, Santa Marta, and the rural mining areas of western Colombia. In January 1573 the City Council of Cartagena issued a disposition,

> ordering that no black, male or female, can get together to sing or dance with drums in the streets, unless it be on a site chosen by the Council, and with the proper license to dance, play, sing, and to do their festivals according to their tradition only until sunset, unless otherwise ordered by justice.[9]

Music, song, and dance were very important sources of affirmation of identity for slaves outside their African communities. In Cartagena during the seventeenth century this can be seen in the zeal with which Pedro Claver, a Jesuit missionary, tried to alienate slaves from their chants, musical instruments, rituals, and gatherings during his residence in Cartagena between 1615 and 1654. When he found blacks singing, dancing, or celebrating any ritual activity, Claver often confiscated the drums, and, with a cross in his hand, whipped the musicians and dancers.[10]

The zeal in incorporating slaves into Hispanic-Catholic culture is clearly manifest in some of the genres of the music used in Spain, Portugal, and the Hispanic colonies during this period. The *villancicos de negros, negritos, guineos* were very popular at the time for the celebration of important Catholic festivities like Christmas, Epiphany, and the Holy Sacrament. Robert Stevenson has shown the popularity and frequency of these events in the extant colonial musical repertoire and has pointed out the first appearance of these genres in America.[11] In the case of Colombia, a musical piece now at the Archivo Capitular of the Bogotá Cathedral reveals some possible knowledge of the characteristics of African ritual music and its use (as syncretic material) to indoctrinate slaves and shake their cultural resistance during the seventeenth and early eighteenth centuries. The text of this piece, a Negro de Navidad, *Toca la flauta*, contains the usual *habla de negro* which refers to the Spanish *criollo* dialect of slaves.[12] There is also a mention of Guinea as a place of origin, and the following verses may allude to a knowledge of how to use the apparently insignificant words *que le, le, le* which can be recognized in several African languages:[13]

> ...*al siquiyo aleglalémo*
> *mil cosita le tlaelémo*
> *y a la Glolia cantalémo:*
> *que le le le, que le le le*
> *al sonsonetillo del zambacaté*

> *(We will make this little boy happy*
> *We will bring him a thousand things*
> *And we will sing to the Glory:*
> *Que le le le, que le le le*
> *To the jangling sound of the zambacaté)*

In 1770, the dances of the population of the area became again an object of suspicion and investigation. A report sent to the king in that year by the Spanish governor of Cartagena states that:

> The dances ... called *bundes* ... are basically a circle half made by men and half by women, in the center, to the sound of a drum and the singing of various *coplas*.... A man and a woman dance until another couple replaces them

> doing so again and again to their wish .... In this dance there
> is nothing unnatural or dishonest, because the man does
> not touch the woman and the *coplas* are not indecent.[14]

Similar mentions appear during the nineteenth century, and the contemporary ethnomusicological evidence suggests a continuity in some practices, but obviously in the musical contexts they are the result of very complex processes of racial and cultural syncretism that continue nowadays.

African and Other Influences - Past and Present
African Retentions

In the Palenque de San Basilio, some funeral songs are performed only in burials of people who belong to the *Cabildo Lumbalú*, one of the several *cuagros* (age groups) which are a central feature of the social organization of the village. Their existence possibly corresponds to the continuity of gatherings of members of the same ethnic or linguistic affiliations. The *Lumbalú* group uses a large ritual drum (*pechiche*) and songs which contain African words not fully under-stood nowadays by the community. Most of these words (*ambwe, berequé, bonga, bwenda, calunga, cambamba, cambé, engwenda, icanda, lwango, lumbalú, mamé, quisilá, reambé, tantué, yombo*, besides *Angola* and *Congo*) have a very probable (80-90 percent) Bantu origin. Their responsorial style of singing is common to *bullerengue* style and the use and function of drums (except the *pechiche*) are the same as in the other ensembles of the region. It is interesting to note that in the funeral dance (*baile e' mueto*) of people belonging to other *cuagros*, normal *bullerengues* are used.[15]

The text of some of these chants contains the above-mentioned morpheme *o le le* or *le le le*. William Megenney and other authors have recognized the morpheme *lele* (and its variations) in several African languages. It appears with different meanings in Yoruba, Ewe, Fon, and several others of the Bantu family. A ritual significance can be inferred from several examples, although references to other meanings may not help to reinforce the hypothesis about the continuity of any ritual meaning.

If the textual African retentions point to an Angola-Congo origin, there is another musical element which points to Central West Africa and its inland. This is the three key-leg xylophone (called *marimba de pie*) common in places like Guinea, Senegal, Ivory Coast, Benin, Togo,

Central African Republic, Malawi, and even Madagascar.[16] Another significant African musical instrument used in San Basilio until recently was the musical bow (also called *marimba*) and the long cylindrical drum used in the funeral chanting, both of which have a larger area of Africa as their origin.[17]

Blacks, Indians, and Mestizos

Inter-ethnic relations between black and Indian communities in the Pacific lowlands have been studied by Friedemann.[18] She concludes that this interaction is now expressed in their ideology, material culture, and even social organization. The Embera groups of that region display a very interesting ritual paraphernalia of mixed African and Amerindian origin. For instance, the ritual sticks carved out of hardwood, representing one of the most important elements of the *jaibaná* (Embera shaman) have the same features of similar sticks made in Angola and Zaïre. This confluence of cultures is also present in their music.

Besides the singing, we can hear the music of cylindrical wooden trumpets (*fotutos*) and drums playing patterns similar to those heard in Lumbalú examples. The drums are conical and barrel shaped, with some African features such as the lacing and use of wedges for tension. The style of chant bears as well some resemblance to the chanting of the "Canto de Lumbalú," although it is freer and in a recitative style.

In other cases, such as that of the Colombian islands of Old Providence, San Andrés and Catalina (which share the Anglo-Caribbean musical culture of Trinidad and Jamaica), it is possible to detect repercussions of the strong Colombian political and cultural centralism of the last quarter of the nineteenth century and first part of the twentieth century, which imposed "mestizo" culture upon this ethnic, religious, and linguistic minority.

In the musical tradition of the Colombian inland provinces the *pasillo* (or *baile del país*) is a transformation of the European *waltz*, syncopated and faster. When it changed from a dance piece to a pure instrumental one, it acquired a virtuoso style very appropriate to the piano. Afterwards this music began to be played on string instruments such as the *bandola, tiple,* and guitar. The mandolin and violin are the main melodic instruments of the ensemble of the archipelago, accompanied by guitars, maracas, the jawbone, and the tub-bass. As a result of direct influence from mainland Colombia, the *pasillo* was added to its repertoire, which consisted of polkas, mazurkas, schotisches, quadrilles, and other dances; this is played and considered an original part of their musical tradition. The additional repertoire of this ensemble consists of calypsos, romantic songs, and Caribbean dance music.[19]

New Trends

The relationship between certain Afro-Colombian musical styles and radio stations and the recording industry has been very close since the 1930s. Around that time, a new style of dance music was formed based on the adoption of the instrumentation of the American big band for playing the rhythmically complex repertoire of ensembles, such as the *gaiteros* or *cañamilleros*. This is the origin of the internationally recognized *cumbia*, still popular all over Latin America. In the mid-1960s New York *salsa* began to be important in Colombia, and still today that tradition is maintained through the activity of several internationally recognized Colombian *salsa* groups like Niche, Fruko y sus Tesos, and Guayacán, among others. In the 1970s, and for political reasons (the creation of a new *departamento* in the Vallenato region), *vallenato* music was promoted by the media and local and central powers, and it became Colombian music *par excellence*. However, *salsa* preserved its status, and only in the last five years, musical groups from all over the Caribbean, which regularly attend the *Festival de Música del Caribe* and the *Green Moon Festival* held respectively in Cartagena and San Andrés, have brought reggae, *soca*, and other Caribbean styles to the Colombian public.

From the perspective of international *salsa* style and following the example of authors such as Rubén Blades and their "socially engaged" *salsa*, one of the most important hits of Joe Arroyo and his band is "Rebelión," a pseudo-historical piece, apparently naive but with a strong affective charge against the lack of equal opportunities and the discrimination blacks face nowadays in Colombian society.

As a recent phenomenon, in the marginal areas of cities like Cartagena, Barranquilla, and the island of San Andrés, young people dance to what they call *terapia* and *champeta*, in both cases a mixture of elements of rap, reggae, and bits and pieces of African *juju, soukus,* and other elements taken from new Caribbean musical styles from all over the English and French Antilles, and from Latin music from the United States, Panamá, and Venezuela. Circulation of the bulk of this repertoire is through pirated cassettes, and its performance takes place mostly in high-powered public sound equipment called *picó* (from the English pick-up), very popular in the villages and in the marginal areas of the big coastal cities of Barranquilla, Santa Marta, and Cartagena.[20]

Conclusions

The status of music as an element of identity in Afro-Colombian marginal communities is ambiguous. In Santa Rosa de Saija (Pacific lowlands) the community and its musicians recognized as their own some pieces of Senegalese *balafon* music brought to them by Nina de Friedemann.[21] On the other hand, they listen and dance mostly to *salsa* and Caribbean dance. This contradiction represents the simultaneous strength and fragility of their rich musical heritage. On the Atlantic coast, *vallenato* and *salsa* prevail. The function of the traditional ensembles is most often limited to their participation in the yearly festivals sponsored by the liquor, soft drinks, and other important local industries; these events are also used by politicians to consolidate their local power. Some of these musicians have been forced to emigrate to the main cities (Barranquilla, Cartagena, Bogotá) and perform with "folkloric" groups and ballets in hotels and in the nationalistic shows characteristic of beauty contests and petty political rallies. The marginality of the Pacific black groups has helped preserve the style and function of the music. However, this music is only partially alive, as the younger generations do not identify it as totally their own and prefer Colombian and Latin American music broadcast by radio and television stations.

Regarding syncretism, some Colombian musical styles mentioned here, notably the "Cantos de Lumbalú" and the "Embera feast music," do not exhibit the degree of homogeneity and coherence one could expect of syncretic styles. The vocal style of the Lumbalú clearly resembles European church chanting, and is probably based on chant formulas taught by missionaries. It is, however, significant to note that it is also performed in a responsorial way bearing little relation to the rhythmic drum basis. We could better describe this as a "superposition" of styles. The same is noticeable in the Embera-Chamí music, although its vocal part is more Amerindian in style. Nevertheless it features the same lack of connection with the musical patterns of the drums and cylindrical trumpets. These cases postulate further reflection on the nature of the concept of syncretism. Following Mintz and Price, we can propose that communities of runaway slaves could create their culture and identities only after a process of cultural change in which syncretism (at least linguistic and musical) of this sort was the constant.[22]

An alternative reading of the lack of consistency found in the examples mentioned here could interpret it as a symbol of cultural resistance and ethnic survival. In these syncretic musical styles, elements coexist from different traditions, but the tension between them results from cultural and social tensions. This perhaps may better reflect the contradictory nature of Afro-American and Latin American culture.

Notes

1. For a wider treatment of the problem in the case of Colombia, see López de la Roche 1989, 283-307.

2. *Music and Poetry in a Colombian Village*, (Bloomington: Indiana University Press, 1983).

3. *El folklore musical de Colombia*, (Bogotá: Revista de Indias, 1949).

4. For these articles, see Morales Gómez 1978 and Ortega Ricaurte 1973, 83-255.

5. See West 1952 and Escalante 1954, 207-351.

6. "Música y relaciones sociales en las tierras bajas colombianas y ecuatorianas del Pacífico: estudio sobre micro-evolución sociocultural," 635-665.

7. De Granda 1971, 1-11, and de Granda 1978; de Friedemann 1981; de Friedemann and Rosselli 1983; and Meggeney 1986.

8. See de Friedemann 1991, 65-86, which includes Schewgler's conclusions.

9. "El cabildo ordenó que ningún negro ni negra se junten a cantar y a bailar por las calles con tambores, si no fuere en la parte donde el cabildo lo señalare y allí se les dé licencia que puedan bailar, taner y cantar y hacer sus regocijos, según sus costumbres hasta que se ponga el sol y no mas, si no fuere con licencia de la justicia" (see Valtierra 1980, 452).

10. See Valtierra 1980, 213.

11. Stevenson 1970 and Stevenson 1968, 475-502. See also Esses 1988, 107-114.

12. For a discussion of the origins and characteristics of the *habla de negros*, see de Granda 1969.

13. These words are mixed with the courteous Spanish expression "usia" and "usie" and with others used for lamenting, such as "ay, ay." These intrusions can allude to a linguistic syncretism in the creole language spoken by slaves and blacks in general, besides the already mentioned deformations of pronunciation transliterated in the text. Obviously the *villancicos de negros*, the *negrillas* and *guineos* constituted also a literary genre in sixteenth- and seventeenth-century Spain and Hispanic America to which also belong the texts under discussion. The author of the piece is identified in the manuscript as M[aestr]o Torices.

14. See Valtierra 1980, 219.

15. The information is not totally clear regarding this point. Some people say that in all wakes (*velorios*) they sing *baile e'mueto*, some say only when very old people die, and some allude to a problem of social discrimination whereby people of high standing would not use it because they consider it old-fashioned and belonging to the lower strata of the village.

16. See Anderson 1984, 872-3.

17. For a wider treatment of this topic, see Egberto Bermúdez, "Cumbia" (in press) and "Los cantos rituales del Palenque de San Basilio: Una aproximación musicológica" (in press).

18. De Friedemann 1977, 68-78, and de Friedemann and Arocha 1987.

19. See also Bermúdez 1992b.

20. See Bermúdez 1992a.

21. De Friedemann 1989, and for a discussion of the problem of identity in the Colombian *negro*.

22. See Mintz and Price 1976, 9-10.

References

Anderson, Lois Ann. 1984. "Xylophone-Africa." In Vol. 3 of *The New Grove Dictionary of Musical Instruments*, 872-3. London: Macmillan.

Bermúdez, Egberto. 1992a. "Música, Identidad y Creatividad en las culturas Afro-Americanas: El Caso de Colombia." *América Negra* 3 (June): 57-68.

Bermúdez, Egberto. 1992b. "Música e Identidad en San Andrés y Providencia." *Boletín-Expedición Humana* (Bogotá) 12.

Bermúdez, Egberto. Forthcoming. "Cumbia." *Musik Geschichte und Gegenwart.* Kassel: Bärenreiter Verlag.

Bermúdez, Egberto. Forthcoming. "Los cantos rituales del Palenque de San Basilio: Una aproximación musicológica." *Congreso de Antropología en Colombia.* Manuscript. Bogotá.

Escalante, Aquiles. 1954. "Notas sobre el Palenque de San Basilio una comunidad negra en Colombia." In *Divulgaciones Etnológicas* 3:207-351.

Esses, Maurice. 1988. "Black Dance Types in Spanish Dominions 1540-1820." *Inter-American Music Review* 9(2)(Spring-Summer): 107-114.

de Friedemann, Nina S. 1977. "La fiesta del Indio en Quibdo: Un caso de relaciones interétnicas en Colombia." *Revista Colombiana de Antropología* 19:68-78.

de Friedemann, Nina S. 1981. *Ma Ngombe: Guerreros y Ganaderos en Palenque.* Bogotá: Carlos Valencia Editores.

de Friedemann, Nina S. 1989. *Criele criele son-Del Pacifico Negro.* Bogotá: Planeta.

de Friedemann, Nina S. 1991. "Lumbalu: ritos de muerte en el Palenque de San Basilio." *América Negra* 1 (June): 65-86.

de Friedemann, Nina S., and Carlos Patino Rosselli. 1983. *Lengua y Sociedad en el Palenque de San Basilio.* Bogotá: Instituto Caro y Cuervo.

de Granda, German. 1969. "Posibles vías directas de introducción de africanismos en el 'habla de negro' literaria castellana." *Thesaurus* 24.

de Granda, German. 1971. "Sobre la procedencia africana del habla criolla de San Basilio de Palenque (Bolívar, Colombia)." *Thesaurus* 26:1-11.

de Granda, German. 1978. *Estudios lingüísticos hispánicos, afrohispánicos y criollos.* Madrid: Ed. Gredos.

List, George. 1983. *Music and Poetry in a Colombian Village.* Bloomington, Ind.: Indiana University Press.

López de la Roche, Fabio. 1989. "Colombia: búsqueda infructuosa de una identidad." *Memorias del Simposio "Identidad Étnica, Identidad Regional, Identidad Nacional,"* 283-307; V Congreso Nacional de Antropología, Villa de Leyva. Bogotá: ICFES.

Megenney, William. 1986. *El Palenquero: Un lenguaje post-criollo de Colombia.* Bogotá: Instituto Caro y Cuervo.

Mintz, Sidney W., and Richard Price. 1976. *An Anthropological Approach to the Afro-American Past: A Caribbean Perspective,* 9-10. Philadelphia: ISHI.

Morales Gómez, Jorge. 1978. *Contribución a la Bibliografía del Folclore Colombiano.* Bogotá: Author's Edition.

Ortega Ricaurte, Carmen. 1973. "Contribución a la bibliografía de la Música en Colombia." *UN-Revista de la Dirección de Divulgación Cultural-Universidad Nacional de Colombia* 12 (August): 83-255.

Stevenson, R. 1968. "The Afro-American Musical Legacy to 1800." *Musical Quarterly* 54(4)(October): 475-502.

Stevenson, R. 1970. *Renaissance and Baroque Musical Sources in the Americas.* Washington, D.C.: Organization of American States-General Secretariat.

Valtierra S.I., Angel. 1980. *Pedro Claver. El Santo Redentor de los Negros.* Bogotá: Banco de la República.

Wade, Peter. 1991. "The Language of Race, Place, and Nation in Colombia." *América Negra* (Bogotá) 2 (December): 41-68.

West, Robert. 1952. *Colonial Placer Mining in Colombia.* Baton Rouge, La.: Louisiana State University Press.

West, Robert. 1957. *The Pacific Lowlands of Colombia.* Baton Rouge, La.: Louisiana State University Press.

Whitten Jr., Norman. 1967. "Música y relaciones sociales en las tierras bajas colombianas y ecuatorianas del Pacífico: estudio sobre micro-evolución sociocultural." *América Indígena* 27:635-665.

Zamudio, Daniel. 1949. *El folclore musical de Colombia.* Bogotá: Revista de Indias.

Arroz Colorao:
Los Congos of Panama

Ronald R. Smith

Introduction

Congo in Panama is a complex and multi-faceted society. Among people of Afro-Hispanic descent, especially in the Atlantic region, this tradition has continued to grow since the early days of the conquest of tierra firme and has developed into an important cultural manifestation.

Throughout Latin America, the observance of carnival and its many variants has become a major event during the pre-Lenten season. Not until the end of Holy Week are people permitted such spontaneous joy and unbridled pleasures. *Congo*, as now practiced in Panama, emphasizes mimetic dance-theater, outrageous costumes, and songs rich in oral history and contemporary observation. Groups form in small coastal towns such as Salud, Palmas Bellas, María Chiquita, Portobelo, Río Indio, and Cuango. There are also important groups who perform *congadas* in the terminal city of Colon, and at times in the capital, Panama. Characteristically, *congo* groups organize before the beginning of carnival festivities. However, there are groups that maintain a communal sense of society throughout the year and exhibit a cohesiveness that often permits greater artistic development of both the group and individuals within the tradition. The majority of material collected for this study was from congo groups in Colón. The music of the Congo is vibrant, pulsating, and filled with the emotion and history of their struggles.

The core from which energy flows during performance consists of song and dance. Within *congo* tradition, there is rarely dance without song or song without dance. During performances of dance-theater,

239

there exists a symbiotic relationship between them. Song is intimately bound to its drum accompaniment and dance; however, singers often perform songs to the accompaniment of clapping hands. Occasionally, drummers exercise some measure of rhythmic and metric freedom in improvisatory flourishes and do not merely provide accompaniment figures; they weave a tapestry of intricate rhythms with the voices and handclaps. Therefore, song is important both as part of the dance accompaniment and as a means to make public general observations and expound upon traditional values. Although not unique to congo society, songs are an indispensable and primary vehicle of group expression.

The music collected touches very importantly upon the question of ethnicity — who we are, who decides, and how we negotiate our identities. In Panama there has been, for many years, a week of "folklore observations": performances, lectures, and other public events to honor the memory of Manuel Francisco Zárate, Panama's most famous folklorist. Although his professional area of expertise was physical science, perhaps chemistry, he conducted numerous field trips and collected both musical and textual materials over a range of genres and regions of Panama. Zárate especially valued the folklore of his native region, Azuero, and the town of Los Santos. Los Santos is the heart of the central provinces of Panama and an area of concentration of mestizo people. This is an important factor in the negotiation of racial and ethnic identity within the folkloric community of Panama.

The *Semana Folklórica de Manuel F. Zárate*[1] includes concerts of décima singing, art exhibits, special radio broadcasts, and folkloric performances within the capital city, especially at the Museo del Hombre Panameño. During one of the evening activities, an important folkloric troupe performed a *congada*. The Congos of Colón, a very famous group and a long-time favorite of the Zárates, came to dance and sing in his honor because he was very important in assisting this group in attaining both local and national recognition. *Congadas* once were dance-theater performances held behind buildings, in old courtyards, and on the beach in Colón (La Playita). For many years, city officials required that a police permit be obtained before they could drum, dance, and sing, since a full *congada* often lasted throughout the night. Inhabitants of Colón often rejected, feared, and despised the *congos*. Zárate, in some sense "*blanqueó*" (whitened) los congos for the general public. The first *copla* comes from a song, "Arroz Colorao."

In this song we can begin to see a facet of the conflict that characterizes race relations in Panama and other Caribbean republics.

Revellín:	Soloist:
Los blancos no van al cielo	*Whites don't go to Heaven*
por una solita mañá;	*for even one day;*
Coro:	Chorus:
Los blancos no van al cielo	*Whites don't go to Heaven*
por una solita maña;	*for even one day;*
Revellín:	Soloist:
les gusta comer panela	*they like to eat sweet bread*
sin haber sembrado caña.	*without having sown sugar cane.*

(Smith, 1976:245)

The quality of laziness or irresponsibility attributed to whites in the copla cited above is sometimes directed towards men within the congo group. The group sings the *copla* with the word hombres (men) in place of blancos (whites). The woman soloist (revellín) then sings:

> *"Siembren arroz mujeres,*
> *Siembren arroz colorao"*
> *(Sow rice women, sow brown rice!).*

When the Congos performed this song at the *Semana Folklórica*, the queen, Lilia Perea, quickly corrected her women's chorus and substituted, in a strong voice, the words: "los hombres (men)," for "mujeres los hombres." At that point the queen enters the room with a full retinue of drummers, dancers, and singers with their full dresses flowing like the giant wings of birds. The chorus answers taking the same text as their refrain. The version that I recorded in the field and the rendition recorded by Lila Cheville use the words *hombres* and *blancos* respectively. These *coplas* also extol the virtue of self-reliance among women. Within *congo* drama women are quite important and have a special strength and prominence.

Societal values that are inherent in programmatic aspects of the *juego de congo* (mimetic theater), as well as in social aspects of the society, are often expressed both figuratively and symbolically through song texts. Similarly, congos openly express antagonism against both whites and men, symbolic of colonial Spanish oppression, in one of the more popular *coplas* within the tradition. If this be true, then why did Queen Perea instruct her women to change the words? Perhaps they censored their lyrics on this specific occasion because they were performing in honor of Manuel Zárate and under the patronage of both Dora Zárate and the national museum. The queen and her court within the *congada*, in *La Playita*, would have sung what they were accustomed to singing. However, she was also very aware of the political implication of "slapping your host in the face" in public, so "*los hombres*" was the preferred text at that time. At other times the *los señores* is substituted for *blancos* or *hombres*.

One of the problems experienced by some Panamanians is a duality or ambivalence about who they are and how to negotiate divisions between the various racial and ethnic identities which constitute the country's population. The predicament is that Panama has always been a land of transit, and much of its fortunes have depended upon decisions made by people and administrative centers outside its territorial boundaries and control. Panama has been owned and occupied by many since the time of the first encounters with Europe in the 16th century. The republic of Panama did not actually become a political entity, as we know it today, until 1903, and even then, the U.S. government encouraged Panamanians to emancipate themselves from Colombia.

The most famous part of Panama's real estate is, of course, its inter-oceanic canal. According to the renegotiated treaty, jurisdiction and full control of the canal and the five-mile-wide zone that borders both shores for its entire length will revert to Panamanian rule in the year 2000. When I first visited Panama, I did not fully understand some of the internal social and political conflicts. For instance, when I changed American dollars the transaction was taxed and I received *balboas* in exchange. However, the actual currency received was U.S. dollar bills.

My attempts to describe my research topic of *música Afro-Panameña* also met with some disbelief and often correction. My statements were frequently met with the comment "There is none." When speaking of the music performed in Garachiné, a town on the gulf of Garachiné in the Darién jungle, or on the Isla del Rey, the largest island in the Pacific archipelago, we might be permitted to call this "black" or "Afro" music. Only when I spoke directly of *los congos* did my focus become clear to the general public. I was soon aware that the categories and concepts that I sought to investigate were not suitable within the Panamanian context. The term "Afro" could not be used; it was something people did not accept. So I learned to describe my research and musical interests in terms such as *música folklórica* or *música tradicional.* These terms were greeted with "Oh fine, then you want to go to the Azuero peninsula to hear the music of the *décima,* the *punto,* and the *tamborito.*"

Although there seems to be a national consensus that Panama's folklore is best represented and appreciated through the traditions of the central provinces, a major thrust of the folkloric work completed by Zárate, the musical substructures of many genres are distinctly African derived. What we find is a mixture of Spanish texts; African drums, movement style and values and costumes derived from both African slave dress and campesino clothing. With only one exception,[2] drums used in accompaniment of dances in Panama are of African derivation, as is the style of the dancing. The national dance, *el tamborito,* a couple dance accompanied by a consort of four drums, and *la cumbia,* a group dance in which couples move in a counterclockwise circle, are excellent examples of the kind of music and movement that characterize many Afro-Latin dances throughout the Americas.

Obviously, the early inhabitants of the isthmus of Panama were various Native American groups, a few of which still maintain some of their traditions.[3] However, in contemporary Panama, and on the national scene, they play a very minor role. The roots of the population may be found in the interbreeding of native peoples, Spaniards, and an enormous number of African slaves who not only performed tasks that supported and built the towns and cities of the isthmus, but also provided the labor force that worked the ships and mines that opened western South America.

In Panama City, differing perceptions of race and ethnicity are important for individual interaction and also form a part of some genres associated with Panama's expressive culture. For instance, both ordinary interactions and the historical literature suggest that two different kinds of African peoples are recognized in Panama: *negro colonial* (colonial negro) and *negro antillano* (Antillean negro). The distinction stems from the historical manner in which African peoples were brought to the isthmus. Those people who are descended from African slaves brought directly to the peninsula during the colonial period are termed coloniales, and for the most part are Spanish dominant, while those descended from peoples who arrived later from English-speaking Caribbean islands such as Jamaica are called *antillanos*. Many people in this latter group were brought to Panama during the 18th and 19th centuries to work in the construction of the trans-isthmian railroad and the inter-oceanic canal.

These distinctions, though in some way arbitrary, are in fact believed and have formed a conduit for personal and social interaction. Local scholarly studies have authenticated these concepts and terminology, and the speaking of English and the practice of Protestant religious beliefs among the *antillanos* still prevail. Thus, the separation is now deeply rooted in the minds of the general public, though much intermarriage and mixing has taken place over the years.

Of the thousands of slaves brought to Panama, most were to be transported somewhere else, although a sizable number became the inhabitants of Atlantic coastal towns, major port cities, and the capital. The port of entry on the Atlantic coast, Portobelo, was a major link in the chain between Panama City and Seville, Spain. African slaves worked as stevedores on the flotillas of Spanish galleons (*ferias*) that visited each year, plied the mule trains that carried gold, silver, timber, and other goods to and from western South America, manned the boats on the Chagres River, and carried all sorts of merchandise on the Camino Real between Panama City, on the Pacific, and Portobelo, on the Atlantic. A major consequence of this constant human flow of Africans has been a historical concentration of African-derived cultural traditions in this part of Panama.

Historical, folkloristic, and anthropological studies of Panama's people of African descent are not numerous. In fact, there are still serious lacunae, especially in the areas of music, dance, folklore, and other domains of expressive culture. The West Indians (*antillanos*) have been subjected to the least amount of investigation. George Westermann, a journalist and descendant of this group, has completed some studies, and there are a few older inquiries. However, in regard to music, there is very little with which to assess the interrelationship of African and European traditions. Research into the traditions of *negros coloniales* has been of greater interest. The champion of this study, Armando Fortune, has produced a long list of well-documented and researched articles over a period of more than twenty years. Although Fortune's historical work is not well known outside of Panama, and none of his work appears in English, it is interesting and important, and it provides us with a window on the colonial era. Fortune wrote extensively, but appears not to have utilized colonial documents in Seville, and he never left Panama. While Zárate has investigated Panama's mestizo traditions, other researchers have not provided similar documentation of the aesthetic and religious contributions that African people have made to the life of the country.

In essence, differences between *negros antillanos* and *negros coloniales* are both real and imagined. It is clear that one cannot understand the relationship of music and the African experience in Panama without examining both actual and perceived barriers to social interaction among Afro-Panamanians and the population in general. Historically, *antillanos* are English dominant and worship in the Anglican Church, while *coloniales* are Spanish dominant and worship with the majority in the Catholic faith. Cultural and social boundaries are permeable, and thus, total separation of groups is not as complete as one might imagine. Although it is now common for many families to consist of members who are descended from both groups, there is a tendency for bilingual speakers to use both languages in the home, but only Spanish in public or in official situations. There is still a strong affiliation with the Anglican Church, especially in Panama City. It is not uncommon for people who feel that they live on the periphery of a larger and better-connected majority to believe their voices are not heard. Often they will look inward, toward their group members, for support and ethnic definitions. For many years, *antillanos* were primarily residents within the Canal Zone, where they were educated in English and came into daily contact with the social values and perspectives of North Americans. Some people never really learned to speak Spanish, and, when the governments of Panama and the United States signed the new canal treaty, full Panamanian sovereignty was extended to the "Zone" in all areas. Those who had not lived in Panama and who were functionally monolingual realized that there would be problems with their full integration into Panamanian life and culture. At the same time, they wanted to maintain some semblance of their former lives and social cohesion.

In the late 1970s, a group of *antillanos* adopted a proactive stance that they hoped would serve to better integrate them into Panamanian society. They supported issues that were important to the society at large, and hoped to erode barriers to social and linguistic interaction among *antillanos* and coloniales, as well as Panamanians who did not belong to these groups. Antillano leaders emulated the principles and values of the Black Power movement, then very strong among African-Americans in the United States. Students, housewives, architects, clergy, lawyers, medical personnel, laborers, teachers, and many others subscribed to values which they believed were shared by the general society. "Acción Reivindicación del Negro Panameño" (*"Revindication" for the Panamanian Negro*) is the phrase they used to give philosophical form to their movement; however, they named the organization UNNEP (La Unión Nacional del Negro Panameño) (National Panamanian Negro Union).

The group's document of principles, entitled "Qué es UNNEP?" (What is UNNEP?),[4] reads in part as follows:

La Unión Nacional del Negro Panameño (UNNEP), es la organización que recoge en su seno a obreros, empleados públicos, profesionales, estudiantes, intelectuales, empresarios negros de ascendencia antillana y colonial, y sus principios fundamentales son:

- Luchar por la igualdad de las razas.
- Luchar por mejorar las condiciones de vida y trabajo del negro Panameño, del campesino, del indígena, del obrero, del pueblo en general.
- Luchar para las paz entre pueblos.
- Elevar el nivel cultural y política del negro Panameño y del pueblo en general.
- Luchar por la unidad de todos los negros y junto al campesino, obrero, al indio, luchar en contra de la opresión imperialista y por la liberación nacional.
- Restablecer el aporte económico, cultural y político 'del negro a la liberación nacional.'[5]

Leaders underscored important principles in the document described above, such as contributions by Afro-Panamanians to Panama. "Sus objetivos son: - Divulgación en nuestro país de la cultura tradicional de los negros y los aportes sociales económicos y político en nuestro país. - Propiciar la unidad y hermandad con las organizaciones negras de otros países que al igual que UNNEP luchen contra el colonialismo."[6] Not only did UNNEP leaders elaborate upon the philosophical basis of the organization, they adopted goals (to help humanity), symbols (the national emblem and flag of the Panamanian Republic), and colors (red, green, and black).

Musically, UNNEP and its leaders also tried to define an artistic or culturally relevant stance to support their goal of unity. On 10 June 1979, musicians, poets, political activists, and the general public gathered in the auditorium of the Episcopal School of San Cristóbal[7] (Parque Lefevre, Panama City) for the first calypso contest. The *antillanos* made a conscious effort to underscore their historical and cultural ties with the English Caribbean and the genre of calypso; however, on this occasion they sang calypsos in both English and Spanish. Some performers sang lyrics that focused upon issues of local importance, while others contained more overt political messages. Instrumental musicians played guitars and drums. It should be noted that on this occasion members of Los Congos also danced and sang and a number of young poets read their poetry. An important feature of the first and subsequent events[8] was the bilingual presentation of both music and poetry. There was a strong feeling of solidarity for participants and audience alike. For many people, UNNEP signaled a beginning of reconciliation as well as a means through which to incorporate all citizens as Panameños, and thus erase some of their distinctions.

During the event of 10 June, Walter Smith Barroja, an *antillano* who worked within the medical establishment of the Canal Zone, presented a poem he had written. This is an important poem, since it provides a glimpse of the inner feelings and conflicts that motivated the actions described above.

> *¡Despierta!*
> *¡Despierta!*
> *¡Negro, despierta!*
> *El barco ya zarpó*
> *Y te has quedado atrás.*
> *¡Despierta!*
> *Negro...*
> *Tienes que despertar*
> *Y tu canoa tallar.*
> *Tienes que echarla al mar,*
> *Y ponerte a remar.*
> *Remar, remar y remar...*
> *Solo así, prodrás alcanzar*
> *el barco, que a la rezaga*
> *te dejó*
> *¡Despierta!*
> *¡Negro, despierta!*
>
> Walter E. Smith Barroja[9] 1975

"Wake up," he says, "Wake up, Negro, wake up! The boat has gone and left you behind. Wake up! You must wake up and carve out your canoe[10] and launch it into the sea. Begin to row, row, row, and row. Only thus will you be able to reach the boat that left you in its wake. Wake up! Negro, wake up!." This is a very powerful statement of the deep-seated feelings of isolation and rejection experienced by *antillanos.* In their own country they did not feel at home and felt left out. Compounding the problem is the fact that Americans exported to Panama some of their worst racial attitudes and biases.

Antillanos have, in effect, redefined their cultural reality in Panama. Instead of traditional songs, calypsos and quadrilles of Jamaica, Trinidad, and Antigua that they performed many years ago, musicians and poets communicate bilingually and prefer sounds and images that draw them closer to the mass of Afro-Panamanian society. Religious observances and the singing of Protestant hymns have, however, not been lost. Cultural identity is important in Panama where everyone has a music, a dance, and a costume.

I began this paper with a short introduction to the music and values of *los congos.* The African heritage of Panama can best be seen in the royal court of the queen, mimetic dance-theater, animal characters, and pulsating drum rhythms of this negro colonial tradition. It is not surprising, then, that other Afro-Panamanian groups have adopted this musical style as an emblem of "African-ness" in Panama.

A prominent figure of conflict and deceit in *congo* tradition is the Devil. For example, variants of a text that might be sung for the Devil's dance clearly describe both the *congo* vision of this supernatural being and measures that they take against him.

> *Anoche soñé con un hombre*
> *de dientes de oro*
> *y me quiso llevá*
> *ayayai!*
> *el diablo tum-tum...*
>
> (Zárate 1971,128)[11]

Congos are afraid of this golden-toothed devil and are on constant alert against the abduction of members of their court by him. Gold, though a symbol of riches for some, is almost synonymous with evil in this instance as well as other dramatic tableaux. *Pajarito* (little bird), son of the Queen María Merce and the chief messenger of the court, and *Amarrador,* a guardian figure that later binds the devil, are supposed to protect the princesses (mininas). The function of *Amarrador* is to capture the devil so that he can be baptized by a priest and thus be returned to a state of grace. Among some groups, *Pajarito* betrays his people and mother for the promise of gold. Heroic actions against such a powerful figure are represented in this variant.

> *El diablo de Vicente...*
> *ese diablo tan malo...*
> *Vamo a amarralo*
> *a ese diablo tum-tum...*
> *Ayayai..!*
> *el diablo tum-tum.*
>
> *The devil of Vincent...*
> *That devil so bad...*
> *Let's tie up*
> *This devil tum-tum...*
> *Ayayai..!*
> *The devil tum-tum.*
>   (Zárate 1971, 127)[12]

There seems to be no universal mechanism for the judgment of songs as either good or bad in themselves. Relative value seems more a function of their suitability to the immediate situation, popularity of the subject treated, and the *revellín's* quality of presentation in performance. It should also be noted that the choral response and ensemble of drummers play important roles in the judging of effectiveness.

Realistically speaking, *congo* song repertoire is unlimited in number and subject matter. Relatively simple techniques of construction in both melodic and textual lines permit numerous combinations and variations which, though similar at times, still allow singers flexibility and even subtle manipulation of language. Although new songs may be generated almost every time a group performs, there are some which seem to be part of a common repertoire and appear time after time in many groups. These songs are most often connected to specific characters within the drama or recurrent situations. The most important subjects are the queen, *Pajarito,* the flag (or emblem of the group) and those songs which deal with pleasure and the comical activities of groups during carnival.

Dr. Lila Cheville, a specialist in dance and author of several books that deal with traditional dance in Panama, initially spent the years 1962-65 in the Republic of Panama documenting a variety of folkloric dance traditions that culminated in her dissertation. She has continued to the present in similar research. Part of her work included recording of *congo* dances, both choreographic aspects and the music which was used to accompany *congadas.* During frequent field trips to Panama, I was also fortunate to record (on film and audiotape) members of the group and songs that had been recorded some ten years earlier by Dr. Cheville. More than one hundred songs gathered during both our trips are the basis for many of the following stylistic judgments. In addition, my personal experiences with members of various groups and other informants have added much to my understanding of *congo* aesthetic, musical style, and practices.

Medium

On the one hand, there is a wide variety of songs. On the other, the variety of media used for musical expression is somewhat limited, concentrating solely upon voice and drums with handclapping functioning as both an organizing device and a percussive element within the ensemble. Each component of the total musical ensemble (voices and drum group) is, within itself, an integrated ensemble whose members function in specific ways and according to predetermined relationships.

The vocal group, consisting of a *revellín* (song leader) and the *segundas* (chorus), is always composed of women. It is not uncommon for the segundas to include young women and small girls (meninas or princesas). These same women are also members of the queen's court; they leave their singing positions behind the drummers freely during the *congada* to dance in the central area. The energy and excitement brought to their performance is a major ingredient in each congo song. The responsibility for animating much of each event rests upon them. From time to time, depending on the availability of women and the size of the entire *congo* group, men might join the singing of the chorus. Only in the rarest of cases will a man be selected to lead a song. I have seen (and recorded) men in this role; however, the groups concerned are not very traditional and do not function with the same consistency as do *congos* who were my major informants. The one group that I saw, which was totally composed of men (in the town of Chepo), functioned only sporadically and did not exhibit the complex social organization or theatrical manifestations characteristic of other groups.

Singing style is relatively uniform from group to group, with the greatest amount of variation occurring in individual vocal ability and stamina of the *revellín*. One overriding aspect of vocal style is the use of the dynamic of forte for each song in the repertoire. There is almost no relief from this high level of volume, either during a specific composition or at any point during the *congada*. Vocal stamina is considered, among congo groups, a desirable attribute in a good *revellín*. She must be able to perform for extended periods of time (a *congada* may last all night or at the least several hours) as well as project both her melodic material and text over both the chorus and instruments. The number of segundas may vary at times, while the instrumental ensemble always consists of four drums. Extraneous noises, sounds of the court, and spectators all add to the general soundscape and competition. From the moment she sets the tonality of a selection and its beginning tempo, the *revellín* throws her voice forward with unflagging energy, continuing in this manner until the end of the composition. The segundas must also have a good deal of stamina, though their role is not as demanding as that of their leader, for they too sing during the entire congada. The dynamic level of the refrain which they sing is also very high; however, the larger number of voices permits each individual to conserve more energy than does the leader. The special sound of a *congo* woman's voice is not produced solely by a preoccupation with loud singing. Extensive use of the upper range of the voice, no vibrato and extreme vocal tension produce a timbre which can best be described as strident and penetrating. Singing in this manner does not permit much vocal coloring or subtle musical effects. Excitement and musical interest is produced, however, by combining this penetrating vocal quality with rhythmic syncopation and percussive effects in the vocal line. Vocal ornamentation is not particularly important in the style. The few ornaments which do exist consist of small falling melodic motifs usually found at the ends of phrases, vocables with no semantic meaning, and a variety of exclamations which are merely vehicles for the expression of emotion during participation in both song and dance.

Although specific drum names may vary from group to group, the ensemble always consist of four instruments. Performers usually sit while holding their drums between their knees, except for the caja which is held on the thigh or rested on the ground. They are so arranged that each occupies a specific position relative to the other. The *caja,* a cylindrical two-headed drum and the only one played with sticks, provides a steady background of unchanging rhythmic patterns to which the other drums play; it is very important but receives little attention from most spectators. The *hondo (jondo), seco,* or *llano,* each of which can occupy the role of principal drum, carry the weight of rhythmic improvisation and tonal variation. Each of these drums is somewhat conical and has a single head. Their construction, playing style, and integration are closely related to central African traditions. In theory, the principal drum does not have to adhere to a specific rhythmic pattern and can improvise. Of course, he must maintain a connection to the basic meter and closely observe movements of the dancers within the central area of the *palacio.* The other drummers play complementary patterns that vary with less frequency or variety. Their relationships are more or less set and maintained by drummers in the ensemble. In actuality, however, drummers can switch drum positions and even instruments from performance to performance. Since all drums, except the *caja,* are of similar design and size, one may perform in the role of the other with a minimum of difficulty. In addition, some individual performers are so highly regarded for their ability and excellence that they may dominate a performance even as a secondary drummer.

Individual drummers can play in such a manner that the tonal quality produced by the drum does not vary to any great extent; concentration is then upon rhythmic variety. There are others who work diligently to produce tonal and timbral changes during a composition. A variety of effects are achieved by striking the drum at different points on the head, using the hand to mute the head while it is being struck with the other, and rapid alternation of hands or fingers as they strike the head along the edge. Elevating the drum from the floor or the ground by lifting it with the knees causes some degree of variation in the resonance and is often utilized by the drummer who occupies the lead position. During rapid eight-note passages of the lead drum (when the drum is said to *repicar),* the drum is raised slightly from the ground and produces a high-pitched, bell-like tone which carries throughout the ensemble. As in the vocal ensemble, the dynamic of forte is ever present. Due to the fact that there is no text for them to manipulate, performers must make variations in timbre, pitch, and rhythm through quite different means.

Themes

Themes in *congo* song may vary greatly and often touch upon quite diverse aspects of congo and everyday life. As Queen Lilia Perea once said: "*Congos* do not keep secrets. They see something and immediately sing about it." On the surface, her statement is quite true; however, there are important secrets among the *congos* that are not shared with outsiders. Thus, when they comment on the world about them, they sing of what they observe about others and maintain a closeness about those parts of their tradition that must remain in-group knowledge. Although songs are sung in Spanish, words and phrases from a special *congo* dialect are often used. Outsiders cannot understand this speech and think it merely consists of unimportant vocables. As a result, the range of subjects is great and includes everyday occurrences, individual characters in the juego, and incumbents of the various roles. Sometimes there are even songs about important visitors or members of the general Panamanian community who have come in contact with *congo* society.

It is difficult to make a clear typology for the thematic material of congo repertoire except to say that most songs may be grouped into several broad categories. But there is another problem when one actually begins to arrange the material. *Congo* songs, as with other songs sung for drum dances (*bailes de tambor*) in Panama, are usually named for the lines of the refrains and not the verses sung by the *revellín*. In some cases this is the same textual material; in other instances there is a marked difference. Often, a *revellín* will begin by singing the refrain (sometimes with the chorus and sometimes as a means to give them the desired pitch, tempo, and spirit). She is then free to improvise new lines upon the theme and/or recombine parts of lines she has sung on other occasions. Textual material, though returning to the main refrain from time to time, may range far afield during the composition.

The general areas of congo thematic material are songs that discuss major or minor personages in the *juego:*

> *Anda buscando al Drake (Sir Francis Drake, the pirate, is an ally of the cimarrones in congo juegos.)*
> *Hojarasquín*
> *Antonio pico pico (a version of Hojarasquín)*
> *Pajarito venía volando*
> *Dame la mano prima (song for the queen)*

> *Dame la vida angué (queen's song)*
> *Viva la Reina*
> *Lilia là Reina*[13]
> *El Diablo, tum, tum*

Animal characters

> *Ave Gavilán*
> *Paloma*
> *Culebra*
> *Tengo mi caballo*
> *El torito*

Individuals

> *Cristina Sierra llorará*
> *Inglés*
> *La Sirena*
> *Manuel*
> *Micaela*
> *Morena (version of Micaela)*
> *Los embajadores*[14]
> *Que viva mi General!*
> *Que viva la Guardia Nacional*

Songs which deal with congo activity and emotions

> *Siembren arroz colorao*
> *La Libertad*
> *Dale la bandera*
> *Mamá yo estoy llorando*
> *Arriba la bandera*
> *Ola de la mar*
> *Auxilio señores*
> *Sabe la vida buena*
> *Corazón llorar*
> *Tiene que querer la monte*
> *Esa Panameña quiere tomar*
> *Vámonos*
> *Yo soy marinera*
> *Yo me voy por la mañana*
> *Yo soy feliz*
> *Y soy boiteña*

It might be possible to subdivide the categories even more; however, it would not be very profitable, nor would it really give us much more information as to the nature of these songs. Although none of the songs is totally programmatic, some do provide a measure of support for the theatrical situation. Very often the themes of mimetic-dance and textual material do not coincide.

A few of the songs mentioned above show the mechanism of text composition more clearly than do other songs in the tradition. As mentioned earlier, institutions or individuals who come in contact with congos and are accepted or disliked by them can be integrated thematically into the song repertoire. This was precisely the case with the songs "Los Embajadores," "Que Viva mi General," and "La Universidad."

Each of these songs referred to recent occasions that were then still fresh in the minds of *congo* members. The Congos of Colón had performed for the first time in an organized public folkloric festival under the aegis of Manuel Zárate, at the University of Panama. This most important occasion for them was commemorated in song by the *congos* who still sing of the time with great joy and excitement.

General of the Brigade Omar Torrijos Herrera was once the most powerful military figure in Panama. Lilia Perea and her Congo group in Colón were most successful in maintaining a very friendly relationship with officers of the National Guard stationed in their city. Torrijos, through his subordinates, cooperated to the extent that he often provided a National Guard bus for transport of the congo group when it was invited to perform in the interior of the country. On these occasions the group was always accompanied by an official driver and an officer of the Guard. Lilia Perea's group is the only *congo* group that seems to have been given this type of official recognition, and in the song "Que Viva mi General!"[15] they celebrate their relationship with General Omar Torrijos.

One immediately notices that there is a minimum of real information in the text. The general is neither described, named, or even discussed throughout the song which lasted some two minutes, 36 seconds on this particular performance. For members of the *congo* group, as well as the general population, there is no ambiguity, for Omar Torrijos is "the" general in the National Guard of Panama. This composition, sung in what *congos* call the "terrible" meter (2/4), conforms to traditional *congo* style in all respects; however, it is more interesting from a musical, rather than textual point of view. The extensively used vocables sometimes function mainly as rhythmic filler, while at other times they provide time and an opportunity for the *revellín* to think of new material that she wishes to sing. Through the use of vocables she can also project the capabilities of her voice. She starts very slowly and intones the first few lines, outlining the tonic minor triad. The tonality of the song is readily established as E minor. The tempo and meter are not completely fixed, however, and do not become fully evident until at least the fourth verse sung by the *revellín*. At this point the drums enter, and the women of the chorus attain a steady tempo with their handclapping. When the meter was finally established, after the *revellín's* rhapsodic introduction, the metronome marking was ascertained to be 132 at the end of the composition. The song began at a marking near 121. Throughout this composition both the *revellín* and the chorus sing the same melody, which is not always the case in *congo* song.

Another song which clearly shows the *congo* penchant for encapsulating immediate surroundings into song is "Los Embajadores." Although the song text deals only with two people, Julio Cesar Schara (a former cultural attaché of the Mexican Embassy) and Claude Leman (a French exchange professor of mathematics), there were in fact at least five persons in the committee which came to visit Lilia Perea. Dora Zárate (referred to as "la profesora" in the song) and Mr. Barrera were also part of the group which came to Colón to arrange the participation of Lilia's *congo* group in yet another festival of music from the province of Colón and the Atlantic coastal region. The Congos were very impressed and honored by the appearance of two foreign guests and thus immortalized the event in song.

This example, approximately of the same duration (2' 23") as the previous example, and also in the "terrible meter" (2/4), presents quite a different picture of Congo compositional skill. This time the *revellín's* goal is to give very specific information about an event of some importance to the group. Although the *revellín* utilizes the same melodic material as the chorus, she does not, in this case, repeat any of the textual material until the very end of the song. The description of the visit, the participants, the purpose, the menu, and its consequences, as well as the possible publicity to be achieved (via television) are well documented in this song. The importance of the message in this song is highlighted by minute detail and a more limited use of vocables as well as the decreased tempo (mm 96-108). In addition, the drum ensemble and chorus begin immediately at their customary places (they enter with the first singing of the refrain by the chorus). The entire composition is very regular and predictable, from a Congo viewpoint. There is, however, an interesting phenomenon which occurs in the leader's performance. Word accents have been distorted to meet musical demands, sometimes creating semantic problems. The use of Congo dialect (for example, *desate = desastre)* and the tendency to drop or to accent the final syllable of words further confuses the issue. These aspects of Congo speech cannot be dealt with here, but form an important link with other Afro-Hispanic communities and language.

Both songs presented above are relatively short in total duration when compared to most songs in performance; their duration is more a function of time strictures connected with public performances. At other times the lack of fecundity of the *revellín's* powers to improvise may shorten a song. The author has had the opportunity to record some songs (in typical circumstances) that have lasted more than ten minutes. If the *revellín* has a good grasp of the material (having sung it many times before) and there are no time limitations, such as is the case in a normal *congada,* it is quite possible for one song to last fifteen minutes. Such extensions of this type may also be partially due to a greater emphasis on dance. The creative use of vocables, recombination of segments of previous verses, and ordinary repetition permit a *revellín* to sing for extended periods of time.

Structure

The basic structural technique of Congo song may be described as additive. The term additive in this work is used to designate a technique in which each verse of new line sung by the *revellín* may be interchangeable with another. Even in the case of the composition "Los Embajadores," it is possible to rearrange sections of the text and still tell the story efficiently. The technique is even more clear in "Que Viva mi General!." Within this system of composition, we find two basic types of text organization. In the simplest form of song, the *revellín* sings one or two lines of text and is immediately answered by the chorus. The chorus response may also be one or two lines. When the *revellín* sings two lines in succession, they usually complement each other or complete a thought. However, when she sings one line and is answered directly by the chorus, her succeeding line may not complete a thought and often is the same line repeated. In this form, the melodic material of leader and chorus often also complement each other. Such techniques may thus permit the development of compositions of substantial length. In the more complicated form of text organization, the *revellín* sings a full quatrain (*copla)* and is answered by a *copla* from the chorus. The textual material may be composed on one complete thought or may be constructed of a recurrent phrase which precedes, follows, or is interspersed with the new material. It is obvious that many more variations on this model are possible. Therein lies the excitement and vitality of Congo song.

The entrance song of *Pajarito* clearly exhibits the former additive technique of composition. The *revellín* and chorus play upon the assonance and recurrent final accented syllable (*asonancia aguda*) of the words *dolor* (pain), *gorrion* (sparrow), *comay* (*comadre* = godmother or intimate woman friend) and *compay* (*compadre* = godfather) in their extension of the material.

Changes which occur in the refrain textually may result from confusion and the unprepared combination of variants by members of the chorus. Though not very common, it is also not a disruptive force in the compositional process.

The songs in which the *revellín* sings a complete *copla* before the chorus answers are not as prevalent as the former type. They are, however, some of the most interesting, for they allow a greater degree of variation on the part of the soloist. The structure of a *copla* also permits the presentation of narrative songs in a more concentrated manner. Simple organization sometimes causes a fragmentation of the narrative and a consequent disorganization and separation of related thoughts. "Los Embajadores" is an excellent example of the narrative techniques which can be exercised in *copla* form. An example of the use of the recurrent phrase in the *copla* form is clearly shown in the composition "Ola de la mar."

There is no predetermined agreement on which strophe or *copla* is final; the composition merely ends when the *revellín* and the group decide it should. Remember that this song performance, as others presented here, was recorded in public performance and thus suffers from strictures of time.

Another important structural aspect of Congo song is that of word accent and stress. It is clear from the examples already shown that there is a preponderance of stress upon the final syllable of the final word of each sentence and phrase. Often this stress violates normal word prosody or speech mode. Such emphasis upon final syllables is found in all Congo songs and in their dialect. At times there is also confusion in meaning which may be attributed to the final accent not coinciding with normal speech stress. There is another more subtle aspect of stress, being the relative line accents present in the copla form of song. The final accents of lines one and two are often strong, while that of line three is weaker. Line four is also strong, making a pattern of strong, strong, weak, strong. This effect is often mirrored in the musical material by a lengthening of the note at the end of the phrase which occurs on the accented syllable.

Rhyme does not seem to hold too much importance in Congo tradition. Simpler selections do not restrict themselves to an exclusive use of either consonant or assonant rhyme. *Copla* versions, however, are constructed so that most often there is a series of assonant rhymes. *Congo* textual style accentuates this propensity by the use of the final syllable stress.

Musical Materials

Congo concept of meter, though not very complex, seems to have a definite pattern of utilization and preference between the two meters used. The predominant meter is "terrible" (2/4). Most songs and dances are performed in this meter. In addition to strong accents that are played by the *caja*, always outlining the basic pulse, the women's handclapping reinforces the main subdivisions. Often, at the beginning of the composition, handclaps mark only the first beat of each measure. Another important characteristic is a tendency within the ensemble to increase the tempo almost immediately. Entrance of drums and chorus (most often simultaneously) is only one stage in the process of acceleration. Each subsequent entrance of the *revellín* or *segundas* is occasion for a slight increase in tempo. Although most songs accelerate during performance, there is no regulation nor standardization of the process or rate of increase in speed. At times the drummers act as brakes, holding the entire ensemble in a state of equilibrium by maintaining their tempo and resisting attempts of the singers to accelerate. When the composition has reached a state of equilibrium, the women clap only on the main subdivisions of the measure. Music in *congo* tradition is basically isometric; however, subtle shifting musical and textural accents often contribute to an effect approaching multiple meter. This phenomenon is not as systematic as in West African music and thus can occur at any point during the composition. Shifts in metrical accent occur most often in the solo melodic line, although the chorus refrain may be set off against the major drum accents also creating a dynamic rhythmic tension.

The "*atravesao*" meter (6/8) is not as common as "terrible" and appears approximately in only ten percent of the examples. Despite its low profile, *atravesao* is used for two of the most important characters and dance sequences. Among topical songs sung in *atravesao* are found one for the queen — "Dame la mano prima" — and another for her son *Pajarito*— "Pajarito venía a volá." There are, of course, a few other songs that use the same meter and treat all sorts of themes. It is important to note here that *atravesao* meter is also accompanied by a dance with different choreographic organization than "terrible." Although *Pajarito* dances in both meters, his theme songs are cast in *atravesao.*

Congas tend to think of the two meters as having different aesthetic characteristics and describe them in terms of their relative tempi. *Atravesao* is considered to be the faster of the two. Analysis of recorded examples show that there is no consistently appreciable difference in the two meters; either in their lower tempi or in the final and highest metronome marking. The perception of speed is probably a function of the greater density of actual notes in 6/8 as compared with 2/4. Dancers perform their basic movements on the principal subdivisions of the measure as do the women who clap their hands (first and fourth eighth notes). During the *atravesao,* drummers play running eighth note figures above the basic patter kept by the *caja.*

Metronome indications range from approximately 86 beats per minute to 135. Songs such as "Pajarito venía volá" (112-120 MM; "Inglés" (120 MM); "Rol Inglés (134); "Amo Amo" (92-116 MM); and "Christina Sierra Llorar" (104-132 MM) are among the fastest in the repertoire that I found and are all in the 6/8 meter. However, there are songs in 2/4 performed at these tempi. An average range of variation within the tradition is approximately 10 points (i.e., 92-102 MM) per composition.

Congo melodic material is characterized by a syllabic setting of the text which is always sung in unison. None of the examples recorded by Dr. Cheville or myself, nor any that I heard in Panama, used the technique of chordal harmony. All songs are cast in the diatonic scale, with the vast majority being sung in major mode. They often vary in tonality according to the capabilities of the soloist's voice and her vocal range. She chooses a key spontaneously each time a song is sung, using her experience and knowledge of the range and nature of melodic movement to condition her choice. However, there have been times when the *revellín* began too high to complete the song comfortably and thus had to stop, since modulation to other keys is not practiced in this tradition. At times, the range is also too wide for chorus members and thus adds to the stridency of the upper part of their tessitura. There seems to be no correlation between textual themes or song types and either the mode or tonality chosen. It should be noted that songs in the minor mode constitute approximately only ten percent of the sample repertoire.

Most songs fit comfortably within the range of an octave, yet there are some that encompass a range of an octave and a third or fifth ("Que viva mi General!"). Problems with range often arise from development strategies of the *revellín*. Recurrent lines, especially when they have little rhythmic or textual variation, may be sung an octave higher than they first appear in the song. This type of variation is always found in the simpler song form, since the message load of text is much lower and sometimes obscured by the extreme tightness of the voice. Use of the upper octave increases both the distortion and stridency of the leader, she being the only member of the ensemble who uses this technique. Syncopation is sometimes found concurrently with the technique of octave displacement of the local line (singing the same or similar material an octave higher).

Phrase structure in Congo song is very predictable and most often regular. Whether the meter is 6/8 or 2/4, the practice consists of using a binary phrase structure. Thus, the *revellín* sings her opening phrase and is then answered in a phrase of equal length by the chorus. These musical phrases may contain varying numbers of syllables or words; however, they are adjusted musically so that they take the same amount of metrical time. The simpler song form exhibits a two-measure phrase sung by the *revellín,* which is subsequently answered by a two-measure phrase sung by the chorus. The only variation of this form occurs at the beginning of songs in which the *revellín* sings a two-line antecedent phrase, which is answered by the one-line refrain characteristic of the form. In the *copla* form, phrases are also binary in structure. The antecedent phrase (soloist) is longer and may assume a length of eight measures. Again, the consequent phrase sung by the chorus will be of equal length. Slight variations in the length of phrases of each part in the ensemble are due to the use of upbeats and overlapping phrases between the *revellín* and the chorus. These are only minor variations and do not in any way change the basic binary structure or feeling of symmetry achieved within the song.

The shape of a characteristic melodic line can best be described as sharply ascending in the antecedent phrase and rapidly descending during the refrain to the point from which it arose. Some songs display a terraced-like form in both the ascent and descent. There seems to be no significant deviation from this general plan, although there are variations in degree. In *copla* form, the first three lines may be handled in a much more flexible manner (the first still ascending, often to the highest note of the *revellín's* line); however, the last line closes by descending to the lowest point of the composition. This note is most often the tonic or key tone. Phrases end in various ways with a decided preference for cadences that incorporate descending seconds and thirds.

On the whole, *congo* style incorporates spontaneous variation and improvisation of both text and melody at its core. There are also conservative forces within the compositional practice that counteract this tendency. Two of these factors are the call-and-response vocal style that rests heavily upon the ostinato refrain of the chorus and the identification of a group of songs with specific characters. The choral ostinato, more often than not, is more complex melodically and rhythmically than the soloist's lines. Songs most often take their titles from the words sung in the refrain. Thus, they seem to change less often and dramatically over a period of time. The sheer number of times a refrain appears in a song tends to fix its text and melody firmly in the minds of both performers and spectators. Minor word substitution does not affect the overall pattern. The more complex *copla* refrains are, however, subject to greater variation, although the line(s) from which the title or theme is chosen tend to remain more fixed.

There is a remarkable consistency of both text and melodic material between versions of songs for *Pajarito* and the queen over a number of years. One of several reasons might be that both roles are essential to the proper functioning of the society and theatrical episodes. In addition, cohesiveness of this specific group and consolidation of *congo* activity has added to what might be called a re-fertilization of the tradition.

African musical heritage, in the form of drums and musical practices, has become so intertwined with musical traditions of Panama that it is difficult to separate them from what most people recognize as *"música folklórica."* The contribution of Africans and their descendants in Panama has been great and constitutes a veritable river of aesthetic power that deeply feeds the Panamanian artistic soul.

Notes

1.   The annual festival is often held in the month of February and has been chaired annually by his widow, Doña Dora Pérez de Zárate.

2.   Some forms of the *caja* or the larger *redoblante* (both double-headed cylindrical drums played with sticks) are quite similar to European military field drums. Differences may be found in the manner in which the heads are attached and whether the head is held by a wooden rim or wrapped with a twisted vine (*bejuco*).

3.   The most prominent group, the Cuna, resides in *Las Mulatas* Islands off the Atlantic coast and has maintained a measure of independence and integrity of their traditions throughout Panama's history. The men have long been involved in activities that have brought them into close contact with other members of Panamanian society and have taken to wearing western clothes. The women, on the other hand, still wear traditional dress, gold earrings, and bright-colored cords binding their ankles, even when they have taken up residence in the capital with their husbands. Other groups are the Guaymi in the province of Bocas del Toro, and the Chocó in the region of Darién.

4.   UNNEP was founded 20 August 1979 in Panama City. The unpublished, mimeographed document from which the principles are quoted was not dated.

5.   Advocate the equality of races.

> Advocate the improvement of life and work conditions for Panamanian blacks, native peoples, agricultural workers, and people in general.

> Advocate peace among peoples.

> Elevate the cultural and political level of Panamanian negroes and the general public.

> Struggle for the unity of all negroes and, with agricultural workers, other workers, and native people, fight against imperialist oppression and for national liberation.

> Reestablish economic, cultural, and political support for the Negro as part of national liberation.

6.   "Whose objectives are: To promote better understanding in our country of black traditional culture and their social, economic, and political contributions. To promote unity and brotherhood with black organizations of other countries that, like UNNEP, struggle against colonialism."

7. The Episcopal school and church, San Cristóbal, has served as an important center for *antillano* cultural and religious activities for many years. Instruction in the school is given in both English and Spanish.

8. On Father's Day (17 June 1979), performers again presented a concert at San Cristóbal. A reporter from the Spanish-language newspaper *La Estrella de Panamá* reported on both events.

9. To my knowledge, this poem and others that I received from Mr. Smith have never been published. They were given to me on the same mimeographed sheets that contain the fundamental principles of UNNEP.

10. The verb *"tallar"* means to sculpt, and in Panama, this would mean to construct a boat from the trunk of a tree. The dugout canoe is very widely utilized, and people have been known to travel more than fifty miles to sea in them using power motors.

11. Dora Pérez de Zárate, *Textos del Tamborito Panameño* (Panama: Impresora Panamá, S.A., 1971).

12. Zárate 1971. I did not include the *estribillo* which would be sung by the chorus of women. The reference to Vicente is to an actual participant in Portobelo who became well-known for his activity in this role.

13. This song is part of the repertoire of the group headed by Lilia Perea of Colón. The inclusion of the title in the listing above merely indicates the practice of composing songs for the incumbent of the queen's position.

14. This song was composed especially by the group of Lilia Perea in honor of the visit of the Cultural Attaché of the Mexican Embassy in Panama and a professor of Mathematics from France who was teaching at the University of Panamá in 1973.

15. Composed in honor of General Omar Torrijos Herrera and the Panamanian National Guard, who had been very helpful to Lilia Perea's group.

References

Bastide, Roger. 1969. *Las Américas Negras*. Transl. Patricio Azcarate. Madrid: Alianza Editorial, S.A.

Biesanz, John and Mavis. 1955. *The People of Panama*. New York: Columbia University Press.

Cheville, Lila and Richard. 1977. *Festivals And Dances of Panama*. Panama: Lila and Richard Cheville.

Drolet, Patricia L. 1980. "The Congo Ritual of Northeastern Panama: An Afro-American Expressive Structure of Cultural Adaptation." Ph.D. diss., University of Illinois.

Fortune, Armando. 1957. "Población de la Provincia de Panamá al Comienzo del Siglo XVII." *Lotería* (Panama) 2(25): 55-72.

Fortune, Armando. 1958. "Cosarios y Cimarrones en Panamá." *Lotería* (Panama) 3(33)(August).

Fortune, Armando. 1960. "Los Orígenes Africanos del Negro Panameño y Composición Étnica a Comienzos del Siglo XVIII." *Lotería* (Panama) 5(56)(July): 113-128.

Fortune, Armando. 1965. "La Sociedad de Estudios Afro-Panameños." *Lotería* (Panama) 10 (120-121): 83-85.

Fortune, Armando. 1966a. "El Prejuicio y la Discriminación Como Causas de Disturbios y Conflictos de la Personalidad. Efectos del Prejuicio y la Discriminación Sobre los Individuos Discriminados." *Lotería* (Panama) 11(128): 79-96.

Fortune, Armando. 1966b. "El Prejuicio y la Discriminación Como Causas de Disturbios Y Conflictos de la Personalidad. Efectos del Prejuicio y la Discriminación Sobre los Individuos que Imponen el Prejuicio." *Lotería* (Panama) 11(129): 64 -82.

Fortune, Armando. 1973. *Presencia Africana en la Música Panameña*. Panama: Dirección Nacional del Patrimonio Histórico, Instituto Nacional de Cultura.

Joly, Luz G. 1981. "One is None and Two is One: Development from Above and Below in North Central Panama." Ph.D. diss., University of Florida.

Smith, Ronald R. 1976. "The Society of Los Congos of Panama: An Ethnomusicological Study of the Music and Dance Theater of an Afro-Panamanian Group." Ph.D. diss., Folklore Institute, Indiana University, Bloomington, Indiana.

Torres de Arauz, Reina. 1975. *Darién: Etnoecología de una región histórica [Grupo Negro Mestizo o Afro-Colonial].* Panama: Instituto Nacional de Cultura, Dirección Nacional del Patrimonio Histórico.

Westerman, George W. 1961. "Historical Notes on West Indians of the Isthmus of Panama," *Phylon* 22:340-350.

Westerman, George W. 1975. "Blacks in the Panamanian Culture." In *The Star and Herald of Panama.*

Westerman, George W. 1980. "Los Inmigrantes Antillanos en Panamá." In *La Nación* of Panama.

Zárate, Manuel F. 1963. "Tambores de Panamá." *Folklore Americano* 11-12:5-21.

Zárate, Manuel F., and Dora P. de Zárate. 1962. *Tambor y Socavón.* Panama: Imprenta Nacional.

African Drumming from Rural Communities around Caracas and Its Impact on Venezuelan Music and Ethnic Identity

Max H. Brandt

Venezuela has been more thoroughly touched by African culture, and particularly African music, than is generally known by the outside world. Venezuelans from a variety of ethnic backgrounds are generally proud of the African side of their national cultural identity, and many express this feeling through participation in African-derived drum ensembles, either as dancers, singers, hand clappers, or actively involved spectators at traditional performances. The sense of an African past is especially evident today among young Venezuelans living in the capital city of Caracas, and particularly among students who have had some instruction in the role of Africa in Venezuelan history and ethnic composition (see Pollak-Eltz 1991). The drum ensembles with which these people are most familiar are those found in rural communities within an hour or two by highway from their home in the capital city. What are these ensembles, and how have they affected both the people who call this their own ethnic music and those people in urban areas who also feel it is a part of their cultural heritage?

North Central Venezuela and Its Subregions of Traditional Music

The central coastal region of this Caribbean and South American country, encompassing its capital city of Caracas, has been an important nucleus of African-inspired musical development since early colonial days. It was this part of Venezuela that served as the country's major gateway for most of the Africans brought either directly from Africa or indirectly from other Latin American and Caribbean locations. Within a radius of approximately 150 kilometers from Caracas, in a crescent-shaped area comprising the Federal District, the State of Miranda, and parts of the State of Aragua, exist related African-Venezuelan musical forms and instruments which have had a major impact on the national musical psyche, especially the music of the drum ensembles. Within this region are four distinct subregions, each having been prominently influenced by African music: the Litoral, Barlovento, the upper Tuy Valley, and the Valley of Guatire and Guarenas. Each has distinct but related musical traditions which are fairly well known to the large number of Venezuelans who live in this central coastal region. The patron saint of the African-Venezuelans who live here is San Juan Bautista (Saint John the Baptist), who is greatly venerated through music and dance.

NORTH CENTRAL VENEZUELA

© North-South Center

The Litoral is a coastal strip which comprises much of the Federal District. It stretches from Puerto La Mar in the west, to Chuspa in the east, with La Guaira, the port city for Caracas, at its approximate center. These towns — and others such as Catia La Mar, Naiguata, Los Caracas, La Sabana, and Caruao — have the Caribbean Sea to the north and a mountain range immediately to the south which separates them from the valley where Caracas is located. The communities along this seaside belt, which stretches for approximately 150 kilometers but is less than one or two kilometers wide in places, are significantly populated by Venezuelans of predominantly African descent. The most distinctive African-derived musical instruments of this coastal strip are very large drums most commonly referred to as *cumacos.*

Barlovento, another one of the subregions, takes its name from the Spanish word meaning "windward" or "the place from where the winds come." It lies southeast of the Litoral and is a triangular-shaped area bounded by mountains on two sides and the Caribbean Sea on a third. At its center is the delta of the Tuy River; its principal towns are Araguita, Caucagua, Panaquire, El Clavo, San José de Rio Chico, Tacarigua de Mamporal, Higuerote, and Curiepe. Up until only fifty years or so ago, before a national highway was established through its center, it was a remote region, culturally isolated from the influence of the nation's capital city. Though an important agricultural area, especially for the production of cacao, its absentee landlords and their families living in Caracas were usually reluctant to visit this region because of its reputation for malaria and other tropical maladies. Barlovento is best known for two drum types, the *mina* and *redondo* drums, and a set of bamboo stamping tubes called *quitiplás* (see Brandt 1988).

South of the Litoral and southwest from Barlovento, in neighboring areas of the states of Miranda and Aragua, are two other subregions containing distinctive musical forms and instruments which are not as well known nationally as those of the Litoral and Barlovento. The first, southwest from the coastal mountain range that separates it from Barlovento, is a valley formed by the upper Tuy River comprising, among others, the communities of Cua, Charallave, Ocumare del Tuy, San Francisco de Yare, Santa Teresa, and Santa Lucia. Here the principal musical instruments of African origin are drums closely related to the family of *redondo* drums of Barlovento, although somewhat smaller in length.

The fourth subregion, marked by another large valley between that of Caracas and the delta region of Barlovento, is dominated by two cities, Guarenas and Guatire, which only decades ago were small towns with distinctive but related musical traditions. Although these latter two subregions exhibit important African-derived music, their musical forms and instruments are not as prominent nor as renowned as those of the Litoral and Barlovento. Guatire and Guarenas are communities perhaps best known for the fiesta of San Pedro (Saint Peter) on 29 June, during which time small drums called *tamboras* are played. San Juan is also venerated here, and at one time *redondo* drums similar to those of Barlovento were used to venerate this much admired saint, but these drums were replaced by the smaller *tamboras* sometime earlier in the present century (Aretz 1967, 92).

The central region is also noted for an ensemble featuring a diatonic, Spanish-derived harp and a distinct style of music that accompanies the regional rendition of the national dance, *el joropo.* The music of this ensemble is quite different from the harp music of the plains states. The music of this ensemble, which also includes maracas and a solo male singer, is thought by some to be more African in performance style than that of the *joropo* ensemble from the plains which also features the diatonic harp.

The central coast was not the only gateway to Venezuela from Africa, of course. There were other ports of entry, and numerous African-Venezuelan musical traditions exist in various parts of the country. In Zulia, around the eastern side of Lake Maracaibo, the well-known *chimbangale* drums of San Benito are played. Further east, in the states of Falcón and Lara, *cumaco*-type drums of various names and sizes are found. Somewhat closer to Caracas are the states of Carabobo and Yaracuy, where San Juan is also the patron saint of the people. The *cumaco* type of drum is also found in some regions of the plains states, particularly in Guarico. At the eastern end of Venezuela's Caribbean coast is the State of Sucre where significant cultural interaction with the island of Trinidad has taken place. In both Sucre, around the city of Cumana, and in the nearby nation of Trinidad and Tobago, drums made from barrels of wooden staves are common.

It is the combined area of the Litoral and Barlovento, though, that has had the most influential musical impact of African significance on the country as a whole, especially through the drum ensembles. These traditions have definitely influenced the musical identity and tastes of a majority of the region's citizens, especially in recent decades. This is in large part because of the location, history, and political prominence of Venezuela's capital city, Caracas, which is at the center of this musical region, and the significant migration of Venezuelans from other parts of the country to this area during the latter part of the present century. A close look at the instruments themselves tells us more about this important link with Africa.

The Drum Types of the Region

Even a cursory examination of the basic instrumental characteristics of the region reveals obvious African influences. While Africa is noted for its vast array of musical instruments beyond the realm of membranophones, it is the drum that dominates the major ensembles of this region, as in so many other bastions of African influence in the New World. Four major drum types can be found in and around Barlovento and the Litoral.

The first is a very large drum, usually approximately two meters in length and approximately 35 to 40 centimeters in diameter which is most commonly know by the name *el cumaco*. It is either placed directly on the ground in performance or is played in an inclined position supported by two crossed poles, sometimes referred to as "scissors." In some communities of the Litoral two or three *cumacos*, placed directly on the ground for performance, are played at the same time. The largest of these drums is also know as the *burro negro* (black donkey) in some communities. On the Litoral the drum skin is always nailed to one end of the instrument. In contrast, in Barlovento, where it is always played in an inclined position, and where the drum skin is always held in place by ropes attached to pegs, it is called either *el tambor grande* (the large drum) or *el mina*. This drum is invariably made from a hardwood tree that has been hollowed out by natural means before being felled.

The shorter corresponding drums of this ensemble are made from the same log as the large drum. In some communities the smaller drum is the only one of the ensemble that stands upright during performance. In Barlovento, where no more than two drums are ever part of this ensemble, the *curbata* stands upright in traditional performance practice; the only exception to this, reported in the town of Curiepe, is when both the *mina* and the *curbata* are laid flat on the ground in the "quichimba" style of playing, which seems to be an imitation of standard performance practice of the Litoral. Like the *mina*, the *curbata* has a drum skin only at one end. It is approximately one meter in length and stands on three legs — sometimes four — that are cut from its bottom end. It also has a drum skin held in place by ropes attached to pegs. The wooden body of the larger of the two drums is almost always struck during performance by sticks called *laures*, usually by two or more musicians holding a stick in each hand.

The second drum type of the region is a friction drum that is similar in size and shape to the *curbata*. It stands upright on three or four legs cut from its body, but rather than being struck with two sticks like the *curbata*, it has a stick resting on the center of the drum skin which is rubbed in a downward motion either by bare hands or a piece of cloth. This friction drum is called *el furruco* and is probably related to the Spanish *zambomba* as well as to friction drums of African origin. It is always played in conjunction with Christmas music and is found in various forms throughout the Caribbean area of Venezuela.

The third drum type, most often referred to as the *redondo* drum, is not found in the Litoral. It has a drum skin on both ends of its body, is usually made from the light-weighted *lano* or balsa tree, and is usually around one meter in length. In playing position it is held between the legs of standing musicians and is struck with a stick held in one hand and by the fingers of the other. The tension on the drum skins is produced by strings running the length of the drum to the edges of each skin, and the inside of this drum is hourglass in shape. The term *redondo* is not taken from the round shape of the instrument itself but from the round or circular motion of its dance and the circular arena formed by spectators. It is also called *tamborcito*, meaning small drum (to distinguish it from the *tambor grande* or *mina*) and *culepuya* or *culo 'e puya* — a name that conjures up many possible meanings. Similar drums with comparable music are also found in the Tuy Valley where they are usually much shorter than the ones in Barlovento.

The fourth drum type, most often called *la tambora criolla* in Barlovento and sometimes *la tamborita* in the Litoral, is a small double-headed drum which is similar in construction to the *redondo* drum, with cords that crisscross the body of the instrument to hold the heads in place. It is normally played under the arm by a standing musician in the *aguinaldo* ensemble in conjunction with the *furruco*. A smaller *tambora* is used to accompany the singing of *fulias* and is held between the legs of seated musicians. Like the *redondo* drums, the *tambora* is made with the soft and light wood of the *lano* tree and is struck with one stick and one bare hand. Like the two other drums described above, this drum type is found throughout the region as well as in many other parts of the country.

Although technically not drums, bamboo stamping tubes called *quitiplas* are often referred to as drums by Barloventeños. These idiophones play the same rhythms and accompany the same songs and dances as the *redondo* drums. The only other drum type found in this region is a barrel drum called the *pipa* which is found only in a few communities along the Litoral, most notably in the town of Naiguata.

Ensembles of Barlovento and their Contexts

When making geographical comparisons of the four subregions, one becomes aware that the population of Barlovento is more concentrated and consolidated than that of the others and especially the Litoral, where communities are stretched along a ribbon of coastline that extends for over one hundred kilometers. Subsequently, the African musical traditions of Barlovento are somewhat more integrated than those of the other subregions, which in many respects makes Barlovento a more interesting location for musical research. Barlovento has therefore been chosen for somewhat more detailed inspection to help us understand the makeup of African-derived ensembles, their repertory, and their cultural context.

In Barlovento the four types of membranophones described above are used in varying combinations to form four distinct ensembles with specific performance contexts. These include the *mina* drum ensemble, the *redondo* drum ensemble, the *velorio* ensemble accompanied by tamboras, and the *aguinaldo* ensemble accompanied by one or more *tamboras* and a *furruco*. There is a fifth ensemble if we consider the *quitiplás* as drums, but we should keep in mind that these bamboo stamping tubes replicate the music of the *redondo* drums. Whether it be four or five, this many distinct drum ensembles in various towns and villages of one subregion is unique in Venezuela and is unusual for African-American communities of the New World as a whole.

As mentioned earlier, San Juan is the patron saint of Barlovento as well as of most African-Venezuelan communities stretching from the State of Miranda westerly to the Federal District and the states of Aragua, Carabobo, and Yaracuy. That 24 June also happens to coincide with the summer solstice may account for San Juan's popularity with the newly arrived Africans who may have had traditional festivals at this time of year. Many Venezuelan scholars, especially Juan Liscano, have documented the importance of and the reasons for the devotion to San Juan Bautista on the coast of Venezuela (Liscano 1973).

Image of San Juan Bautista

In most parts of Venezuela San Juan is depicted as a cherub-like child, as we see him here in Barlovento. He is also called San Juan Guaricongo, suggesting African roots, and San Juan Borrachero (Saint John the Imbiber or Drunkard), among other names, and is known to appreciate not only music and dancing but also *aguardiente* (hard liquor) and rum during his fiesta. Two of the Barlovento drum ensembles mentioned above are particularly associated with San Juan: the *mina* and the *redondo* ensembles. It is also common to hear the *quitiplás* ensembles being played around this time of year.

The *redondo* ensemble is composed of three drums, one or two maracas, a specific song genre, and a specific dance. The names of the drums vary somewhat from community to community, but commonly the smallest, highest sounding, and lead drum (first to sound) of the ensemble is called the *la hembra* (female). In some communities it is also called the *la prima* (first or prime) or *la quitimba*, a word of African origin whose original meaning has been lost. The largest and the lowest-sounding drum, and the one that does most of the improvising, is called *el macho* (the male) or *el pujao*. The drum of middle pitch and size is almost always referred to as *el cruzao* (the hybrid or the one that crosses).

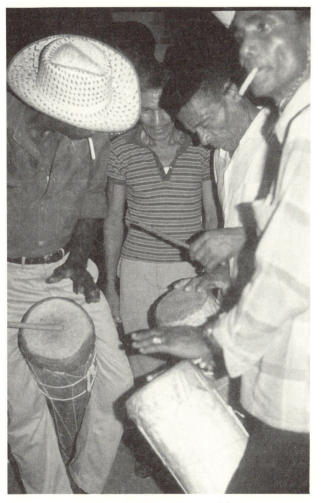

Redondo Drum Ensemble

All three drums are played with a stick in one hand. The *cruzao* and *macho* alternate playing the drum head with a regular stick beat to the side of the drum which serves as the principle pulse within a 6/ 8 metric framework to which the singing and dancing relates. To the contrary, the *hembra*, which is the first drum to sound at the beginning of a performance, plays a regular two-pulse offbeat against the sharp-sounding stick strokes played on the sides of the other two drums.

The *redondo* songs, as all traditional songs in Barlovento, are sung in Spanish with an occasional word or syllable that may reveal African roots. Only one couple dances at a time, with successive entries by male and females dancers to keep things moving and allow for a number of different people to participate. Most scholars believe that the *redondo* drums and the music associated with them have strong central African roots.

The same dance and songs can be performed to the sound of the *quitiplás*, which are often played by children to learn the rhythms of the *redondo* drums. The lead player (first to sound) of this ensemble holds a bamboo tube in each hand, hitting one to the ground and then the next, which sound much like the two tones of the lead *redondo* drum, and then completes the ternary pattern by hitting the tubes together, producing a sound much like that made by the stick strokes to the side of the *cruzao* and *macho* drums. Two or three other performers hold a bamboo tube in one hand and use the other hand for cupping it to get different sonorities as it is struck on the pavement, usually a cement floor. The term "quitiplás" is onomatopoeic, imitating the sound of the two tubes of the lead musician: qui-ti-pla, qui-ti-pla, qui-ti-pla, qui-ti-pla.

Quitiplás Ensemble

During the San Juan festival, when moving from one location to another, a simple ternary beat in unison is played on the *redondo* drums as the participants sing a song known as *malembe* or *melembe*, a bantu term meaning "softly, slowly," or "take it easy." It should also be pointed out that *redondo* and *quitiplás* music is not restricted to the San Juan fiesta. This music can be played at any time of year, but is most commonly performed around the time of the San Juan fiesta, either during devotional ceremonies dedicated to San Juan or for social entertainment unrelated to San Juan festivities.

Mina Drum Ensemble

The *mina* ensemble can also be performed at any time of the year for unspecified social occasions but, as with the *redondo* ensemble, it is most commonly associated with the fiesta of San Juan. There are three rhythmic components to this ensemble: the *mina* drum, its smaller upright companion the *curbata*, and the *laures* that are played on the side of the *mina* drum. In this ensemble all of the musicians play with a stick in each hand.

While *redondo* music is noted for its duple and triple juxtapositions, recalling the hemiola or sesquialtera of much Caribbean and Latin American music, the *mina* rhythms and its singing and dancing are primarily in duple meter. *Mina* drumming accompanies a song form that is distinct from the *redondo* songs and the *fulias*. It also has its own dance, which is more of a communal exercise with many people dancing at the same time, than is the couple dance of the *redondo* drums.

The original meaning of the term "mina" has been lost to the inhabitants of Barlovento, but some scholars believe it has connections to West Africa, perhaps even to the old slave port of Elmina in present-day Ghana. While in some communities of Barlovento such as Curiepe the same musicians have mastered both *mina* and *redondo* drumming, in most towns and villages musicians and their families are usually advocates of only one of the two traditions. We could speculate that during an earlier period of history specific ethnic groups of recent African derivation may have aligned themselves to one or the other drum ensemble. There is no recollection by today's inhabitants of Barlovento, however, of such a division based on specific ethnic and music lines.

It is interesting to note that in those communities of Barlovento where there are *mina* drums but no *redondo* drums, *redondo* rhythms are sometimes played on the *mina* drums to accompany *redondo* singing and dancing, something that is never done in the communities of Barlovento that have both *mina* and *redondo* drums. The same phenomenon takes place in the Litoral, where *redondo*-type drums have never been part of the instrumental tradition.

A third ensemble is that which accompanies the *velorios* or night watches in honor of the Holy Cross or a particular saint. Such *velorios* are usually originated by families or neighborhoods that invite people to a private home where festivities are held. A table with an image of a saint or a cross serves as an altar around which the musicians are seated. The main tribute to the altar are the songs known as *fulias*, the most complex and perhaps most beautiful song genre of the region. The principal instruments are three or four *tamboras* which are held between the legs of the seated musicians and played in a manner very reminiscent of the *redondo* playing technique, with comparable rhythms. Other instruments of secondary importance include one *cuatro*, the four-string national instrument of Venezuela, maracas, a pewter plate which is scraped with an eating utensil, and hand clapping.

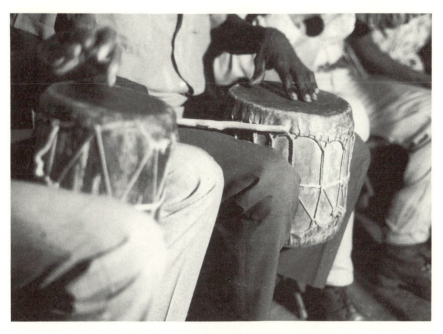

Tamboras of the Fulia Ensemble

Sets of drumming and singing are interspersed with participants' reciting of *decimas*, ten-lined poetry, often with revealing texts that date back to early colonial days. The *fulia* melodies may have somewhat more traces of Spanish influence than the *mina* and *redondo* songs, but the *tambora* accompaniment is definitely African in character as is the solo and chorus singing style.

The fourth ensemble of Barlovento that utilizes drums features a Christmas song form known as the *aguinaldo*. The *aguinaldo* melodies also have Spanish characteristics, but these songs do not necessarily have the expected religious themes and texts of European

Christmas carols. They do feature the characteristics of the African-style rhythmic accompaniment and solo and chorus singing. Each *aguinaldo* ensemble generally centers around one *furruco* or friction drum and one *tambora*, usually larger in size than the ones used at *velorios*. The *furruco* may be related to both the Spanish *zambomba* and African precedents (Aretz 1967, 104-107). *Aguinaldo* ensembles, like the *velorio* ensembles, are similar from one community to another throughout the region and are also found in other parts of Venezuela.

Furruco and Tambora of the Aguinaldo Ensemble

African Drums and Implications of Ethnicity

Organological and musicological analysis of the drum ensembles and their music clearly identifies a fusion of African and European elements, even though many of the musicians demonstrate Native American physical characteristics. The most African of musical traits found in these ensembles are the instruments and their manner of performance. Also, while some of the singing and poetry have Iberian characteristics, African influence can be determined by the solo and chorus format of most of the vocal music. When asked about the origins of these musical traditions, though, a majority of the informants, regardless of racial background, thought that it came from the *indios* or Indians.

The answer to the above question is somewhat more complex then one might initially think. The term "indio" as used by someone from Barlovento does not necessarily mean Amerindian or Native American. The use of the Spanish word for Indian in Barlovento can imply a remote and foreign past that is not restricted to Native Americans. Until encounters with visiting scholars in the past half century, most Barloventeños had lost contact with their African past. To this day, many of the older people of Barlovento are still quite vague about the historical and cultural differences between Africans, Europeans, and Native Americans. Perhaps one of the reasons for this is that Venezuelans do not have the advantage of being able to point to specific ethnic groups of Africa for purposes of national identity. Cubans and Brazilians, for example, can lay claim to the Yoruba and other recognizable ethnic groups from Africa. It is more difficult for Venezuelans to make such connections. The slave trade came to a halt in Venezuela during the early nineteenth century, about the time of the battles for independence, and there seems not to have been any major ethnic group that dominated African-Venezuelan societies as in other Latin American countries. Instead we have an important African-American region of the New World where the most common distinctions are vague references to something west or central African, although most scholars suggest that Bantu-speaking people from the central part of Africa were the principal figures in this sad migration of people from one continent to another.

Clearly a rebirth in pride among African-Americans from this region has taken place over the past few decades, and the drum ensembles are often the main focus of this African past. Visitors from abroad, better education, new channels of communication between Venezuela and Africa, and journeys to Africa by a few people from Barlovento are just a few of the things that have made these people more cognizant of their African ancestry. Furthermore, pride and proficiency in these art forms extend beyond the boundaries of race. Although most of the musicians and participants in drum ensemble performances in the central region seem to be predominantly descendants of Africans, this is not always the case. While admitting it is not very scientific to make attempts at determining biological descendence through visual observation, some of the musicians interviewed in Barlovento during the field research had physical characteristics that were obviously more Native American and European than African. These informants, though in a minority, were not merely peripheral adjuncts to these ensembles, but key musicians, singers, and leaders. The musicians of light complexion, however, never suggested anything unusual about this during conversations, unless probed on the subject which was done on occasion. Even then, it did not seem of much significance to them. Nor are these musicians seen as anything unusual or less than musical by their fellow musicians of more African physical identity. In other words, race does not seem to play an important part in the dissemination of this African-Venezuelan musical tradition, even though it is obvious to scholars that the instrumental and rhythmic components of these ensembles are African.

We can broaden this discussion and move to Caracas, a major capital city of the world with somewhere between two and three million inhabitants. Most people living in the capital who hear mention of the towns of Curiepe and La Sabana immediately experience images of African-Venezuelan drum ensembles, and they identify these art forms as something that belongs to them, even though they may not have a trace of African blood in their veins. They do know that Africa has affected them culturally in some way and are generally very proud of this association. Most people in the capital are familiar with the words "mina," "curbata," and "culoepuya," and almost everyone can sing most of the words to the popular merengue entitled "Barlovento" whose text refers to the drums of that region by name.

Musicologists still have much to do to further demonstrate relationships between African-derived music from this region and other forms of both traditional and popular music in Venezuela. For example, much of traditional Venezuelan music from various regions of the country can be transcribed or written in 6/8 time, and much of this 6/8 music has a percussive stroke on every third beat. We find much of this in music performed on the national instrument, the *cuatro*, where every third beat in a measure of six pulses is a percussive scraping of the strings, something the Venezuelans call *rasgueo*. We find the very same musical technique used on both the *redondo* drums, with stick beats to the side of the *cruzao* and *pujao* on every third pulse, and the *quitiplás*, where the lead musician clicks his two bamboo tubes together on every third pulse of the phrase. Did the *redondo* drums and *quitiplás* percussion tubes of Barlovento give this musical technique to the rest of the country, or did it evolve in various places of Venezuela at the same time? It may well have been introduced to Venezuela by Africans brought to Barlovento many generations ago and was dispersed to other parts of the country from there. If so, millions of Venezuelans, regardless of ethnic ancestry, are masters at a musical technique that is inherently African.

The drum ensembles described here are undergoing great change. The region of Barlovento, for example, now under two hours by paved road from Caracas, has been experiencing profound sociological change over the past few decades. More people from the capital are using this subregion as a weekend playground, with more condominiums being built every day on former cacao plantations, while many of the African-Venezuelan youth indigenous to the subregion are now moving to Caracas for better schooling, health care, and job opportunities. This is having an impact upon young people learning traditional forms of music which are just not practiced in the city. Furthermore, even the youth who stay in Barlovento are more involved in the electronic transmission of music than in traditional musical instruments. Making drums from scratch is no easy task, but most young people have easy access to radios and recordings of enticing music from faraway places. Therefore, the role of these traditional ensembles in the future is questionable.

Nevertheless, they have already made their impact. It is up to those of us who are interested in the future development of music in Venezuela to study how these ensembles might continue to enrich both music and ethnic identity in this country with such a rich African heritage.

References

Aretz, Isabel. 1967. *Instrumentos musicales de Venezuela*. Cumaná: Universidad de Oriente.

Brandt, Max. 1988. *Estudio etnomusicológico de tres conjuntos de tambores afro-venezolanos de Barlovento*. Caracas: CCPYT-CIDEF.

Liscano, Juan. 1973. *La fiesta de San Juan el Bautista*. Caracas: Monte Avila Ed.

Pollack-Eltz, Angelina. 1991. *La negritud en Venezuela*. Caracas: Lagoven.

Los Hermanos Congo y Milton Tadeo *Ten Years Later: Evolution of an African-Ecuadorian Tradition of the* Valle del Chota, *Highland Ecuador*

John M. Schechter

On October 27, 1979, one of his musician-colleagues introduced me to Germán Congo, excellent lead guitarist of the ensemble, "Conjunto Rondador." Named for the unique single-rank panpipe of the Ecuadorian highlands, this internationally traveled ensemble was performing in a restaurant patio in Ibarra, capital of Imbabura Province, in northern highland Ecuador. Germán invited me to come visit him and his musician-brothers in the Chota Valley nearby. Some months later, on March 1, 1980, my friend, Don Valerio, from Cotacachi, Imbabura, my wife, Janis, and I journeyed to Chota.

After traveling for some time along the Pan American Highway north of Ibarra, we saw Germán's village through a notch carved deep in the dry hillside. It was located on a dry, flat plain, but with avocado trees close behind it. Just before noon, we arrived at Germán Congo's mother's house where, we were told, Germán also lived; the doors were locked. Suddenly, a man came over, introducing himself as Germán's brother; he led us to his own thatch-covered home.

I explained the circumstances of our visit. He listened courteously, then invited us to accompany him to find some of his musical companions. We walked a short distance to a clean, concrete-walled room next to a tavern, and we sat on low benches. For the next three hours, Eleuterio Congo, the brother of Germán, his other brother, Fabián, and their compatriots, Milton Tadeo and Segundo Padilla, played guitar and sang, typically two musicians playing any one song, with one of them also singing. As we tape-recorded during these hours, we also exchanged English lessons — requested by Eleuterio — and made a tri-cultural recording (also at Eleuterio's request): an American ethnomusicologist, singing an Imbabura Quichua sanjuán (a genre to be discussed briefly below; see also Schechter 1987), with accompaniment of Chota African-Ecuadorian guitarists. See Figure 1, a photograph taken in Carpuela on March 1, 1980. At the invitation of Eleuterio and Milton, Janis and I returned two weeks later, on March 15, for further work with the Congo brothers and other Chota musician-colleagues.

Figure 1. (left to right) a woman of Carpuela, Janis O'Driscoll Schechter, Segundo Padilla, Eleuterio Congo, Milton Tadeo, and Don Valerio

Fabián Congo, his brothers, Germán and Segundo Eleuterio, and their colleague, Milton Tadeo, are composer-musicians of Carpuela, Imbabura, in the Chota River Valley of highland Ecuador. Although

Ecuador does not often come to mind when one thinks of Latin American regions with large populations of African-Americans, as much as 25 percent of the population of the country is African-Ecuadorian. The heaviest concentration of blacks is in coastal Esmeraldas Province, neighboring Imbabura. The first black Africans arrived in Ecuador in the sixteenth century; thereafter, Jesuit missionaries brought in large numbers of African slaves to work on plantations both on the coast and in the central highlands: indigenous labor was difficult to find in some areas and unwilling to serve as slaves in others. The relatively small pocket of approximately fifteen thousand African-Ecuadorians of Carpuela and some ten to fifteen neighboring villages has an unclear origin. Most widely accepted is the belief that they are descended from slaves held by Jesuits on their highland plantations (Lipski 1987, 157-8).

The Congo brothers are the third generation of composer-musicians in their family, beginning with their maternal grandfather, Lucho Campos. With Milton — a friend of Fabián's since childhood, they are today the most celebrated musicians of Chota. Around 1980, according to Milton (Tadeo and Mendes León 1990), he and the Congo brothers were agriculturalists; they did not yet consider themselves "musicians," although they would get together to make music. Milton himself began on *bomba* (double-headed drum, discussed below), then moved to guitar, ultimately achieving acclaim as a vocalist. Although they consider themselves and are locally regarded as the premier ensemble of Carpuela, they then performed largely locally, for such events as weddings, baptisms, and school programs (electricity for sound systems only arrived in Carpuela about 1982). It should be noted that, like their Quichua-speaking neighbors in the province, and like Roman Catholic African-Americans and Iberian-Americans throughout Latin America (Schechter 1983, 1988), the residents of Chota celebrate the festive child's wake, which, Fabián and Milton informed me, is known locally as *wawallo*.

By 1990, their names had become household words throughout Imbabura and even beyond. Their ensemble, Grupo Ecuador, had produced six long-playing records in the previous eight years. Figure 2 is a photograph taken after our recording session October 21, 1990, outside an Ibarra-area community house, close to Germán Congo's home; from left to right, the musicians are Ermundo Mendes León, güiro, Germán Congo, Milton Tadeo, and Fabián Congo; Eleuterio Congo, seated, plays the bomba. Milton noted in our October 31 interview that they no longer "worked" (in agriculture), but rather derived their entire income from making music; Milton's brother works Milton's land and the brothers share the harvest, an arrangement typical of the ensemble as a whole. Grupo Ecuador's regular weekend concert dates involving travel throughout Ecuador and into southwestern Colombia, their high concert fees, and their television appearances attest to a distinguished regional reputation. Milton and Ermundo commented on their changed image among their Chota neighbors, who now see the musicians as "different people," with changed dress and lifestyles.

Figure 2. Grupo Ecuador

The Chota region claims as its own the genre *bomba*. The bomba as a Chota-area membranophone appeared in the literature by the late nineteenth century; the bomba as a musical genre was described by the mid-twentieth century (Carvalho-Neto 1964, 99; Bueno 1991, 172). When questioned about the history of the genre, Milton Tadeo expressed the view (Tadeo and León 1990) that the music of the bomba had emerged from the culture of the *molienda,* (mill) of the *trapiche* (sugar mill) of the older generation in Chota. In this regard, Lipski notes:

> Until the middle of the eighteenth century, Jesuit wealth was considerable in Ecuador, including a number of sugar

plantations in Carchi [close by Carpuela] and Imbabura. Many of these estates still exist, as do the settlements that arose around them, and when the Jesuits were expelled from Ecuador in 1767, most of the slaves simply changed masters as these lands were taken over by Ecuadoran owners. These slaves and freedmen formed the population nuclei of the Chota Valley.... When slavery was abolished in Ecuador in 1852, the Choteños continued working on the large land-holdings that form the economic backbone of the region...the majority of the Choteños share a history of more than 250 years of residence in the central highlands (1987,158).

Milton continued, during this interview, citing one traditional bomba text (a variant of which Coba Andrade published, as well; see Coba Andrade 1980, 191f.) that came from this way of life: "A la culebra verde, negrita, no hagas caso, mete caña al trapiche, chupa y bota gabazo." (Don't pay attention to the green snake, dear woman; put cane to the sugar mill, suck on it, and throw away the waste pulp.) Ermundo and Milton added that, in earlier times prior to the advent of the guitar in Chota, Choteños would perform bombas on *cabuya* (cactus) leaves, together with *puros* (different-sized gourd aerophones and idiophones — still performed today in the village of Chalguayacu; see Coba Andrade 1979, 72, "sonajeros de calabazas" and "sonajeros de puros," and 87, "calabazas: puros pequeños, puros medianos, puros bajos, and puros contrabajos," and Schechter 1984: "Banda mocha").

In his monograph on African-Ecuadorian folklore, Carlos Coba Andrade (1980, 185) notes that the bomba, a dance typical of the Chota Valley, is an "indo-hispano-afroecuatoriana" hybrid. He comments, for example, with regard to the bomba "La Bomba Manuela," recorded in 1975, that it employs the bomba drum, using Africanate rhythms in its performance; that it incorporates the term, *chicha* — a beverage associated with Andean Native American culture — in its lyric; that it also incorporates *aguardiente* — a beverage associated with Iberian-American culture, in the highlands (Coba Andrade 1980, 48). He later adds, by way of summation, that, in his view, the tricultural nature of the Chota bomba lies in its juxtaposition of African rhythm, indigenous pentatony, and European (verse) structure: estrofa-estribillo-estrofa — A-B-A' (Coba Andrade 1980, 48-49). In my own investigations of the bomba "Vamos pa' Manabí" (Schechter 1992, 423-425), I have pointed to a distinctively African-American freedom of expression, a markedly syncopated manner of interpretation by both singer and guitarists; Spanish couplets; and a particularly Quichua-resonant form of relative major-relative minor bimodality, together with one word from the Quichua lexicon. Lipski (1987, 158) remarks on the relative isolation of the Chota Valley and states that, in the language of Chota one perceives an "...overwhelming linguistic influence of the surrounding highland dialects."

Musical example 1

1) Simple duple bomba drum accompanimental pattern for "Una naranja partida " and "Negra linda":

2) Sesquiáltera bomba drum accompanimental pattern for "Este pañuelito" :

Song text 1 (see appended song texts) is the bomba "Una naranja partida," performed March 15, 1980 in an *estanco* (tavern) in Piquiucho, Carchi, close by the Chota River bridge at the village of El Juncal, within walking distance of Carpuela — the bridge being at the juncture of Carchi province and Imbabura province. The three musicians were Rigoberto Borja, lead singer and first *requinto* guitar, Atiliano Campos, response singer and second requinto guitar, and Arturo Campos, bomba drum. A native of Piquiucho, Atiliano Campos is a cousin of

Fabián Congo. Figure 2 shows the performance posture for the double-headed bomba.

The tempo in Musical Example 1 was dotted-quarter = 104-112. The call-and-response texture, the use of the bomba drum (same name in Puerto Rico) held between the knees, the antecedent-consequent phrasing, the repetitive nature of the melody, and the simple duple meter of the percussion, at least, recalled, to different degrees, the bomba of coastal Puerto Rico, notably as it has been interpreted by Puerto Rican musicians in New York City (e.g., "Bomba Calindé" on the LP Caliente = Hot, 1977). The relative major/relative minor bimodality — with excursion into the major subdominant, and the compound duple character of the melodic line, resonated with the albazo of the neighboring Iberian-American population in Imbabura.

Me gus - ta la le - che　me gus - tael ca - fé
pe - ro - más me gus - ta　lo que　tie - neUs - ted

Musical Example 2. The sanjuán, "Me gusta la leche" of the Congos of Chota

Further to ground the Congos' own bomba style is one other regional bomba, "Negra linda," recorded in 1975 — dotted-quarter = 114-118 — by Carlos Alberto Coba Andrade, together with José Peñín and Ronny Velásquez of the Instituto Otavaleño de Antropología staff, and published on the Instituto's 1990 two-disc LP, *Música etnográfica y folklórica del Ecuador* (reviewed by J. Schechter, 1991). Coba informed me in 1990 about the three musicians playing here; they are from Juncal, I was informed by Fabián in 1990. The piece was recorded in Carpuela, however. This text — along with those of other bombas — was published in Coba's 1980 monograph, *Literatura popular afroecuatoriana*. In Musical Example 2, the call-and-response exchange was eschewed; nevertheless, other features were shared with "Una naranja partida": the rigorous syncopation, the repetitive melody, the integral bimodal harmony with excursion into the major subdominant, and even the same keys for the two pieces: A/f#/D. Lastly, both bombas recorded five years apart employed the same pentatonic (again, see Coba Andrade 1980, 49) tonal gamut — f#-a-b-c#-e — expanded, during subdominant sections, to include also d.

Other bombas in other performances, such as "Este pañuelito," have a clear sesquiáltera meter, due to the bomba's outlining not a simple duple meter (2/4) via three different membranophone pitch levels, as was the case both with "Naranja partida" and "Negra linda," but rather a 3/4//6/8 pattern; see Musical Example 1. Due to this sesquiáltera superposition of 6/8 in voices and 3/4//6/8 in percussion accompaniment, *these* bombas now *closely* approximate the character both of the *albazo* of the Spanish-speaking mestizo population and of the *pareja* of the Imbabura Quichua population; see Schechter 1982, 488-544 for fuller discussion — with transcriptions of parejas — of both of these genres. Fabián and Milton consider the slightly quicker, more sentimental bomba to be in fact the parent genre and albazo the derivative. Moreno Andrade, who provided a transcription, in 6/8 meter, of a "La Bomba" from Chota (1930, 217), pointed out the relationship between albazo and an unnamed Quichua genre: "El albazo posee — por lo general — un ritmo caprichoso y elegante, cuyo origen puede encontrarse en ciertas melodias autoctonas de figuración sincopada...." (The albazo possesses — in general — a whimsical and elegant rhythm, whose origin may be found in certain autochthonous melodies with syncopated figuration...) (Moreno Adrade 1930, 213). It is very possible Moreno Andrade had been listening to Quichua pareja. Thus the sesquiáltera bombas "sound" more distinctly highland Ecuadorian — in fact, Imbabureño — than do the merely duple bimetric (compound duple in treble, simple duple in percussion accompaniment) bombas. The harmonic scheme outlined for the earlier bombas, however, remains identical, with "Pañuelito." It is to be noted that Fabián and Milton were careful to term the albazos they sing "albazos" and to acknowledge that these pieces are "borrowed," not native to Chota. Musical Example 3 featured Eleuterio Congo, on guitar, and Milton Tadeo on guitar and vocals, singing the sesquiáltera traditional bomba "Este pañuelito," recorded during my first visit to Chota, on March 1, 1980. The bomba role was here taken by a Carpuela colleague playing a large gasoline container. (The actual bomba is made from the trunk of the cabuya cactus, I was informed on October 31, 1990 by Milton and Ermundo.)

The 1980 "Pañuelito" moved at dotted-quarter = 102-108. Ten years later, on October 21, 1990, Eleuterio (now on the bomba drum) and Milton were joined by their brother Fabián, on guitar and baritone vocals, by their other brother Germán, on lead/requinto guitar, and by percussionist Ermundo Mendes León on güiro, playing "Pañuelito" again. They were recorded — in stereo now — in the casa comunal close to Germán's home outside Ibarra, capital of Imbabura. Note that the dotted-quarter has now slowed to 94-98.

Beyond the question of the slightly more sedate tempo, there is a new dimension to this Congo performance: first, the exquisite requinto counterpoint work of Germán, eldest brother and a professional guitarist with international touring experience, as part of Conjunto Rondador; second, the special character — and blend — of the two voices, Fabián, baritone, and Milton, tenor — friends since their soccer-playing childhood. Remarkable is the fact that these voices blend beautifully, as well as being distinctive solo timbres, as I have documented in recordings of, for example, Milton, with the 1980 "Pañuelito" and a 1980 bomba vocal solo by Fabián, "Vamos pa' Manabí" (Schechter 1992, Recorded Selection 61). In a discussion 31 October 1990, Milton told me that the distinctive guitar technique of the ensemble originated with the requinto — that, in effect, the requinto was the fulcrum of the ensemble. When asked this same day what he felt was distinctive about the sound of the ensemble, Milton responded that theirs was the sound of the bomba — that this sound had a certain *"sabor," "sentimiento," "dulzura,"* or *"alegría"* (Tadeo 1990; see also below). He repeated, moreover, that, without the requinto, there was no "dulzura" or "alegría." During this interview, Ermundo Mendes León, also present, noted that, were the bomba (drum) to be absent from a performance, the presentation would be next to worthless. It should be noted that this ensemble, with six LP's under their belts by this time, appeared polished, though not lacking enthusiasm.

As we shall shortly observe, the Congos are actively involved currently with the composition of topically oriented songs. Yet they stubbornly acknowledge their continuing debt — and commitment — to the past, to the music-traditions of their beloved Chota. Said Fabián on October 24, 1990: "The old songs are those that have the most sentiment, right up to today. We are of course now recording the latest hits, but, to be frank, I am aware of the fact that the earlier songs had more import than those of today" (Congo and Tadeo 1990). He cites as an example the pasillo "Triste sepultura," recorded on the 1985 LP *A Bailar la Bomba*, con los hermanos Congo. A touching sentiment set in contrasts, it speaks of a parent confronting death, speaking to a daughter about to be married; it was composed by the Congos' mother, Luz-María Campos. Ermundo admitted that "always, one remembers that which has been sung first" (Tadeo and León 1990). Milton noted that, despite the ensemble's new material, they maintain the traditional repertoire because "the first song-texts have made one famous, and all the people ask for the old music" (Tadeo and León 1990). Fabián remarked on October 24 that, despite their *cumbia, pasillos,* and *albazos,* they *are* still composing bombas: "We cannot be far from the bombas, since the bombas characterize us." Milton added (October 31), "The way we play, is bomba. It has a flavor, a sentiment — we have that sentiment in our playing, no? For that reason we have that sweetness...the joy, we have that joy in playing." The old songs, such as the sanjuán "Me gusta la leche" (composed, Fabián said, by an unnamed "ancestor"), Fabián noted, were composed solely about "what the people lived," not, like today, with a few grains "invented," in order to embellish a text.

Eleuterio and Milton (vocal soloist) performed the Imbabura sanjuán from the Valle del Chota, "Me gusta la leche," on March 1, 1980. The Congos' Grupo Ecuador sang the same piece on October 21, 1990 in the same casa comunal outside Ibarra. Interestingly, the two performances ten years apart both have quarter-note = 84.

Despite its slower tempo (Imbabura Quichua sanjuán frequently moves at quarter-note = 92-108), this "Leche" of the Congos — 1980 or 1990 version — clearly draws on the regional sanjuán of the Quichua indigenous population, who share Imbabura province with the African-Ecuadorians and Iberian-Ecuadorians. Beyond the obvious points of closely approximating tempi and shared simple duple meter, it is phrase structure, rhythm, and a particular pattern of bimodality, which most clearly mark "Leche" a member of the Imbabura sanjuán family. Imbabura Quichua sanjuán (see Schechter 1992 [Examples 9-7, 9-8, 9-9, and 9-10], 396-401, for transcriptions of *sanjuan* with melody and accompaniment, melodic lines only, and characteristic rhythmic figures) is in two phrases of simple duple meter, with the first phrase frequently emphasizing, or cadencing in, the major, the second phrase its relative minor; "Leche" meets this criterion. Secondly, Quichua sanjuán has the rhythm of the two phrases identical or nearly so, something which "Leche" also approximates; see Musical Example 2. Third, although Quichua sanjuán never has four consecutive sixteenth-notes, Imbabura mestizo (Iberian-Ecuadorian) sanjuanito — an adaptation of Quichua sanjuán — *does* often use four running sixteenths. Finally, the motif: sixteenth-eighth-sixteenth is highly characteristic of Quichua sanjuán; it appears in "Leche's" second phrase.

Before summarizing the music-evolutionary tendencies of the Congos and Milton, I note that "La Viudita," a Mexican children's song (a circle dance), has a nearly identical text to that of "Me gusta la leche": "Me gusta la leche, Me gusta el café; Pero más me gustan, Los ojos de usted" (Moncada García 1985, 108; published earlier in *The Spanish-American Song and Game Book*, [1942] 1976, 40); the music is dissimilar, however.

In the evolution of their performance style with regard to traditional repertoire, it would seem that, with regard to sanjuán ("Leche"), tempo appears unchanged. Although "Leche" may be traditional in Chota, it is beyond serious question that, as a genre, sanjuán is indigenous to the regional Quichua, not the regional African-Ecuadorian culture (Schechter 1982, 247-251). The musical character of what is, ultimately, then, a borrowed music, has been maintained notably intact over ten years. With regard to the *Congos'* bomba performance practice, as illustrated by "Pañuelito" and by the albazo/bomba "Robando me he de casar" (dotted-quarter = 106 in 1980, and 96 in 1990) — not discussed in this paper, tempo has appeared to slow down; in comparison with the call-and-response and pre-1980 bombas of their cousins and neighbors, quite noticeably. Whereas Fabián considers the Chota bomba "más caliente" than their neighbors' albazo, of late the temperatures of the neighboring genres have begun to closely approximate one another. This may reflect the fact that the Congos are now addressing a broader cultural audience than in former times and that thus they have begun to assimilate their Chota bomba into the broader albazo sesquiáltera character of the highlands at large. Indeed, Quichua indigenous musicians are performing albazos on LPs, as well, such as Conjunto Indígena Peguche performing "Aires de mi tierra," (on the LP Folklore de mi tierra, 1977) again, to appeal to the broader commercial market. Fabián is clear on his wish, in fact, that the unique sound of the music of Chota — of which Grupo Ecuador is widely acknowledged the most excellent exponent — spread as far as possible. When asked about his goals for the next ten years, he answered: "First, we wish to spread all of our music; hopefully, it will reach many sectors of the world .... We are sharing our tradition with all humankind."

Regarding rates of change for bombas (for example, "Este pañuelito") versus for Chota sanjuán ("Leche"), among the Congos: Nettl (1983, 195) has spoken of the concept of the density of a particular repertory: "By density, I mean the degree to which separate units of a repertory are similar.... *Or,* putting it another way, how close or how far apart, musically, the units, pieces, songs, may be from each other." Specifically pertinent to this discussion, he subsequently defined "historical density" as "...the rate at which a piece or a repertory changes...while one song may change very quickly, another might undergo the same changes but with the process requiring much more time" (Nettl 1983, 196). Preliminary research produces the hypothesis, then, that, for the African-Ecuadorians of Chota, the historical density for pieces pertaining to their own genre, the bomba, is somewhat sparser than that for an "imported" but maintained genre, the sanjuán. Another way of viewing the phenomenon might be from the perspective of the Congos themselves: For Fabián, his brothers, and Milton, maintaining the historical density for the imported sanjuán is an issue, a preoccupation. With regard to their own bombas, they entertain a willingness to allow a sparser historical density, a somewhat greater compositional flexibility — particularly pertaining to tempo — in the name of commercial exposure to a potentially broader audience.

Finally, there are the Congos' new compositions. Whereas traditional bomba texts and the sanjuán "Leche" may deal with themes of love — of woman, or of their native tierra, Carpuela, Fabián, his brothers Germán and Eleuterio, and Milton, are now composing songs — in both bomba and borrowed forms such as Colombian cumbia — with distinctly political content. In his bomba "Promesas políticas," Fabián expresses the growing disillusionment of the people with the unfulfilled promises of their governments. Fabián's "Deber y Dolor," a cumbia, expresses gratitude to the guards of the nearby border with Colombia for their sometimes painful (but required by their job) efforts to halt the flow of illicit merchandise into Ecuador. Song text 7 is Germán's cumbia "El Ecuador y Colombia," in which the Congo musician sings of his and his brothers' consciousness of the special geography of Chota — both within highland Imbabura, Ecuador, and close by the Colombian border. Milton commented on October 31 that, as time passes, the group continues to change and evolve, and to compose new songs, with the goal of making more LPs. (Milton and Ermundo added, on this same day, that the younger generation in Carpuela care little today for the bomba, but are consumed by "ró[c]" — American rock 'n roll — and salsa.) The Congos are confronting their current stylistic dilemma — the demand by their public for texts "of the moment," in Fabián's words, versus the debt they feel to the old (literally the old: it is those of the older generation in Chota who continue to demand of them the traditional bombas [Tadeo and León 1990]) — by a planned compromise in their forthcoming recordings: they intend to record an LP with six traditional songs (not yet sung on LP, though recorded in 1980 and 1990 with me) and six "current" ones.

The recent compositions of Fabián Congo and his brothers and colleagues look outward — expressing regional pride and consciousness. The Congos and Milton Tadeo are presently walking a stylistic tightrope: seeking to incorporate in their songs current, real concerns — springing from their political stance and from their own geography, while also feeling constrained to maintain the music-genre traditions of their native Carpuela. They appear to be confronting a conflict in their self-image, a conflict which can be viewed in terms of a pull between forces both regional and nonregional, or supraregional. Specifically, the musicians of Grupo Ecuador are involved with an interaction of regionality, generation, and individual contribution. Both the music-stylistic proximity of the Chota bomba to Imbabura Province albazo (mestizo population) and pareja (Quichua Native American population), and the close parallels in tempo, meter, phrase structure, rhythm, and particular usage of bimodality between the Congos' "Leche" and Imbabura sanjuán firmly establish the musical *tone* of the Congos' traditional pieces, at least, as pertaining to the region of Imbabura, northern highland Ecuador. Yet this regional grounding is challenged by forces that impinge on regionality: generation and individuality. The Congos and Milton are in fact on the cusp of the younger and older generations in the Chota Valley. While they have inherited — and acknowledge a debt to — the repertory of their parents' and grandparents' generation, they are simultaneously considered role-models by numbers of younger Chota musicians. The Congos reflect their involvement with the momentum of the younger generation by their recent use of international genres, such as cumbia, in newly composed songs that express views that are innately supra-regional: unity across borders ("El Ecuador y Colombia"), history

(Fabián's cumbia "Recuerdos del Santo Papa," fixing in song the January 1985 visit of the Pope to Ecuador [on Side B of Los Grandes de la Bomba, 1989]), justice, and oppression — themes prevalent in the music of Nueva Canción.

In Jorge de Carvalho's terms, explained in "The Construction of Black Ethnicity in Ritual and Popular Music of African Origin in Brazil" (de Carvalho 1992), the maintenance of historically dense sanjuán and traditional bombas such as "Pañuelito" in their repertoire reflects the conservatism of a "power/traditional" model: the Congos' preservative effort, their intention to reproduce a cultural history, to freeze it in time. By contrast, the Congos' opening themselves aesthetically to outside influences — beyond Imbabura, beyond Ecuador — and their intention to introduce historical and geographical facets into their newer compositions reflect de Carvalho's third model: in his context, the umbanda, or macumba, model, one of syncretism, one which implies the potential for a constantly expandable repertoire. In sum, the Congos are active at once in both a closed canon and an open canon.

Anthony Seeger (1992) notes that group formation (ethnicity) often involves an image. For the blacks of Chota, that image has been up until recent times the bomba genre; however, one now senses a restlessness among the Congos with that self-image. The Congos are now less concerned with "bomba," more concerned with finding a genre — whatever that might be — to express their latest textual ideas — a Pope's visit, brotherhood between Ecuador and Colombia, disillusionment with the government, and so on. It is possible that visiting ethnomusicologists might do a disservice to the effort to change that self-image by suggesting that they try to keep active the traditional repertoire.

If ethnicity is to be defined, as Kubik (1992) does, as a "new consciousness about ethnic attachment," then "ethnicity" may not apply to a group like the blacks of Chota, who for 250 years have been self-contained and not a cimarrón group (see Lipski 1987, 165), in the same area where their ancestors were brought by the Jesuits. Their language — suggestive, as John Lipski suggests, of an earlier period when a partially Africanized Spanish was spoken in Chota — and their bomba drum are deeply rooted in the region. In the Chota Valley, blacks are not a sub-culture, but the dominant culture — though they are not even a great minority in Ecuador, where, as has already been noted, as much as 25 percent of the population are African-American.

For Angel Quintero-Rivera (1992), the (Puerto Rican) bomba rhythm he finds in the introduction to the band La Selecta's piece "Somos el son" may have symbolic value in Puerto Rico as evocative of the period of black slavery. The Chota bomba — which shares textural, organological, phrasing, metric, and tempo aspects with the Puerto Rican bomba — is *not*, I believe, singled out for its value as being symbolic of an oppressed past. On the contrary, the Chota bomba has been *continuous* in performance, *positively* symbolic, and perhaps the genre-archetype for related regional genres: albazo and pareja — or at least the bomba is very much in the vein of Imbabura regional musics, notably for its firm bimodality, pentatonic gamut, and sesquiáltera meter. In fact, the musical "distance" between what appears "clearly" an Africanate music (call-and-response, bomba drum held between the knees, repetitive melody, simple duple percussion patterning) and what suddenly seems Imbabura-regional *mestizo* music is not great: eliminate the call-and-response, and make the percussion sesquiáltera, and you are suddenly in Ecuador-wide — even continent-wide — sesquiáltera. Finally, the culture-personality is not, in Chota, a self-deprecatory one (cimarronaje — "fleeing" character), but one with a strong self-image. The Congos of Chota are *of* the bomba, are proud of it, and know they are the best practitioners of their music-culture. In Chota, there has not been any "camouflage."

Victoria Eli Rodríguez (1992) notes that it was the central African Congo people that have made a signal contribution to Cuban music-culture. Stutzman (1979, 100) remarked that, inasmuch as slave-traders did not know slaves' real family names and did not understand African dialects, they would give slaves names that pertained to the particular ethnic group or port of origin. Stutzman's survey of blacks living in the Ibarra area revealed some 122 different surnames; among those surnames with African provenance, "Congo" was one. It is interesting to find that, over three generations, "Congos" (surname) have played leading musical roles in Chota.

Martha Ellen Davis (1992) discusses the notion that, in the Dominican Republic, one can find the *nation* as an ethnic group. In some ways, this can be said, also, for a country like Ecuador, where *cousin*-genres such as bomba (blacks of Chota) — albazo (mestizos) — pareja (Quichua) can serve as, at least, markers of a "*highland* [Ecuadorian] *nation*": all three musics are loved, preeminent, much developed, and continuously utilized over a spectrum of contexts.

There is a kind of "highland ethnicity," then, which is transcultural and regional. That is, regionality can supersede in importance "ethnicity," viewed in a narrow, or strictly racial, sense.

Egberto Bermúdez's chapter (1992) is pertinent to my Chota research in his "interethnic perspective." Specifically, Native Americans' borrowing stick-types and responsorial chant-practices from neighboring blacks in Palenque de San Basilio, Colombia, may have some parallels in Chota, Ecuador. In Chota, it may well be that mestizos have borrowed the bomba *genre* for their own albazo, while the Chota blacks have borrowed *lexicon* from their Quichua-speaking neighbors, as well as *genre* (sanjuán). Interethnic borrowing seems a way of life in Imbabura.

Figure 3. Grupo Ecuador

The Congos' music has always expressed a strong love for local genre, village, and region. Figure 3 shows the musicians of Grupo Ecuador after our 21 October 1990 recording session, photographed in front of German Congo's home outside Ibarra. Only the future will tell if their newer musical expressions will carry the same popularity — and, more profoundly, the same symbolic weight — as the bombas of the past.

Song Texts

S ong text 1: "Una naranja partida." Genre: bomba. Ensemble: Rigoberto Borja, Atiliano Campos, and Arturo Campos. Recorded 15 March 1980, in situ.

> *C' una naranja partida*
> *Y un limón hic' una sopa*
> *C' una naranja partida*
> *Y un limón hic' una sopa*

Call: Y el besito que me diste.

Response: Me lo quitaste boca y boca.

Song text 2: "Negra linda." Genre: bomba. Ensemble: Israel Caravalí, Angel Guerrón, and Amílcar Lozano. Recorded 1975, in situ.

> *A mi negra linda*
> *Yo le tengo enamorada*
> *Porque es tan bonita*
> *No me niega su mirada.*
>
> *Carlos Alberto Coba A.*
> *Literatura popular afroecuatoriana* (1980, 203)

Song texts 3 and 4: "Este pañuelito." Genre: bomba. Ensembles: 1 March 1980, Carpuela: Eleuterio Congo, Milton Tadeo, & Carpuela colleague on bomba drum.

21 October 1990, outside Ibarra: Grupo Ecuador de los Hermanos Congo y Milton Tadeo.

> *Este pañuelito te mandé a bordar*
> *Este pañuelito te mandé a bordar*
>
> *Son dos corazones para no olvidar*
> *Son dos corazones para no olvidar*
>
> *Por el mundo voy en busca de vos*
> *Por el mundo voy en busca de vos*
>
> *Llevando ilusión de mi corazón*
> *Llevando ilusión de mi corazón.*

Song texts 5 and 6: "Me gusta la leche." Genre: sanjuán. Ensembles: 1 March 1980, Carpuela: Eleuterio Congo, Milton Tadeo, and Carpuela colleague on bomba drum.

21 October 1990, outside Ibarra: Grupo Ecuador de los Hermanos Congo y Milton Tadeo.

Me gusta la leche, me gusta el café
Pero más me gusta, lo que tiene Usted.
Me gusta la leche, me gusta el café
Pero más me gusta, lo que tiene Usted.

Así negra linda de mi corazón
Cuando yo te veo me muero de ilusión.
Así negra linda de mi corazón
Cuando yo te veo me muero de ilusión.

Song text 7: "El Ecuador y Colombia." Genre: cumbia. Ensemble: Los Grandes de la Bomba, con Fabián Congo y Milton Tadeo. 1989. Novedades, LP 323102.

El Ecuador y Colombia
Son dos países hermanos.
El Ecuador y Colombia
Son dos países hermanos.

Por eso es que yo le canto
A la tierra colombiana;
Por eso es que yo le canto
A mi tierra ecuatoriana.

¡Viva, mi Colombia!
¡Viva, mi Ecuador!

References

A bailar la bomba. Con los Hermanos Congo. 1985. Quito: Famosa-Fadiso, 700211.

A bailar la bomba. Hermanos Congo. 1986. Vol.2. Guayaquil: Producciones Maldonado-IFESA, 339-5881.

Bermúdez, Egberto. 1992. "Ethnicity and Syncretism in Colombian Afro-American Musical Traditions." Paper presented at international symposium, *Music and Black Ethnicity in the Caribbean and South America,* January 18, 1992, at the University of Miami.

Bueno, Julio. 1991. "La Bomba en la Cuenca del Chota-Mira: Sincretismo o Nueva Realidad?" *SARANCE: Revista del Instituto Otavaleño de Antropología* 15 (15) (August): 171-193.

Carvalho, José Jorge de. 1992. "The Construction of Black Ethnicity in Ritual and Popular Music of African Origin in Brazil." Paper presented at international symposium, *Music and Black Ethnicity in the Caribbean and South America,* January 18, 1992, at the University of Miami.

Carvalho-Neto, Paulo de. 1964. *Diccionario del folklore ecuatoriano.* Tratado del Folklore Ecuatoriano. 1. Quito: Editorial Casa de la Cultura Ecuatoriana.

Coba Andrade, Carlos Alberto. 1979. "Instrumentos musicales ecuatorianos." *SARANCE* 7 (October): 70-95.

Coba Andrade, Carlos Alberto. 1980. *Literatura Popular Afroecuatoriana.* Otavalo, Ecuador: Instituto Otavaleño de Antropología.

Congo, Fabián, and Milton Tadeo. Interview with author. Ibarra, Imbabura, Ecuador, October 24, 1990.

Davis, Martha Ellen. 1992. "Music and Cultural Identity in the Dominican Republic." Paper presented at international symposium, *Music and Black Ethnicity in the Caribbean and South America,* January 17, 1992 at the University of Miami.

Folklore de mi Tierra: Conjunto Indígena "Peguche." 1977. Indústria Fonográfica Ecuatoriana S.A. (IFESA). Orion 330-0063. Guayaquil, Ecuador, Dist. by Emporio Musical S.A., Guayaquil and Psje. Amador, Quito.

Los Grandes de la Bomba. Con Fabián Congo y Milton Tadeo. 1989. Novedades, LP 323102 [no city].

Kubik, Gerhard. 1992. "Ethnicity, Cultural Identity and the Psychology of Culture Contact." Paper presented at international symposium, *Music and Black Ethnicity in the Caribbean and South America*, January 17, 1992, at the University of Miami.

Lipski, John M. 1987. "The Chota Valley: Afro-Hispanic Language in Highland Ecuador." *Latin American Research Review* 22(1): 155-170.

Moncada García, Francisco. 1985. *Juegos infantiles tradicionales.* Toluca, México, D.F.: Librería Imagen Editores, S.A., de C.V.

Moreno Andrade, Segundo Luis. 1930. "La Música en el Ecuador." In *El Ecuador en Cien Años de Independencia: 1830-1930*, ed. J. Gonzalo Orellana, 2: 187-276. Quito: Imprenta de la Escuela de Artes y Oficios.

Música etnográfica y folklórica del Ecuador: Culturas: Shuar, Chachi, Quichua, Afro, Mestizo. 1990. Rec. by José Peñín, Ronny Velásquez, and Carlos Coba A. 2 LPs, 6 pages of notes by Carlos Alberto Coba Andrade. Otavalo: Instituto Otavaleño de Antropología.

Nettl, Bruno. 1983. *The Study of Ethnomusicology: Twenty-nine Issues and Concepts.* Urbana: University of Illinois Press.

Quintero-Rivera, Angel. 1992. "La melodización de ritmos en el lenguaje musical puertorriqueño: Transformaciones en la etnicidad." Paper presented at international symposium, *Music and Black Ethnicity in the Caribbean and South America*, January 17, 1992, at the University of Miami.

Rodríguez, Victoria Eli. 1992. "Música y etnicidad cubanas: Consideraciones históricas." Paper presented at international symposium, *Music and Black Ethnicity in the Caribbean and South America*, January 17, 1992, at the University of Miami.

Schechter, John M. 1982. "Music in a Northern Ecuadorian Highland Locus: Diatonic Harp, Genres, Harpists, and Their Ritual Junction in the Quechua Child's Wake." 3 vols. The University of Texas at Austin. UMI No. 8217936.

Schechter, John M. 1983. "Corona y baile: Music in the Child's Wake of Ecuador and Hispanic South America, Past and Present." *Latin American Music Review* 4(1): 1-80.

Schechter, John M. 1987. "Quechua Sanjuán in Northern Highland Ecuador: Harp Music as Structural Metaphor on Purina." *Journal of Latin American Lore* 13(1): 27-46.

Schechter, John M. 1984. "Banda mocha." *In The New Grove Dictionary of Musical Instruments*, ed. Stanley Sadie, 1:143.

Schechter, John M. 1988. "Velorio de Angelito / Baquiné / Wawa Velorio: The Emblematic Nature of the Transcultural, Yet Local, Latin American Child's Wake." Latin American Studies Working Paper No. 3, September. Santa Cruz: University of California, Santa Cruz.

Schechter, John M. 1991. Review of *Música etnográfica y folklórica del Ecuador. Latin American Music Review* 12(2): 204-216.

Schechter, John M. 1992. "Latin America/Ecuador." In *Worlds of Music: An Introduction to the Music of the World's Peoples*, 2nd ed. 376-428. New York: Schirmer Books.

Seeger, Anthony. 1992. "Whoever We are Today, We Can Sing a Song about it." Paper presented at international symposium, *Music and Black Ethnicity in the Caribbean and South America*, January 17, 1992, at the University of Miami.

Singer, Roberta, and Robert Friedman. 1977. "Caliente = Hot: Puerto Rican and Cuban Musical Expression in New York." New World Records, NW 244.

The Spanish-American Song and Game Book. [1942] 1976. Illustrated. Compiled by Workers of the Writers' Program, Music Program, and Art Program of the Work Projects Administration in the State of New Mexico. New York: A.S. Barnes and Company. Reprint. New York: AMS Press.

Stutzman, Ronald L. 1979. "La gente morena de Ibarra y la sierra septentrional." *SARANCE* 7 (October): 96-110.

Tadeo, Milton, and Ermundo Mendes León. 1990. Interview with author. El Ejido, outside Cotacachi, Imbabura, Ecuador, October 31, 1990.

El Valle del Chota y su música. 1984. Bombas del Chota. Conjunto Estrella [including Milton Tadeo]. Arreglos y dirección: Segundo Rosero. Guayaquil: IFESA: Sarita, 339-320l, S-9300-PRO-12, S-9301-PRO-12.

Black Music and Identity in Peru: Reconstruction and Revival of Afro-Peruvian Musical Traditions

Raúl R. Romero

Peru and Mexico were two of the most important centers of black slavery in the colonial period in the New World (Bowser 1977, 11). However, these countries are seldom included in surveys of black musical traditions in Latin America. The reason for this omission is twofold: 1) The black population in these nations almost disappeared after the abolition of slavery in the nineteenth century, and 2) the cultural roots of these countries are more dependent on the contributions of their indigenous populations than on the few survivals of slave cultures. In contrast, the black presence in the United States, the Caribbean countries, and Brazil, is culturally and demographically much more significant.

In Peru, black slaves arrived between 1524 and 1528 with the first expeditions of the Spanish army of conquest. Francisco Pizarro himself in 1529 obtained an official permit to bring with him in one of his travels to Peru two slaves for his personal service (Bowser 1977, 21-22). After that time, the number of slaves introduced to Peru became increasingly important. By the mid-eighteenth century, almost half of the population of Lima was black (Estenssoro 1988, 161), and in comparison with other countries, Peru was among the colonies with larger amounts of black slaves in the New World (Uya 1989, 161).

But in contemporary Peru, at least since the turn of the century, which is the period described in this article, despite their small numbers, blacks have made significant cultural contributions in specific areas of Peruvian urban culture. The black presence, for example, is notable in many expressions of popular urban music; in very popular sports like soccer, and in women's Olympic volleyball, the most successful and competitive sport in Peru. The role of blacks in the making of traditional foods is also acknowledged by historians and researchers. The writer Fernando Romero has recently published 400 African-derived words (*Afro-Negrismos*) currently used by Spanish-speaking Peruvians (Romero 1980). On the literary scene, old and contemporary coastal black lifestyles are depicted in the novels of authors Gregorio Martínez and Galvez Ronceros.[1] Last but not least, the emergence of a massive urban popular religious cult such as the Lord of the Miracles, which currently draws thousands of followers in Lima in the month of October, is principally indebted to an urban black brotherhood which initiated this cult in the nineteenth century (Stockes 1987, 219). Concentrations of blacks in various rural coastal towns like Zaña, Chincha, Cañete, and Aucallama have also provided refuges for the preservation of old and dying black cultural expressions, which have been only partially documented (Vásquez 1982, Matos Mar and Carbajal 1974, Rocca 1985).

The black presence in these important expressions of Peruvian urban culture does not correspond to the demographics of the black minority in Peru. According to the 1940 census — the last one which considered the racial factor — only 0.48 percent of the population was black (Mac-Lean 1948, 146). Why, then, is the presence of blacks in urban Peru so notable?

This article will describe and analyze the recent revival and reconstruction of black musical traditions since the late 1950s in Lima.[2] This musical revival is indeed the most recent and best-known case of intensive promotion of a black cultural presence at a national level through the mass media (TV, radio, records and cassettes). Also addressed herein are questions concerning ethnicity and identity among Peruvian blacks. Do blacks in Peru perceive themselves as a minority group with a common destiny and problems to solve? How does the dominant culture perceive them? Do blacks in Peru have a distinct cultural identity? Is music a basic identity emblem for blacks in Peru?

Afro-Peruvians and the National Society

Could one consider the black sector in Peru an ethnic unit within the national society at large? An ethnic group has been considered a specific social group existing within a larger social system, unified by common traits such as race, nationality, or culture (Morris 1975, 253). The ideal type of an ethnic group, according to Fredrik Barth (1976, 11), consists of a community that must 1) self-reproduce itself biologically, 2) share common values, 3) communicate and interact, and 4) have an identity — that is, they must identify themselves as a group and the rest of the society should perceive them as such.[3] In fact, blacks in Peru do not constitute an ethnic group as it has been conceptually defined above. One of the main problems in dealing with the issue of black identity in Peru is that, as historian Flores Galindo has concluded, blacks appear as an "undifferentiated mass" instead of as a social class or ethnic group (Flores Galindo 1984, 128). Black culture, according to Flores Galindo, does not exhibit clear features (Flores Galindo 1984, 137).

Regarding the first condition, since the days of slavery blacks in Peru never followed strict endogenous marriage practices. Miscegenation was a strategy for upward social mobility, and it ultimately contributed to dissolve African traditions, as happened also in other Latin American countries. The colonial society imposed fewer barriers to a mulatto than to a black. The less dark the person was, the better he or she was treated (Bowser 1977, 391). Various censuses demonstrate how the black population since the seventeenth century decreased in numbers, while the number of mestizos and castes (*castas*: descendants of mixed marriages) increased. For example, in the seventeenth century there were almost 20,000 blacks in Peru, while in the 1908 census fewer than 7,000 were declared as such, (Stockes 1987, 183). Conversely, compared with 900 castas declared in the seventeenth century, 10,000 were declared in the eighteenth century (Flores Galindo 1984, 101-102). The traveler Middendorf in the nineteenth century examined the information in several censuses in Lima. According to these, in 1820 45 percent of Lima's population was black, whereas in 1836 only 10 percent was declared black, and in 1876, only 9 percent. This suggests that the process of racial mixture was intense, and that the sons and daughters of mixed marriages declared themselves as mestizos (Middendorf 1973, 143). The proportion of mixed marriages is still high in the present century: Almost 40 percent of black men marry white women, and almost 25 percent of black women marry whites (Stockes 1987, 186). In a context of racial discrimination and unequal opportunities, blacks saw, and still see, racial mixing as a way to secure better opportunities in life.

The second and third conditions — to share common values, communicate, and interact — were also lost since the early colonial times. Most urban black slaves were isolated from each other because their main occupation was that of servants in Spanish households. At the end of the eighteenth century, 82.39 percent of black slaves in Lima were servants (Flores Galindo 1984, 121). Also, the fierce competition among freed black slaves for jobs with incomes prevented them from forming common identity bonds. Occupational diversity, therefore, divided slaves and prevented them from concerted action (Galindo 1984, 121).

Residential dissociation added more difficulties for black communication and interaction. After the abolition of slavery (1854), and until the beginnings of the twentieth century, there were specific districts in Lima with a strong black population, such as *La Victoria* district, traditionally known and considered among *limeños* as a black district. Over the last decades, however, blacks have moved away from these urban districts without establishing other obvious residential patterns. The situation in the rural black towns of the coast is not entirely different. The experience of the United States, the Caribbean countries, and Brazil where huge plantations could congregate massive numbers of slaves was not operative in rural Peru. Rather, small or middle sized plantations with a small number of slaves who had scarce contacts with each other prevailed (Flores Galindo 1984, 108-109; Stockes 1987, 178-9). The coastal *haciendas* did not have more than 40 slaves each (Bowser 1977, 136-137). This is one of the strongest reasons Peruvian rural slaves did not find the conditions for preserving their original traditional cultures and musical expressions. In the present century as well, coastal towns with strong black populations have not maintained cultural exchanges with each other.

Another factor is that slaves came to Peru from different tribal origins. Some were brought from the Caribbean region (already Creole blacks adapted to Spanish culture), and others called bozales came directly from Africa. Groups like the *Terranovos, Lucumíes, Mandingas, Aubundes, Carabalíes, Cangaes, Chalas, Huarochiries, Congos,* and *Mirangas* are cited in several colonial and republican sources. Not all of these terms were derived from African tribal languages; some were local terms (Fuentes 1925, 81). These heterogeneous origins also prevented the cultural emergence of a common black identity.

The fourth condition (to have an identity, to identify oneself with a group) is the most difficult to evaluate. The 1940s national census was the last to include the ethnic origin of the population; hence, there are no statistics available on the proportion of blacks living in Peru today. In addition, most of the research on blacks has been historically oriented, focusing mainly on the colonial period and the study of the black slavery. No in-depth studies on the issue of contemporary black ethnicity and identity have been published to date. Based on numerous interviews and testimonials from young and older blacks in Peru, they do not view themselves as a group distinguishable from others. Blacks have traditionally identified themselves as Creoles and have historically avoided considering themselves as a separate and independent group. An outside observer could affirm, as a result, that they seldom interact as an ethnically or culturally defined group. On the other hand, Peruvian society grants them a status from which they cannot escape. It considers them a separate group through racial discrimination, which, though not supported by official posture, in fact exists and is one of the main complaints of almost every Peruvian black. Thus, they are in an ambiguous situation: While they want to consider themselves part of the Creole culture — which is predominantly white or mestizo — they are viewed by the national society as blacks, who are ultimately subject to racial discrimination.

Discriminatory policy is, of course, not official and will rarely be recognized in a public or private realm. Racial discrimination in Peru is a subtle phenomenon, and in the majority of the cases it is applied in a manner more circumstantial than systematic. The fact that the state and its institutions have never recognized racial discrimination against blacks implies that they have never acknowledged the existence of a "black problem" in the way they did since the beginnings of the century with the "Indian problem." As Serbin has suggested (1991), the recognition of that conflict permitted Indian peasants a surge of *indigenismo*, an official as well as an intellectual and artistic movement which aimed to fight for the human rights of Indians, who were discriminated and exploited by the official culture. No movement like that has ever emerged in the case of black culture in Peru or Latin America at large (Serbin 1991, 155).

The attempt of blacks to integrate into the dominant society is a process, as mentioned above, of a long historical date. From the beginnings of the conquest, blacks were always closer to the conquerors than to the other ethnic dominated group — the Indians. Blacks spoke Spanish, served the conquerors in very specialized and qualified activities, and many times acted as intermediaries between them and the defeated Indians. Blacks even fought in the regular armies of the conquerors and participated in the civil wars between them (Bowser 1977, 27-28). The Indians themselves perceived blacks as members of the victorious army (Millones 1971, 603). Blacks had a special status, higher than Indians and mestizos, because most of them lived in the homes of the Spaniards; owning them was a sign of prestige because they were expensive; in urban fiestas they were a main attraction; and the black was the confidant, accomplice and private messenger of the Spaniard (Millones 1973, 26).

The ethnic bonds of blacks in Peru have tended to disappear due to processes of dissociation and creolization, but some symbols of black contributions to the national culture are still recognized as such by the dominant culture. Today, besides the already mentioned black presence in religion and sports, music and dance appear as the principal identity markers of a struggling ethnic entity. The persistence of such survivals of black culture in Peru, and the danger of its disappearance, partly explain why in the late 1950s a process of collecting, revival, and reconstruction of black music occurred.

The African Heritage in Afro-Peruvian Music

The practice and performance of African music, dances, and rituals by the black slaves in Peru since the early years of the conquest is well established in numerous colonial and republican written sources. The continuing participation in street fiestas during the colony by black musicians and dancers is well documented since the early sixteenth century;[4] the most important of these fiestas are those of the Virgin of Rosary, the Lord of the Miracles, and Corpus Christi (Estenssoro 1988, 162). There were numerous attempts to repress the black slaves' cultural expressions in the fiestas in Lima, through explicit prohibitions from the Lima municipality and the Church. As early as in 1549, the municipality of Lima had ordered the black slaves to perform their fiestas in only two main plazas in Lima (Romero 1939). Despite these restrictions, however, the slaves managed to continue participating in urban Catholic fiestas and processions until the eighteenth century. A very detailed description of the music and dance of the *bozales* published in the eighteenth century in the influential journal *Mercurio Peruano* mentioned their intense body movements, the circle and erotic choreographies between men and women, the use of drums and *marimba*, and the use of a jawbone as a musical instrument.[5] The institution of the *cofradía* (brotherhoods), the first of which appeared in 1540 (Millones 1973, 37), was of great importance in uniting black slaves in a highly structured hierarchical organization.

During the sixteenth and seventeenth centuries, music and dances were heavily influenced by African roots, especially with the continuing arrival of the slave *bozales*. The eighteenth century marks the beginning of the creolization of black music (Romero 1939). With the integration of blacks into the dominant Creole society, Creole cultural and musical expressions began to be accepted and adopted. During the nineteenth century, after the abolition of slavery, blacks intensified this process.

The process of creolization of the music brought by the African slaves was, nonetheless, not abrupt. Since the seventeenth century, blacks had already incorporated the European guitar and the harp in their street fiestas (Estenssoro 1988, 163), and the appearance of instruments such as the *cajita*, the jawbone, and later the *cajón*, resulted from the creative initiative of Peruvian blacks and the processes of cultural syncretism between African and Spanish-Creole traditions in Peru. The role of blacks as music professors for Lima's aristocracy and the slow but confident acceptance of specific music played by the blacks were signs of this creolization process. Another factor was the learning of Western musical techniques by black slaves (Stevenson 1968, 304; Bowser 1977, 246). The disappearance of African drums and marimba during the eighteenth century was an expression of abandonment of African roots, as was the disappearance of the institution of the *cofradía*.

By the beginnings of the twentieth century, the African traits of most of the black Creole musical genres were difficult to distinguish, if they were present at all, and only few ceremonial expressions related to, but not original with, the black sectors persisted in the rural areas such as the theatrical representation of the "Doce Pares de Francia" in Aucallama (Matos Mar 1974), the "Hatajo de Negritos" in Chincha (Tompkins 1981, Vásquez 1982) and the narrative form of the *décima*. In urban areas, the song genres associated with blacks began a slow process of disappearance. By the mid-twentieth century, only a few were remembered by a few specialists, and the repertoire was reduced to a minimum. While the main melodies were more easily remembered by some performers, the choreographies from most of them were completely forgotten.

Before the movement of revival and reconstruction of the "Afro-Peruvian" repertoire, which began in the late 1950s, it could have been concluded that in terms of musical form and structure, contemporary black musical repertoire in Peru was based more on European-Hispanic than on African musical structures and forms (Romero 1942, 122; Tompkins 1981, 111), and that its practice and performance, while primarily by blacks, was not reserved exclusively for them since many of its expressions had been also adopted by white Creoles and mestizos — another sign of black integration into the national society at large.[6] The majority of the so-considered Peruvian black musical expressions were song genres of homophonic texture, accompanied primarily by the guitar and the *cajón*. The guitar provided a basic harmonic base for a Western-European-designed melodic line. The rhythmic motifs of the percussion instruments were easily identified by Peruvian Creoles as black, but hardly any other African trait could have been detected.

Revival and Reconstruction

The revival and reconstruction of ancient and almost forgotten "Afro-Peruvian" song-genres began in the late 1950s. Rather than originating in a popular spontaneous movement, this was initiated by local intellectuals interested in the revival and recognition of the contribution of blacks to Peruvian culture. The late historian José Durand (1935-1990), along with Nicomedes Santa Cruz (1925-1992) and his sister Victoria Santa Cruz (1992) were the main collectors, producers, and promoters of black performances during this period. One of the first requirements for this revival movement was the isolation of those genres associated with blacks, which in the past integrated the Creole repertoire of the Peruvian coast, and were sung by whites, mestizos, and blacks and performed intermingled with white Creole song genres such as waltzes, polkas, and marineras. Only since the 1950s, therefore, and due primarily to the efforts of the above-mentioned intellectuals, were those genres separated from the Creole repertoire and considered and labeled exclusively "Afro-Peruvian" (Romero 1985, 265).

There are two specific pieces of evidence from the beginning of the twentieth century that document this analysis. First, the well-known folk collector Rosa Mercedes de Morales in her collection

Antiguos Pregones de Lima (Lima, 1937) intermingled the Andean *huayno*, the *yaraví*, and the Creole *marinera* with genres which are now considered Afro-Peruvian, such as the *festejo*, the *socabón*, and the *agua de nieve*. Second, the Peruvian historian Jorge Basadre mentioned that in one of the first important concerts in Lima in 1912, entitled "Peruvian Music," the well-known white creole guitarist Alejandro Ayarza included the creole waltz and marinera, together with the *agua de nieve* and the *zaña* (Basadre 196, 142), also later to be considered typical Afro-Peruvian genres.

This process of revival, however, was not abrupt. The first recordings of Afro-Peruvian music produced by Nicomedes Santa Cruz, issued in the late 1950s, included the Creole waltz among its featured genres. Much later, in 1971, Victoria Santa Cruz included in an LP six Creole waltzes (from a total of ten examples). Thus, the process of isolation of a black repertoire peaked during the 1970s, soon after which the revival movement faded and commercialism became the main force behind Afro-Peruvian performances.

Peruvian black musicians, therefore, were accustomed to performing Creole repertoire, and, in fact, considered themselves part of the Creole culture. As Millones has affirmed, both blacks and mestizos "demand for themselves the condition of Creoles," and the urban colonial culture that prevails in Peru puts Creoles and blacks in the same sector, in contrast to the Indian, mestizo and *cholo* sectors (Millones 1978, 62-63). It is understandable, then, that the revival movement of black musical culture had to break this identification between blacks and Creoles and isolate a previously non-existent specific Afro-Peruvian repertoire.

One may well ask why this revival movement took place, what were the conditions that permitted it to occur, how the reconstruction of extinct black song genres and dances was possible, and how this effort was received by Peruvian society.

This movement grew out of the individual initiative of a few Peruvian artists and intellectuals interested in the revival and revaluation of the contributions of the black minority to Peruvian national culture. Scholar José Durand is frequently cited as having organized in 1956 the first representation of black-associated genres in the municipal theater of Lima. He entitled this representation "Estampas de Pancho Fierro" (Vásquez 1982, 37). Also in the late 1950s, Nicomedes Santa Cruz and his sister, Victoria, composers and lyricists who sang and wrote their own scripts, began producing black dramas and musical representations. Nicomedes himself produced the first commercial LPs of Afro-Peruvian music with his group *Cumanana*. It would not be an exaggeration to affirm that the main force behind the revival movement of black music in Peru came henceforth from the initiatives and activities of Nicomedes and Victoria Santa Cruz.

Born in Lima, Nicomedes and Victoria Santa Cruz were introduced to black musical traditions at an older age; they were raised in a black family of intellectuals and artists. Their father, Nicomedes (1871-1957), was a writer, and their grandfather, José Milagros Gamarra (1850-1923), a Creole painter and design artist. According to Victoria Santa Cruz, an encounter between Nicomedes and Porfirio Vásquez, an old black musician from the rural town of Aucallama, was crucial for them to discover the extant black musical traditions. From Vásquez and other old black musicians living in Lima, Nicomedes and Victoria learned various songs and dances which were usually performed by blacks. The repertoire was scant, and sometimes the songs were incomplete. Reconstruction of the repertoire was, thus, a logical alternative and a requisite for its revival. The "innate" sense of rhythm of blacks, and the belief in the moral right of African descendants to use elements from African contemporary music, were the basic resources Victoria Santa Cruz utilized for the reconstruction and revival of the then-virtually extinct black musical traditions.[7]

Nicomedes Santa Cruz has stated in two of his most important record productions (*Cumanana* and *Socabón*) his main thoughts on the early origins and recent revival of black music in Peru. One of his main justifications for the process of revival and reconstruction of an Afro-Peruvian repertoire is that the music of the Peruvian blacks originated from music brought by African slaves.

One of the most important African elements brought to Peru by the *bozales*, according to Nicomedes, is a choreographic figure in which the dancers bump pelvises together simulating a sexual encounter, a movement called *umbigada* in Brazil, and *vacunao* in Cuba (the existence of this figure had been mentioned in the above-cited edition of the *Mercurio Peruano* in the eighteenth century). Based on this citation, Nicomedes elaborated a very personal theory, largely based on speculation. He affirmed that this choreographic figure was the basis for the *landó*, the *zamacueca*, and almost all the Peruvian black genres. While there was no historical evidence or citation for the existence of the *landó* in Peru, Nicomedes presented it as an Afro-Peruvian genre and affirmed that it had derived from the Brazilian *lundú*.[8] Following his speculative trend, he further affirmed that the *landó* had developed into the *zamba-landó*, and finally into the *zamacueca*.

The *zamacueca*, however, permitted Nicomedes to elaborate a more scientific assumption. It was a well-documented genre, and its origins and social associations could be rigorously sought in historical written sources. It is mentioned in several documents of the nineteenth century, and it is probably the best-documented genre among all of the Peruvian black musical expressions.[9] The well-known Peruvian drama writer Manuel Ascencio Segura mentioned it in 1842 in his theater piece *La Moza*, citing it as an *erotic*, indecent dance; and in 1829, Felipe Pardo y Aliaga's comedy *Frutos de la Educación* (The Fruits of Education) features a girl breaking up with her fiancé because she had danced the *zamacueca* (Tompkins 1981, 61-62). The excellent description of François Magrin de Collogny from the beginnings of the nineteenth century mentions other choreographic traits: swinging hips, twisting, rapid steps, the use of a handkerchief, the body movement of approaching and retreating, naked breasts, the use of the European vihuela and, of course, the Spanish texts (Tompkins 1981, 71).

Even the academic composer Claudio Rebagliati included the zamacueca in his *Album Sudamericano*, one of the most important musical works of the nineteenth century. He arranged various popular *zamacuecas* according to Western academic standards. Although the term *zamacueca*, as well as its other alternative terms, was later abandoned for the term *marinera* after the war with Chile (1879-1884), it was still in use until the turn of the present century. Manuel Atanasio Fuentes has mentioned a performance of the *zamacueca* in the festival of Amancaes in Lima, performed with harp and guitar (Fuentes 1925, 151). The *zamacueca* was not a black dance genre *per se*, but there are enough sources that confirm that the genre was the favorite one for the blacks, and it was generally identified with them. Travelers like Wilkes (1839), Radriguet (1841), Wiever (1877), Botinilau (1850), Pradier (1897), Bresson (1872), and Zapiola (1812) mentioned the *zamacueca* linked with black performers (Romero 1939).

The case of the *zamacueca*, therefore, permitted Nicomedes to base his conclusions upon hard evidence. Based on the previously cited written sources and the excellent cited description of its choreography by Collogny, which prompted him to conclude that the bumping of the pelvis (*golpe de frente*) was part of its choreography, and in view of its frequent description by writers as having an erotic and "indecent" quality. Nicomedes affirmed that it was clearly of African origins. Many others have disagreed with this conclusion; Assuncao, for example, demonstrates that indecency or sexual symbolism is not an exclusive African trait, citing that case of the Spaniard *zarabanda*, described by many as pantomimic of sexual intercourse (Assuncao 1970, 26-27).

At any rate, by producing the first records of Afro-Peruvian music in the late 1950s and beginning of the 1960s, Nicomedes established the genres which were to be considered by the general public as black in origin and character. Genres such as the *festejo, ingá, socabón, zapateo* (shoe tapping), *marinera, cumanana, pregón* and *panalivio* were featured in his first records of the late 1950s. His subsequent, more documented records were *Cumanana* (1964) and *Socabón* (1975), in which he included genres such as the *landó* or *zamba-landó, son de los diablos, habanera, zaña, samba-malato, agua de nieve* and the *alcatraz*— in all, nearly fifteen different types of musical forms considered as the Afro-Peruvian repertoire.[10]

Looking into the issue of the African roots of these genres, one could conclude that the strongest historical evidence for the existence of Afro-Peruvian forms prior to the twentieth century pertains to the dance of the *zamacueca* and to the representation of the *son de los diablos*. Colonial documentary evidence of genres such as *agua de nieve*, the *panalivio*, the *toro-mata*, and even a sole mention of the *zamba-landó* do exist, but without any useful or even minimal description of the music or dance. Absolute reconstruction has occurred with these forms, as well as with the music and/or choreography of genres created in the twentieth century. The latter include the *festejo, landó* (or its variant *zamba-landó*), and satirical and joyful dance-plays such as the *ingá* and *alcatraz* which are not genres in themselves but theatrical dance-representations based on the musical form of the *festejo* (Tompkins 1981, 239). Genres like the *habanera*, on the other hand, were never performed in Peru. Nicomedes himself acknowledged that the *habanera* was from Cuba and that after hearing it he decided to record it and introduce it as part of the Afro-Peruvian repertoire for his album *Socabón* (Santa Cruz 1975). Whatever its origins, the Santa Cruz siblings reconstructed old melodies that were remembered only partially by old black performers, and they recreated choreographies where they did not exist or reconstructed them on the basis of the few available historical sources. The result is that an Afro-Peruvian repertoire was established, and for general audiences these musical genres were thought, from then on, to be directly or indirectly derived from African roots and to constitute an exclusive cultural expression of Peruvian blacks.

Nicomedes, however, had never attempted to deny the fact that most of these genres were recreated, explicitly recognizing in his disc notes the early disappearance of their choreographies. The dance of the *festejo*, for example, while some melodies apparently survived, was recreated by black professors of dance in the early twentieth century in local private academies. Specifically, Nicomedes affirmed that Porfirio Vásquez had recreated the basic steps of the current *festejo* in his capacity as a dance professor in the Academy in Lima (Santa Cruz 1982, 108). Victoria Santa Cruz consolidated its reconstruction and disseminated it widely.

Victoria Santa Cruz was responsible for all the choreographic recreation and reconstruction of these Afro-Peruvian genres and had an intense activity of her own. In 1959 she founded a group called "Peruvian Theater and Black Dances" which initiated local performances of black music and dance in theaters and open scenarios in the city. Her first works of this period were "Callejón de un solo caño," "Escuela Folklórica" and "Malató," in which she combined theatrical segments with music and dance. This period of her work concluded in 1962, when she took a French government scholarship to study theater and choreography in France.[11]

In 1966, she returned to Lima and resumed her work with the group, calling on all interested blacks and mixed-race blacks to participate in a theater and dance production. She has described the response as overwhelming.[12] All variations of the black race were present, a sign she interpreted as positive because it meant that a clearer mulatto, for example, did not any longer mind being explicitly considered as black. Victoria Santa Cruz believed that the young blacks who responded to her call were starting to look for their own identities and to cease to be embarrassed about being black. In 1971 she produced an LP which synthesized most of her work during that period. From 1973 until 1982, she was director of the National Folklore Company, the most important governmental folklore performance group for many decades.

The younger generation of urban blacks in the early 1960s had not heard about the existence of an Afro-Peruvian repertoire. Many who joined Victoria Santa Cruz's dance group learned from the very beginning level. An excellent background for them was that they were used to dancing to different Caribbean rhythms, currently called *salsa*, very popular in Peru. Victoria Santa Cruz has said that Peruvian blacks feel the African roots they have in their own collective memory: "Rhythm combinations that we [blacks] perform since we were little kids sound African, without having ever been there." In relation to her recreation work, she has stated that she felt the latent harmonies and rhythms of the extant melodies and proceeded to their reconstruction: "The melody and the rhythmical combination is asking for something.... So, if you want to feel it, you feel it, percussion is within us. To recreate from an ancestral memory is just a remembrance."

Santa Cruz said that this movement began as a result of the impact of foreign black dance companies which performed in Lima during those initial years. Convinced that something similar could be done in Peru, her main objectives were to disseminate black contributions among the general public and to contribute to the emergence of a black cultural identity. Racial discrimination and hostility toward blacks also motivated the fight for the revaluation of black contributions to Peruvian society, which were seldom recognized by the official and dominant culture: "Before looking for the guilty ones, we had to discover who we were!" Victoria has stated. In one of her theater pieces, she introduced African deities like *Shangó*, so that younger Peruvian blacks could come to know their African heritage.

The use of various instruments related to the music of black heritage slaves, such as the *quijada* (jawbone) and the *cajita* (small wooden box), played an important role (confirmed by diverse written and iconographic colonial sources). An instrument of later origins, the *cajón*, is said to have replaced the functions of the African drum lost during the colonial period. Other modern and foreign percussion instruments such as the *conga*, the cowbell, and the *bongós*, widely disseminated in Peru due to the immense popularity of Caribbean rhythms, were incorporated by the Santa Cruz siblings to the instrumental corpus of the Afro-Peruvian repertoire. The European guitar, on the other hand, continued to be the preferred harmonic instrument.

No attempt was made to revive the harp or the different types of membranophones used by the colonial black slaves. No attempt was made, either, to reintroduce the marimba, which was undoubtedly used by the slaves at least until the eighteenth century.[13]

Musical Revival and Cultural Identity

As blacks in Peru did not conform to a strictly defined ethnic group, it is understandable that the revived Afro-Peruvian repertoire was not widely adopted by blacks as an identity emblem. With no links to political and social demands (one of the main drawbacks of this revival movement in the long run), the movement dissolved into the realm of mere commercial entertainment in the 1980s. Nevertheless, the black music revival had an impact on national society through the important and frequent presence of Afro-Peruvian music in the mass media, an influence that encompasses all social and ethnic sectors. It is performed by black professional groups for a variety of urban audiences, but not specifically black.

Only since the late 1970s have groups of blacks interested in social and political problems and demands appeared. Two new associations for the revival of black culture as a whole were the most important. ACEJUNEP (Cultural Association for the Black Peruvian Youth) called on young blacks to analyze and discuss their problems as a social group within Peruvian society. Their predecessor was the Harlem Group, founded in the traditional district of *La Victoria* as early as the 1930s (Luciano 1987, 208). Some of the young blacks who went to ACEJUNEP later accepted the call of Victoria Santa Cruz to become members of her music and dance group.[14] According to the founders of ACEJUNEP, the cultural resistance of Peruvian blacks must be recognized. This resistance permitted, for example, 1) disguising their religion; 2) permeating African spirits with Creole music and dance; and 3) influencing medical practices and popular foods (Luciano 1987, 207). ACEJUNEP recognized the subordinate position of blacks, who worked in low-paid and unqualified jobs, resided in the poorest neighborhoods in the city or in scattered rural villages, and generally were poorly qualified workers with a high degree of illiteracy (Luciano 1987, 208). The group's main objectives were to organize activities to benefit the black ethnic group and to elaborate a social examination of themselves. Unfortunately, these aims were not fully carried out.

In the mid-1980s the Movimiento Francisco Congo (founded in 1986) published a manifesto, also noting that blacks were among the poorest and most impoverished sectors of the Peruvian social classes and were not accepted as equals. They recognized that blacks were exploited and marginal.[15] In spite of this, blacks have maintained a cultural resistance and artistic creativity, especially in the music realm. The manifesto mentioned the most important exponents of black culture in Peru, highlighting the contributions of Nicomedes and Victoria Santa Cruz and the black influence on Creole cuisine, sports, and the community life of some neighborhoods of Lima. The group's aims are 1) to promote union among blacks, 2) to defend their rights, 3) to fight for equality and dignity, and 4) to develop and motivate the artistic creativity of the black people.

The movement did not attract enough supporters, however, and so it could not unite a significant portion of the black population of Lima. Only a handful of members currently belong to the group, and they lack financial support. In better moments, however, they organized several activities. They produced an event called "Black Christmas" which since then has been a frequent spectacle in Lima. In 1987 they organized a "black carnival" in the traditional black district of *La Victoria*, a festival of black music, a conference of young blacks, and the recreation of the street dance *Son de los Diablos* which was reenacted in the streets of Lima during three consecutive years. The group aims to change the negative image of blacks and revive the historical role of cultural resistance among Peruvian blacks, following the examples of the *palenques* and the *cimarrones* and pursuing its contributions to sports, music and dance, and foods.[16]

These movements, therefore, have not succeeded in uniting a majority of blacks in Peru. Black integration into national society implied their "creolization," and this process limited the possibilities for the individual black to identify himself as such, to recognize himself as a member of a group different from that of the dominant culture, and consequently, to demand and denounce social marginality and racial discrimination. In several interviews, the frequent and common complaint was the existence of racial discrimination, but other factors were hardly mentioned. Peruvian blacks avoid speaking about the condition of blacks as an ethnic group, which confirms their option for assimilation in the official culture through miscegenation and/or cultural integration. Only blacks associated with revival or specific artistic groups seem conscious of their ethnic origins.

The musical revival movement of Nicomedes and Victoria Santa Cruz did not find a sufficiently strong social base. It remained within musical and choreographic dimensions, without incorporating other aspects of Peruvian black culture. Hence, once the reintroduction of Afro-American genres was consolidated, the movement faded out. Today, the revived black genres are performed exclusively by professionals and are disseminated only through the commercial circuit. Though revived and reconstructed, the genres were not popularized, that is, they were not accepted by the black people as their own expression or identity icon. Even Nicomedes explicitly recognized that, in the case of the *festejo,* for example, these genres received and reconstructed by an elite, were not adopted spontaneously by the common people: "This choreography *(festejo)* did not become popular, the people did not dance to it spontaneously, not even in social gatherings" (Santa Cruz 1970, 61). In fact, this was a statement that could be applied to other genres as well, and probably to the whole movement. The process of reconstruction in itself did succeed, but it did not help at that time to confirm a black identity in Peru.

Conclusions

There were several limitations on the movement of revival and reconstruction of Afro-Peruvian musical traditions. One of the most important is that these musical genres did not become popular among the general audiences. Rather, they were mainly performed by professional musicians and dancers in commercial settings (restaurants and mass media commercial channels such as radio, TV, records and cassettes).

Why did the process end in such a way? One hypothesis is that the movement did not address the social and political problems of Peruvian blacks as a whole, focusing only on the artistic aspect. Peruvian blacks thus did not deeply identify themselves with the movement, because their problems went further than these artistic interests. Racial discrimination, poverty, and lack of education and economic resources were realities that overcame their concern for music and dance. Only in the 1980s did politically oriented black groups appear, as young, intellectual blacks met to inaugurate movements with broader goals than in the past decades, encompassing the whole universe of black reality in Peru. Unfortunately, these also remained in the hands of an elite unable to get popular support.

In this sense, both attempts had similarities: Neither of these movements was able to overcome its intellectual approach, and both were incapable of satisfying the popular taste and needs. The Santa Cruz movement was indeed not a popular and/or democratic movement. Its leadership was based on a vertical authority, which imposed a strict discipline among its musicians and dancers. The leaders knew the philosophy of the movement, but did not share it with their staff, who remained only as interpreters and performers. The young followers learned the formal aspects of the music and choreographies, but were not introduced to the philosophical and historical knowledge of their leaders. The Santa Cruzes, therefore, could not transmit their knowledge to their followers. This is the most important reason why the musicians, without their leaders, began performing commercially. Another reason is that the reconstructed choreographic forms were too complex to be performed by an average person, and their musical accompaniment did not catch on with the various Peruvian classes and sectors. The Peruvian public watch, like, and even admire black musical genres, but they still consider them as exotic attractions.[17]

Finally, because the black minority in Peru is not an ethnic group *per se*, it has not been able to produce or maintain a traditional musical culture. The straightforwardness of this fact could prevent us from paying attention to the positive and thought-provoking aspects of this revival and reconstruction process, but the black presence in Peru is evident and is still present in the collective minds of many Creole Peruvians. The positive aspects of this movement include, first, the preservation of many musical and choreographic genres which at the beginnings of the present century were virtually extinct. The Santa Cruzes collected these and stimulated the performers gathered around them to continue interpreting these genres. Despite the drawbacks mentioned herein, these black expressions would have been forgotten already were it not for their work. Their intense collecting, though not always systematic, resulted in the dissemination of these genres among the whole population. Arranging, composing, and choreographing new forms prepared them to be recorded and broadcasted throughout the country.

Second, the presence of black musical forms and dances in the Peruvian cultural scene has given the Peruvian black an identity symbol which — though it may not be currently attractive or useful because no ethnic bond now joins Peruvian blacks — could be an important cultural symbol in the future. These forms, alive today in the commercial arena, could go from there to play a more active role among blacks in the near future.

An important facet in this identity issue is that Peruvian blacks who consider themselves members of Creole society could use this identity marker in the future, not to be differentiated from other sectors, but to be accepted by the dominant Peruvian society, as they apparently wish. As stated earlier, blacks and white Creoles have historically formed a group opposed to Indians and mestizos. Even as slaves of the Spanish conquerors, blacks since colonial times have felt the need to integrate into the white dominant Creole society. The attempt to separate black music as an independent repertoire (an Afro-Peruvian corpus) could have been a reflection of their desire to be widely accepted into the dominant groups of Peruvian society.[18]

In that sense, one could say that new groups like *Francisco Congo*, in fighting against discrimination, were actually fighting for their recognition, for their acceptance into the dominant society. This goal has been overshadowed in recent times by the movement of Andean peasants to Peruvian cities and the astonishing takeover of Peru's economy by Andean migrants, which has changed the traditional social and ethnic divisions of Peru (Creole/black versus Indian/mestizo). Now the "dominant" culture in Lima is predominantly Andean, not Creole. Amidst these changes the black minority will have to search for its identity — or continue to accept desegregation and discrimination and being mixed with other minority groups located below the poverty level.

Finally, the fact that the official spheres did not, and do not, acknowledge a black problem in Peru (in contrast to their recognition of the "Indian problem" in the 1920s), and that a cultural revival movement like *indigenismo* never existed for the blacks in Peru, suggests that there is still enough ground for blacks to argue for recognition of their cultural presence and for abolition of all racial and social discrimination against them.

The musical reconstruction and revival movement of the Santa Cruzes and other intellectuals contributed substantially to this possibility by preserving, recreating, reconstructing, and disseminating black musical and choreographic expressions. This involvement probably will be seen in the future as one of Peruvian blacks' most significant cultural actions and symbols.

Notes

1. As suggested by Luis Millones, personal communication.

2. I want to thank Pilar Albareda L. for her assistance in the biblio-graphical investigation for this article and for the interviews she held with specific informants.

3. Fredrik Barth, however, cites this ideal definition of an ethnic group in a critical way, recognizing that while it is useful for many anthropologists, it sometimes prevents the analyzer from understanding the role and place of the ethnic group within human societies and cultures (Barth 1976, 11-12).

4. See, for example, the *Libro de Cabildos* from 5 May 1586, (Lima: Consejo Provincial de Lima, Vol. X, 343).

5. See *Mercurio Peruano*, June 16, 1791.

6. In rural black towns, for example, narrative forms such as the *décima*, or its regional derivations such as the *cumanana* or the *socabón*, which are usually associated with blacks, are also performed by white Creoles or mestizos (Santa Cruz 1982, 17-18).

7. Personal interview with Victoria Santa Cruz, Lima, August 10, 1991.

8. In fact, a form called *ondú* has been mentioned by such Peruvian authors as Ricardo Palma, José Galvez, and Manuel A. Segrua. Only Manuel A. Fuentes mentions the existence of a *londu floreado* in the nineteenth century (Tompkins 1981, 292).

9. The *zamacueca* was also named in diverse ways, including *toro-mata*, *maicito*, *moza-mala*, and *zanguaraña* (see Romero 1939).

10. For a very complete definition, musical description, and history of each genre (as well as a discography) the reader should consult Tompkins' dissertation on the topic, thus far the best and most complete survey of black musical culture in Peru (Tompkins 1981).

11. As stated in the program notes of the recital "Victoria Santa Cruz: Adiós al Perú," Lima, Teatro Municipal, October 11, 1982.

12. This and all the data regarding Victoria Santa Cruz's viewpoints and statements on the Afro-Peruvian movement were obtained during a personal interview with her in Lima, August 10, 1991.

13. See *Mercurio Peruano*, 16 June 1791, and the drawing number 142 of Bishop Martínez Compañon (work of the late eighteenth century).

14. Interview with Professor Gladys González, a black dancer and former member of the National Folklore Company directed by Victoria Santa Cruz, in Lima, November 27, 1991.

15. A section of the manifesto says: "The majority of us are among the impoverished and oppressed sectors of the Peruvian people. Moreover, we are subject of a socially negative treatment" (Movimiento Negro Francisco Congo 1986, 2).

16. Interview with Guillermo Nuñez, member of the black movement Francisco Congo, in Lima, December 1991.

17. The introduction in the Afro-Peruvian repertoire of African-derived percussion instruments such as the cowbell, the *tumba*, and the *bongó*, and the omission of instruments such as specific membranophones (and the *marimba*) whose existence is well documented in historical written sources, brings to mind that there were several other options for reconstructing Peruvian black musical expressions. Were their options and choices the ideal ones? Was their "re-Africanization" theory overemphasized to the detriment of a more practical study of historically proven Peruvian/African musical roots?

18. As suggested by Gisela Canepa Koch, personal communication.

References

Assuncao, Fernando. 1970. "Aportes para un Estudio sobre los Orígenes de la Zamacueca." *Folklore Americano* 18(16): 5-39.

Basadre, Jorge. 1964. "Notas sobre la Música en el Perú." In *Historia de la República del Perú, vol. 10*, 4603-4619. Lima: Editorial Universitaria.

Barth, Fredrik. 1976. "Introducción." In *Los Grupos Etnicos y sus Fronteras, la organización social de las diferencias culturales*, ed. Fredrik Barth, 19-49. México: Fondo de Cultura Económica.

Bowser, Frederik P. 1977. El *Esclavo Africano en el Perú Colonial, 1524-1650*. México: Siglo XXI Editores.

Estenssoro, Juan Carlos. 1988. "Música y Comportamiento Festivo de la Población Negra en Lima Colonial." *Cuadernos Hispanoamericanos* 451-452:161-166.

Flores Galino, Alberto. 1984. *Aristocracia y Plebe: Lima 1760-1830*. Lima: Mosca Azul Editores.

Fuentes, Manuel Atanasio. 1925. *Lima: Apuntes Históricos, Descriptivos, Estadísticos y de Costumbres*. Lima: Librería Escolar E. Moreno.

Jiménez Borja, Arturo. 1939. "Danzas de Lima." *Turismo* 14(135): 10-11.

Luciano, José. 1987. "Apuntes para una interpretación crítica sobre la presencia africana en el Perú." In *Primer Seminario sobre Poblaciones Inmigrantes*. Actas, 1:197-209. Lima: Consejo Nacional de Ciencias y Tecnología-CONCYTEC.

Mac-Lean y Estnós, Roberto. 1948. *Negros en el Nuevo Mundo*. Lima: Imprenta Domingo Miranda.

Matos Mar, José y Jorge A. Carbajal H. 1974. *Erasmo: Yanacón del Valle de Chancay*. Lima: Instituto de Estudios Peruanos.

Middendorf, E. W. 1973. *Perú. Observaciones y Estudios del País y sus Habitantes Durante una Permanencia de 25 Años*. Vol. 1. Lima: Universidad Nacional Mayor de San Marcos.

Millones, Luis. 1971. "Gente Negra en el Perú: Esclavos y Conquistadores." *América Indígena* 31(3): 593-624.

Millones, Luis. 1973. "La Población Negra en el Perú: Análisis de la Posición Social del negro durante la Dominación española." In *Minorías Etnicas en el Perú*, ed. Luis Millones, 17-47. Lima: Pontificia Universidad Católica del Perú.

Millones, Luis. 1978. *Tugurio: La Cultura de Los Marginados.* Lima: Instituto Nacional de Cultura.

Morris, H. S. 1975. "Grupos Etnicos." In *Enciclopedia Internacional de las Ciencias Sociales*, ed. Edward Sills, 253-257. Madrid: Editorial Aguilar.

Movimiento Negro Francisco Congo. 1987. *Manifiesto, Plataforma, Estatutos.* Lima: Movimiento Negro Francisco Congo.

Rocca, Luis. 1985. *La Otra Historia.* Lima: Instituto de Apoyo Agrario.

Romero, Fernando. 1939. "Ritmo Negro de la Costa Zamba." *Turismo* 135.

Romero, Fernando. 1939. "Instrumentos Africanos de la Costa Zamba." *Turismo* 137.

Romero, Fernando. 1939. "La Zamba, Abuela de la Marinera." *Turismo* 141.

Romero, Fernando. 1939. "Cómo era la Zamacueca Zamba." *Turismo* 146.

Romero, Fernando. 1942. "De la Zamba de Africa a la Marinera del Perú." *Actas y Trabajos Científicos de XXVII Congreso Internacional de Americanistas (Lima)* 2:105-40.

Romero, Fernando. 1980. *Quimba, Fa, Malambo, Ñeque. Afronegrismos en el Perú.* Lima: Instituto de Estudios Peruanos.

Romero, Raúl R. 1985. "La Música Tradicional y Popular." In *La Música en el Perú*, 215-283. Lima: Patronato Popular y Porvenir Pro Música Clásica.

Santa Cruz, Nicomedes. 1982. *La Décima en el Perú.* Lima: Instituto de Estudios Peruanos.

Santa Cruz, Nicomedes. 1964. "Cumanana: Poemas y Canciones" [LP disc notes]. Lima: Phillips-El Virrey [First Edition].

Santa Cruz, Nicomedes. 1970. "Cumanana: Antología Afroperuana, Décimas y Poemas, Danzas y Canciones" [LP disc notes]. Lima: El Virrey [Third Revised Edition].

Santa Cruz, Nicomedes. 1975. "Socabón" [LP disc notes] Lima: Virrey VIR 948-949.

Serbin, Andrés. 1991. "Porqué no Existe el Poder Negro en América Latina?" *Nueva Sociedad* 111:148-157.

Stevenson, Robert. 1968. *Music in Aztec and Inca Territory.* Berkeley: University of California Press.

Stockes, Susan C. 1987. "Etnicidad y Clase Social: Los Afro-peruanos de Lima., 1900-1930." In *Lima Obrera 1900-1930,* ed. Steve Stein, vol. 2, 171-252. Lima: Ediciones El Virrey.

Tompkins, William D. 1981. *The Musical Traditions of the Blacks of Coastal Peru.* Ph.D. Dissertation in Music. University of California, Los Angeles.

Uya, Okon Edet. 1989. *Historia de la Esclavitud Negra en las Américas y el Caribe.* Argentina: Editorial Claridad.

Vásquez, Rosa Elena. 1982. *La Práctica Musical de la Población Negra en el Perú.* Cuba: Casa de las Americas.

Contributors

Olavo Alén Rodríguez, from Havana, Cuba, graduated from the Escuela Nacional de Artes in Havana as a pianist in 1969. He studied musicology and ethnomusicology at the Humboldt University in Berlin and received his doctorate there in 1979, having defended his thesis on the Tumba Francesa Societies in Cuba. He is founding director of the Centro para la Investigación y Desarrollo de la Música Cubana in Havana. Since 1980, he has been a faculty member of the Instituto Superior de Arte, teaching organology, historiography of Cuban music, and musical transcription.

Gage Averill is a professor of ethnomusicology at Wesleyan University, Middletown, Connecticut. He received his Ph.D. from the University of Washington where he wrote his dissertation on "Haitian Dance Band Music: The Political Economy of Exuberance." He is a regular columnist on Haitian music for *The Beat* magazine and directs the Pandemonium Steel Band. In 1990-1991, he was a member of the Organization of American States Electoral Mission to Haiti. His research has concentrated on Haitian popular music, Haitian rara (traditional festival) music, and on North American barbershop harmony.

Gerard H. Béhague has been a professor of musicology and ethnomusicology at the University of Texas at Austin since 1974, where he holds the Virginia Murchison Regents Professorship in Fine Arts. He graduated from the National School of Music of the University of Brazil and the Brazilian Conservatory of Music. He studied musicology at the University of Paris. In 1963 he joined Gilbert Chase's Inter-American Institute for Musical Research at Tulane University (New Orleans) for his doctoral studies and received a Ph.D. in 1966. Before his affiliation with the University of Texas, he taught at the School of Music of the University of Illinois. A past president of the Society for Ethnomusicology, he was the editor of *Ethnomusicology* and founded the *Latin American Music Review* (1980) that he has edited ever since. His main research interests have been the theory and methods of musical research as applied especially to the musical traditions of Latin America, which he has studied as both music historian and ethnomusicologist.

Egberto Bermúdez, from Colombia, is professor of musicology and ethnomusicology at the Universidad Nacional in Bogotá. He received both his M.A. and Ph.D. degrees in musicology from the University of London, King's College. He has published numerous articles dealing with Colombian colonial music, musical instruments, and traditional music.

Max H. Brandt is director of academic affairs for the Semester at Sea Program, University of Pittsburgh. After graduating from the University of Southern Maine, he served in the Peace Corps in Nigeria from 1963 to 1965, where he surveyed music in the Ibadan primary schools and the Yoruba children's songs. His M.A. degree in ethnomusicology from the University of California, Los Angeles, emphasizes drum ensemble performance with African American children. As a researcher at the Instituto Interamericano de Etnomusicología y Folklore in Caracas (1973-1979), he concentrated on African-derived drum ensembles of the central Venezuelan coast. His doctorate in ethnomusicology is from the Queen's University of Belfast, Northern Ireland. Since 1984, he has served in the Semester at Sea Program and has taught courses on the music of Latin America and introduction to world musics at the University of Pittsburgh.

José Jorge de Carvalho holds degrees in music, ethnomusicology, and social anthropology from the University of Brasilia and the Queen's University of Belfast, Northern Ireland. He is a lecturer in the Department of Anthropology at the University of Brasilia and a researcher for the National Research Council of Brazil. He has published several works on ethnomusicology, symbolic studies, mythology, anthropology of art, popular culture, and comparative religions. His main fieldwork is on the Xangô cults of Recife, Pernambuco, Brazil.

Martha Ellen Davis is an anthropologist and ethnomusicologist and a research associate at the Center for Latin American and Caribbean Studies, Indiana University. She is a visiting professor at the University of California at Berkeley; at the Autonomous University of Santo

Domingo; and at the Queen's University of Belfast. She has been a Bunting Fellow at Harvard University and carried out field research in the Dominican Republic, Puerto Rico, Spain, and Trinidad, funded by Fulbright and other grants. Her most recent book is *La otra ciencia: El vodú dominicano como religión y medicina populares.*

Jorge Duany is associate professor of social sciences at the Universidad del Sagrado Corazón in Santurce, Puerto Rico. Prior to this position, he was director of the Academic Research Center at the same institution and assistant director of the Center for Latin American Studies at the University of Florida. He earned a Ph.D. in Latin American studies at the University of California at Berkeley, specializing in cultural anthropology. His main research interests are Caribbean migration, ethnic identity, and popular culture. In 1990, he edited the book *Los Dominicanos en Puerto Rico: Migración en la Semi-Periferia.*

Victoria Eli Rodríguez, Cuban musicologist, is the head of the Department of Basic Research at the Centro de Investigación y Desarrollo de la Música Cubana and professor of music history at the Instituto Superior de Arte de Cuba. She studied at the University of Havana and the Instituto Superior de Arte and earned her doctoral degree in 1987 from Humboldt University in Berlin. She has published extensively in numerous music journals worldwide on various aspects of Cuban musical creation (1959-1980) and Cuban music history. She is the Cuban coordinator for the forthcoming *Dictionary of Spanish Music and Hispanic-American Music.*

Gerhard Kubik, professor at the University of Vienna, is one of the best-known Africanist ethnomusicologists. He has achieved wide recognition for his work, especially in Angola, Mozambique, Malawi, and Namibia. He has also worked in Afro-Brazilian music. An extremely prolific scholar, he has published on many African topics and on African fieldwork in oral literature in Namibia, in cooperation with the oral literature research program in Chileka, Malawi, with which he is affiliated.

Kazadi wa Mukuna, ethnomusicologist from Zaire, is assistant professor of ethnomusicology at Kent State University. He is a graduate of the University of California, Los Angeles, with a Ph.D. in ethnomusicology and the Universidade de São Paulo with a doctorate in sociology. He has taught at the National University of Zaire, Michigan State University, the Universidade de São Paulo, and the Universidade Federal do

Maranhão in Brazil. At the Smithsonian Institution, he researched and coordinated cultural programs for the national Festival of American Folklife. As a scholar, he is best known for his contributions in the field of traditional African music on the continent and in the diaspora and of urban music in Zaire and Brazil. His publications in these areas have appeared in several languages and countries.

Angel G. Quintero-Rivera, from Puerto Rico, received his Ph.D. from the University of London. Since 1970, he has been project director at the Social Science Research Center and professor at the University of Puerto Rico at Río Piedras. He has been a visiting professor and researcher at the University of Illinois, Chicago, and at the Centre for Caribbean Studies at the University of Warwick, England. His numerous books and articles address critical social issues of Puerto Rico, Latin America, and the Caribbean. He is a frequent invited lecturer and panelist at institutes and colloquia in academic and intellectual circles in the Americas and Europe.

Raúl R. Romero, Peruvian ethnomusicologist, earned his master's degree in ethnomusicology at Columbia University. He is associate professor at San Marcos University in Lima, Peru, and head of the Archive of Traditional Andean Music (ATAM) at the Catholic University of Peru. He has published various articles and chapters in books on traditional Andean music. His wide experience as a field worker in various provinces of Peru allowed him to act as producer of the outstanding archive of the ATAM record series. He is pursuing a doctoral degree in ethnomusicology at Harvard University.

John M. Schechter is on the faculty at the University of California, Santa Cruz. He received a Ph.D. in ethnomusicology from the University of Texas at Austin, where he studied ethnomusicology under Gerard H. Béhague, Andean anthropology under Richard Schaedel, and Quichuan language under Louisa Stark and Guillermo Delgado. He carried out fieldwork among Quichua Indians and Afro-Ecuadorians in the Andes of Ecuador. His articles on Quichua music and culture, Inca musical culture, the Latin American child's wake, and Latin American musical instruments have appeared in a number of journals in the United States and Latin America. His most recent book, *The Indispensable Harp*, was published by Kent State University Press (1992).

Anthony Seeger is an anthropologist, ethnomusicologist, archivist, and musician. He received a B.A. from Harvard University and an M.A. and Ph.D. in anthropology from the University of Chicago. His research has concentrated on the music of Amazonian Indians. He lived in Brazil for nearly ten years between 1970 and 1982, and for much of that time served as a member of the Graduate Faculty of the Department of Anthropology at the National Museum in Rio de Janeiro, where he was chairman of that department as well as coordinator of its Graduate Program. In 1982 he returned to the United States as associate professor of anthropology and director of the Indiana University Archives of Traditional Music. In 1988 he moved to the Smithsonian Institution to assume the direction of Folkways Records and to become the curator of the archival collection. He is the author of four books and many articles on anthropological, ethnomusicological, archival, and Indian rights issues, including several on ethnicity and musical performance.

Ronald R. Smith is associate dean, Indiana University Graduate School, and associate professor of Folklore and Ethnomusicology at Indiana University's Folklore Institute. He has conducted extensive fieldwork among peoples of African descent in the Caribbean, especially in Panama. His interests are in musical transcription, festival, religious music and dramatic events, musical instruments, and the use of technology in the study of the humanities. His most recent research in Spain, Archivo de Indias, focuses on historical documentation of religious brotherhoods established for slaves and free blacks in colonial Panama.

Production Notes

This book was printed on 60 lb. Glatfelter Natural text stock with a 10 point C1S cover stock, film laminated.

The text of was set in Garamond for the North-South Center's Publication Department, using Aldus Pagemaker 5.0, on a Macintosh Centris 650 computer. It was designed and formatted by Stephanie True Moss.

The cover was created by Mary M. Mapes using Aldus Freehand 3.1 to create the illustration and exported to Quark XPress 3.3 for the composition and color separation.

The book was edited by Karen Payne, Kathleen A. Hamman, Jayne M. Weisblatt, and Diane C. Duys. Special thanks to Mary D'Leon for research on the map of Venezuela.

It was printed by Edwards Brothers, Inc. of Ann Arbor, Michigan, U.S.A.